NO SURE VICTORY

No Sure Victory

MEASURING U.S. ARMY EFFECTIVENESS AND PROGRESS
IN THE VIETNAM WAR

Gregory A. Daddis

OXFORD
UNIVERSITY PRESS

UNIVERSITY PRESS

Oxford University Press, Inc., publishes works that further
Oxford University's objective of excellence
in research, scholarship, and education.

Oxford New York
Auckland   Cape Town   Dar es Salaam   Hong Kong   Karachi
Kuala Lumpur   Madrid   Melbourne   Mexico City   Nairobi
New Delhi   Shanghai   Taipei   Toronto

With offices in
Argentina   Austria   Brazil   Chile   Czech Republic   France   Greece
Guatemala   Hungary   Italy   Japan   Poland   Portugal   Singapore
South Korea   Switzerland   Thailand   Turkey   Ukraine   Vietnam

Copyright © 2011 by Gregory A. Daddis

Published by Oxford University Press, Inc.
198 Madison Avenue, New York, New York 10016

www.oup.com

Oxford is a registered trademark of Oxford University Press

All rights reserved. No part of this publication may be reproduced,
stored in a retrieval system, or transmitted, in any form or by any means,
electronic, mechanical, photocopying, recording, or otherwise,
without the prior permission of Oxford University Press.

Library of Congress Cataloging-in-Publication Data
Daddis, Gregory A., 1967–
No sure victory : measuring U.S. Army effectiveness and progress in the Vietnam War / Gregory A. Daddis.
   p.   cm.
Includes bibliographical references.
ISBN 978-0-19-974687-3 (acid-free paper) 1. Vietnam War, 1961–1975—United States 2. United States. Army—Evaluation.
3. United States. Army—History—Vietnam War, 1961–1975. I. Title.
DS558.2.D34   2011
959.704′3420973—dc22   2010027311

1 3 5 7 9 8 6 4 2
Printed in the United States of America
on acid-free paper

To my father, Robert G. Daddis

Contents

Acknowledgments ix
List of Abbreviations xiii
Maps xv

Introduction 3
1. Of Questions Not Asked: Measuring Effectiveness in the Counterinsurgency Era 19
2. Measurements Without Objectives: America Goes to War in Southeast Asia 39
3. An "Unprecedented Victory": The Problem of Defining Success 63
4. Metrics in the Year of American Firepower 87
5. "We Are Winning Slowly but Steadily" 109
6. The Year of Tet: Victory, Defeat, or Stalemate? 133
7. "A Time for Testing" 157
8. Soldiers' Interlude: The Symptoms of Withdrawal 181
9. Staggering to the Finish 201
    Conclusion 223

Notes 237
Bibliography 303
Illustration Credits 327
Index 329

Acknowledgments

IN 2005, THE command group of the Multi-National Corps-Iraq (MNC-I) asked West Point's Department of History to compose vignettes on past counterinsurgencies that might inform current U.S. military operations in Iraq. As part of the project, a colleague and I drafted two short essays, one on the French-Indochina War, another on the American war in Vietnam. Our department head collected the ten or so papers and dispatched them to Baghdad. Weeks later, a Special Forces group commander, recently arrived in Iraq for his second combat tour in as many years, responded to our work by asking for any useful information on measuring progress in a counterinsurgency environment. I thought it unusual at first that a senior officer was struggling to delineate metrics after having so recently served in Iraq. I found quickly, however, that the inquiry proved much more complex than I first had assumed. As I conducted research on how the U.S. Army in Vietnam dealt with such a problem, the more sympathetic I became to the group commander's query.

Four years later, I had the privilege of serving as the command historian for MNC-I. In the interim I continued working on the historical question of how a conventional army measured its progress and effectiveness in an unconventional environment. From my perspective as both a historian and a professional officer, this underemphasized aspect of the Vietnam War seemed to anticipate facets of warfare in the early twenty-first century. In Iraq, I saw firsthand the difficulties commanders and staffs faced in gauging progress, even after years of combat and occupation. The problem of evaluating unconventional warfare in foreign lands appeared endemic not just to the fighting in Vietnam or Iraq but to insurgencies in general.

Comparisons between Vietnam, Iraq, and Afghanistan have been made by many historians, military professionals, and even general critics in recent years. At its core, this work is historical, not comparative, in nature. Still, it is my desire that the scholarship within has some relevance for contemporary issues. While any "lessons" from Vietnam should be treated with caution and skepticism, I hope that what I recount here is suggestive about America's experiences in more modern wars. The process, if not very idea, of measuring progress against an unconventional enemy is exceedingly complicated and is often fraught with potential pitfalls. Too many times in Vietnam, American commanders fell into such traps. What follows, then, is what I believe to be a much-needed addition to the history of the Vietnam War and, hopefully, a valuable perspective on waging unconventional warfare more broadly.

Throughout the process of completing this work I have been privileged to be associated with two of the finest history departments in the United States. At the University of North Carolina at Chapel Hill, Richard H. Kohn provided wonderful counsel and taught me the importance of asking the question "So what?" I owe Dick special thanks—he has been a role model in so many ways. Joe Glatthaar, a terrific friend and mentor, read through each chapter with an experienced eye and gave expert feedback. So too did Wayne Lee, Michael Hunt, and Duke University's Alex Roland. I have learned a remarkable amount about the profession of arms from this stellar collection of historians.

At the United States Military Academy at West Point, I have served with an equally impressive group of scholars. Colonels Lance Betros, Matthew Moten, Ty Seidule, Gian Gentile, and Kevin Farrell all have offered splendid guidance and support over the last five years. Professors Cliff Rogers, Steve Waddell, and Chuck Steele not only served as sounding boards for my early ideas but, more importantly, have been tremendous colleagues and friends. Chuck, now at the U.S. Air Force Academy, was especially helpful in outlining an initial framework for historical analysis, as was Major John Walmsley. I owe another special thanks (and lots of chocolate fudge) to Professor Jen Kiesling. Jen read every page of the manuscript and offered invaluable feedback, most of it coming, it always seemed, while swimming or riding.

I also have relied on, and been humbled by, the extraordinary generosity of a number of others: Andrew Birtle, Dale Andrade, Frank Shirer, and Sherry Dowdy of the U.S. Army Center of Military History; Dave Keough of the U.S. Army Heritage and Education Center; Richard Boylan of the National Archives at College Park; Kathy Buker of the U.S. Army Combined Arms Research Library; and Jill Redington of the U.S. Army Aviation Center of Excellence. Paul Miles of Princeton

University took a special interest in my work and has provided so many insights and recommendations that I will be indebted to him for some time to come. The Omar N. Bradley Foundation granted me a research fellowship that greatly aided my work. Dave McBride and the staff at Oxford have been a pleasure to work with through the editorial process. I also owe thanks to Susan Ferber for allowing me to pitch my ideas to her during a visit to North Carolina.

Lastly, I would like to acknowledge the tremendous support I have received from my friends and family. Rob Young and the McNulty family not only offered me a place to stay while conducting research in Washington, D.C., but have been marvelous friends for years. So too have been the Puryears. The entire Turschak family made my own family's Chapel Hill experience, quite simply, special. To my mom and Robert, I cannot express fully how important it is to have you in my life. To my wife, Susan, and my daughter, Cameron (and, yes, to our cat, Lucky), I could not have asked for anyone better. I am both a proud husband and a proud father. Finally, this book is dedicated to my father, who over the last year in battling cancer has demonstrated a degree of courage, a level of determination, and a depth of character that I doubt I ever will equal.

List of Abbreviations Used in the Text

AFQT	Armed Forces Qualification Test
APC	Accelerated Pacification Campaign
ARCOV	United States Army Combat Operations in Vietnam
ARVN	Army of the Republic of Vietnam
CGSC	Command and General Staff College
CIA	Central Intelligence Agency
CINCPAC	Commander in Chief, U.S. Pacific Command
CIP	Counterinsurgency Plan
CJCS	Chairman of the Joint Chiefs of Staff
COMUSMACV	Commander, United States Military Assistance Command, Vietnam
CORDS	Civil Operations and Revolutionary Development Support
COSVN	Central Office of South Vietnam
CTZ	Corps Tactical Zone
DMZ	Demilitarized Zone
DoD	Department of Defense
DRV	Democratic Republic of Vietnam
FLN	Algerian National Liberation Front
FM	Field Manual
FWMAF	Free World Military Assistance Forces
GVN	Government of South Vietnam
HES	Hamlet Evaluation System
JCS	Joint Chiefs of Staff
JUSMAPG	Joint United States Military Advisory and Planning Group
KIA	Killed in Action
LZ	Landing zones
MAAG	Military Assistance Advisory Group
MACV	Military Assistance Command, Vietnam
MCP	Malayan Communist Party
NCO	Noncommissioned Officer
NLF	National Front for the Liberation of South Vietnam
NSC	National Security Council

NSSM	National Security Study Memorandum
NVA	North Vietnamese Army
PAAS	Pacification Attitude Analysis System
PAVN	People's Army of Vietnam; see also NVA
PLAF	People's Liberation Armed Forces; see also VC
PRG	Provisional Revolutionary Government
PROVN	Program for the Pacification and Long-Term Development of South Vietnam
RD	Revolutionary Development
RF/PF	Regional Forces/Popular Forces
ROAD	Reorganization Objectives Army Division
RVN	Republic of Vietnam
RVNAF	Republic of Vietnam Armed Forces
SAME	Senior Advisor's Monthly Evaluation
SEER	System for Evaluating the Effectiveness of RVNAF
TCK-TKN	*Tong Cong Kich–Tong Khoi Nghia* (General Offensive-General Uprising)
TFES	Territorial Forces Evaluation System
VC	Vietnamese Communist, Vietcong
VCI	Vietcong Infrastructure
USAID	United States Agency for International Development

LIST OF ABBREVIATIONS USED IN THE NOTES

CARL	Combined Arms Research Library. Fort Leavenworth, Kansas.
CMH	U.S. Army Center of Military History. Fort McNair, Washington, D.C.
FRUS	*Foreign Relations of the United States*. U.S. Department of State.
LBJL	Lyndon B. Johnson Library Oral History Collection. Austin, Texas.
JCSHO	Joint Chiefs of Staff History Office. The Pentagon, Washington, D.C.
MHI	U.S. Army Military History Institute. Carlisle Barracks, Pennsylvania.
NARA	National Archives and Records Administration. College Park, Maryland.
OSDHO	Office of the Secretary of Defense Historical Office. Washington, D.C.
TTUVA	The Vietnam Archive, Texas Tech University. Lubbock, Texas.
USAASL	U.S. Army Armor School Library. Fort Knox, Kentucky.
USAAWCL	U.S. Army Aviation Warfighting Center, Aviation Technical Library. Fort Rucker, Alabama.
USMA	United States Military Academy, West Point, New York
VNIT	Vietnam Interview Tape Collection, CMH. Fort McNair, Washington, D.C.
WCWP	William C. Westmoreland Papers
WPSC	Special Collections, United States Military Academy Library. West Point, New York.

This work expresses the opinions of the author, and does not represent the views of the Department of Defense, the Department of Army, or the United States Military Academy.

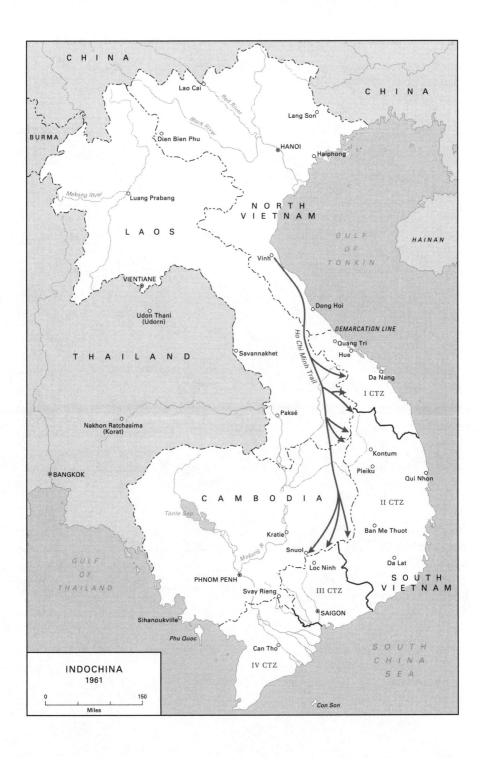

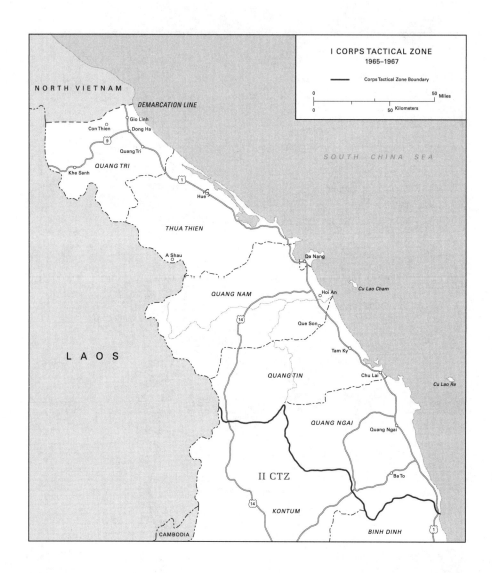

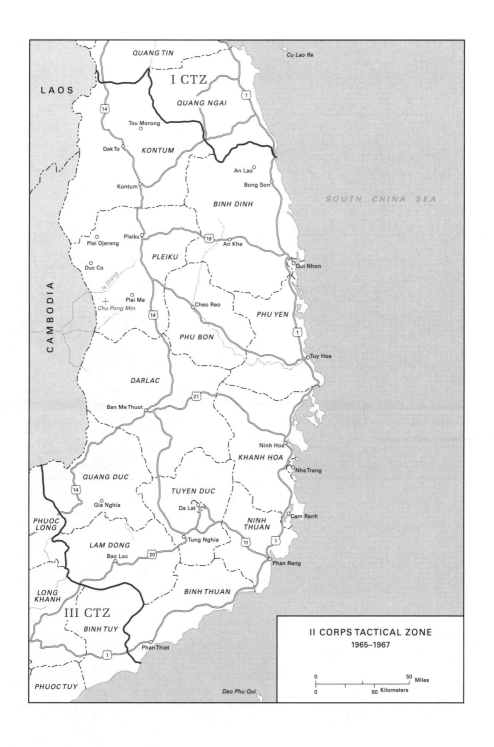

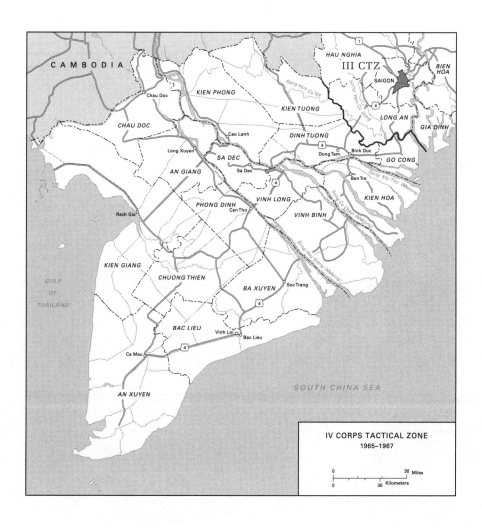

NO SURE VICTORY

"Then, no matter what we do in the military field there is no sure victory?"
—President LYNDON B. JOHNSON
"That's right. We have been too optimistic."
—Secretary Of Defense ROBERT S. MCNAMARA
White House Meeting, December 18, 1965

Introduction

ON JUNE 6, 1944, American, British, and Canadian forces launched their amphibious invasion against Hitler's Atlantic Wall. Determined to secure a foothold on French soil, Allied soldiers labored through the English Channel's surf, only to be met by mines, obstacles, and the covering fire of German defenders. One American combat engineer in the Easy Red sector of Omaha Beach articulated the fears of many Allied commanders fretting the lack of progress on the 1st Infantry Division assault beaches. "We were really just pinned down and couldn't really see anyone to shoot at. Around ten o'clock things looked hopeless on our part of the beach."[1] By mid-day, Lieutenant General Omar N. Bradley, the U.S. First Army's commander, was becoming increasingly alarmed over stagnating conditions on the beachheads. Fragmentary reports from Leonard T. Gerow's V Corps created added confusion. Bradley recalled that as the Omaha landings fell "hours and hours behind schedule" the Allied command faced an "imminent crisis" about whether and how to deploy follow-up forces. Throughout the day, Bradley and his officers agonized over potential German counterattacks.[2]

On the beaches, small groups of infantrymen struggled to make their way inland under withering German fire. Carnage was everywhere. A lieutenant in the U.S. 29th Infantry Division estimated that for every 100 yards of beach, 35 to 50 corpses lay slumped on the sand.[3] Despite the damage they suffered, the Americans slowly but perceptibly began pushing back the German defenders. Just before 1:30 P.M. Bradley received his first bit of good news from V Corps headquarters. *"Troops formerly pinned down on beaches Easy Red, Easy Green, Fox Red advancing up heights behind beaches."*[4] As midnight approached, the Americans held a tenuous grip on the French mainland. They were, however, still far short of their objectives outlined in the original Overlord plans. The 4,649 casualties sustained in Bradley's First Army on June 6 clearly indicated that putting 55,000 men ashore had been no simple task—despite the beach codenames of Easy Red and Easy Green.[5] But signs of progress did exist. By the end of D-Day, eight Allied divisions and three armored brigades had made it safely ashore. By D+1, over 177,000 troops had landed on four beachheads secured by an increasingly sturdy defensive perimeter supported by Allied air and naval power.

Over the next few weeks, American and Allied forces made even more tangible progress. After consolidating its hold on the Normandy beaches, Bradley's First Army captured Carentan on June 12, effecting a link-up between the Utah and Omaha beachheads. On June 14, Major General J. Lawton Collins's VII Corps launched an offensive to seize the port facilities at Cherbourg, which fell on June 27. All the while, logistical buildup on the original landing beaches continued at a steady pace, despite severe July storms in the English Channel. As Bradley later wrote, "France was supposed to be liberated in phases and we now stood at the brink of the first: a swift push from the grassy pasture lands of Normandy to the sleepy banks of the Seine."[6]

This next phase in the Allied operation advanced less smoothly than the First Army Commander envisioned. U.S. forces, now confronting Germans defending from a series of hedgerows, bogged down in the French inland *bocage*. Collins, studying the terrain on the VII Corps front, knew his subordinate units were in for "tough sledding," and his calculations proved accurate. The 83rd Infantry Division, leading the corps attack on July 4, lost nearly 1,400 men and failed to achieve its objective of Sainteney.[7] The Americans made scant progress on the second day, and a sense of frustration began to permeate the Allied high command. Supreme Allied Commander Dwight D. Eisenhower recalled, "In temporary stalemates . . . there always exists the problem of maintaining morale among fighting men while they are suffering losses and are meanwhile hearing their commanders criticized."[8] For the next three weeks, the Allies measured their progress in the number of hedgerows taken, hardly a basis for sustaining troop morale or displacing the Germans from French soil.

The deadlock finally broke when Operation Cobra, launched on July 25, smashed through the German defenses at St. Lô and beyond. Allied difficulties in establishing and expanding the beachhead and breaking out of the Norman hedgerows provoked important operational and institutional questions. Combat commanders in particular reflected on how best to assess their effectiveness and progress. In short, how did they know if they were winning? Terrain arguably served as the most visible scorecard. In fact, during the Normandy campaign, unit effectiveness and forward progress could be determined using a number of quantitative indicators—the number of troops or units ashore in France, the amount of territory under Allied control, the number of phase lines passed, or the number of Germans killed, wounded, or captured. American commanders considered their troops effective because they were making progress in capturing territory and killing the enemy, both of which led to ultimate victory.

Less than a quarter of a century after the D-Day landings at Normandy, assessing wartime progress and effectiveness proved much more challenging. When United States Regular Army and Marine forces arrived in the Republic of South Vietnam in 1965 they confronted a war in which useful metrics for success or failure were not readily identifiable. With a ubiquitous enemy and no clearly defined front lines, U.S. soldiers and commanders struggled to devise substitutes for gauging progress and effectiveness. Their conventional World War II experiences offered few useful perspectives. Occupying terrain no longer indicated military success. The political context of fighting an insurgency complicated the process of counting destroyed enemy units or determining if hamlets and villages were secured or pacified. In short, the metrics for assessing progress and effectiveness in World War II no longer sufficed for counterinsurgency operations. Operation Attleboro, fought between September 14 and November 24, 1966, typified the complexities of evaluating unit effectiveness and operational progress in an unconventional environment. It would be a problem that would plague American leaders for the duration of their war in Vietnam.

Dubious Metrics in Vietnam

In February 1966, the commander of the U.S. Military Assistance Command, Vietnam (MACV), General William C. Westmoreland, arrived at Honolulu for a presidential summit meeting to receive formal guidance for the coming year. Westmoreland had been in command for over eighteen months and had supervised the buildup of American forces in Vietnam. In the dark days of 1965, when South Vietnam seemed on the verge of collapse, he had managed the allied riposte to the dual threat of North Vietnamese Army (NVA) units and southern communist revolutionary forces (Vietcong[9]). By year's end, a wave of optimism swept through the American mission in South Vietnam. The U.S. 1st Cavalry Division had won an apparently stunning victory over NVA regulars in the Central Highlands' Ia Drang

Valley. Other American units were aggressively pursuing southern insurgent forces. After a series of coups between 1963 and 1965 that wracked the South Vietnamese government, political stability finally seemed to be emerging in Saigon.

At Honolulu, Secretary of Defense Robert S. McNamara and Secretary of State Dean Rusk assigned Westmoreland a number of goals to help gauge American progress for the coming year. Among the primary strategic objectives, increasing the percentage of South Vietnam's population living in secure areas ranked high. So too did multiplying base areas denied to the Vietcong and pacifying high-priority locales. These were hardly new goals. However, with the introduction of American ground combat forces in mid-1965, McNamara and Rusk believed they finally had the tools to make substantial progress in all fields. Westmoreland, though, viewed his overall mission as a sequential process. To MACV's commander, the summit meeting's first strategic objective of "attrit[ing] . . . Viet Cong and North Vietnamese forces at a rate as high as their capability to put men into the field" preceded any major efforts toward pacification or population security. While President Lyndon B. Johnson had hoped that the conference would spur social and domestic reform in South Vietnam, military operations took center stage in 1966.[10]

Westmoreland set his sights on the northwest portion of South Vietnam's III Corps Tactical Zone. From there, the communists drew strength from their inviolable base areas inside the Cambodian border while maintaining pressure on Saigon.[11] Westmoreland's prime target was the 9th People's Liberation Armed Forces (PLAF) Division. A major Vietcong unit supporting the NVA, the 9th had parried local U.S. forces for months. If the division were destroyed, MACV argued, pacification of the countryside could begin in earnest. Preoccupied with searching for and destroying enemy formations, the Americans overlooked that much of the Vietcong's power derived from its political organization in the rural villages and hamlets outside of Saigon. Based on their conventional experiences from World War II and the Korean War, many U.S. commanders viewed attrition of the enemy as a necessary first step to achieving their larger strategic ends. Westmoreland clearly thought along these lines when he ordered Operation Attleboro launched in the fall of 1966.[12]

The battles comprising Operation Attleboro illustrated the ephemeral nature of American gains against the Vietcong. Brigadier General Edward H. de Saussure's 196th Brigade moved into Tay Ninh province in mid-September and immediately began a series of battalion-sized probing operations searching for supply caches and enemy base camps. The 196th had been in country for less than two months, and enemy contact during the campaign's first weeks had been light. On November 3, de Saussure stumbled into the lead reconnaissance company of the 9th Division. Enemy machine gun and rocket fire ripped into the American formations.[13] De Saussure's soldiers, slowed by command and control difficulties, groped blindly through the dense jungle, taking casualties from mines, booby traps, and constant sniper fire. For the 196th, the actions in Tay Ninh were a sobering initiation to insurgent combat. Despite these initial troubles, Attleboro quickly expanded into a full-blown search-and-destroy operation. Major General William E. DePuy, commander of the 1st Infantry Division, took control of the fighting as brigades from the 4th and 25th Infantry Divisions rushed into Tay Ninh province. On November 6, artillery and Air Force B-52 bombers pummeled suspected enemy locations. For a loss of one killed and 23 wounded, the Americans had inflicted 170 enemy casualties.[14]

Over the next three weeks, the 9th PLAF Division sparred with the growing number of American units inside War Zone C. By Attleboro's conclusion on 24 November, eighteen U.S. and three South Vietnamese infantry battalions, along with twenty-four batteries of artillery, had participated in the operation. The Americans received support from an impressive array of logistical and fire support assets. Nearly 8,900 tons of supplies were flown into Tay Ninh during Attleboro, while U.S. airmen flew over 1,600 sorties and dropped 12,000 tons of ordnance. On one day of fighting alone, November 8, artillerymen fired over 14,000 rounds of ammunition.[15]

General DePuy found Attleboro's results extremely satisfying. American units reportedly inflicted 1,016 casualties on the 9th Division during the nearly two-month long battle. Relying on body counts in Vietnam, however, was problematic at best, fraught with intentional inaccuracies at worst. Possible kills, double-counting, estimations, exaggerations, and difficult terrain all made body counting an imprecise technique for measuring progress. In a war partly concerned with enemy attrition, though, there seemed to be few alternatives. As Westmoreland's chief intelligence officer curtly stated, "To obtain the attrition rate, enemy bodies had to be counted."[16]

While attrition formed an important element of American strategy in Vietnam, it hardly served as the guiding principle. Westmoreland believed that destroying enemy forces would help lead to larger political ends. Even before Westmoreland's tenure, MACV had realized that quantitative reporting of enemy kills insufficiently measured progress in an unconventional environment. Body counts did not necessarily produce reliable qualitative assessments of the enemy's military and political strength. While General DePuy thought that Attleboro had crippled the 9th PLAF Division, after the first week of November the Vietcong simply refused to fight. They instead withdrew west, closer to their Cambodian bases. Once DePuy's combat units left, the VC quietly returned. Reducing the Vietcong's fighting power had not diminished their political influence within the local hamlets and villages. Killing the enemy was one thing. Defeating him politically was something altogether different. Attleboro did not break the Vietcong's political hold in Tay Ninh province, a point that few American commanders realized at the time.[17]

If estimating progress during Operation Attleboro proved difficult, so too did assessing unit and soldier effectiveness in the jungles and dense thickets of Tay Ninh province. During the fighting's opening rounds in early November, American units quickly became separated from one another and disoriented in the harsh terrain. Westmoreland relieved General de Saussure on November 14 and MACV reluctantly concluded that the 196th Infantry Brigade had "cracked" under the pressures of combat.[18] Clearly, unit and soldier performance under fire concerned MACV, but other problems existed as well. If killing the enemy did not translate into political progress, how could MACV accurately measure effectiveness and progress at all? How would MACV know if an area was "pacified?" How should commanders define "security?" If intelligence officers were unable to provide precise assessments of enemy strength levels, how would field commanders know if the Vietcong and North Vietnamese forces were in fact succumbing to attrition? In a counterinsurgency environment, how did American officers and soldiers know whether or not they were making progress over time? It is upon these questions, and most importantly the last, which this study looks to shed light.

Measuring Counterinsurgency Effectiveness

Separating the assessment of military effectiveness from that of operational and strategic progress is critical to both army operations and organizational learning. Progress often validates unit effectiveness, doctrine, training, and an army's tactical approach to fighting. Progress on a conventional, linear battlefield is often clearly discernable. An army on the offense is either moving forward or not, killing enemy troops or not. A defending army is either holding its ground or retiring before the enemy. Progress, of course, is not constant. Stalled offensives can recover momentum, just as crumbling defenses can recuperate after early setbacks. The Allied breakout from the Norman *bocage* region and the subsequent hardening of German defenses along the Siegfried Line illustrated how success and failure can be fleeting. Still, in most conventional operations, progress is tangible—to the combatants, to the civilian populace, and to both sides' political leadership. Such is usually not the case in counterinsurgencies.[19]

In fact, the unconventional nature of the Vietnam War created innumerable problems for those measuring progress and military effectiveness. MACV, to its credit, realized early on that it needed to develop assessment metrics for fighting an insurgency. The military staff, however, produced an unmanageable system. MACV's monthly "Measurement of Progress" reports covered innumerable aspects of the fighting in Vietnam—force ratios, VC/NVA incidents, tactical air sorties, weapons losses, security of base areas and roads, population control, area control, and hamlet defenses. Though kill ratios became a central yardstick for many U.S. combat units, even contemporary officers sensed that they were inadequate. In a 1974 survey of army generals who served in Vietnam, 55 percent noted that the kill ratio was a "misleading device to estimate progress."[20]

Given the complexities of establishing appropriate metrics in a counterinsurgency environment, this work evaluates how the American army in Vietnam defined and measured its own progress and effectiveness. It argues that the U.S. Army component of MACV failed to accurately gauge performance and progress because, as an organization, it was unable to identify what Scott S. Gartner has called "dominant indicators" within the complex operating environment of Southeast Asia. In developing the dominant indicator approach for assessing wartime effectiveness, Gartner has argued that military organizations often misjudge how they are performing because a host of variable factors influence combat. Contradictory evaluations frequently result. For Gartner, the "modern battlefield produces too much information for individuals to assess fully. So they reduce the available information to specific indictors." Dominant indicators thus "represent an organization's central measure of performance."[21] While much of the Vietnam historiography maintains that "body counts" served as the U.S. Army's only indicator of success in Vietnam, this argument is too simplistic and unsupported by the vast number of reports generated by MACV in attempting to measure wartime progress.[22]

In revealing how American officers and soldiers, particularly those assigned to MACV, assessed both their effectiveness and progress in Vietnam, this study argues that the U.S. Army's ineffective approach to establishing functional metrics resulted from two primary factors. First, few officers possessed any real knowledge on how to gauge progress in an unconventional environment, particularly within the distinct setting of South Vietnam. While officers understood the basics of political-military coordination in countering insurgencies, and faithfully attempted to implement such an approach in Vietnam, the majority held only a superficial appreciation of the intricacies involved in unconventional warfare. Most American officers serving in MACV deployed to Southeast Asia with limited knowledge or practical experience in assessing counterinsurgency operations. They possessed even less understanding of the cultural landscape on which they were fighting. As the Attleboro experience implies, notions of one's own effectiveness mattered as much as the reality of that effectiveness. MACV's process of establishing what was thought to be useful performance metrics thus becomes an important undercurrent within this work.

Second, the U.S. Army in Vietnam often stumbled through the conflict without a consensus on its strategy. In its inability to develop coherent strategic objectives supporting broad policy goals, MACV never conveyed to its officers in the field how best to defeat the communist insurgency. Almost by default, American combat operations centered on three tasks—search and destroy, clearing operations, and security.[23] While MACV designed these missions to support pacification and the re-establishment of governmental control in South Vietnam, their wide range undermined efforts at measuring progress. Metrics for a search-and-destroy mission in 1966 might not be practical for a pacification mission in 1969. The body count made sense when fighting NVA regiments in the Central Highlands. It served little use, however, in determining how much progress a Mekong Delta village was making in freeing itself from insurgent influence. MACV never articulated how field commanders should prioritize their efforts, for in large part it never agreed on where the main threat lay. Pacification and civic action missions often conflicted with the competing tasks of defeating North Vietnamese main force units. The unresolved debate lasted throughout the United States' involvement in Southeast Asia and left MACV without a clear strategy to assess.

Left with insufficient foundational knowledge of counterinsurgencies and vague strategic objectives, MACV embraced Secretary of Defense McNamara's advice that everything that was measurable should in fact be measured. The problem of gauging effectiveness and progress stemmed not from a lack of effort on the part of army officers or a single-minded commitment to counting bodies. Rather, complications followed from collecting too many data points without evaluating how accurately such data reflected progress on the battlefield. Few within the American mission analyzed the data to develop meaningful trends. Senior officers thus had no way of accurately assessing their level of success in counterinsurgency operations. Rarely did MACV staff officers link their metrics to their strategic objectives. Consequently, MACV—and much of DoD—went about measuring everything and, in a real sense, measured nothing. In the process of data collection, the data had become an end unto itself. Ultimately, this failure in establishing functional metrics of effectiveness and progress played a significant role in undermining the American conduct of the war in Southeast Asia.[24]

In Search of Relevant Metrics

In the late 1980s, Allan R. Millet, Williamson Murray, and Kenneth H. Watman developed a comprehensive framework for gauging the effectiveness of military organizations. The authors defined military effectiveness as "the process by which armed forces convert resources into fighting power. A fully effective military is one that derives maximum combat power from the resources physically and politically available."²⁵ They characterized combat power as "the ability to destroy the enemy while limiting the damage that he can inflict in return." Millet, Murray, and Watman then outlined a way to assess effectiveness at the political, strategic, operational, and tactical levels of war. Political effectiveness consisted of securing resources in the required quantity and quality. Strategic effectiveness meant the ability to obtain politically derived national goals using those resources. At the operational level, the authors posited that effective military organizations flexibly integrated combat arms to achieve their strategic objectives. Finally, they defined tactical effectiveness in terms of battlefield movement, destruction of enemy forces, and logistical support for tactical engagements.²⁶

While appropriate for conventional military operations such as the 1944 Normandy invasion, the above framework seems insufficient for assessing counterinsurgency effectiveness. Political efficacy has less to do with mobilizing national resources at home than coordinating political and military actions within the theater of conflict. Even the definitions of military effectiveness and combat power appear inappropriate for unconventional warfare. Destruction of enemy forces does not necessarily translate into operational or strategic success. The ability to hold or gain ground—a measure of effectiveness in Trevor N. Dupuy's *Numbers, Predictions and War*—may mean little within the political conflict between insurgents and the population.²⁷

If more recent literature offers little guidance for measuring counterinsurgency effectiveness, Vietnam-era American officers had few historical resources and even less practical experience upon which to draw. This is not to say that counterinsurgency was unstudied in the late 1950s and early 1960s. Changes in U.S. and Soviet Cold War strategies created an upsurge in insurgency literature. In January 1961, Soviet Premier Nikita Khrushchev pledged support to countries waging "wars of national liberation" against Western influence. President John F. Kennedy, Jr., countered, having already renounced the Eisenhower administration's reliance on strategic nuclear deterrence. In its place, Kennedy sought a more balanced approach (flexible response) to the American strategy of containment, increasing conventional ground forces and emphasizing the use of Special Forces.²⁸ The changing political environment encouraged a spurt of treatises and commentary on unconventional warfare. Interpretations of guerrilla warfare and counterinsurgency operations flourished, from Cuban Che Guevara to Briton Robert Thompson and a host of "specialists" in between. The expanding literature provoked Vietnam expert Bernard B. Fall to lament that "too many amateur counter-insurgency cooks have had their hands in stirring the revolutionary warfare broth."²⁹

Fall himself would maintain "the difference between defeat and victory in Revolutionary War" was that "the people and the army must 'emerge on the same side of the fight.'"³⁰ This political dimension of insurgency did not lie outside the intellectual capacity of U.S. Army officers in the early 1960s. Several commentators thought the French had lost in Indochina during the 1950s because of their inability to gain the political support of an increasingly nationalistic civilian population.³¹ British experiences in Malaya and the U.S. advisory role in Greece also seemed to indicate that revolutionary warfare would be an essential part of modern conflict and that strategy must include more than military elements.³² Reflective officers grasped the need to coordinate military and political actions. The answer, wrote Major General Edward G. Lansdale in 1964, "is to oppose the Communist idea with a better idea."³³ For commanders on the ground, however, implementing such a proposal was not so straightforward. How could a division commander devise and offer a "better idea" once he was deployed to Southeast Asia and engaged in combat operations? Once occupied in searching for and destroying enemy units, there often seemed little incentive to devote time and resources away from actual fighting.

American officers largely dismissed British and French experiences for their seeming irrelevance to tactical combat operations in Vietnam. Westmoreland believed that Malaya's unique environment and political situation offered few lessons for MACV.³⁴ Thus, despite a rising interest on the subject, U.S. officers came across few suggestions for measuring success in counterinsurgencies. Most understood the political element of unconventional warfare but struggled to find advice on integrating military operations into the larger political context of fighting against insurgencies. In spite of the mass of counterinsurgency writings, military officers possessed few practical texts on the political-military relationships of revolutionary warfare. Even fewer sources discussed measuring effectiveness once military units were engaged in fighting insurgents.

Given the dearth of resources on measuring counterinsurgency effectiveness, it seems no wonder that U.S. officers found it difficult to evaluate their efforts in Vietnam. Achieving political objectives using military tools was a complicated task. Most officers deploying to Vietnam knew population security to be an important task within the political realm of counterinsurgency. The question remained of how commanders could discern whether their units were making progress. Robert Thompson illustrated the problems in establishing criteria based on hostile incident rates. A decrease in enemy incidents might mean the government was in control but might also mean the insurgents were so established politically they no longer needed to fight. Thompson did propose that the quality of information voluntarily gained from the population was an important gauge, perhaps indicating that qualitative standards were more important than quantitative ones in determining progress. As he noted in 1969, "In the end an insurgency is only defeated by good government which attracts voluntary popular support."³⁵ For young American officers and soldiers hardly operating in the same political universe as Vietnamese villagers, such metrics certainly were difficult to measure accurately.

The nature of combat in Vietnam compounded these difficulties. No two battles or engagements were identical. Environmental, behavioral, and political circumstances all varied in ways that may have seemed haphazard to Americans unfamiliar with unconventional warfare.[36] Further muddying the waters was the "mosaic" nature of revolutionary warfare in Vietnam. As Westmoreland's chief intelligence officer persuasively asserted, depending on the balance between military and political struggles, insurgents often avoided combat in one area while seeking it in another. Consequently, what might have been an effective counterinsurgency technique in one province or district might be irrelevant or even counterproductive in another portion of the country.[37] This mosaic nature, which many American senior officers seemed to have overlooked, made assessing army progress in Vietnam all the more daunting.

So too did the nature of the American military experience in Southeast Asia. U.S. Army policies for the rotation of personnel did little to promote either transmission of lessons or thoughtful analysis of unit effectiveness. As one observer noted, the "shortness of tours for staff and commanding officers (while sound for the troops on grounds of morale), together with the conformity of the system, led to a dependence on statistical results."[38] The validity of these statistics often depended entirely upon the reporting commander. With tours of duty rarely extending beyond one year, a commander's perceptions could be a significant variable in determining organizational effectiveness.

No less important was the MACV change of command between William Westmoreland and Creighton Abrams. While many accounts overstate the differences between Westmoreland and Abrams, an important point remains. Shifts in command focus and in national strategy objectives required changes to metrics for determining the effectiveness of MACV's own operational plans. Since MACV never made such modifications, its system for measuring progress and effectiveness became increasingly irrelevant as the war proceeded.[39]

Doctrinal gaps added yet another element of uncertainty. Commanders could not even turn to their own field manuals to determine military effectiveness in a counterinsurgency environment. Department of the Army Field Manual 31–16, *Counterguerrilla Operations*, while comprehensive, offered scant advice on how to gauge progress in an unconventional war. The manual did counsel commanders and staffs to develop detailed estimates of both the civil and military situation in their areas of operation. This included analyzing weather and terrain, the population, the guerrilla forces, and what resources the host country could offer. The doctrine counseled staffs to assess the effectiveness of the guerrilla, his relation to the population, and the effectiveness of his communications and intelligence networks. At the same time, FM 31–16 recommended that planners assess the "effectiveness of measures to deny the guerrilla access to resources required by him."[40] Left unanswered was the question of "how?"

As the war proceeded, few if any Americans truly knew if they were winning or losing. Operating blindly made it nearly impossible for MACV to make prudent adjustments to tactical and operational procedures. Such confusion made it equally difficult for administration officials to provide strategic focus as the war proceeded. Frustration became palpable at the highest levels of command in Vietnam. Major General Frederick C. Weyand, commander of II Field Force, offered his assessments to a visiting Washington official in late 1967. "Before I came out here a year ago, I thought we were at zero. I was wrong. We were at minus fifty. Now we're at zero."[41]

A Framework for Assessment

All this raises the question of whether one can even quantify something as abstract as a counterinsurgency campaign. In such an environment, what is a measurable standard? One could make the argument that metrics in counterinsurgency operations are pointless. Political will, loyalty of the population, and an individual's sense of security cannot be accurately measured. But if there are no measurable standards in a counterinsurgency operation, do senior officials simply measure progress based on a military commander's instinct within his area of responsibility? This appears problematic, regardless of how much senior officers trust their subordinate leaders' judgments. Certainly commanders' personal assessments are important, but relying solely on intuition in determining progress is just as troubling as relying exclusively on statistics such as body counts.

In revealing how American officers and soldiers assessed their effectiveness and progress in Vietnam, this study looks beyond body counts. MACV established a host of other metrics that often contradicted one another and provided a false sense of progress. General DuPuy's evaluation of Operation Attleboro suggests that relying on the wrong indicators can result not only in contradictory assessments but inaccurate ones as well. Reports exaggerated the damage inflicted on the 9th PLAF Division, damage that hardly upset the Vietcong's political hold in Tay Ninh province. This relationship between indicators and resultant staff estimates and command decisions serves as the principal framework for analysis of this study. It will examine three main areas in which officers and soldiers defined and evaluated their effectiveness in counterinsurgency operations during their time in Vietnam.

The first area of analysis can be defined as *metrics of mission success* and takes a broad interpretation of combat power, expanding the definition to include political, social, and cultural aspects. Naturally, the overall objective of military operations in Vietnam was important for measuring mission success. As historian Russell Weigley stressed, "to answer the question of whether an institution is effective, we must first ask the further question: effective in pursuit of what purposes?"[42] Even while prosecuting his strategy of attrition, Westmoreland argued that pacification efforts remained the crucial element of American policy. Despite this assertion, body counts seemingly became the prominent index of progress in a war without front lines and territorial objectives.[43] This study uncovers the host of other metrics used by MACV to measure its progress. It examines how officers defined and measured pacification security, how they evaluated the effectiveness of their Army of the Republic of Vietnam (ARVN) training programs, and how they assessed the damage being inflicted on the enemy's political infrastructure.

Finding dominant indicators for mission success became increasingly difficult as MACV added further metrics to evaluate local support and popular attitudes. In exploring these metrics, this study will consider how MACV measured the population's trust and cooperation. It probes how U.S. officers assessed voluntary aid from villagers and to what extent local residents trusted their governmental officials or feared insurgents, who so often reemerged when American forces departed. This study additionally reveals the problems MACV faced in rating its performance in winning the intelligence war, arguably a prerequisite for winning the larger war in Vietnam. Army officers too often stressed quantity over quality in their reporting systems. In the process, they at times missed the importance of information being voluntarily provided as a metric of mission success. Villagers trusting U.S. advisors enough to identify insurgents within their hamlets seemed an important indicator of progress. If American forces were pursuing insurgent units without local assistance, conceivably their offensive operations mattered little. Broken Vietcong cells simply would be replaced by a sympathetic or frightened population.

Perhaps clear measures of ineffectiveness were equally as important as measures of success. *Metrics of mission failures* thus comprise the second area in which this study analyzes MACV's system for assessing effectiveness and progress. Such metrics should have covered a wide range of potential missteps—unwarranted "collateral damage," wrongful detentions, or civilian deaths based on faulty intelligence, or enemy initiated battlefield contact. While arguably a negative approach to gauging progress, it seems a vital element of confronting an insurgency. U.S. strategy in Vietnam depended on units operating within legal boundaries to maintain legitimacy among the population. Contemporary counterinsurgency literature discussed the importance of operating within these bounds, and keeping track of transgressions may have helped to refine military operations in a given area. Surely it would have been advisable for officers to measure untoward acts of violence on those civilians they were charged to protect.

The final area of analysis can be described as *metrics of organizational effectiveness* and considers how the U.S. Army assessed itself as an institution. Both historians and former officers have held varying perspectives on the army's performance during the Vietnam War, especially in the conflict's latter years. This study probes that debate, asking if the quality of American ground combat troops eroded over time. This institutional-based metric rests largely on factors internal to the U.S. Army, such as morale, unit cohesion, and the will to fight. As such, commanders' assessments of their units loom large. Determining a unit's level of motivation and morale were among the most intangible aspects of assessing military effectiveness in Vietnam. These are critical areas to explore, however, because they affected the army's capacity to accomplish its assigned missions.

Measuring organizational effectiveness is further warranted because of its relationship to the metrics of mission success and failure. Here, one must distinguish between—and separate—the terms "effectiveness" and "progress," especially for counterinsurgencies. As this work demonstrates, the two concepts, while related, are not the same. American commanders in Vietnam, however, often conflated and confused the terms. Throughout the war, they trumpeted the combat effectiveness of their troops on the battlefield, believing that such effectiveness equated to progress in the overall war effort. Yet in the complex political-military environment of Vietnam, effectively killing the enemy did not guarantee progress toward strategic objectives. Therefore, this study explores not only how MACV defined and perceived organizational effectiveness but how senior officers related these notions to their broader evaluations of progress.

Finally, this last area of analysis investigates whether there was a decline of unit effectiveness within the U.S. Army over time. Poor race relations, drug problems, and contentious officer-enlisted relations epitomized the final years of American involvement in Vietnam. This study asks if these issues truly eroded the army's effectiveness. It seems important to ask if ostensible changes within the U.S. Army's ranks in the early 1970s altered how senior officers wrestled with measuring success.

Limits of the Study

Counterinsurgencies are complex affairs. Former advisor Dave R. Palmer claimed that the American war in Vietnam in 1966 included four components: "the air campaign against North Vietnam; a nation-building effort within South Vietnam; a diplomatic offensive to put pressure on Hanoi to cease its aggression; and Westmoreland's ground battle in the South."[44] While modern ground combat rarely, if ever, occurs in a vacuum, this study will limit its focus to the U.S. Army experience during the Vietnam War. External variables such as air power and the performance of ARVN allies certainly influenced the U.S. Army's ability to achieve its objectives. However, these areas will be considered only to the extent that they shaped the army's perceptions of its own progress and effectiveness. As an example, this study will not evaluate air power effectiveness in Vietnam. Rather, it will assess how army officers viewed air power as a means for increasing their own effectiveness in winning the war.[45]

Clearly, U.S. Army combat units were not the only American forces operating in South Vietnam. American advisors, working with both ARVN units and local district and provincial chiefs, were intricately involved in missions of pacification and Vietnamization. Their efforts in measuring effectiveness had a marked influence on command and staff perceptions at MACV. The Hamlet Evaluation System (HES), established in January 1967, attempted to gauge progress in the pacification effort and fed directly into the Civil Operations and Revolutionary Development Support (CORDS) directorate at MACV. While a thorough discussion of the American advisory effort falls outside the parameters of this study, U.S. district and provincial advisors and those training ARVN units supplied a wealth of data to MACV. How well MACV thought evaluation tools such as HES helped assess overall progress during the war is crucial to understanding the relationship between pacification programs and American strategy.

U.S. Marine Corps operations also fall outside the purview of this study, even though the Corps operated under the MACV command structure. Despite their influence on certain campaigns and battles, and their oftentimes innovative way of approaching pacification missions, the marines ultimately did little to alter the course of American strategy or the way in which the command measured progress and effectiveness. They often served only as an auxiliary to MACV planning and operations. As an example, the pioneering approach of Combined Action Platoons, a combination of marine volunteers and Vietnamese militia living inside villages and working primarily on civic action projects, failed to take hold at the strategic level. More importantly, the marines were responsible for a limited geographical area and could not affect the insurgency's attack on large portions of the country or the stability of the Saigon government. Though the marines offered creditable alternatives to fighting the insurgency in Vietnam and fought valiantly in some of the heaviest fighting of the war, their efforts, from MACV's perspective, too often remained of a secondary nature.

In the end, this is a study of how the U.S. Army component of the Military Assistance Command in Vietnam assessed its progress and effectiveness throughout a long war in Southeast Asia. Without existing evaluation models for counterinsurgency operations, the army struggled to measure if and how much progress was being made against an enemy committed to revolutionary warfare. Searching always for discernible signs of progress, either on the military or political front, MACV and its field commanders labored to develop accurate metrics of success for an unconventional environment. They never succeeded. The conventional benchmarks of World War II no longer applied. That the army never could determine if it was winning or losing goes far in explaining the final outcome of the war in Vietnam.

"There are three kinds of lies: lies, damned lies and statistics."
—MARK TWAIN, *Autobiography*

1 Of Questions Not Asked: Measuring Effectiveness in the Counterinsurgency Era

BY THE MID-1950S it seemed increasingly possible that war might no longer be practical in an atomic age. Recent experiences in the Korean War had left U.S. Army officers unsatisfied with the outcome and academic theorists exploring the dangers of escalation. Fighting a massive, national war with few restraints, akin to World War II, not only seemed ill-suited for curbing the global communist threat but risked nuclear annihilation. In 1957, the University of Chicago's Robert Osgood entered the debate, publishing *Limited War: The Challenge to American Strategy*. Osgood claimed that "total war" was both impractical and dangerous. The Chicago professor acknowledged that "the limitation of war is morally and emotionally repugnant to the American people." He argued forcefully, however, for the capacity to wage war in which belligerents rationally could limit and control both political policy and military operations. Only by realizing the "principle of political primacy" could Americans successfully check communist aggressors bent on increasing their sphere of global influence.[1]

While Osgood's arguments made political sense, army officers struggled with applying military power in the context of limited conflict. Fighting limited wars depended not only on technical and tactical acumen but also on balancing the relationship between national power and international politics. Such relationships seemed particularly murky. For many officers, the Korean War had ended in an inconclusive draw in large part because it was a limited conflict.[2] Further causing concern,

World War II had disrupted the social and political fabric of European colonial holdings. The French army's expulsion from Indochina in 1954 appeared to support Mao Tse Tung's November 1957 proclamation that the "East Wind prevails over the West Wind." A rash of assassinations and terrorist attacks in South Vietnam did little to assuage American officials. At the same time, the Soviet Sputnik launch and the threat of atomic war cast a long shadow over political and military thinking, underscoring the growing complexity of employing effective military power in the Cold War era.[3]

To their credit, many U.S. Army officers realized the political and technological challenges facing their profession. The imprint of conventional ground combat in World War II and Korea, as well as institutional cultural preferences for traditional battle, surely made a mark on the officer corps. Still, officers did contemplate changes affecting their profession. Within the army served officers who addressed the unresolved tactical and strategic problems of both nuclear and limited war throughout the mid-1950s and early 1960s.[4] Contrary to arguments that almost all officers wedded themselves to a concept of conventional battle on the European plains, the army made serious and thoughtful attempts to develop unconventional warfare doctrine that addressed both military and nonmilitary matters.[5] Missing was not an appreciation for balancing political and military action in a counterinsurgency environment. Rather, officers had yet to define a system for evaluating their efforts when engaging irregular forces and insurgents.

Professional journals and army doctrine reinforced many of Osgood's arguments on the need for a limited war capacity.[6] Yet while army officers appreciated the complexities of irregular warfare, they could turn to few sources offering advice on how best to gauge success in an unconventional, revolutionary environment. At a time when systems analysis became increasingly accepted throughout the Department of Defense, computer-based research methods presented a valuable tool to compensate for the dearth of suitable yardsticks. Officers setting out to Vietnam thus deployed with only a modest intellectual foundation for measuring effectiveness in a counterinsurgency environment. At the same time, they were becoming gradually more tolerant of and comfortable with systems analysis programs aiding their assessments of wartime progress. This confluence of doctrinal deficiencies and technological advances would shape how the U.S. Army defined and measured progress throughout the war in Vietnam.

Theory over Time

The problems of revolutionary insurgencies posed undeniable challenges for American strategists at a time when communists seemed to be fomenting insurrection in World War II's aftermath. Nonetheless, small wars, popular rebellions, and irregular warfare had been a part of armed struggle for centuries. Historical commentaries on such conflicts—from the likes of Carl von Clausewitz, Denis Davydov, and T. E. Lawrence—offered useful perspectives for American officers during the Cold War. Within this vast literature, however, imprecise language often plagued interpretations of regular armies fighting against unconventional or popular forces. Clausewitz, as an example, characterized effective insurgencies as those in which "the element of resistance" existed "everywhere and nowhere." Like many of his contemporaries, the Prussian theorist conflated political insurgents with both militia bands and sympathetic civilians involved in a general uprising.[7]

Early twentieth-century writers were no more discriminating in defining unconventional warfare. British Colonel C. E. Callwell's treatise on the subject vaguely defined "small wars" as "all campaigns other than those where both the opposing sides consist of regular troops." Neither Clausewitz nor Callwell offered comprehensive prescriptions for the modern counterinsurgent. Few historical tomes provided insights into determining how best to gauge effectiveness in an unconventional environment. Callwell argued for "bold and resolute procedure" (a consistent theme in U.S. Army counterinsurgency literature) yet furnished little rationale for how aggressiveness necessarily led to effectiveness.[8] Likewise, T. E. Lawrence's writings on Arab insurgencies stressed the importance of mobility, security, and converting the masses to "friendliness" yet left unanswered how to achieve and measure progress toward such ends.[9]

Despite these historical examples, some U.S. Army officers, doctrine writers in particular, appreciated the political nature of counterinsurgency operations. A 1962 publication by Fort Benning's Infantry School, titled "Selected Readings on Guerrilla Warfare," provided twenty historical instances in which nations "had been foresighted enough to plan for . . . [unconventional] activities." "Selected Readings" covered a wide historical spectrum—partisan warfare in the American Revolutionary South, Spanish guerrilla resistance against Napoleon, and the French *maquis* in World War II. Terse commentaries explored how guerrillas and insurgents had achieved success throughout history. Many of the case studies focused on military actions, such as infiltration techniques during the Trojan War. Several accounts, however, offered insights on non-military factors and demonstrated the importance of integrating political and psychological operations into the overall context of counterinsurgencies. Regarding Lawrence's participation in the Arab War, the authors commented upon the "relative unimportance of killing the enemy."[10]

Army doctrine writers comprehended the political nature of insurgencies, even if their terminology lacked precision. Throughout the late 1950s and early 1960s, most counterinsurgency literature made few distinctions among such terms as guerrilla, partisan, and insurgent.[11] Ambiguity complicated analysis. How could one successfully counter an insurgency without accurately identifying the threat? Still, at a foundational level, army field manuals recognized the need to coordinate military, political, social, and economic efforts. Published in January 1953, Field Manual (FM) 31–15, *Operations against Airborne Attack, Guerilla Action, and Infiltration*, offered wise counsel. "Failure to recognize and apply necessary nonmilitary measures may render military operations ineffective, regardless of how well these operations are planned and conducted." A decade later, army doctrine still espoused the role of political ideology and the importance of the civilian population's support. Simply killing or capturing the enemy guerrilla force would not "prevent the resurgence of the resistance movement."[12]

The army's appreciation for political-military coordination was well founded, given the appeal of national independence movements in the wake of World War II. Retired Marine Brigadier General Samuel B. Griffith in 1961 thought it "probable that guerrilla war, nationalist and revolutionary in nature, will flare up in one or more of half a dozen countries during the next few years." Griffith believed that few, if any, of these uprisings would be communist inspired. He contended, however, that such outbreaks would "receive the moral support and vocal encouragement of international Communism, and where circumstances permit, expert advice and material assistance as well."[13] The army's officer corps slowly began to embrace this point, with more of its professional journal articles pondering the theory behind and characteristics of unconventional warfare. One 1957 *Military Review* essay thoughtfully assessed Mao Tse-tung's theories and the basic principles for communist warfare in Asia. "Guerrilla warfare has come to stay," the author concluded. "It has revolutionized the conception of war."[14] Other articles followed as officers wrestled with the political and cultural aspects of what they simply termed "guerrilla warfare." By 1960, one *Military Review* contributor believed that guerrilla warfare had become a "major mainstay of all Communists" even if it was "not regarded as either a dominant or decisive method of operating."[15] All the while, the British and the French, and to a lesser extent the Americans themselves, were gaining experience in counterinsurgency.

Actions at the Edges

In a poignant scene from Gillo Pontecorvo's 1966 movie *The Battle of Algiers*, French Lieutenant Colonel Philippe Mathieu insists during a press conference that his paratroopers, having fought in the resistance during World War II, having survived Dachau and Buchenwald, and having battled for years in Indochina, are now serving in Algeria to do what their nation has asked: to crush the National Liberation Front

(FLN) resistance. Controversial tactics aside—the French viewed torture as an integral part of their tactical repertoire—the fictional Mathieu represented a professional body well-versed in counterinsurgency. The French army had amassed a wealth of practical knowledge, and their officers had published some of the best monographs on unconventional warfare. These accounts, though, offered few clues for measuring progress and effectiveness in such environments. Even when they did, strained Franco-American relations undercut any chances for sharing lessons between the two armies. As one American scoffed, "The French haven't won a war since Napoleon. What can we learn from them?"[16]

The French, of course, had learned. Ho Chi Minh's Vietnamese declaration of independence of September 2, 1945, led inexorably to the First Indochina War. Upon the outbreak of hostilities in late 1946, the French army battled Vietminh rebels who artfully employed Mao's theories of protracted warfare. Unwilling to concede Vietnamese independence, France found itself embroiled in a nationalist and popular war that became even more complex after the 1949 communist victory in China. Henri Navarre, who took command of French forces in Indochina in May 1953, realized the war's many domains—military, political, diplomatic, psychological, social, and economic.[17] Jean de Lattre de Tassigny, Navarre's predecessor, had thought it vital for indigenous military forces to serve as the foundation for defeating the Vietminh insurgents. De Tassigny argued that in "pacification work especially," Vietnamese soldiers needed to "fill the gap between the people and the leaders, to be a human link between the rural masses and the central government."[18] Unfortunately for the French, these accurate conceptions of the war never blossomed at the operational and tactical levels, a point for which American commentators leveled harsh criticism against their European allies.

French prosecution of the war, however flawed, demonstrated honest efforts to succeed within the complex parameters of an insurgency. Pacification planning included the *tache d'huile* (oil slick) tactic of expanding military and political control from key population centers into surrounding areas using a *quadrillage* system. This "gridding of the countryside" consisted of "each grid being carefully 'raked over' (the '*ratissage*') by troops thoroughly familiar with the area or guided by experts who knew the area well." In application, the system foundered on inadequate troop strength and lack of a compelling political message that could compete with Vietminh indoctrination at the village level.[19] Worse, French military strategy drifted. Officers pursued countless objectives—defeating General Vo Nguyen Giap's regular army divisions in open battle, preventing Vietminh infiltration into the strategically vital Tonkin Delta region, constructing a chain of defensive positions (known as the "de Lattre Line") to free units for offensive campaigns, employing river craft units called *dinassauts* to penetrate the country's interior, and accelerating training of the

Vietnamese National Army. The disjointed strategy dissipated French strength and led ultimately to the catastrophic defeat at Dien Bien Phu in May 1954. Peace negotiations at Geneva soon followed in July.[20]

The U.S. Army swiftly dismissed the French experience in Southeast Asia. One study of guerrilla warfare in the Indochina War provided an inventory of failures that left readers doubtful of any French military proficiency. The "short list" included poor intelligence, underestimating the enemy, lack of a positive political program, a defensive-minded attitude, reluctance to get into the jungle, and undue reliance on air support.[21] Surely, given the chance, Americans would never make such foolish mistakes. As one U.S. colonel maintained, "two good American divisions with the normal aggressive American spirit could clean up the situation in the Tonkin Delta in ten months."[22] William C. Westmoreland's chief intelligence officer would remark after his own war in Vietnam that the "French made no effort to fight the political war—the war to win the support of the Vietnamese people."[23] In the process, the U.S. Army categorically rejected any insights the French might have offered into measuring effectiveness in Indochina.

Unlike Indochina, the French experience in the Algerian war for independence from 1954–1962 drew more American attention. French operations in Algeria not only were more recent but appeared more successful.[24] In fact, if the Americans had not learned from the war in Indochina, the French certainly had. Officers distilled lessons in countering the Vietminh and developed the theory of *guerre révolutionnaire*. By 1956, its concepts were influencing a large portion of the French officer corps. Advocating the interdependence of political, military, and psychological facets in revolutionary warfare (certainly nothing new in French military theory), *guerre révolutionnaire* rested on the principle of regaining control of the population. Military action pertained only as a subset of a larger integrated framework for defeating insurgencies.[25]

The French in Algeria undertook serious efforts to evaluate their effectiveness in breaking the insurgents' hold on the population. Officers assembled card catalogue files on all household occupants in their district for use in village spot checks and house-to-house searches. Simply cataloguing houses, of course, was relatively easy. Assessing the insurgency's strength proved more difficult. One study, completed by a French colonel after the 1957–1958 Opération Pilote, made "plain that pacification is a term of very relative meaning, including some features as continued rebel movement through the area and continued need for information from the local inhabitants."[26] A 1964 RAND report on counterinsurgency in Algeria specifically highlighted such evaluation problems. Noting the difficulty of assessing population attitudes, the report argued that not only was information difficult to evaluate, it often was just as difficult to obtain. "The best indications are the number of native soldiers on the side of the established power, the extent of desertions, and especially the quality and quantity of information obtained."[27]

While assessing popular attitudes proved nettlesome, evaluating military effectiveness remained no less complicated. The RAND report found "the evaluation of military successes against rebel bands is in itself quite difficult. The number of rebels killed (often swollen by civilians counted among the dead rebels) is less important than the number of military weapons seized, the number of prisoners and especially of recruits."[28] Experiences on the ground corroborated the analytical problems of using dead bodies and captured weapons as metrics for success. Jean-Jacques Servan-Schreiber, the famous French intellectual then lieutenant, held little faith in the weapons-counting process. "This question of arms involved us in a veritable acrobatics of accountancy. The regulations laid down that together with the dead counted after each 'engagement' the nature of the arms recovered should be specified." Servan-Schreiber found that administrative audits discovered "these entries were often pure imagination and the arms fictitious." Americans soon would be facing similar scrutiny for their own counting procedures in Vietnam.[29]

Prior to the U.S. commitment of ground troops to Vietnam, however, two French officers skillfully examined the complexity of counterinsurgency operations as expressed by Servan-Schreiber. David Galula, whose *Counterinsurgency Warfare: Theory and Practice* remains one of the subject's most incisive works, argued for a systematic approach in developing a counterinsurgency strategy. Outlining a prescriptive eight-step procedure, Galula argued that local civilians should not be treated as the enemy. Ultimate victory required the "permanent isolation of the insurgent from the population, isolation not enforced on the population but maintained by and with the population." By following a step-by-step approach, Galula believed the counterinsurgent provided "himself with a way of assessing at any time the situation and the progress made."[30]

Roger Trinquier similarly advocated a methodical approach to counterinsurgency. Here was contentious advice for U.S. officers who believed that the French army's lack of aggressiveness factored heavily in their loss to the Vietminh. Trinquier, however, saw steady progress essential for eliminating insurgent influence over the population. "The fight against the guerrilla must be organized methodically and conducted with unremitting patience and resolution. Except for the rare exception, *it will never achieve spectacular results, so dear to laurel-seeking military leaders.*"[31] Still, assessing the extent of popular support, as well as the insurgency's influence, remained problematic. How, for example, could the counterinsurgent accurately measure intimidation? Galula considered "political organization at the grass roots" an important indicator. His personal account on pacification in

Algeria offered more concrete metrics—how often his soldiers fired their weapons, how safely he could move from post to post, how accurate his population census was, and how often mayors shared information with him on rebel activities. For military commanders accustomed to relying upon terrain seized and enemy killed, Galula and Trinquier's counsel underscored the intricacies of counterinsurgency warfare.[32]

Among commentators of the French experience in Southeast Asia, Bernard B. Fall ranked first in American thinking. Born in France and a professor of international relations at Howard University, Fall had spent nearly fifteen years in Indochina, becoming one of its most respected scholars. His 1961 publication, *Street Without Joy*, a classic of the eight-year French-Indochina War, influenced a wide range of American officers preparing for deployment to Vietnam. Fall defined victory in revolutionary war as "the people and the army . . . emerg[ing] on the same side of the fight."[33] He realized that assessing progress toward victory required relevant indicators. The French criteria for "control" often had "no real meaning when it came to giving a factual picture of who owned what (or whom) throughout the Vietnamese countryside inside the French battle line, much less outside."[34] Fall argued that trends in levels of security and population control could be plotted objectively on a map given accurate reporting of assassinations, insurgent raids, and taxation by the Vietcong. Measuring "administrative control," however difficult, if done properly, provided military commanders with the most accurate assessment of their progress.[35]

While authorities like Galula and Fall offered several indicators for measuring success, U.S. officers also turned to other nations for insights on revolutionary warfare. The Malaya Emergency from 1948–1960 served as an attractive case study. British forces offered a seemingly textbook example for successful counterinsurgency operations. Socially and physically isolating the Malayan Communist Party (MCP) insurgents from the population, British officers effectively integrated civil service, police, and military programs. They adopted a strategy that emphasized gaining support of the people rather than defeating the insurgents through use of force.[36] British successes rested on building effective intelligence organizations, improving prosperity at the village level, and ensuring that the population "became increasingly confident that they would be protected if they took the risk of giving information" to government forces.[37]

However alluring the British triumph in Malaya, exceptional circumstances favored the implementation of their much-touted "Briggs Plan." At the end of a long peninsula, Malaya's geographic isolation made insurgent resupply from cross-border sanctuaries nearly impossible. A generally honest Malayan political system also aided British officers in bringing the population to their side. Perhaps most importantly, MCP insurgents were almost exclusively Chinese, an ethnic minority in Malaya, hindering their ability to "swim invisibly in the sea of society."[38] These geographic, political, and demographic features were not lost on outside observers. Bernard Fall agreed that the British experience in Malaya was close to the physical environment of the fighting in Vietnam, "but [was] totally different in the sociological, political, and ethnic factors so crucial to winning such a battle."[39] William Westmoreland later defended his own indifference to the British Advisory Mission in Vietnam from 1961 to 1965. "The Malaysia experience had some but not much relevance to ours. The British were fighting an insurgency force that was different ethnically from the Malaysians.... Secondly, the insurgents had no well established source of reinforcement and supply from outside. Third, they [the British] had a unified command."[40] Thus, as with much of the French experience in Indochina, British counterinsurgency efforts made relatively little impact on how the U.S. Army's officer corps determined ways to establish metrics for success in Vietnam.[41]

U.S. Army officers naturally looked to their own history in dealing with small wars. From the pacification campaign in the Philippines at the opening of the twentieth century to providing advice and support in Greece and again in the Philippines after World War II, American officers had developed a certain appreciation for counterinsurgency operations. The communist-led Greek insurrection in 1945 offered American officers a chance to cut their teeth on the problems of revolutionary warfare in the nascent Cold War era. Working under the Joint United States Military Advisory and Planning Group (JUSMAPG), advisors advocated aggressive "search-and-clear" operations while concurrently implementing progressive civil reforms to alleviate economic and social concerns.[42] General James Van Fleet, head of JUSMAPG, found valuable lessons in the Greek Civil War regarding "the mobilization and organization of foreign armies." More importantly, Van Fleet considered "the knowledge and experience gained" to be of "great value in the event of guerrilla warfare elsewhere."[43]

Contemporary counterinsurgency literature on the Greek Civil War emphasized the political. One American officer noted that for an insurgency to be successful "it must appeal to the fundamental political, moral, and ethical values of the people."[44] Practice, however, more often focused on tactical military execution. U.S. advisors criticized Greeks for their timidity and lack of aggressiveness in seeking out and destroying insurgents. However important political and social reform, U.S. Army officers found heavy firepower, close air support, and mobility as effective against insurgents as against the conventional forces they had fought in World War II. The defeat of the Greek communists in 1949 offered little incentive to assess the more difficult questions of how to measure effectiveness and progress on the nonmilitary front. Although officers outwardly accepted General George Grivas's conclusion that "Who wins over the people, has won half the battle," few sought ways to evaluate movement toward winning that critical half.[45]

The Hukbalahap insurgency in the Philippines swiftly followed, if not overlapped, American achievements in Greece. As the military arm of the Philippine Communist Party, the Huks challenged the landed-class political domination of a country devastated by World War II fighting. While Americans established an advisory group in 1947, not until 1950 did it become more active in advising the Filipino government and its armed forces against the Huks. As in Greece, Americans recognized the value of politico-military synchronization. A member of the army's military history office maintained that the "principal reason for the initial failure of counterinsurgency activities from the days when the Hukbalahap first began to make trouble was the fact that purely military operations were overemphasized." Arguably, the leadership of Minister of Defense Ramón Magsaysay most influenced events in the Philippines. Deftly coordinating political and economic reform with military campaigns, Magsaysay demonstrated the vital importance of inspired local administration (rather than simple military might) in defeating insurgent movements.[46]

Commentary on the Huk campaign discussed ways to measure effectiveness in countering the communist insurgents. One study offered a comprehensive summary of lessons addressing intelligence, civilian cooperation, leadership, security, and psychological warfare.[47] Two officers, one Filipino and one American, published an insightful history of the Huk campaign in 1962. Though Napoleon Valeriano and Charles Bohannan's *Counter-Guerrilla Operations: The Philippine Experience* gained little traction in the development of American counterinsurgency doctrine, its authors asked valuable questions for analyzing the effectiveness of counterinsurgency forces. Valeriano and Bohannan discussed how the transfer of political power could serve as useful information to the counterinsurgent. "Is the transfer of power authorized through elections?" "Do the voters take elections seriously? If not, why?" "Who is entitled to vote? How many do? Are their votes counted?" The two officers also sought ways to assess the composition, equipment, and state of training of governmental armed forces. The authors contended, however, that evaluation of an indigenous army's "strong and weak points is more difficult, since it so largely depends on the evaluator's appreciation of the requirements for successful counterguerrilla warfare."[48] In hindsight, Valeriano and Bohannan's questions for evaluating intelligence services, popular attitudes, and governmental agencies offered a promising yet unexploited framework for gauging counterinsurgency effectiveness.[49]

Thus, as the U.S. Army considered the possibility of counterinsurgency becoming a principal mission, its officers encountered few suggestions for measuring success in an unconventional setting. The French in Algeria had come closest to developing a systematic approach, yet Americans too often discounted their experiences. The joint Filipino-American campaign against the Huks held similar clues, but it went unnoticed by much of the army's officer corps.[50] Still, at least a few officers realized their operational environment was changing. One lieutenant colonel, reflecting on counterinsurgency in 1964, noted how army officers and civilian officials alike were gaining valuable experience in countries plagued by insurgency. "The major problem before us is to orchestrate the magnificent counterinsurgency resources we have into a single symphony."[51] For those looking to concentrate on counterinsurgency operations, the Cold War unfortunately demanded musicians elsewhere.

The Efficacy and Difficulties of Limited Warfare

If resources to combat insurgencies seemed plentiful in 1964, such was hardly the case in the early 1950s. The Truman Doctrine had expanded American global responsibilities by implementing a policy of Soviet containment to help "free peoples" around the world oppose "totalitarian regimes." The possibility of intervening in other nations' civil wars required both a systematic approach to foreign policy and a commitment to spend an increasing amount of capital on international commitments. The 1950 National Security Council (NSC) Report 68 served as a blueprint for Truman's assertive foreign policy. NSC-68 not only cemented the perception of a global communist menace throughout the 1950s and early 1960s but created a host of problems for the U.S. Army.[52] National objectives now demanded military proficiency in two seemingly unrelated fields—conventional war on a nuclear battlefield and counterinsurgency. Cold War–era officers still embraced the need, if not desire, to prepare for conventional war in Europe yet worried how training for unconventional warfare would affect army readiness. As the 1951 edition of FM 31–20, *Operations Against Guerrilla Forces*, contended: "All troops, both combat and service, committed to areas threatened by a guerilla menace must be trained in the special aspects of guerilla warfare and the active and passive countermeasures to be employed."[53]

Army Chief of Staff General George C. Decker agreed, arguing that units designed for conventional and tactical nuclear warfare were obviously "not the proper response to a band of guerrillas which in a flash will transform itself into a scattering of 'farmers.'"[54] Recent history, though, indicated that unconventional warfare rarely occurred in isolation. Army doctrine writers interviewed German officers to mine their experiences battling Soviet partisans on World War II's Eastern Front for insights into counterguerrilla operations on a conventional battlefield. While some professional journal studies offered advice on combating guerrillas in conventional war—one noting that the "anti-guerrilla" must simultaneously defend vital installations, attack the guerrillas, and win the support of the population—most studies proved generic. Though one assessment tangentially considered partisan effectiveness on the Eastern Front, American officers found little in the way of assessing the same for the counterinsurgent.[55]

The Korean conflict from 1950–1953 equally saw the use of partisans on a conventional battlefield, though North Korean and Chinese regulars clearly presented the gravest danger. In relation to metrics, geography served as a practical scorecard during the war's early maneuver phases. In the relatively static operations after 1951, however, ground gained or lost meant little. Commanders aimed only to maintain their defensive lines and inflict high numbers of enemy casualties during ongoing negotiations. As General Matthew B. Ridgway, the Eighth U.S. Army commander, noted, units should "have as their objective not the seizure of terrain but the maximum destruction of hostile persons and materiel at minimum cost to our forces."[56] Counting enemy losses quickly became a benchmark for success in this kind of war. Relying on objects that could be counted—enemy casualties, ammunition expended, patrols conducted—the army set a precedent for gathering figures and statistics that would persist into Vietnam.[57]

Frustrations with fighting in Korea underlined the difficulties of preparing for limited conventional conflict in the nuclear era while simultaneously grappling with the problems of revolutionary war. Friction arose over where best to focus the army's organization, training, and education for the next war.[58] One lieutenant colonel, writing in response to *Army* magazine's 1961 translation of Che Guevara's *Guerrilla Warfare*, discounted all the recent commotion over unconventional war. As the officer argued, "It appears that guerrilla warfare is, as I have long suspected, the application of sound military principles by a force organized and supported by expediency. Why further confound ourselves by surrounding this too, with an air of complexity?" Furthermore, if both Mao and Guevara acknowledged that revolutionary war ended in a conventional war of movement—"even though its origins are in the guerrilla army"—the U.S. Army certainly could wade its way through the early stages of a revolutionary conflict and eventually emerge at a point where its aptitude in conventional warfare would win the day.[59]

This need to maintain effectiveness and expertise across a wide military spectrum underscored the tensions within modern counterinsurgency doctrine and theory. Frenchmen like Galula and Trinquier stressed the importance of a methodical, systematic approach against insurgents, yet much of the U.S. Army's doctrine, literature, and training emphasized seizing the initiative and being aggressive.[60] To some, sound military principles precluded the need for developing a unique set of counterinsurgency skills. While some contemporary officers derided their profession's "cultural distaste for intellectual pursuit," the evolution of counterinsurgency doctrine suggested some appreciation for the complexities of unconventional warfare.[61] Still, for officers seeking insights into measuring progress and effectiveness in this environment, a significant gap remained within the army's field manuals and professional military education.

Questions Not Asked: Counterinsurgency Doctrine and Education

Beginning with the February 1951 publication of FM 31–20, *Operations Against Guerrilla Forces*, the army possessed a thoughtful field manual on resistance movements and guerrilla warfare. Advocating the coordination of political, administrative, and military actions, FM 31–20 set the general tone of counterinsurgency doctrine for years to come. The manual's author, Lieutenant Colonel Russell W. Volckmann, articulated three basic objectives of anti-guerrilla operations: isolating guerrilla forces from the civilian population, denying guerrillas contact with and support from the national government, and finally destroying the guerrilla forces.[62] While refraining from prescriptive recommendations (each insurrection was unique), FM 31–20 noted the importance of aggressive offensive operations, effective propaganda, impartial administrative measures, and detailed intelligence. No less salient, Volckmann emphasized the need for continuity in policy and personnel and the requirement of regional commanders to coordinate their actions.

Subsequent manuals pressed similar themes. FM 31–15, *Operations Against Airborne Attack, Guerrilla Action, and Infiltration*, published in January 1953, observed how effective guerrilla movements relied upon a sympathetic population. Mimicking earlier doctrinal advice for controlling the civilian populace, FM 31–15 contended that it was "much easier and more economical to prevent the outbreak of resistance and guerrilla warfare than to cope with it after it has developed."[63] FM 31–21, *Guerrilla Warfare*, opined in May 1955 that for anti-guerrilla actions to be successful, they "should be based on a detailed analysis of the country, national characteristics, the customs, beliefs, cares, hopes, and desires of the people."[64] By May 1961, FM 31–15, now entitled *Operations Against Irregular Forces*, introduced "ideological bases for resistance" and "civic action" into the doctrinal lexicon. Aggressiveness and constant pressure against the guerrilla, however, remained the hallmark of combat operations. Still, doctrinal manuals recommended that commanders understand the relationship between large-scale resistance movements and local sources of political, social, and economic dissatisfaction.[65]

By the time the Infantry School completed work on FM 31–16, *Counterguerrilla Operations*, in 1963, a certain continuity had emerged within the army's counterinsurgency doctrine. Field manuals stressed the importance of integrating political and military action in order to separate the insurrectionist from the population. Successful counterguerrilla operations relied upon superior mobility and intelligence, aggressive and imaginative leadership, and a comprehensive analysis and understanding of the civilian population. Doctrine revealed a growing appreciation for counterinsurgency's complexities. While FM 31–16 (1963) emphasized relentless pressure in harassing guerrilla forces, it also grasped that guerrillas often dispersed under that pressure. "Since the probable guerrilla force reaction to applied pressure is to move to another area or 'lie low' until the vigor of current counteraction has lessened, commanders must be particularly alert to consider the force not yet destroyed merely because opposition has halted."[66] Guerrilla forces might be lacking resources but not necessarily resourcefulness.

This realization persisted as one of the very few instances in which American counterinsurgency doctrine hinted at the problems of assessing effectiveness and progress in an unconventional environment. How was a commander to know if his units had succeeded in forcing the guerrilla to cease operations or merely suspend them until the conventional threat had passed? If terrain held little tactical value, how could commanders keep score of their progress against the guerrillas? Finally, how was a commander to assess the guerrillas' hold on the population? On these questions, doctrine remained silent. In fact, in none of the army's field manuals written during the 1950s or 1960s was any mention of developing measures for effectiveness or progress in counterinsurgency operations.

This gap in the doctrinal literature illustrated a larger problem within the army's views on counterinsurgency. In an attempt to refrain from prescription, doctrine remained unsatisfactorily generic. Of course, revolutionary wars usually evolved as unique events, largely because of each one's distinct political and social environments. Soviet partisan experiences in World War II offered only one set of circumstances when compared to the FLN in Algeria or the Vietminh in Indochina. Many American officers, though, rarely delved into such details and only scratched at the surface when thinking about counterinsurgencies. Such intellectual shortfalls would inhibit the army's ability to assess its organizational performance once committed to Vietnam.[67]

Professional military education within the army school system followed the path of counterinsurgency doctrinal development, though at a perceptibly slower pace. Not until 1958, a full seven years after the publication of FM 31–20, did the Command and General Staff College (CGSC) at Fort Leavenworth establish a Department of Unconventional Warfare and revise its curriculum to incorporate lessons on insurgencies. That year, school commandant Lieutenant General Lionel C. McGarr, who soon would head the Military Assistance Advisory Group (MAAG) in Vietnam, added instruction on guerrillas in limited war, unconventional warfare planning and operations, and anti-guerrilla operations. By the 1959–1960 academic year, CGSC students were receiving thirty-three hours of instruction on unconventional warfare during the thirty-eight week course. (By 1969, instruction increased to 222 hours.) As with doctrine, the devil lay in the details. Upon arrival in Saigon, McGarr asked the staff college to send him "everything we had" on unconventional warfare. The general recalled he was "a little taken aback of how little we had in the implementing phase." CGSC, McGarr conceded, had been "built on [the] high level approach. Not the implementation."[68]

While CGSC taught army field grade officers unconventional warfare theory, younger officers received even less practical instruction. The Infantry School at Fort Benning waited until 1962 to begin presenting information on Vietnam. To its credit, the education system quickly began integrating counterinsurgency lessons into curricula. Vietnam veterans spoke as guest lecturers, faculty modified small arms instruction to better prepare soldiers for jungle ambushes, and by 1965 the Infantry School had even constructed two mock South Vietnamese villages for instructional use.[69] At Fort Knox, young armor officers did not see an increased emphasis on counterinsurgency until 1964, when time devoted to unconventional warfare topics doubled from twelve to twenty-four hours for the captains' career course. By 1965, the Armor School's Officer Candidate Course was using Bernard Fall's *The Two Vietnams*, George Tanham's *Communist Revolutionary Warfare*, and Truong Chinh's *Primer for Revolt* in its insurgency lessons.[70]

If the army lacked comprehensive counterinsurgency instruction and training, it was not from of a lack of effort or even interest. Officers increasingly accepted unconventional warfare, despite their obligations to master conventional fighting on a potentially nuclear battlefield. As with doctrine, however, the problem remained one of implementation. Here, not all officers agreed upon the best course for the army to take. When West Point Superintendent William C. Westmoreland established a Counterinsurgency Training Committee in April 1962, Commandant of Cadets Richard G. Stillwell thought it "infeasible" to begin a specific counterinsurgency course "as it could only be affected at the expense of some portion of solid foundation it is our mission to provide the graduates."[71] That same year, in a speech at Fordham University, General Earle G. Wheeler, soon to be Army Chief of Staff, noted with derision that it was "fashionable in some quarters to say that the problems in Southeast Asia are primarily political and economic rather than military. I do not agree. The essence of the problem in Vietnam is military."[72] On the eve of deploying ground troops to Vietnam, the army's officer corps seemed uncertain about how best to educate, train for, and implement counterinsurgency.

Within this debate between counterinsurgency and conventional operations, most officers never tackled the problems of measuring effectiveness and progress in an unconventional environment. Attempts at providing answers were ambiguous at best. One 1962 RAND report titled "Notes on Non-Military Measures in Control of Insurgency" came to the unsatisfying conclusion that in "successful counterinsurgency, control of the population is a most important factor."[73] The report never articulated how to define or measure such "control." Similarly, the only professional journal article dealing explicitly with measuring effectiveness characterized the problem in fundamentally conventional terms. In 1962, Colonel Wesley W. Yale, writing on the evaluation of combat effectiveness for *Army* magazine, defined success as "the ratio of damage inflicted on the enemy against damage sustained while doing so." As Robert Taber perceptively wrote soon afterward, such a definition could prove irrelevant or even counterproductive in an environment where psychological and political objectives stood paramount. "Local military successes will serve no purpose," Taber argued, unless linked to a political objective.[74]

In its quest to measure progress in a war without fronts, the army gradually, if reluctantly, turned to systems analysis.[75] While the army demonstrated a willingness to learn about counterinsurgency in the late 1950s and early 1960s, none of its doctrine, education, or practice provided meaningful insights into the problem of unconventional warfare metrics. However much the army became interested in fighting insurgents on the eve of the Vietnam War, its officers had only come to a shallow appreciation of counterinsurgency warfare. More importantly, they had overlooked completely the need for gauging success in such a complex political-military environment. The apparent solution for this oversight came not from within the army's ranks, but rather from the Department of Defense.

Bureaucracy to the Rescue

Revolutions are inherently turbulent affairs, and Robert S. McNamara's "management revolution" against Department of Defense inefficiencies in the early 1960s proved no exception. In January 1961, newly appointed Secretary of Defense McNamara found an "absence of the essential management tools needed to make sound decisions on the really crucial issues of national security."[76] Relying on a staff of like-minded intellectuals and analysts—the infamous "whiz kids"—McNamara incorporated the relatively new techniques of operations analysis into defense decision-making processes. A former Harvard Business School student and statistical control officer for the U.S. Army Air Forces in World War II, the new secretary swore by statistical analysis tools in helping make "cost effective" decisions for the enormously complex defense department. McNamara ruthlessly investigated whether defense programs warranted their costs, his decisions informed by a program budgeting application relying on quantitative comparisons and statistical inputs.[77]

Trusting in modern analytical methods to reconcile defense expenditures and requirements, McNamara formalized defense budgeting so as to assess costs and needs simultaneously. The new Secretary also expected the armed services, obeying directives from civilian superiors, to supply accurate data needed for his analysis.[78] To institutionalize this new management system, McNamara established the Systems Analysis Office under the aegis of Alain C. Enthoven, himself a champion of quantitative analysis. Enthoven heard the criticisms leveled against his office, of unnecessarily slowing down the decision-making process, but argued that systems analysis was a "reasoned approach to highly complicated problems of choice in a context of much uncertainty." Charles J. Hitch, one of the most influential whiz kids, warned, however, that systems analysis studies offered no panacea for the department's problems. "Measuring effectiveness of military worth poses a much more difficult problem," Hitch counseled. "Reliable quantitative data are often not available. And even when such data are available, there is usually no common standard of measurement."[79]

Hitch's awareness of system analysis limitations scarcely dampened enthusiasm for its use among McNamara's inner circle. His assessment, though, hinted at the potential risks of applying quantitative research outside the budgeting process. Sound analysis depended on choosing appropriate goals and objectives and then selecting accurate criteria to measure effectiveness. At times, qualitative standards for measurement eluded analysts. Human judgment weighed heavily in deciding which factors were most relevant when comparing alternative actions. Uncertainty persisted no matter how detailed the analyst's model. Criteria errors also could potentially undermine precision, for matters of preference clearly influenced criteria selection. Similarly, standards used for analyzing one problem might not be relevant when applied to a different problem. One RAND analyst recommended that when comparing "systems in terms of more than one test," one should "look for dominance with respect to these tests."[80] If a system of deterrence, as an example, rated highest among several different tests, that system could be labeled dominant. How such tests quantified uncertainty remained largely unresolved.

Threatened by the potential usurping of military decision-making, senior military officers quickly drew attention to the shortcomings of systems analysis. The whiz kids' perceived arrogance helped little. Enthoven once told a general that he had fought in as many nuclear wars as had the officer. Air Force Chief of Staff Curtis E. LeMay cursed these statistical "experts" in a field "where they have no experience [and] propose strategies based upon hopes and fears rather than upon facts and seasoned judgments." Other officers grumbled about the "use of computers versus military judgment." Criticism of the whiz kids within the senior officer corps grew as the arguments of civilian analysts gained traction throughout DoD.[81] Rote adherence to numbers, officers argued, never could account for the intangibles of war. Fearful that systems analysis mindlessly equated to decision by computer, many among the higher ranking brass resisted the integration of operations research into defense programming and budgeting.

McNamara pressed ahead, undeterred by demurring senior officers. Systems analysis filtered down into the lower levels of the Department of Defense's management structure with the objective of reducing uncertainty throughout the defense establishment. Officers saw nothing less than a full-scale assault on the Pentagon's operating procedures. Still, McNamara's coterie advocated exchanging information and techniques. Sharing program assessments and cost effectiveness data arguably would help minimize parochialism and organizational bias. As Hitch claimed, perhaps too ardently, "This is one of the great merits of the scientific method—it is an open, explicit, verifiable, and self-correcting process."[82] While McNamara contended that factual data had not supplanted judgment based on military experience or intuition, senior uniformed officials perceived their expertise being minimized as systems analysis took hold within DoD.

Interestingly, the military's lower-ranking officers did not share their chiefs' reticence toward or suspicion of systems analysis. In fact, the army's younger officers appear to have tentatively accepted the utility of quantitative methods. In 1965 alone, *Military Review* published three articles advocating the use of systems analysis, and in April, the Army War College conducted a symposium on operations research and the systematic approach of measuring costs and effectiveness. A colonel who participated in the symposium maintained that while "most military problems contain a great deal of uncertainty," analysts could help devise methods to quantitatively measure effectiveness during war. "Breakthroughs in effectiveness measurement could be the difference between victory or defeat in the future."[83] Two months after the War College conference, a lieutenant colonel declared that conclusive evidence "abounds" supporting the "general thesis of the relationship between strategy and systems analysis."[84]

The development of operations research in World War II already had established a precedent for measuring battlefield effectiveness through quantitative means. Advances in systems analysis in the early 1960s served only to strengthen this organizational predilection for measuring progress in a time of war. Given the professional dialogue and doctrinal evolution regarding counterinsurgency, officers probably viewed unconventional conflicts as ones that defied simple measurements due to the range of intangible non-military factors—political allegiance, population security, and ideological strength. Systems analysis became a method to compensate for these imponderables. Naturally, some observers remained unconvinced of relying on such a quantitative approach. Bernard Fall believed past experience in Vietnam illustrated the limitations of "hard statistics . . . their futility in many cases, their inaccuracy in others, and their meaninglessness most of the time." Westmoreland accepted Fall's logic but seemed at a loss for an alternative. "Statistics were, admittedly, an imperfect gauge of progress," he wrote after the war, "yet in the absence of conventional front lines, how else to measure it?"[85]

Convergence in Vietnam

The same year that Robert Osgood published his treatise on limited war, journalist Ellen Hammer offered a "Progress Report on Southern Viet Nam" in *Pacific Affairs* (1957). An accomplished student of Southeast Asia, Hammer observed "substantial achievement" since the 1954 Geneva Conference arbitrarily had divided Vietnam at the seventeenth parallel. "With independence accomplished, the first prerequisite to meeting the Communist challenge, the new government turned next to the question of how to achieve stability in the south." Despite several quarters questioning President Ngo Dinh Diem's methods, Hammer believed the "initial emergency" had passed and "very real elements of economic and social stability" existed south of the seventeenth parallel.[86] Within five years, though, U.S. Army soldiers found themselves combating a growing insurgency inside South Vietnam. In less than ten years, American infantry divisions would be conducting full-scale combat operations throughout the Vietnamese countryside. Hammer's inaccurate assessment augured future problems for those less familiar with Vietnamese culture and politics.

As the United States moved toward its own war in South Vietnam, the U.S. Army had only begun to appreciate the complexities of counterinsurgency theory and principles. Though open to learning about unconventional warfare, officers too often read generic summaries filled with imprecise, if not misleading, terminology. Their training and education was no different. Advice to remain aggressive against insurgents offered little meaningful insights when doctrine admitted the primacy of political action in revolutionary war. Perhaps most importantly, none of the army's field manuals or professional journals provided counsel on how to gauge success in a war without fronts. Perspectives from the French and British experiences went largely unheeded. In a real sense, the army was unprepared intellectually to consider the problems of measuring progress and effectiveness in a counterinsurgency environment. Though resisted by higher-ranking officers in the early days of the Kennedy administration, systems analysis techniques quickly would fill this intellectual void in Vietnam. Even before U.S. ground troops began streaming into the Vietnamese peninsula, quantitative reports were measuring innumerable data points on the progress of American forces and their Asian allies.

> "I am an optimist, and I am not going to allow my staff to be pessimistic."
> —General PAUL D. HARKINS, MACV Commander, quoted in *Time*

2 Measurements without Objectives: America Goes to War in Southeast Asia

IN APRIL 1962, five years after Ellen Hammer's misleading progress report, twelve U.S. and allied officers and civilians gathered in Washington, D.C., for a five-day symposium on the growing communist insurgency in South Vietnam. Each presenter held personal experience in guerrilla or counterinsurgency warfare, having served in Algeria, Greece, Malaya, or the Philippines. During the event's final meeting, Stephen T. Hosmer of the RAND Corporation, the symposium's chairman, posed a multifaceted question that would stymie American officers throughout their war in Vietnam. "How do you measure whether or not you are winning a counterguerrilla struggle?" Hosmer queried. "What are the precise factors to be included in a yardstick? What weight would you give, for example, to numbers of casualties or to the incident rate of terrorism and guerrilla attacks? What are the most significant measurements?"[1]

David Galula, the French counterinsurgency theorist who had served in Algeria, listed several objective markers: number of ambushes against friendly convoys, number of enemy weapons captured, rate of desertions, and strength of enemy forces for military operations. He then offered a more penetrating analysis on nonmilitary indicators. Galula maintained that the most significant gauges of the civilian population's actions and attitudes were the number of volunteers within the counterinsurgent's forces, the amount of information willingly offered by civilians, and the people's readiness to break with insurgent demands. Two other panel members agreed. The "people's voluntary cooperation and their disregard for the guerrilla's orders," they noted, "were important signs of progress, and indeed perhaps the only reliable ones."[2]

Clearly, the RAND conference was intended to illuminate problems that the United States might face as it committed military forces to South Vietnam. In March 1962, one month before the symposium, U.S. forces in Vietnam had reached a total of 5,400 troops. American pilots began flying "combat training" missions with the South Vietnamese Air Force. By December, U.S. presence had more than doubled. Yet as the army wrote and spoke of counterinsurgency while sending more of its troops to South Vietnam, the diverse nature of the communist threat posed several dilemmas for both American policymakers and uniformed officers.[3] Should the U.S. armed forces prepare for conventional warfare on the European battlefields or for wars of national liberation on the periphery of American interests? Was there any such thing as a periphery in the context of a global war to contain communism? To what extent would conventional forces suffice to deal with the threat in Southeast Asia? Most pertinent to South Vietnam, was the main threat from a foreign, communist-supported aggressor or from internal revolutionaries aiming to overthrow their own government?

For the army in Vietnam, these questions on strategic and operational aims remained unsettled for the duration of the war despite the counsel of its doctrine. In February 1962, the Department of the Army published a revision of its principal field manual, FM 100–5. *Operations* described both how the army fought and the relationship between strategy and military force. FM 100–5 advised that "because the purpose of war is the attainment of national objectives, military strategy must be geared to these objectives." Highlighting the primacy of the political nature of war, *Operations* maintained that regardless of the form of conflict, military objectives had to be compatible with national policies. "A military operation is futile unless it is directed toward attainment of the objective set for it, no matter what else it may accomplish."[4] Thus, judged by the standard of its own doctrine, the army in Vietnam, as well as those civilian leaders directing national policy, failed to establish the foundation for which success could be both measured and achieved. Military objectives quite simply lacked connectivity to the political aim. As Americans picked up the gauntlet left by the French in Southeast Asia, they could agree neither on the nature of the war nor the methods for prosecuting it.[5]

This inability to conceptualize a coherent counterinsurgency strategy—one that balanced the complex problems of political stability and governance with security, pacification, and economic development—found its outgrowth in a reliance on statistical indicators. For the U.S. Military Assistance Command, Vietnam (MACV), statistics became a substitute for a fuller comprehension of the war's larger political-military problems. Well before the term "body count" became an established part of public discourse on the war, MACV's commanders and staff had cemented the framework for assessing progress and effectiveness in Southeast Asia. Astonishingly, the framework's faulty construction would remain unchanged for most of the war. The U.S. command simply gathered numbers to prove that it was making progress against both North Vietnamese regulars and South Vietnamese insurgents. Despite all the data obtained and quantified, MACV's figures never captured the vicissitudes of a war that continued to perplex American officers. Hosmer's final symposium question on how counterinsurgents knew if they were winning or losing would remain largely unanswered.

A Lacuna in America's Cold War Strategy

Divided along the 17th Parallel by the July 1954 Geneva Accords, the Vietnamese peninsula had entered into an uneasy truce after the defeat of the French at Dien Bien Phu. In the north, communist supporters consolidated their power under Ho Chi Minh. In the south, the non-communist Ngo Dinh Diem confronted an internal political power struggle. The population's religious, ethnic, and geographical diversity posed significant challenges for building a popular, self-sustaining government.[6] The creation of a parallel communist government in the south presented perhaps the greatest challenge. This political infrastructure, called the Vietcong (VC) by a contemptuous Diem, was well-versed in insurgent warfare and spread a potent message of nationalism and Marxist ideology among the village peasantry. Increasingly, it undertook a sophisticated campaign of political and armed opposition to Diem's regime. Diem responded harshly, his repressive tactics helping only to create more domestic adversaries.[7]

Because of Diem's staunch anti-communist views, the United States committed itself to the Republic of Vietnam's survival. Formal assistance to South Vietnam began in the early 1950s with the creation of a Military Assistance Advisory Group (MAAG) in Indochina. As U.S. Army advisors began training the Vietnamese army after the Geneva Accords—mainly in conventional tactics should the North Vietnamese invade—American money flowed into the unstable country. Still, the Vietcong threat grew. In 1959 the Central Committee of North Vietnam's Communist Party took advantage of the south's internal weaknesses and moved from political consolidation to armed opposition.[8] By early 1960 Diem's rural political structure nearly buckled under the combined pressures of increased subversion, terrorism, and assassinations. A May 1961 U.S. Department of Defense memorandum warned that the "internal security situation in South Viet-Nam has become critical." In spite of increased efforts by South Vietnamese forces, the "number of violent incidents per month now averages 650," the report noted. Though moving toward armed struggle, terrorism did not dominate the communist approach. As Bernard Fall wrote, sound propaganda, "like the 'Three Withs' program ('a good cadre lives with, eats with, works with the population')," complemented VC military actions.[9]

Despite the growing insurgency, fears of conventional invasion reminiscent of the Korean War shaped many U.S. Army officers' perceptions of the Vietnamese threat. Not all, of course, were blinded to the realities of the southern insurgency. Lieutenant General Lionel C. McGarr, head of MAAG from 1960 to 1962, strongly emphasized counterinsurgency, publishing a lengthy guide for opposing the insurgent menace. The former head of the Command and General Staff College argued for the "absolute necessity to separate the people from the Viet Cong" and for the "cohesive employment of both conventional and unconventional military forces."[10] Insightful on numerous levels, McGarr's "Tactics and Techniques of Counter-Insurgent Operations" offered advice consistent with contemporary army discourse and doctrine on counterinsurgency warfare. Clearly, neither the insurgents nor the regular units could be ignored, but few officers or civilian officials could agree upon the most pressing danger. Even Diem himself claimed, "We can handle the guerrillas. What we can't handle is the main force units which are going to be built up and built up and built up until an invasion takes place."[11]

The communists' effectiveness in integrating political and military elements into one synergistic campaign confounded Diem and helped undermine his authority and legitimacy in the countryside. In December 1960, the National Front for the Liberation of South Vietnam (NLF) announced its program of open resistance against Diem and his American backers. The NLF appealed to a largely neglected rural society at odds with both an oligarchic government in Saigon and large landholders living in the cities.[12] One landless peasant in Long An province, representative of many southerners, found compelling the NLF's propaganda message. "They said that . . . the poor had become slaves of the landlords. The cadres told us that if the poor people don't stand up to the rich people, we would be dominated by them forever. The only way to ensure freedom and a sufficient way of life was to overthrow them."[13] With increasing communist infiltration from the north along the Ho Chi Minh Trail, the NLF's political organization and military buildup spread throughout the South Vietnamese countryside.

Upon his January 1961 inauguration, John F. Kennedy inherited a growing commitment to South Vietnam that had become integral to Cold War containment policies. Eisenhower had left the new president a Counterinsurgency Plan (CIP) that advocated augmenting American forces in Vietnam and following a program for internal social reform. In October, Kennedy dispatched advisors General Maxwell

Taylor and Walt Rostow to Vietnam, where they found a "double crisis in confidence: doubt that the U.S. is determined to save Southeast Asia; doubt that Diem's methods can frustrate and defeat Communist purposes."[14] When Kennedy spoke to West Point's graduating class on June 6, 1962, of a war requiring a "wholly new kind of strategy," the American commitment to Vietnam had grown considerably. During his first year in office alone, the president tripled the number of military advisors in Vietnam.[15] Kennedy meanwhile pressed the army to develop further its counterinsurgency forces and doctrine.

Despite both the White House and McGarr emphasizing counterinsurgency, the growing American advisory effort naturally leaned toward training its Vietnamese charges for a conventional threat. After a spring inspection trip to Vietnam in 1961, General Lyman Lemnitzer, the Chairman of the Joint Chiefs, reported that "too much emphasis on counter-guerrilla activities would impair the ability of the South Vietnamese Army to meet a conventional assault like the attack on South Korea."[16] Images of North Korean and Chinese regulars streaming across the 38th parallel stifled the thinking of conventional-minded officers like Lemnitzer. Underscoring the contradictory approach to formulating military strategy in Vietnam, MAAG published a command directive on "Concepts of Pacification Efforts" soon after the chairman's visit. Nonetheless, U.S. officers continued to preside over the formation of a heavily mechanized, Western-style army of corps and divisions. Pacification would have to wait. As one former advisor recalled, "The question was not *whether* to help; it was *how* to help."[17] This uncertainty in the operational environment, disagreement on the nature of the threat, and ambiguity within the overarching strategic framework led to immense frustrations on the ground.

As his political reforms waned and Vietcong attacks mounted in both frequency and magnitude, Diem turned increasingly to trusted army officers to stem the communist tide. Though McGarr argued for an "inter play and . . . application of all elements of national power . . . on the overall pacification effort," soldiers quickly became the face of Saigon's government in the rural areas.[18] The dichotomy between friendly and enemy approaches did not go unnoticed. Reporter David Halberstam saw the Vietcong's methodology as "entirely political: its military aspects were simply a means to permit them to practice their political techniques." Veteran journalist Stanley Karnow, who believed that Diem's army "operated as if they were in enemy territory," reported that the "villages, open to Diem's troops by day, were run by the Vietcong at night." Diem seemed unfazed. A CIA memorandum reviewing the war's progress indicated that the "overall effectiveness of the counterinsurgency effort . . . continues to be blunted by the government's political modus operandi."[19] If Vietnam was to be a test case of American resolve against the spread of communism, clearly Diem required greater assistance.

Infusion of American money, personnel, and equipment appeared to check the Vietcong offensive in late 1961 and early 1962. The gains proved fleeting. American dollars failed to address the political discontent among South Vietnam's rural population. Despite an increase in U.S. advisors and the formal establishment of a United States Military Assistance Command in February 1962, neither the level nor intensity of Vietcong operations abated. MACV's new commander, General Paul D. Harkins, reported that "we have taken the military, psychological, economic and political initiative from the enemy" yet confessed in the same dispatch that the "VC are still everywhere."[20] Nearing sixty, Harkins had been Deputy Chief of Staff for Patton's Third Army in World War II. A perpetual optimist and product of conventional military training and experiences, the nuances of counterinsurgency eluded him throughout his tenure in MACV. He was completely unprepared for commanding in an unconventional environment.

Officially established on February 8 as a subordinate of Pacific Command, MACV assumed broad responsibilities for U.S. military policy, operations, and assistance in Vietnam. Its mission statement underlined the wide spectrum of U.S. commitments, as well as the unresolved debate on the nature of the threat. Pacific Command directed Harkins to "assist and support the Government of Vietnam in its efforts to provide for its internal security, defeat communist insurgency, and resist overt aggression."[21] The problem now became one of developing a coherent strategy to fulfill this broad mission. Harkins was ill-prepared for the task. The new MACV commander recalled, "it was something new to all of us. It was an entirely different type of military operation than we'd ever been in on.... There wasn't any front line, it was no place; it was everyplace. It was in your kitchen, in your backyard."[22] Faced with a clear political-military threat inside South Vietnam, risk of invasion from North Vietnam, and weak political leadership in Saigon, an overwhelmed Harkins failed to establish coherent goals and programs to support MACV's mission. From the very start, MACV's strategy was diffuse and disjointed.

South Vietnam's diversity only added to Harkins's predicament. Forty-three provinces, akin to small states, composed a country of more than 65,000 square miles (approximately the size of Washington state). Its geography included the rugged Annamese Cordillera mountain chain in the north, a vast central plateau, and the Mekong delta and plains dominating the south. Eighty percent of the population lived in rural villages, disconnected physically and culturally from Saigon. Within these villages, the Vietcong built their political base, achieving legitimacy with rural peasants that the ruling elite in Saigon seemed either unwilling or unable to contest. Hawkins recalled that when armed opposition broke out in late 1959 and early 1960, the communists initiated a dispersed yet interconnected uprising. "That's when the war started in forty-three different provinces, and they had forty-three wars going on."[23]

Arguably, U.S advisors confronted their most vexing strategic dilemma in determining how internal security and political stability complemented one another. Was security a necessary prerequisite for political stability or vice versa? Senator Mike Mansfield expressed doubt after visiting Southeast Asia in late 1962 that the Saigon government had the capacity to "carry out the task of social engineering." Less than two years later, the Deputy Chief of Mission at the American Embassy reported that he did not see in the present regime "or any conceivable successor much hope in providing the real political and social leadership or the just and effective country-wide administration so essential to the success of our counter-insurgency program." Robert W. Komer, soon to head MACV's civil operations effort, remarked after the war that "despite all the help provided, the regimes we backed proved incapable of coping with the threat they faced."[24] Army officers struggled to build an effective strategy providing for internal security, a specified task in MACV's mission statement, on such a shaky foundation. Certainly, country-wide security would be unsustainable if the government in Saigon lacked legitimacy with the population.

Exploiting Diem's political weaknesses, the Vietcong integrated their armed and political efforts into a coordinated struggle (*dau tranh*) encompassing a wide range of military and nonmilitary power. MACV well recognized the disparity between ally and enemy. In a briefing on the National Campaign Plan for 1963, MACV's staff acknowledged the "VC organization is complete. It runs the gamut of all governmental functions from political to military to economic and sociological. Action against him, then, must also be all-inclusive to be successful. It is not enough, for example, to destroy his military apparatus."[25] Wedded to a host regime incapable of providing a competitive political effort, American officers increasingly relied upon military operations to realize their strategic goals. Even MACV noted, though, that winning battles alone would little further their strategic designs. Analyst Douglas Pike well depicted the U.S. Army's strategic quandary. "If you win, if you defeat armed struggle, you merely give yourself an opportunity to defeat the political struggle. And until you do that you don't win."[26] Simply put, the Americans and South Vietnamese could not defeat the insurgency unless they won the people to their side. Military and political goals had to be achieved simultaneously.

Still, military objectives, like training the Army of the Republic of Vietnam (ARVN), remained an important part of MACV's approach to fulfilling its mission. With aggressiveness a hallmark of U.S. Army counterinsurgency theory, ARVN appeared to many American officers an unimpressive tool for weeding out communist insurgents. Advisors frequently lamented that ARVN was chronically slow, casualty averse, and reluctant to pursue the enemy. Of course, the Americans themselves partly were responsible for the army they were building and training. As MACV's Deputy Commander recalled, "There was a notable lack of urgency or concern or desire to get the job done. There was a notable lack of good training methods with respect to the individual soldier and as far as training officers was concerned."[27] Despite these grievances, positive reports emanated from Vietnam, portending future credibility issues for the army. In November 1963, Major General C. J. Timmes, chief of MAAG—MAAG would become subsumed into MACV before the introduction of ground combat forces in 1965—reported that "our job here was to train an army for the Government of Viet-Nam. I feel we have completed that part. The Vietnamese armed forces are just as professional as you can get."[28]

Timmes's glowing report said more about U.S. Army culture than results on the ground. In fact, the growing advisory effort thus far had failed to produce a turning point, either politically or militarily. On November 16, 1963, the CIA station in Saigon reported the "enemy has only been contained." The overthrow and assassination of President Diem two weeks earlier certainly appeared a turning point of sorts. As Diem battled Buddhist political activists throughout the summer, members of the U.S. mission bickered over his value to the anticommunist struggle. To the many U.S. governmental officials who believed they needed to start anew in Vietnam, Diem's assassination offered hope. Instead of a fresh start after Diem's fall, however, Americans found themselves bound to a country wracked by political instability.[29] A revolving door of South Vietnamese governments in 1964 made it increasingly difficult to resist the NLF's coordinated efforts in the countryside, but President Lyndon B. Johnson decided to stay the course in Vietnam after Kennedy's death on November 22, 1963. As correspondent David Halberstam remarked, not long after Diem's assassination, "we [were] getting deeply involved in a situation where we could be no more effective than the established government."[30]

The Vietcong, on the other hand, pressed their advantages. Propaganda efforts progressed at the village level. Military operations expanded in size and aggressiveness. Increasingly, U.S. troops found themselves and their facilities targeted by Vietcong attacks. In August 1964, when the controversial Gulf of Tonkin incident propelled Vietnam to center stage of American foreign policy, Johnson seemed ready, if not eager, to turn to coercion in dealing with the intractable North.[31] Coercion would provide few results, though, if not linked to a coherent strategy with definable objectives. This was especially true for a war that, as Ambassador Henry Cabot Lodge admitted, "would be won or lost on the basis of the attitude of the rural population."[32] However, articulating and obtaining consensus on such objectives proved exceedingly difficult in the complicated, confusing environment of Vietnam.

U.S. policy makers had outlined broad national objectives, such as South Vietnamese independence and territorial integrity, countering Communist influence and controlling insurgent elements.[33] Clear objectives for the use of military force, though, never accompanied these general goals, leaving the armed forces searching for linkages between strategy and policy. One senior intelligence officer expressed the frustration of many soldiers by arguing that the "Johnson administration attempted to fight the Vietnam War without clear, tangible, or measurable objectives, both military and political." In 1964, two members of the Joint Chiefs of Staff went so far as to submit a memorandum to Chairman Maxwell Taylor "expressing concern over a 'lack of definition, even confusion,' concerning American objectives and possible courses of action in Southeast Asia." A Department of State official working closely with the Government of South Vietnam (GVN) even contended after the Diem coup that there was no "particular strategic conception of how to deal with the problem of the VC."[34]

The origins of this lacuna in strategy, of not assigning clear objectives and plans for an extremely complex mission, could be found in the inability of high-ranking U.S. officials to settle on the true nature of the war in South Vietnam. Members of the Joint Chiefs of Staff, the National Security Council, and Johnson's civilian advisors could not even agree on the nature of the threat. How could they be expected to develop coherent strategic objectives? Civilians and officers alike simply did not balance the military and political responses for combating the growing southern insurgency. Problems also persisted within the army during these early years. Officers read about counterinsurgencies but had accumulated limited personal experience in implementing their doctrine in the post–World War II era. Recognizing counterinsurgency as more than just a military problem was easy. Effectively coordinating political and economic reform with pacification and security efforts in an attempt to mobilize the civilian population against the insurgents, all in a culturally alien country, proved much more difficult.[35]

Without a clear strategy, the question soon arose of what MACV should be measuring to determine if its efforts were effective in making progress toward the endstate of an independent, non-communist South Vietnam. Reliance on a systems analysis approach emerged as the answer. As Thomas Thayer, a senior analyst in the Department of Defense, recalled, *"Vietnam was an unusually statisticized war, precisely because everyone was groping for understanding."*[36] Numbers filled an intellectual and conceptual void among policy makers and army officers equivocating over strategic objectives and supporting military operations. Within this controversy and near-debilitating confusion over strategy lay the seeds of the American army's failure to assess accurately its efforts and effectiveness in Vietnam.

Establishing the Conceptual and Analytical Framework

Lacking clear objectives, Americans in Vietnam increasingly began to question if their exertions were going unrewarded. In October 1961, Edward Lansdale, the Secretary of Defense's Deputy Assistant for Special Operations and one of the more progressive counterinsurgency intellectuals within the U.S. mission, reported from Saigon that perhaps "the truest thing that could be said about the situation in Vietnam today is that the accomplishments do not match the efforts that are being made." Less than one week later, Maxwell Taylor, after an extended visit in country, communicated the need to "engage in a joint survey in the provinces to assess the social, political, intelligence, and military factors bearing on the prosecution of the counter-insurgency in order to reach a common estimate of these factors and a common determination of how to deal with them."[37] Several factors, though, undermined Taylor's advice. The diversity of Vietnam's provinces, the superficial treatment of indicators in both counterinsurgency theory and doctrine, the consistent debate over the nature of the threat, and the overall lack of clarity among MACV's objectives all inhibited the creation of an accurate and practicable measurement system.[38]

McGarr already had developed a crude reporting system at MAAG, directing his intelligence officer to brief him on the "number of incidents, weapons, people killed, and things of that nature. Mainly for information, one. Two, to keep on their toes."[39] While keeping staff officers alert, the reporting system remained an unrefined tool. The systems analysis approach, ostensibly well-suited for complex cost-effectiveness problems within the defense establishment, soon found traction and advocacy among McGarr's successors. As one officer remarked, the approach had become a "fact of life . . . because possible courses of action have multiplied so rapidly and the choices to be made are of such consequence that every tool must be used to reject the poor choices and to help human judgment in picking the right ones."[40] Properly used, here was a tool to gauge progress in a complex environment. Analysts in particular, however, offered patent reminders that systems analysis should serve rather than replace judgment. Yet for military officers unproven in the art of counterinsurgency warfare, reliance on numbers proved an irresistible substitute for a deeper comprehension of a confusing war.

In March 1962, Lansdale offered a "suggested yardstick for measuring Civic Action in Vietnam." Highlighting the importance of earning the people's friendship, Lansdale's report focused on "such things as willing care for the wounded and injured civilians, sharing rice with the hungry, repairing destroyed public structures" all done to "start linking up the villages spiritually as well as mentally . . . and physically . . . with the provincial and national centers." In July, he wrote a trenchant analysis of the "x-factors" in Vietnam with a sample of questions that U.S. officers should ask to gain an understanding of "the real war" among the rural population. Questions ranged from villagers' attitudes toward Vietnamese troops to the "cost" of providing information to ARVN and the effectiveness of VC propaganda in "wooing popular support."[41] These impressive memoranda epitomized Lansdale's appreciation of the political nature of the war zone but foundered in the wake of Robert McNamara's visit to South Vietnam in May.

Rather than concentrating on the "imponderables" of Lansdale's report, MACV instead presented the Secretary of Defense a "practical index for appraising the problem" by focusing on "control—geographic and by population—exercised over the country by the GVN and by the VC." Unlike Galula and Lansdale's focus on population attitudes, Harkins and his staff attempted to gauge the war by using hard numbers. According to the MACV assessment, the GVN controlled only 14.7 percent of the country and 18.1 percent of the population. Despite such low percentages, enthusiasm prevailed during McNamara's visit. So too did the penchant for numbers, which McNamara found much more suitable for measuring progress than any subjective approach. MACV's staff officers fell quickly in line. Rather than embracing the war's complexities, Harkins's staff simply gave McNamara what he wanted to hear.[42]

The rapid influx of American advisors during 1962, from nearly 800 to 10,000, provided Harkins the manpower he needed to gain a better appreciation of VC control in the countryside. His reporting system, however, left much to be desired. The process for selecting measurements of effectiveness was haphazard. Nowhere in their doctrine could MACV staff officers find suggestions for developing meaningful indicators. The May report presented to McNamara incorporated such a wide array of indicators, focused largely on military matters and nowhere linked to MACV's mission statement, as to be nearly incomprehensible. As an example, criteria for a VC controlled or influenced area included "operational contact" with the enemy, the ability to establish "lasting garrisons or outposts," ARVN defection and desertion rates, and a host of other "incident" reports.[43] Worse, the report lacked any true analysis. By September, the proclivity to rely on numbers had intensified. The State Department's Far Eastern Affairs office advised that it "would be desirable to devise indicators which could be made reasonably objective." That same month Taylor was "encouraged to find that there is a more methodical reporting system to check than I had realized."[44] Lansdale meanwhile chaffed at the army's disinterest in comprehending the underlying political, economic, and social reasons behind the VC's success.

In 1963, despite Lansdale's admonitions, MACV solidified the analytical approach to measuring effectiveness that would endure throughout the war. Harkins's command published criteria for a monthly "GVN vs. VC Control Report" in early

January to "evaluate the progress of the battle against the insurgency in South Vietnam." Collating reports from advisors in the field, MACV staff officers plotted villages on maps according to color codes—blue for GVN in control, white for neither the GVN nor VC in control, and red for VC in control. Even with the abundance of "objective" indicators, defining "control" remained subjective at best. A RAND study in November warned that "the input data utilized are neither complete, consistent, nor reliable."[45] The study's warnings went unheeded by MACV headquarters as it concentrated instead on establishing an analytical framework that would illustrate progress in the field. At conferences and in telegrams, Harkins remained ever-optimistic, confident that the wealth of numbers his advisors and staff officers generated were revealing positive trends. Although publicly emphasizing that the "problem is one of people, not statistics," MACV's commander continued to lean on a reporting system that relied heavily on numbers.[46] He was not alone.

Lacking a clearly defined strategy, many MACV officers depended on statistical outputs because of their discomfort with the war's political nature. Defense analysts, however, advised caution. They warned that "effective control of the population and countryside is difficult to measure," that operational data are "almost completely limited to operators' reporting," and that a war without fronts "does not fit neat analytic models."[47] Without solid footing in either counterinsurgency or Asian culture, officers under pressure from McNamara opted for numbers over nuance. As one reporter maintained, Harkins was "probably more willing to settle for the straight 'kill' statistics characteristic of traditional military situations than for the circumstances which produced those statistics."[48] It is important to remember that men like Harkins were Cold Warriors influenced by their personal experiences in World War II and Korea as well as by the conventional threats from the Soviet Union and China. While Harkins may have contended that "war is not all military and that the military should help in civic actions," there was little in his personal or professional background to prepare him for the type of war in Vietnam.[49]

As Harkins neared the end of his tour in June 1964, MACV's reporting system rapidly expanded. In December 1963, the command established a policy to outline procedures for a quarterly review and analysis of their metrics for progress. Although admirably linking indicators to objectives, such as voluntary information on VC activity from local citizens, the reporting system quickly became unwieldy. The nearly eighty indicators rose to over one hundred by April, with no one on the staff prioritizing data collection or validation.[50] The number of reports continued to grow: the MACV daily Situation Report (SITREP), the weekly Military Report (MILREP), a Monthly Evaluation (MONEVAL), and a Quarterly Review and Evaluation. In June, the Secretary of Defense required submission of a Senior Advisor's Monthly Evaluation Report (SAME), and in September, the Ambassador directed that MACV supply a weekly and monthly Military Assessment report.[51] A MACV Information and Reports Working Group devoted six months of full-time analysis in late 1963 and early 1964 reviewing and evaluating the approximately *five hundred* U.S. and Vietnamese reports in an attempt to assess the command's major reporting problems. Data collection was becoming an end unto itself.[52]

The pacification reporting system emerged as one of the more controversial programs in MACV's data collection effort. Adopted in May 1964 as a series of monthly submissions by district chiefs and U.S. advisors, the reports sought to measure the level of security within rural hamlets and villages. Much of the information relied on Vietnamese sources. MACV's Province Reports Center managed the receipt, analysis, and dissemination of the pacification data. Thomas Thayer believed the reporting "oversimplified and of poor quality and exaggerated the amount of security that actually existed in the countryside."[53] The 21st Infantry Division's senior advisor at Bac Lieu confirmed Thayer's assertions. Colonel John H. Cushman had two criteria for a "blue" (GVN controlled) rating in his province: officials moving

FIGURE 2.1 Overwhelmed by data. SP4 Byron Thrasher works in the tape library of the MACV Combined Document Exploitation Center.

Source RG123S, Vietnam Photos, Misc. Collection, U.S. Army, Misc., Intel—IDHS at night without an escort and no open VC taxation. As Cushman recalled, "We'd have our advisers go out and check these areas. They'd say, 'Hey, we've got this blue here, I want to go out and see it.' The Vietnamese would say, 'You can't go there, you'll get shot at.'"[54] Despite hundreds of reports inundating MACV headquarters, the conflict's true nature would continue to elude army officers as long as the quality of their data remained so suspect.

As MACV pursued the competing goals of rural pacification, ARVN training and advising, and defeating the communist insurgency, the Secretary of Defense pressed Harkins to gauge and report his progress in the field. William Colby, the CIA's Chief of Station in Saigon until 1962, remembered that McNamara "really believed that the intangibles and fog of war could be brought under control if they could be reduced to numbers."[55] McNamara's background had instilled confidence in quantitative reporting systems. A Harvard business school alum, he had served with the Army Air Forces during World War II, conducting program and operational analysis for B-29 bombing operations. After the war, his skills as a statistician landed him a job with Ford Motor Company. His energy, command of detailed facts, and skill at systematizing problems served both McNamara and Ford extremely well. Logical, if not unfeeling, decision-making became McNamara's hallmark at the motor company. When he arrived in Washington in 1961, a reputation for rationality preceded him.

This bent for figures had obvious repercussions for uniformed subordinates in Vietnam. As Colby recalled, "briefings and conferences were dominated by slides and graphics in the best military manner, and little time was devoted to trying to deal with the more intangible aspects of the conflict."[56] Army Chief of Staff Harold K. Johnson equally grumbled over the early search for "yardsticks." As Johnson declared, "The Secretary [McNamara] will not be satisfied until he has some kind of clear indication as to progress being made, obstacles to progress and the effort required to eliminate or at least reduce the size of the obstacles. Neither of us will rest easy until some sort of program along that line is developed."[57] Pressure led swiftly to acceptance in the field. From battalion advisors to MACV headquarters, the army staff system first countenanced and then promoted the use of numbers to track progress of their efforts.

Colby's criticism of discounting intangibles made sense in the politically driven environment of Vietnam. The threat was often more political than military—a point thoroughly understood by the NLF—yet McNamara's focus on numbers discouraged a fuller understanding of this threat. Given the limited depth of their counterinsurgency expertise, army officers fell in line, even though they professed to know better. At a May 1964 conference with McNamara, MACV suggested that more of its operations should support pacification. The staff concluded that 86 percent of operations focused on defeating the VC, while only 4 percent aided pacification (the other 10 percent involved road openings, supply operations, and the like).[58] Army efforts obviously lacked balance, but assessing progress in pacification and political "control" eluded easy measurement. Desirous of showing progress, MACV instead relied on statistics that illustrated effectiveness against the Vietcong. In doing so, more and more weighted their efforts to the military rather than the political struggle.

Numbers whetted an appetite for more numbers. One army major commented on the impressive array of reporting and data collection programs. "The Army has not been remiss in establishing measuring schemes: on the contrary, so many criteria of performance, success indicators, and testing systems are in use that they almost overwhelm the unit commander."[59] Even the White House was not immune to this penchant for systems analysis. National Security Council (NSC) staff member Chester L. Cooper found the emphasis on quantification nearly suffocating. "Numbers flowed into Saigon and from there into Washington like the Mekong River during the flood season."[60] This "number mill," as Cooper described it, overburdened the capacity of staffs to analyze whether the reports were useful or even made sense. Any chance of finding dominant indictors that might accurately reflect progress or effectiveness became lost in the sheer volume of information being reported and processed.

This emphasis on data collection concealed the lack of data evaluation at all levels. Innumerable metrics posted statistics in such diverse areas as number of VC-initiated incidents, rate of VC defections, percentage of population under governmental control, number of civil guard companies trained, and percentage of small unit ground actions initiated by GVN forces. The dizzying array of statistics undermined the utility of a systems analysis approach designed to cut through the fog of unconventional war. MACV's staff counted activities and events instead of evaluating the impact or validity of what was being counted. One RAND report suggested that MACV had developed excessive metrics without knowing enough about the situation in Vietnam to accurately evaluate the indicators themselves. Lacking a deep understanding of their operational environment, MACV's staff officers did not rigorously question data input. "The problem," as Thayer recalled, "was that quantification became a huge effort, but analysis remained a trivial one."[61] Statistics could be both encouraging and completely irrelevant.

MACV appraisals, as an example, failed to capture the NLF's nuanced approach to revolutionary warfare. American estimates lacked qualitative analysis of communist strength and organizational effectiveness in the countryside. Hard numbers, often derived from unreliable South Vietnamese sources, failed to capture the war's political realities. Reporting from the Mekong Delta in 1963, David Halberstam found that MACV's figures routinely reflected what senior officers wanted to hear. "There was no differentiation, for instance, between Government forces killed on offensive operations and those killed in static, defensive points, though this would have been one of the truest indicators of how successfully the war was being conducted."[62] Numerical metrics also never explained how villagers regularly lived under two governments: the GVN by day and the Vietcong by night. Control over an area often could change "overnight," allowing many observers to deceive themselves about levels of progress.[63]

Lacking clear strategic objectives and basing their metrics of effectiveness largely on quantitative data, MACV misjudged the undercurrents of Vietnam's political and cultural landscape. Since "nothing was ever very clear-cut" in Asia, one journalist believed that "attitudes were much more important than facts." The army's statistical approach did not account for assessing attitudes until well late into the war.[64] In short, systems analysis became a substitute for understanding the broader problems of Vietnam's growing insurgency. Without an evaluation system in its quest to gather data, MACV wallowed in an ever-growing morass of reports. MACV headquarters, the White House, and the American public all were left to speculate about who was winning or losing in Vietnam.

Winning or Losing: The View from the Ground

Just eight days before the fall of Diem's regime, Brigadier General Frank A. Omanski, a senior MACV staff officer, briefed the annual meeting of the Association of the U.S. Army in Washington, D.C. Omanski highlighted the three-pronged counterinsurgency strategy in Vietnam that clearly was making headway—the strategic hamlet program designed to separate Vietcong insurgents from the population, field operations directed at destroying the VC and their infrastructure, and civic action aimed at improving the citizenry's socioeconomic and political welfare. Despite the wide range of missions within this strategic concept, the general's speech concentrated on the military aspects of killing the enemy. Within these narrow confines, Omanski argued MACV was making progress. "The military events of this past year in the Republic of Vietnam have contributed substantially both to the development of improved counterinsurgency techniques and toward ultimate victory."[65] Within two weeks, however, Diem had been assassinated and the South Vietnamese government lay in shambles. Without political stability, military gains seemed hollow against a coordinated VC effort. Omanski's misplaced optimism underlined the problems of accurately gauging progress and effectiveness in all areas of the Vietnam War—fighting, advising, pacifying, and decision-making.

The January 1963 battle near Ap Bac exemplified the early problems of honestly measuring and reporting progress on Vietnam's battlefields. Located in the Mekong Delta 40 miles southwest of Saigon, Ap Bac symbolized U.S. advisors' frustrations over ARVN shortcomings and defining success in an unconventional environment. Responsible for defending against invasion from the north and defeating insurgents in the south, ARVN mastered neither. U.S. advisors nevertheless pined for a set-piece battle against the elusive Vietcong. Catching and destroying the Vietcong—"a primary objective of counter-insurgency operations rather than a piece of real estate" according to MACV—consumed American advisors.[66] With Saigon looking to contest VC control of the upper Mekong Delta in late 1962, it looked as if the Americans finally might have their chance. As 1963 opened, they landed the battle but hardly the results.

Acting on what would turn out to be faulty intelligence, the ARVN 7th Division and accompanying civil guard units planned a three-pronged offensive on the village of Tan Hoi. Helicopter gunships, M113 armored personnel carriers, and 2,000 soldiers proposed to attack what was thought to be a single VC company. Instead, over 300 Vietcong defended positions between Tan Hoi and the nearby village of Bac. Squandering a nearly ten-to-one advantage, the South Vietnamese attack broke down almost as soon as it began on 2 January. Morning fog and ambiguous command relationships between the three assault elements caused as much mayhem as the defending VC. By noon the Vietcong had downed five American helicopters. Lieutenant Colonel John Paul Vann, the senior U.S. advisor, railed for his ARVN counterparts to encircle the enemy and move in for the kill. Apprehensive of incurring too many casualties, the 7th Division's commander vacillated throughout the day. The VC held their positions until nightfall and then evaporated into the countryside. Over sixty ARVN soldiers and three Americans died in the fighting, another hundred suffering wounds. Scornful of the South Vietnamese officers that day—"a miserable damn performance. . . . They make the same goddam mistakes over and over again in the same way"—an apoplectic Vann soon resigned from the army in disgust.[67]

Given Vann's public remarks, high-ranking American officers hastened to call the battle of Ap Bac a victory since ARVN had retained the field. Senior officials defined success in strict conventional terms. Harkins claimed that while ARVN could have fought better, they had overpowered the VC and pushed them out of their defensive positions. It was a hollow argument. Battles like Ap Bac made only temporary gains since ARVN had not driven the surviving Vietcong away from the local population. Nor did U.S. advisors resolve ARVN deficiencies in aggressiveness, leadership, or enthusiasm for engaging the enemy. A MACV study following Ap Bac found the South Vietnamese army had prosecuted a total of 4,475 small unit operations throughout the country in July, quite a laudable number. "However, on the average," the report concluded, "only 175 of the 4,475 made contact with the enemy." Unsurprisingly, the director of the Defense Intelligence Agency contended at year's end that Saigon had been ineffectual in reducing the strength of the Vietcong in spite of the large number of offensive operations.[68]

ARVN's questionable performance at Ap Bac typified frustrations within the American advisory effort and illustrated the obstacles to admitting problems and honestly reporting effectiveness while training a host country's army for unconventional warfare. Though Harkins partially blamed the French for ARVN's problems, such arguments masked larger issues confronted by U.S. advisors. Lacking an understanding of Vietnamese culture—one junior officer thought his cultural training "shallow and superficial"—advisors often missed the political and social tenor of the revolution sweeping throughout the villages.[69] Americans entering Vietnam found a maturing insurgency fighting a reluctant allied army. Jonathan Ladd arrived in the southern half of the Mekong Delta in June 1962, finding it "pretty well controlled by the Viet Cong.... Larger towns than the villages were controlled by the Vietnamese government, but the vast areas of that particular part of Vietnam, mostly very flat rice lands, and the countryside, was controlled by the Viet Cong."[70] Martin Dockery, a young advisor in 1963, believed the relationship with his South Vietnamese counterpart "was defined by mutual ambivalence.... I was raised in a culture where directness is expected. His culture valued indirectness.... When they said yes, it could mean, 'Yes, I agree' or it could mean, 'Yes, I hear you.'"[71] With their enemies having such a head start and their allies apparently disdainful of help, many advisors wondered if their goals might be unattainable.

Many of these frustrations during MACV's first attempt at Vietnamization emerged in the American reporting system. Officers began using the Senior Advisor's Monthly Evaluation (SAME) of Proficiency, Combat Readiness, Morale, Leadership and Other Factors of ARVN in June 1964. The report consisted of eight pages of statistical information. Only one short paragraph offered advisors the chance to recommend improvements for the effectiveness of evaluated units. While the SAME reports reflected the penchant for numbers over evaluation, enduring themes began to develop in American critiques of South Vietnamese performance. In August 1964, the senior U.S. officer in Binh Tuy province reported a need "for more aggressive night patrolling" by Regional and Popular Forces and of "ineffective" local training. The senior advisor for ARVN's 2nd Infantry Division believed the "Non-Commissioned Officers in these units, with few exceptions, fail to exercise initiative on their own," while in the 1st Division, junior level leaders "do not demonstrate the ability to lead and supervise." By October, Binh Tuy's advisor was complaining of recruiting problems and weapons shortages.[72]

In spite of the ARVN's many problems, U.S. advisors and their counterparts had several incentives to emphasize the positive in their reports. An unfavorable comment by an American officer might damage his relationship with the local ARVN commander or village chief. South Vietnamese officers, serving in an army wracked by political corruption, likewise valued upbeat performance evaluations to remain in favor with Saigon officials. The perennially optimistic Harkins habitually met unfavorable reports with hostility, convincing MACV staff officers to discount or silence any bad news.[73] Reporters Neil Sheehan and David Halberstam, interviewing advisors like John Paul Vann, proclaimed the Vietnamese regular army "was at a loss" in meeting the increasing Vietcong threat. MACV, however, accentuated the most upbeat portions of its heavily statisticized reports to illustrate ARVN's improving battlefield effectiveness.[74] It would not be long before journalists began questioning command optimism as dishonesty.

Optimism aside, defeating the insurgency required more than military action and the training of ARVN forces. Achieving internal security for the population also ranked as a major concern. In late 1961 and early 1962, American and South Vietnamese officials agreed upon an operational approach influenced by the British experience in Malaya. The program, under the direction of Diem's brother Ngo-Dinh Nhu, sought to curb VC contact with the rural population. Inaugurated in Binh Duong province, "Operation Sunrise" aimed at fortifying South Vietnam's villages into defensible communities or "strategic hamlets." Civil defense and regional forces would aid in the defense and pacification of these hamlets, allowing ARVN to pursue VC main force units in the field. Harkins and Diem jointly hoped the strategic hamlet program would serve as the "unifying concept for a strategy designed to pacify rural Vietnam (the Viet Cong's chosen battleground) and to develop support among the peasants for the central government." Strategic hamlets became the primary operational means of isolating the VC while extending the government's authority and services throughout the countryside.[75]

As with larger debates concerning strategic objectives, arguments soon surfaced over the proper implementation of the strategic hamlet program. U.S. Army officers believed local province chiefs could not perform their tasks without military forces keeping the Vietcong "off balance while the hamlets were being developed." American advisors wanted to pursue offensive operations in the field against VC main force units. Members of the British Advisory Mission, however, preferred that ARVN react to local threats against protected hamlets.[76] Both advisory missions squabbled over the definition of "isolating" the insurgents from the population. In an important sense, operational means remained as unsettled as the overarching strategy. Matters on the ground soon worsened as the strategic hamlet program collapsed under the weight of governmental pressures to show progress from a concept that was anything but unifying.

Disregarding the methodical "oil blot" principle of progressing from stable areas only as fast as individual hamlet security allowed, Nhu built hamlets in a fashion that one American described as "willy-nilly."[77] In the process, Saigon alienated dissatisfied villagers. Peasants "paid" for their strategic hamlets through compulsory labor, digging trenches and constructing defensive earthworks. GVN officials rarely spent the night in these new hamlets, a fact that the VC quickly exploited in their propaganda. Roger Donlon, an early American advisor and the first Medal of Honor recipient in the Vietnam War, remembered relocating to the mountains coastal families who had been fishermen for generations. Donlon also found enemy infiltrators moving with the population. "Of the three hundred members of our Strike Force it turned out that about a hundred sympathized with the enemy."[78] Sensing that an effective strategic hamlet program might become a threat, the VC concentrated terrorist attacks on the newly constructed hamlets. Disgruntled villagers blamed Saigon for being forcibly relocated from their traditional homes and for the increased VC attacks. Contemptuous of the peasants' complaints, the GVN forged ahead. The strategic hamlet's original intent had become so perverted that one visiting reporter left with the impression of having "blundered into some sort of prison camp."[79] Despite these problems, U.S. officials reported progress because of the growing number of completed hamlets.

MACV's statistics missed the strategic hamlet program's problems until it was beyond repair. After Maxwell Taylor visited Vietnam in September 1962, he announced "much progress" in "the snowballing of the strategic hamlet program which has resulted in some 5,000 hamlets being fortified or in the process of being fortified."[80] Taylor's report, though, rested on dubious numbers. According to one study on Gia Dinh province, official sources had reported 146 hamlets completed in January 1963, rising to 289 completed in June, and then falling to 266 in July. Furthermore, reports of decreasing enemy "incidents" were misleading. The VC often controlled these hamlets from the inside, sometimes with the villagers' willing support, and thus had no need to order further attacks. An advisor serving in the delta believed 90 percent of reported information untrue. Many "completed" hamlets were nothing more than "piles of barbed wire" and others "just a bunch of peasants all corralled in." State Department's Roger Hilsman asserted that "statistics on the number of strategic hamlets and on the number of villages under effective government control were completely false."[81] Pressure to demonstrate progress thus had sabotaged efforts to actually achieve progress. Perhaps most damaging, U.S. officials based their decisions for prosecuting the war on indicators that rarely captured the true essence of ARVN training, civil pacification, or security in the countryside.

Decision-making based on inaccurate assessments of the war's progress became an unfortunate mainstay of the American effort during the early 1960s. Saigon hosted flocks of U.S. officials, reporters, and analysts, all seeking to decipher who was winning, who was losing, and why. Ever since Maxwell Taylor and Walt Rostow found the "double crisis of confidence" in Saigon in 1961, the White House had regularly dispatched missions to Southeast Asia in hopes of gaining insights from which to make better decisions. Typically, the reports only muddied the waters. After visiting Saigon, Marine Major General Victor Krulak, special assistant to the Joint Chiefs for counterinsurgency, and Joseph A. Mendenhall, a senior Foreign Service officer in the State Department, briefed the White House on September 10, 1963. Krulak maintained that the "shooting war is still going ahead at an impressive pace." Mendenhall stated he had found "a virtual breakdown of the civil government in Saigon as well as a pervasive atmosphere of fear and hate arising from the police reign of terror." When both men completed their briefings, an incredulous President Kennedy asked "The two of you did visit the same country, didn't you?"[82]

For a president weighing further U.S. commitments to Vietnam, the Krulak-Mendenhall report offered few insights into the effectiveness of South Vietnam's counterinsurgency fight or the potential for overall success. Less than two weeks later, Kennedy sent Secretary of Defense McNamara and Chairman of the Joint Chiefs Taylor to South Vietnam for answers. Their 2 October trip report seemed just as inconclusive. While noting that the military campaign had made "great progress," the report also acknowledged "serious political tension in Saigon . . . where the Diem-Nhu government is becoming increasingly unpopular." Military indicators in the report reflected the now standard proclivity for statistics with little analysis of trends—Vietcong killed and defected, weapons captured, and estimations on enemy strength. Despite suggesting that an increasingly effective GVN was making progress, McNamara and Taylor still questioned when final military victory could be achieved. That, they noted, depended on the political situation not impeding their efforts. Back in Washington, McNamara recalled that the White House debate upon his return "reflected a total lack of consensus over where we stood in *meeting our objectives.*"[83]

These high-level visits to Vietnam underscored fundamental shortcomings in MACV's analytical framework. U.S. officials could not depend solely on numbers when assessing the army's advisory effort or the GVN's political viability. Despite tremendous effort spent on data collection, officials often disregarded the reports when the numbers did not suit their needs. The case of Army Chief of Staff Harold K. Johnson is enlightening. Johnson visited Southeast Asia in March and December 1964, reporting after his first trip that he was "most encouraged by the trends which were apparent in Vietnam." In December, he expressed his belief that the "conflict in Vietnam can be brought to a successful conclusion in a military sense, provided some semblance of a national governmental structure can be maintained." In between these two trips, however, MACV published an Indicator Balance Sheet showing a discouraging change in trends. The ratio of GVN weapons losses to VC weapons recovered had increased, while the ratio of Vietcong killed to GVN killed had decreased. MACV concluded that these trends reflected an increasing effectiveness among Vietcong actions and recommended maximum advisory effort on improving the quality of small unit leadership within ARVN. Civilian officials were no doubt left questioning both Johnson's observations and MACV's indicators.[84]

The Interlude Ends

Back in July 1961, Walt Rostow, the President's Deputy Special Assistant for National Security Affairs, proposed a list of questions that a military mission to Southeast Asia might answer. Rostow first sought to determine if "the Vietnamese [were] losing ground, holding their ground, or gaining ground in the war against the Viet Cong?" Three years later, in May 1964, Michael V. Forrestal of the National Security Council staff provided an overview of his impressions developed during a two-week stay in Saigon. On the progress of the war, Forrestal pointedly remarked, "I cannot answer the question of whether we are winning or losing. The situation varies from place to place. If I were forced to sum it up, I would say that there has been a slight improvement overall in the last month, but that trend has definitely not yet turned in our favor."[85] After years of searching for evidence of progress, the view from the ground remained muddled as ever. Interpretations continued to vary. Classifications for contested areas and hamlet security remained highly subjective, even though the reporting system depended on objective numbers and percentages. Despite mountains of data collected and the efforts of thousands of advisors and staff officers, MACV's analytical framework had failed to provide clarity.

By the closing months of 1964, U.S. officials increasingly concluded that their position in Vietnam was becoming untenable. Coups plagued the South Vietnamese government at an alarming rate in spite of rising economic and military support. By December, well over 23,000 U.S. troops were serving throughout the country. Still, the southern insurgency continued to thrive. A bewildered Maxwell Taylor reported on the NLF's resiliency despite its losses over the past four years. "Not only do the Viet-Cong units have the recuperative powers of the phoenix, but they have an amazing ability to maintain morale."[86] With an increased American commitment came growing casualty lists—over 350 dead and 1,500 wounded in 1964 alone. Expanding the war failed to generate momentum. U.S. bombing raids and covert operations targeting North Vietnam produced few results, other than placing the Democratic Republic of Vietnam (DRV) on an increased war footing. Then, alarmingly, as 1965 approached, intelligence officers began tracking entire units of the North Vietnamese Army (NVA) infiltrating southward along the Ho Chi Minh trail. As one officer recalled, "It looked as if the invasion that advisors had expected a decade before was on the way at last."[87] Perhaps advocates of a conventional strategy and of training ARVN for aggression from the north had been right all along.

Still, the U.S. mission was not certain from where the primary threat came. It was a debate that would remain unresolved for the remainder of the 1960s. After years of data collection and statistical analysis, Americans in Vietnam were no closer to understanding the true nature of the conflict then when they started. MACV's analytical framework had failed to unravel the intricacies of revolutionary war in Southeast Asia. Harkins and his staff meanwhile embarked upon a disjointed strategy while failing to identify dominant indicators which might accurately gauge its effectiveness.[88] An enormous data collection system remained unconnected to an incoherent strategy. If most U.S. officers missed this point, at least one of their allies had not. As one ARVN general exclaimed to an American friend, "*Ah, les statistiques!* Your Secretary of Defense loves statistics. We Vietnamese can give him all he wants. If you want them to go up, they will go up. If you want them to go down, they will go down."[89] Clearly, the Americans were off to an inauspicious start.

"We cannot defeat this armed enemy unless we win the people; yet unless we defeat the armed enemy, we cannot win the people."
—MICHAEL MOK, *Life*, November 26, 1965

3 An "Unprecedented Victory:" The Problem of Defining Success

BY THE BEGINNING of 1965, over a decade had passed since the Geneva accords and the U.S. decision to create South Vietnam as a front in its anti-communist struggle. Despite infusions of money and technical advisors, the Americans had failed to either crush the insurgent threat or to help build a stable, responsive Government of South Vietnam (GVN). Indeed, South Vietnam seemed on the verge of a decisive defeat. The Vietcong held both the political and military initiative throughout most of the countryside, increasing their manpower pool at an alarming rate and intensifying their psychological campaign against GVN supporters and uncommitted civilians. Republic of Vietnam Armed Forces (RVNAF) casualty rates were higher in December 1964 than in any other month that year. The government's pacification program had, according to the U.S. Military Assistance Command, Vietnam (MACV), been "brought to a virtual standstill." The debilitating political maneuvering in Saigon continued unabated.[1]

The Americans, of course, stood partially responsible for the deteriorating situation in South Vietnam. General Harkins's unshakable optimism as MACV commander hardly compensated for the failure to translate broad strategic concepts into well-defined operational techniques. The botched Strategic Hamlet Program typified mismanaged counterinsurgency policies that did not fully integrate political and military means and objectives. It seemed that no one was coordinating civil-military efforts in Saigon. The inability to agree on the nature of the threat only complicated matters. At the end of 1964, Harkins's successor, William C. Westmoreland, fretted that GVN ineptness was undercutting his ability to carry out his mission at MACV. Commenting on Hanoi's support of the southern insurgency, Westmoreland concluded, "The external threat we must deal with as soon as some governmental stability is manifest and the counter insurgency campaign makes some progress."[2]

Progress, however, characterized few of the reports emanating from South Vietnam. By early 1965, despite the cumbersome, often contradictory, nature of MACV's reporting system, nearly all observers foretold of an impending GVN collapse. In November 1964, Ambassador Maxwell Taylor described the "deterioration of the pacification program" and reported that "the counterinsurgency program countrywide is bogged down." From the White House, National Security Council staff member Chester Cooper noted in March that the "growing lack of confidence among the GVN leadership ... was a direct result of the apparent superiority of the Viet Cong in the military, political, and psychological fields." Later that spring, William DePuy, MACV's chief operations officer, claimed that the South Vietnamese armed forces were "close to anarchy."[3] Few of these observers questioned whether such reports accurately represented the precarious situation in Saigon. South Vietnam certainly appeared to be tottering on a precipice; however, the reporting system that led many Americans to such a conclusion came under little scrutiny during this crucial year of American escalation.[4]

As President Johnson made the fateful decision to send ground combat troops to South Vietnam, the new MACV commander barely tampered with the command's abundant metrics for progress and effectiveness. Staff officers, in fact, appended more reports to an already cluttered system. Though Westmoreland developed a strategic concept addressing the problems of both pacification and enemy attack, MACV failed to integrate the measurement reporting system into its decision-making processes. Perhaps most noteworthy in this first year of troop commitments, measuring the effectiveness of programs to fulfill Westmoreland's strategy attracted little staff attention. Rather, commanders and staffs worried about how certain units executed an innovative organizational concept built around new technologies. Measuring the effectiveness of airmobility superseded measuring MACV's overall operational and strategic progress. Institutional pressures to test these modern technologies and operational concepts dominated army thinking and established a dangerous precedent for the future conduct of the war and how it was measured.

These pressures led officers in the field and on MACV's staff to accentuate one particular element of Westmoreland's otherwise comprehensive strategy—the search for battle. When troopers from the 1st Cavalry Division found such a battle in the Ia Drang valley of the Central Highlands, their "victory" over North Vietnamese regulars overshadowed how MACV defined progress and success for years to come. The massive data-collection effort for measuring progress and effectiveness that MACV had been working on for years would be dominated by a single marker. As soon as the American cavalrymen had left the Ia Drang battlefield, the body count, already in use in MACV estimates, would eclipse nearly all other metrics and indicators. The way in which success was narrowly defined and measured in this "first" battle obscured many of the underlying problems of the army's counterinsurgency efforts and its preparation for and conception of warfare in Vietnam.[5]

The American Buildup: Decisions Based on Metrics

The decision to deploy U.S. ground combat troops to South Vietnam remains one of the most controversial foreign policy decisions in American history. Having served in an advisory role for over a decade, both civilian and military officials believed they had reached their limit of influence in Saigon. If the GVN were to be saved, Americans would have to take on increased responsibilities. Time, apparently, was not on their side. In early 1965, "it had become clear," as Lyndon Johnson would later remark, "gradually but unmistakably, that Hanoi was moving in for the kill."[6] Nearly every metric used in MACV's reporting system foretold of an impending disaster— ARVN desertions and casualties on the rise, increased tempo of VC attacks on lines of communication, hamlets, and outposts, and escalating numbers of northern infiltrators into the south. Yet in evaluating these trends, MACV inexplicably struck an optimistic tone. After collecting scores of data points, the army staff selectively highlighted those figures that best represented advances in accomplishing strictly military tasks. It seemed as if MACV in early 1965 refused to believe it could be losing a war to peasant insurgents. Hanoi had in fact expanded both political activities and offensive military actions throughout the south. Yet, American planners persisted in focusing on the war's military aspects. All the while, MACV remained unsure if conventional forces or insurgents presented the most pressing threat.[7]

Harder to quantify, though no less critical, was the political infighting in Saigon, which had reached near incapacitating levels. In January, Ambassador Taylor described "a seriously deteriorating situation characterized by continued political turmoil" and blamed the "lack of a stable government, inadequate security against the VC and nationwide war-weariness" as the sources of South Vietnam's problems.[8] Taylor did not explain why ten long years of advisory effort had produced such paltry results. To regress so abruptly from Harkins's optimistic reporting, from "winning" battles like Ap Bac to the very brink of defeat, seemed inconceivable to uniformed officers. Such revelations did not escape the media at home. On January 24, *Washington Post* columnist Joseph Alsop declared that the "specter of a catastrophic American defeat looms larger and larger." "The aimless drift that afflicts our Vietnamese policy making," Alsop cried, "calls out for explanation."[9] Harkins's incoherent strategy, causing innumerable problems in MACV's attempts to measure progress and effectiveness, now was breeding skepticism on the entire American war effort in Vietnam. Alsop's piece portended future domestic problems.

While doubt at home slowly increased, counterinsurgency expert Edward G. Lansdale continued to press the administration for a political rather than military solution. MACV largely ignored these strategic issues, focusing instead on where it was making progress inside Vietnam. As such, MACV's monthly evaluation report, one of its principal interpretive tools, portrayed quite a different picture than Alsop's editorial or Taylor's diplomatic cables. MACV claimed that a review of "military events in January tend to induce a decidedly more optimistic view than has been seen in recent months." The staff cited a sudden decline in VC activity that month, a high intensity of ground operations, and a favorable kill ratio against the enemy. (It conceded, though, that pacification was making little progress.) The January report speculated that if "the RVNAF capability can be underwritten by political stability and durability, a significant turning point in the war could be for forthcoming."[10] Such evaluations underscored the shortcomings of metrics that concentrated narrowly on quantifiable military activities. Unsurprisingly, mixed signals continued to radiate from Saigon. The U.S. ambassador to South Vietnam reported on a "number of unpleasant developments" the same month that MACV found cause for optimism.

The Vietcong raised the stakes on the morning of February 7 with a mortar attack on the U.S. barracks at Pleiku airfield in the central highlands, killing eight Americans and wounding 108. Less than a week later, President Johnson began Operation Rolling Thunder, a retaliatory air campaign against the North that would last well into 1968 and create an entirely different measurement problem—one beyond the scope of this work.[11] On the 21st, Westmoreland requested two battalions of marines to protect the Danang airbase from VC reprisals. MACV's monthly evaluation report for February acknowledged it "is obvious that the complexion of the war has changed." Indicators for RVNAF operational efforts, VC activity, and pacification all exhibited disappointing results. In March, however, events were suddenly "encouraging," and in April friendly forces had apparently "retained the initiative." Such inconsistent reporting from MACV headquarters actually no longer mattered. Pleiku marked a turning point in America's Indochina policy. National security advisor McGeorge Bundy, visiting South Vietnam during the attack, wrote the president that the "United States could no longer 'wait and hope for a stable government' while the VC expanded its control over the RVN.'" Bundy urged Johnson to "use our military power . . . to force a change of Communist policy."[12] The advisory and operational support phase rapidly was coming to an end.

Bundy's argument to LBJ rested on two broad yet widely held assumptions. Representative of the president's inner circle, Bundy presumed that South Vietnam's survival directly affected U.S. national security. The domino theory of containment remained valid and, Bundy believed, prestige abroad factored heavily into communist assessments of American commitment to winning the Cold War. The national security advisor was not alone in this assessment. As the Joint Chiefs argued, "a US withdrawal would have serious consequences."[13] Such conjecture, however, rested on worst-case speculation. Johnson spoke at Johns Hopkins University on April 7 of "increased unrest and instability, and even wider war" throughout Indochina if the United States abandoned South Vietnam. Neither he nor his advisors saw any reason to question the basic assumptions upon which the domino theory rested. America would continue to support South Vietnam because it apparently had no other choice.[14]

The widespread belief that Hanoi was on the verge of launching an all-out offensive served as the second assumption driving escalation. Army Chief of Staff Harold K. Johnson visited Saigon in March and received a gloomy report from embassy officials. Taylor expressed concern over population security, governmental instability, lack of progress in destroying the Vietcong, and the continuing ability of the VC to replace their losses. More importantly, U.S. advisors reported increases in the strength and aggressiveness of communist attacks. If the war had been ill-defined to this point, the American mission believed that a clearer picture was emerging in the spring of 1965. The murky internal political situation might remain baffling to outsiders, but the GVN appeared to be teetering. Though MACV analysts faced continued difficulties in assessing NVA/VC strategy, the communists now seemed poised for a knockout blow.[15]

With North Vietnam evidently abandoning their successful guerrilla tactics and moving to the conventional "third stage" of Mao's protracted warfare, the Joint Chiefs appealed for an increase in ground combat troops. Defense Secretary Robert S. McNamara quickly assented. In March, Westmoreland, who initially had been hesitant to enlarge the role of ground troops, concluded that the war had indeed moved to "a more formalized military conflict" and recommended higher troop levels. At the Honolulu conference in April, he received a commitment for 40,000 more troops. As one officer recalled, the "floodgates were now open."[16] They were about to open still wider as McNamara visited Saigon in mid-July after a month's worth of discouraging field reports. Reversing itself, MACV now reported that its major statistical indicators of progress—population and area control, desertions, weapons losses, terror incidents, price levels, and casualties—all failed to show any significant gains for either GVN or ARVN. McNamara weakly questioned the reports' accuracy. Upon returning home, he recommended to the president, based on Westmoreland's request for forty-four additional maneuver battalions, a substantial deployment of U.S. ground troops to demonstrate to the North "that the odds are against their winning."[17] At the end of July, Johnson announced that 50,000 troops would be dispatched to South Vietnam, raising the total to 125,000. If needed, more would be sent as requested.

This decision to send thousands of additional ground combat troops to Vietnam in mid-1965 rested in large part on assumptions stemming from a disjointed treatment of MACV's measurements of effectiveness and progress. With so many indices for evaluation, inconsistent assessments of the political and military situation in Vietnam seemed predictable. MACV's monthly eval report for July noted that ARVN forces were making progress in some areas and that their "operational effort remained at a high level"[18]—this the same month that McNamara visited Saigon and recommended increased troop deployments based on MACV's estimate of the deteriorating situation throughout South Vietnam. Few, either in MACV or the president's inner circle, questioned the use of statistics. The United States would send American troops to contain communism, plain and simple. Thus, in the first half of 1965, policy debate centered not as much on the proper strategy to achieve the administration's goal of demonstrating the North's incapacity to win, but rather on the number of troops required to do so.[19]

Believing its credibility at stake, the United States rushed headlong into Vietnam with little debate as to how U.S. ground forces would fulfill Johnson's broad policy objectives. Undersecretary of State George Ball, the lone dissenter inside the administration, reviewed for Johnson the recent French-Indochina experience. In critiquing the currently flawed measurement system leading to escalation, Ball cited the successive disappointments since 1961. He then compared the Americans and French. "They quoted the same kind of statistics that guide our opinions," he wrote the president, "statistics as to the number of Viet Minh killed, the number of enemy defectors, the rate of enemy desertions, etc." Lack of a stable political base in Saigon continued to frustrate American efforts, just as in the First Indochina War. Ball argued for "more evidence than we now have that our troops will not bog down in the jungles and rice paddies—while we slowly blow the country to pieces."[20] His arguments fell on deaf ears. The momentum for war pushed logic aside. By June and July, few officials considered if the enormous influx of U.S. ground troops to South Vietnam might actually be counterproductive. Based on selectively chosen indicators, the American mission had convinced the Secretary of Defense, and he the President, that the counterinsurgency campaign over the last few years had been a failure.[21]

A New Strategy?

Ball's articulate dissent attracted few supporters, chiefly because of fears lying at the heart of Johnson's Vietnam policy. As Ball's superior, Secretary of State Dean Rusk, reminded the president, "If the Communist world finds out that we will not pursue our commitments to the end, I don't know where they will stay their hand."[22] To fulfill these promises, the assumptions went, required a complete transition from advisory role to ground combat operations. Security assistance that characterized early American efforts in Vietnam had failed. MACV now required an overhaul in operational concepts and strategy. Westmoreland, who had served as the Deputy COMUSMACV beginning in January 1964 and replaced Harkins that June as the American commander in Vietnam, had nearly eighteen months of experience in the country as he undertook this task of translating the administration's recent plans into sound strategy.[23] Yet the new MACV commander had little more practical knowledge in counterinsurgency than his predecessor.

A South Carolinian and West Point first captain, William Childs Westmoreland seemed destined to wear general's stars. Ramrod straight, hard-working, exceptionally dedicated, the one-time Eagle Scout rarely failed to impress either peers or superior officers. He served with distinction as an artillery commander in Africa and Europe during World War II and commanded an airborne regimental combat team in Korea. He had taught at the Army War College and commanded the 101st Airborne Division before becoming the Superintendent of West Point in 1960. He knew the right people (critics alleged that his career trajectory was influenced in no small way by Maxwell Taylor and the "airborne mafia") and held the right assignments, even attending Harvard's Business School. Westmoreland looked and acted every inch the part of commanding general. His preparation for four-star command was as conventional as that of the U.S. Army since World War I.

Though Westmoreland possessed no practical counterinsurgency experience, he at least seemed open to the complexities of revolutionary war. As Superintendent he instituted a counterinsurgency warfare training program for cadets and organized a series of lectures on low-intensity and insurgency warfare. As Deputy COMUSMACV he headed a mission to Malaya to study British anti-guerrilla tactics. If Westmoreland was not brilliant, he was intelligent and reasonable and grasped the debate over appropriate strategy as American troops streamed into South Vietnam.

FIGURE 3.1 Americanization of the war. General William Westmoreland, Commander, U.S. Army Military Assistance Command, Vietnam.
Source RG124S, SLA Marshall Collection, Box 6, Folder 600

While his impressive qualifications may have been suited for a different kind of war, the fifty-one-year old officer appreciated the magnitude of the task before him.[24]

Westmoreland's first challenge was to develop a comprehensive plan for the American effort in South Vietnam. To a number of officials—newly assigned Ambassador Henry Cabot Lodge, CINCPAC Admiral U. S. Sharp, Marine General Victor Krulak—occupation of key enclaves offered the best opportunity for success. Lodge canvassed in July for the "highly political oil spot procedure, never striving for flashy and misleading statistics, always seeking solid and *durable* gains, however small, however slowly achieved."[25] This enclave strategy mirrored the French *tache d'huile* approach in occupying and defending key areas, building up a secure base of political support, and then gradually expanding outward. Lodge's appeal for slow and small gains unfortunately contradicted a principal element of counterinsurgency doctrine. Quite simply, the enclave strategy was not aggressive enough. It left the NLF to operate at will throughout the countryside, causing the GVN, now led by Air Marshal Nguyen Cao Ky, to lose standing in the eyes of the people. More important for Westmoreland, "it put American troops in the unfortunate position of defending static positions. . . . It also left the decision of ultimate success or failure in the hands of the South Vietnamese troops whose demonstrated inability to defeat the Viet Cong was the reason for committing American troops."[26]

Through the spring and summer, Westmoreland formalized the strategic views that would guide American troop employment for the next three years. The Joint Chiefs, incidentally, presented their "Concept for Vietnam" to the Secretary of Defense in late August but the civilian leadership took no action on the vague document.[27] With the JCS paper failing to gain approval, Westmoreland's proposals solidified into official strategy almost by default. On August 30, MACV issued a three-phase concept for operations. Phase I, lasting through the end of 1965, marked the commitment of forces "necessary to halt the losing trend." Military tasks included security of logistical and military bases, strengthening the RVNAF, and conducting offensive operations against major VC bases. In Phase II, beginning in early 1966, Westmoreland envisioned a "resumption of the offensive" to destroy enemy forces and allow for the expansion of pacification operations. Finally, Phase III, lasting for a year to eighteen months, depending on enemy persistence, would see the final "defeat and destruction of remaining enemy forces and base areas."[28] The American command in Vietnam finally could operate under a coherent, articulate strategy that included specific tasks for each phase of the operation.

Behind the clarity of Westmoreland's plan lay confusion over strategic objectives and military tasks. In this sense, little had changed since the Harkins era. The limited objective of demonstrating the North's inability to win had not changed. Nor had the complexity of the political-military threat. MACV's reporting system still required assessments on the insurgency, the "big unit war," the pacification program, and GVN political and economic stability. One district advisor in Gia Dinh province explained the three distinct aspects of his mission, which required "the delicacies of dealing with allies who desire our support while resenting any hint of interference; the grassroots administration of foreign aid (in terms of ensuring that our aid gets to the people who need it); and the military confrontation of Communist revolutionary warfare."[29] Westmoreland appreciated all of these facets. A strategy to accommodate such wide-ranging features of revolutionary warfare demanded an integrated effort. MACV could not, and did not, simply focus on one aspect of the fight. Equally important, the counterinsurgency campaign required a perceptive appraisal of the kind of warfare being waged in the fluid environment of South Vietnam. Throughout the war, the Vietcong adeptly shifted emphasis between political and military means depending on their own sense of progress. Keeping pace with these changes proved as frustrating for the American command under Westmoreland as it did under Harkins.[30]

While supplying much-needed clarity in linking strategic goals to operational objectives, Westmoreland's three-phase plan remained a broad, if not equivocal, policy document. As such, the U.S. command never blindly pursued search-and-destroy operations at the expense of all other activities. In 1965, MACV's mission required

Westmoreland "to assist and support the RVNAF in their efforts to defeat communist subversive insurgency, and to accelerate effective GVN control over the country."[31] Westmoreland held no illusions that this would be a short conflict. He appreciated early on the problems of "VC lie-low tactics" in which the enemy purposefully avoided American forces. During the escalation period in mid-1965, he placed renewed attention on pacification programs and political stability in Saigon. Yet Westmoreland led an organization that held little practical experience in counterinsurgency and generally disliked unconventional operations. Though Edward Lansdale persisted in crusading for a "reorientation of military thinking to 'make it the No. 1 priority for the military to protect and help the people,'" army forces deploying to Vietnam in 1965 saw civic action and local aid programs as foreign to their core mission of closing with and destroying the enemy.[32]

The spring and early summer debate over the enclave strategy epitomized the dissension over strategy and the proper employment of ground forces in South Vietnam. Westmoreland never retreated from his conviction that Vietcong and NVA regular forces could not be left to roam unopposed through the countryside. To many officers, including COMUSMACV, leaving internal security issues to local troops made sense, given their language and cultural ties. U.S. troops could be better employed on offensive operations shielding the population from attack rather than providing assistance to pacification programs. Westmoreland's strategy was not a matter of choosing search-and-destroy operations over pacification, but rather of emphasizing the use of Americans for one element of a complex and diverse mission.[33] Senior American officials all seemed to agree that security was fundamental to progress in other governmental social and economic programs. How best to achieve security, however, remained contentious. Back in March, Taylor claimed that the lack of security stemmed from ARVN's inability to defeat the VC. John Paul Vann, the American advisor at Ap Bac, thought otherwise. "Emphasis is placed upon the use of physical obstacles to provide population security rather than the fostering of a spirit of resistance."[34] This strategic discord would persist throughout the war, leaving MACV officers uncertain of how to measure progress as emphasis swung from military to nonmilitary programs.

In a large sense, the strategic debate stemmed directly from challenges in gauging the effectiveness of those political and military tasks associated with counterinsurgency. How was security defined and measured? Decreasing incident rates did not necessarily equate to improved security, a fact the French had learned in their war against the Vietminh. How was control defined and measured? Through territory or population? Westmoreland recognized that ARVN operations in a given area often did not produce a corresponding rise in governmental control. After finalizing his strategic plan in late August 1965, Westmoreland issued a command directive explaining his concept for employment of U.S. forces. He noted, "the ultimate aim is to pacify the Republic of Vietnam by destroying the VC ... while at the same time reestablishing the government apparatus, strengthening GVN military forces, rebuilding the administrative machinery, and re-instituting the services of the Government."[35] Which of these tasks were most relevant toward achieving pacification? If MACV was ineffective in one area, did all other areas suffer? Certainly, military tasks could not be abandoned in the pursuit of political, sociological, or economic measures, even if it was difficult to bring Vietcong insurgents to battle.[36]

What confronted Westmoreland, then, was a continuing problem in defining the political-military "battlespace," a notion quite different from delineating the conventional battlefields of World War II and Korea. In Vietnam, the battlefield extended well beyond the villages. Military action mattered, but so too did the training of South Vietnamese forces, the relationship between Saigon officials, provincial chiefs, and religious leaders, and the state of the economy. MACV strategy considered these diverse political-military tasks. Still, lack of coordination between civilian and military agencies, the continuing debate over the true nature of the threat, and the burdens imposed by an escalating American presence all added confusion in defining where the decisive point of the war would be fought.[37]

Westmoreland acknowledged the problem of gauging progress and seemed to appreciate the cumbersome, if not unmanageable, structure of MACV's reporting system. While U.S. advisors in the field bemoaned the growing demands for information, Westmoreland proposed that the more than one hundred indicators be pruned down to a few basic "yardsticks" that could be "employed as primary indicators to measure pacification progress."[38] These yardsticks included population control, area control, communications control, resources control, and both VC and ARVN strength and viability. However, the Research Analysis Corporation, studying MACV's statistical indicators, criticized the staff's data collection efforts—too much to be overwhelming in some instances, not enough in others to be useful. (It is doubtful that district-level advisors would have agreed that MACV's staff was not receiving enough information.) The report also indicated a major gap in strategic planning. It asserted that "the current phase of activity in South Vietnam has been primarily military in character" and that research on non-military parameters "has not been intensive." MACV instead had been paying attention to areas more congenial to conventional-minded officers—casualties, VC order-of-battle and activities, and ARVN ground operations.[39]

This failure to resolve the reporting conundrum before the introduction of ground forces ranked as one of Westmoreland's greatest mistakes as MACV commander. Recognizing the problems of gauging progress in an "area war" with no front lines, Westmoreland nonetheless neglected the bloated, mechanistic reporting structure developed under Harkins. Condensing indicators to five or six vague "yardsticks" hardly served as a solution. Population control still remained largely undefined. Data, much of it still coming from Vietnamese sources, remained questionable. Nowhere did COMUSMACV lay out how his command would measure political and military progress, instead simply stating that all wars of attrition are lengthy affairs.[40] Westmoreland, to his credit, articulated specific tasks to support each phase of his strategic concept. He neglected, however, to connect these tasks to metrics for effectiveness and progress. Left alone, the reporting system continued to focus on more easily quantifiable actions, most of which fell into the military rather than political realm. All of this occurred as the army's newest unit prepared to embark on its first campaign in the South Vietnam central highlands.

Measuring Airmobility's Organizational Effectiveness

The initial ground combat troops sent to Vietnam in the spring and early summer of 1965 deployed overseas before MACV and the Joint Chiefs had agreed on how those soldiers would be used against the enemy. Among the first units resulting from Westmoreland's troop requests in March and April, the 173rd Airborne Brigade arrived from Okinawa in early May. Placed in Bien Hoa, just outside of Saigon, the 173rd immediately began a mobile defense of the province while conducting offensive counterinsurgency operations. The brigade quickly found the VC a wily foe. Unable to sustain contact with the Vietcong, Brigadier General Ellis W. Williamson, the 173rd's commander, griped in September, "I am thoroughly convinced that running into the jungle with a lot of people without a fixed target is a lot of effort, a lot of physical energy expended. A major portion of our effort evaporates into the air."[41] Poor intelligence compounded these frustrations as officers juggled the loads of information pouring into their headquarters yet found most of it too old to be usable. One senior advisor thought "the intelligence . . . absolutely horrible."[42] Despite the incorporation of stirring new organizational concepts, the enemy clearly seemed to hold the initiative in these early contests.

The American command placed high hopes in these new concepts, for airmobility looked as if it might solve the problem of quickly moving soldiers in the often impassable terrain of Vietnam. For the first time in American military history, the 173rd transported four battalions worth of soldiers (two American and two South Vietnamese) to their targets in helicopters. Units might now be able to react to intelligence reports before they became stale. Ambushes might be avoided. Initiative might be regained. Such heady aspirations had been growing since James M. Gavin's

1954 *Harper's* magazine article "Cavalry, and I Don't Mean Horses." Gavin, the popular commander of the 82nd Airborne Division in World War II, believed that stalemate in Korea had resulted in large part from a lack of reconnaissance and mobility that cavalry forces historically provided their armies. Helicopters could serve as the cavalryman's new mount, Gavin declared. Within two years the army's Aviation School at Fort Rucker, Alabama, began weapons tests with Bell H-13 Sioux airframes. In 1956 the army authorized its airborne divisions each a helicopter reconnaissance troop. By the early 1960s, Rucker's air assault proponents looked to their next step—gaining approval and funding for an experimental unit to test the airmobile concept.[43]

The aviators' timing was fortunate. The Kennedy administration was already emphasizing a larger role for conventional forces in its "flexible response" approach to national security. As early as December 1961, U.S. Army helicopter pilots were ferrying South Vietnamese paratroopers into battle near Saigon. After reviewing the results of an Army Aircraft Requirements Board the year prior, the Secretary of Defense indicated in late 1961 his support for procuring additional army aviation assets. In April 1962, McNamara wrote the Secretary of the Army about their potential for tactical mobility. "Air vehicles operating close to, but above, the ground appear to me to offer the possibility of a quantum increase in effectiveness."[44] Within one week, the army's training command assigned Lieutenant General Hamilton W. Howze, the XVIII Airborne Corps commander, to convene the U.S. Army Tactical Mobility Requirements Board. The Howze board consisted of seventeen officers and five civilians. After extensive war games, training exercises, and consideration of opinions from the field, the board submitted its 3,500-page report in late August. While the report reviewed organizational issues, operational techniques, and personnel training, the board's main conclusion left little doubt as to the efficacy of future airmobile operations. "Adoption by the Army of the airmobile concept—however imperfectly it may be described and justified in this report—is necessary and desirable."[45]

The Howze Board's report predictably encountered sharp criticism from a parochial Air Force and more conservative-minded army officers. The escalating war in Vietnam, however, provided compelling incentive to expand upon the airmobility concept. In February 1963, the same month that Chairman of the Joint Chiefs of Staff Earle G. Wheeler stated "the tide is turning in our favor," the 11th Air Assault Division (Test) activated at Fort Benning, Georgia. Handpicked to command the unit, Major General Harry W. Kinnard received instruction to "determine how far and fast the Army can go, and should go, in embracing airmobility."[46] A recipient of the Distinguished Service Cross, the forty-eight-year-old Texan had served in the 101st Airborne at the Battle of the Bulge. The veteran airborne infantryman eagerly accepted his new challenge. Throughout 1963 and 1964 the 11th Division experimented with helicopter tactics, support requirements, and flying techniques. All the while, counterinsurgency considerations cast a long shadow over the evaluations. In February 1964, Wheeler noted that Vietnam's terrain and environment "hold the rate of ground movement to that of the soldier on foot. Thus the addition of the helicopter gives the Army of the Republic of Viet Nam a mobility differential and the advantages that go with it." As the United States inched closer to taking full control of the war effort in 1965, U.S. officers looked to reaping the benefits of their new airmobile organization. In June, McNamara authorized inclusion of an airmobile division into the army's force structure, officially redesignating the 11th as the 1st Cavalry Division (Airmobile).[47]

National media exposure increased institutional pressures to perform. With the army recently completing a reorganization of its divisional structure, from battle groups of the pentomic division to the more flexible supporting-arms brigades of the "Reorganization Objectives Army Division" (ROAD), the 1st Cavalry symbolized the military leadership's commitment to rapid movement. Airmobility seemed perfect for offsetting Vietcong advantages in intelligence and surprise. Kinnard recalled the "Viet Minh had defeated a well trained, well equipped, *ground-bound* French force in the early 1950s."[48] Helicopters, free from the constraints of terrain, ostensibly presented a solution to the military problems of insurgent warfare. American soldiers riding in their new cavalry mounts would not make the same mistakes as their French predecessors a decade earlier. In one sense, this drive to ensure airmobility's relevance to counterinsurgency demonstrated the army's genuine attempt to consider the special requirements of unconventional warfare. Commanders and planners did realize the need for changing tactics and techniques to wage counterinsurgency, even if those changes were not precisely tailored to South Vietnam. As early as 1961, the American mission in Vietnam was debating how best to exploit helicopters in a counterinsurgent role.[49]

Perhaps more importantly, institutional eagerness to validate the helicopter's role in modern warfare intensified pressures to demonstrate the effectiveness of the airmobile division. Intensive field tests accompanied every step in the airmobile division's development. The Howze Board even conducted a large-scale counterguerrilla exercise in North Carolina's Appalachian Mountains to simulate conditions in Laos. "These tests," the board found, "showed that helicopters and fixed-wing aircraft in conventional and counterguerrilla actions would materially enhance combat effectiveness."[50] The Army Concept Team in Vietnam supported the Howze Board's evaluations by examining the effectiveness of helicopters being used to transport ARVN troops in combat during late 1962 and early 1963. Encouraging results stimulated further interest in airmobility—helping solidify the inclusion of the 1st Cavalry

Division into the army force structure—and increased expectations for use in fighting against VC insurgents. A January 1965 Concept Team evaluation report stated unequivocally that the "armed helicopter provided the Army of the Republic of Vietnam with an effective means of collecting and reporting combat information in time to permit appropriate combat action."[51] Thus, as American ground forces entered South Vietnam in the spring and summer of 1965, measuring the effectiveness of helicopters and the airmobile organization was fast becoming as important as measuring the effectiveness of Westmoreland's strategy and the army's counterinsurgency doctrine.

The aspirations of airmobility enthusiasts deeply influenced how the army looked at measuring effectiveness versus progress in its first large-scale ground operation in South Vietnam. Helicopters inspired near delusional expectations like Kinnard's later claim that cavalry finally had been "freed forever from the tyranny of terrain."[52] But the helicopter in Vietnam was no panacea. Technology could not, in itself, change attitudes or defeat an ideology. Airmobility could not, as hoped, compensate for Vietcong advantages in intelligence and political resourcefulness. The French realized this from their recent experiences in Algeria (one officer noting that helicopters "fail strategically ... because they leave the initiative to the guerrillas") but no one in the American mission took notice.[53] The die had been cast with McNamara's decision to formally incorporate the airmobile division into the army's force structure. Too much time, effort, and resources had been expended for the 1st Cavalry to fail under combat conditions. Too many signs pointed to the efficacy of modern airmobile troopers fighting and winning against peasant insurgents. How effective "sky cavalry" would be in the political-military environment of South Vietnam seemed little in doubt.

Establishing the New Benchmark

On July 1, 1965, the 1st Cavalry Division officially came into existence. On August 2, in a feat of logistical and administrative planning, the unit began its deployment to South Vietnam. Westmoreland placed the division near An Khe in western Binh Dinh province in the central highlands. COMUSMACV intended the 1st Cavalry to screen the Cambodian border while preventing North Vietnamese units from controlling the critical Highway 19, which linked Pleiku city in the highlands to Qui Nhon on the eastern coast. Hanoi had been closely monitoring the U.S. buildup and replied by increasing infiltration of its own forces and supplies into South Vietnam. The mountainous, rugged terrain of the central highlands offered advantages as NVA base areas, thanks to its inaccessibility to ground transport, especially in the monsoon season from mid-May to mid-October. MACV considered the area vitally important as well. If North Vietnamese regulars wrested control of Highway 19 from ARVN, they essentially would cut the country in half. Accordingly, 1st Cavalry troopers carved out a base camp at An Khe—nicknamed the "Golf Course"—and immediately began "shakedown" exercises in preparation for their expected baptism of fire with the enemy.[54]

The division did not have to wait long. In early October, as Kinnard's men gradually expanded operations to find the enemy and establish governmental control in the VC-dominated region, Hanoi ordered General Chu Huy Man to undertake a series of engagements around Pleiku. Three North Vietnam Army (NVA) regiments joined the local Vietcong forces. On October 19, they attacked the small U.S. Special Forces Plei Me camp near the Cambodian border. NVA forces quickly pounced on the South Vietnamese relief column that Man correctly had anticipated. On October 23, Kinnard received permission from Westmoreland to transfer his entire 1st Brigade to Pleiku, only 25 miles away. Relying heavily on artillery and tactical air support, the Americans responded with overwhelming firepower. By the 25th, Man decided he had suffered enough and withdrew westward to the northern bank of the River Drang near Cambodia. The MACV monthly evaluation for October cheerfully noted that the engagement "permitted an extensive and effective utilization of Allied air power to strike the Viet Cong force." However, not all participants were so optimistic. One of Kinnard's helicopter pilots recalled, "With all our mobility, the VC still called the shots. We fought on their terms." The young warrant officer's observations were accurate. Man had determined when to attack and when to withdraw.[55]

Having tasted enemy blood—Americans estimated North Vietnamese losses at 850 dead and 1,700 wounded—Kinnard wanted desperately to continue the pursuit. The successful Plei Me defense hardly illustrated the full capacity of the airmobility concept. Lobbying MACV to unleash the division onto the offensive, Kinnard received authorization on October 28 to pursue Man's withdrawing units. UH-1 Huey helicopters swarmed the skies over Pleiku province as 1st Cavalry soldiers roamed the desolate brush in search of enemy forces. Between October 28 and November 14, division troopers only sporadically came into contact with NVA forces, which were being reinforced by nearly 2,000 soldiers from Man's reserve regiment. As the number of American air assaults and artillery moves multiplied, MACV turned greater attention to filling the airmobile division's increasingly critical fuel shortages. Colonel Thomas W. Brown, whose 3rd Brigade relieved the 1st Brigade on November 9, underlined the frustration—"having drawn a blank up to this point, I wasn't sure what we would find or even if we'd find anything."[56] Apparently helicopters had not cracked the puzzle of the intelligence battle. Kinnard continued to press west toward the Cambodian border, directing Lieutenant Colonel Harold G. Moore's 1st Battalion, 7th Cavalry, to search the Ia Drang Valley near the Chu Pong Mountain area. Moore expected to make contact, and on November 4, after an early aerial reconnaissance of prospective landing zones (LZs), his battalion of 431 men began their flights deeper into the western plateau.

Moore's suspicions of enemy presence were well founded. Man in fact had consolidated his forces within the Chu Pong massif, awaiting the Americans' next move. Moore selected his LZ (landing zone), X-Ray, right below the NVA position. The U.S. battalion commander, however, was no easy target. A 1945 West Point graduate, Moore had served as an infantry company commander in the Korean War and held a master's degree in international affairs from George Washington University. The pragmatic forty-three-year-old Kentuckian had read Bernard Fall's *Street Without Joy* and, though exacting in his demands, engendered fierce loyalty in his subordinates. Shortly after landing at X-Ray, one of Moore's patrols captured an enemy prisoner who reported North Vietnamese battalions in the nearby massif. Extending its perimeter toward Chu Pong, B Company collided with two NVA companies triggering some of the most ferocious fighting of the entire war. Dennis Deal, a platoon leader in B Company working up a ravine, remembered that "at any given second there were a thousand bullets coursing through that small area looking for a target—a thousand bullets a second." Correspondent Neil Sheehan recalled X-Ray "was not hard to distinguish from the air on Monday morning. It was an island in a sea of red-orange napalm and exploding bombs and shells."[57]

Despite the Americans' heavy use of firepower, NVA infantrymen continued to surge out of Chu Pong toward Moore's battalion. That the 7th Cavalry traced its lineage to Custer and Little Big Horn was not lost on the embattled troopers. By early afternoon, Moore was fighting three separate actions: defending the landing zone, attacking the North Vietnamese, and attempting to rescue a platoon that had earlier pursued an NVA patrol and had been cut off from the rest of the battalion. Outnumbered, he pulled back to establish a perimeter and called in waves of artillery fire and tactical air strikes to keep the enemy at bay. Moore remembered the shells "falling down in torrents." Helicopter pilots braved the storm of steel enveloping the LZ, transferring ammunition and reinforcements to and the growing number of wounded from the battlefield. So desperate had Moore's position become that MACV authorized the use of B-52 strategic bombers from Guam for close air support. On November 16, unable to break the cavalry's perimeter, the NVA commander, as at Plei Me, decided he could do no more against American firepower and began withdrawing his forces from the landing zone area.[58]

While the fighting at X-Ray died down, the North Vietnamese infantry were not quite done with the Americans. On November 17, Lieutenant Colonel Robert A. McDade's 2nd Battalion, 7th Cavalry, en route to X-Ray as reinforcement, received orders to turn north and sweep the area for enemy soldiers before evacuating from a new LZ code-named Albany. McDade had been in command for only three weeks and took few precautions as he set out. The 8th Battalion of the 66th PAVN Regiment, heading in the same direction, found the American unit through careful scouting and immediately began establishing an ambush. Under deep jungle canopy, McDade's men walked headlong into a trap. The melee, confusing as it was deadly, continued throughout the afternoon as pilots, often unable to distinguish between friend and foe, vainly attempted to provide support through the thick foliage. One soldier recalled, "Men all around me were screaming. The fire now was a continuous roar.... No one knew where the fire was coming from, and so the men were shooting everywhere. Some were in shock and were blazing away at everything they saw or imagined they saw." Throughout the night, the NVA maintained their pressure on the encircled American perimeter. At daybreak they silently melted away. McDade's unit had suffered 151 killed, 121 wounded, and five missing—over 60 percent casualties. Afterward, Kinnard reported that the "cavalry battalion had taken everything the enemy could throw at it, and had turned on him and had smashed and defeated him."[59]

Moore's actions at LZ X-Ray quickly, perhaps predictably, eclipsed McDade's at Albany. Yet was the Ia Drang battle really a victory? U.S. officials quickly hailed it as such, based on familiar metrics. Discounting the catastrophe at Albany, MACV focused on the satisfyingly low ratio of American to enemy casualties. Body counts revealed Moore's troopers killed 634 NVA soldiers—while "estimating" another 1,215—compared to losing 75 killed and 121 wounded. (MACV did not publicize McDade's losses.) To MACV, such casualty ratios demonstrated the validity of the airmobile division's use of firepower and mobility. Body counts also appeared to validate MACV's long-term objective of breaking the enemy's will through a strategy of attrition.[60] Through conventional lens, Westmoreland later celebrated the 1st Cavalry's apparently decisive victory. "We had no Kasserine Pass as in World War II, no costly retreat by hastily committed, understrength occupation troops from Japan into a Pusan perimeter as in Korea."[61] American troops, bearing technologically advanced weaponry, had stood their ground against the finest troops North Vietnam could offer. More, they inflicted a greater number of casualties and sent the enemy fleeing from the battlefield.

Just as predictably, the North Vietnamese embraced a different view of their first large-scale battle with the Americans. Common infantry soldiers had withstood the firestorm of American airpower and heliborne assault tactics. As Moore recalled, by

Hanoi's "yardstick, a draw against such a powerful opponent was the equivalent of a victory."[62] More importantly, American firepower could be effectively countered, as seen during the destruction of McDade's forces at Albany. By closing in tight with the 1st Cavalry troopers, the NVA could negate U.S. advantages in weaponry. One former PLAF general officer remembered "the way to fight the American was to 'grab him by his belt' . . . to get so close that your artillery and air power were useless."[63] While Americans rejoiced in their victory at Ia Drang, they failed to consider that their new airmobile tactics might have an Achilles' heel. It seemed not to faze any of the 1st Cavalry Division or MACV's leadership that B-52 bombers were needed to save Moore's battalion. Hanoi's leadership arguably took a more balanced appraisal of the fighting in Pleiku province. Helicopter assaults could be disrupted successfully but only at a heavy price. It was not yet time to progress into the final conventional phase of revolutionary war.

The 1st Cavalry's spoiling attack into the western central highlands certainly derailed General Man's plan to control Highway 19 and strike toward the coast before U.S. troops gained a significant foothold in South Vietnam. Ia Drang, however, hardly validated airmobility's success in counterinsurgency operations. MACV misinterpreted, if not ignored, a number of significant facts in evaluating Kinnard's Pleiku campaign. At Plei Me, X-Ray, and Albany, the enemy initiated fighting and decided when to withdraw. Further, the North Vietnamese operated in battalion-sized formations, an option they would henceforth consider sparingly. Finally, destruction of enemy forces did not necessarily equate to population control. Tying military success in the central highlands to pacification progress along the coastal plains eluded MACV from the start.[64]

Justifiably inspired by the heroic performance of his young soldiers, Moore likely missed all the subtleties of evaluating progress in an unconventional war. In fact, almost all of MACV's officers chose to define success in November 1965 in narrow, conventional terms—in terms of combat effectiveness exhibited by American forces, rather than of progress in the war against the southern insurgency. The "Significant Victories and Defeats" annex of MACV's eval report that month consisted of five full pages of friendly and Vietcong losses. Nowhere did the annex mention pacification, civil affairs, or training of ARVN forces. Despite Westmoreland's comprehensive strategy, staff officers at MACV made little effort to assess whether such hard statistics yielded any political "victories" against the enemy.[65]

Certainly a few Americans appreciated that helicopters had not wrested the initiative from either the Vietcong or the NVA. If official channels conveyed little doubt, some U.S. soldiers expressed their suspicions of airmobility's touted invincibility to the media. After the Pleiku battles, *New York Times* military correspondent Hanson W. Baldwin recounted how some 1st Cavalry officers questioned both the airmobile division's staying power and the number of ground forces needed to effectively search out and destroy the enemy. Pulitzer Prize–winning journalist and photographer Malcolm W. Browne quoted one U.S. advisor who doubted airmobility's utility in a counterinsurgency environment. The officer noted, "the Viet Cong have no helicopters or airplanes. They didn't have any during the Indochina War either, but they still won." The advisor then offered a veiled critique of the airmobility concept and the larger American approach to revolutionary warfare in Vietnam. "After all, when you come to think of it, the use of helicopters is a tacit admission that we don't control the ground. And in the long run, it's control of the ground that wins or loses wars."[66] Such introspection hardly occurred within MACV's own assessments of the recent Pleiku campaign, speaking volumes to the integrity of the evaluation system that was measuring effectiveness and progress in the field.

In reality, the 1st Cavalry Division's "success" temporarily alleviated the confusion created by MACV's abundant measurements of effectiveness. Ia Drang served to reduce the clutter of excessive metrics and provide army officers with an organizationally and culturally comfortable indictor for success: the exchange ratio. Traditional concepts of firepower and maneuver still mattered. Victory could still be defined by the destruction of any enemy unit. In the aftermath of Ia Drang, many army officers seemed not to consider, as Westmoreland had earlier mused, that if NVA regiments could be so decisively defeated in the field by American firepower, they might realize the futility of fighting conventionally and revert to guerrilla tactics. The U.S. Army simply believed that it could impose its will on a peasant army and society. In the process, MACV took the "estimation" of enemy dead in Moore's after-action report at face value. It appears in late 1965 only Army Chief of Staff Harold K. Johnson questioned the 1st Cavalry Division's battlefield results. Johnson cabled Westmoreland that he believed the NVA had repositioned in early January 1966 "to pounce on the Cavalry. In contrast, the picture painted by the Cavalry is that the PAVN were driven from the field. . . . I now have some rather serious doubts about this."[67]

Johnson's reservations aside, Kinnard's cavalrymen validated for MACV airmobility's effectiveness in a counterinsurgency role. Doctrine stressed aggressiveness in maintaining continuous pressure on enemy forces. "Superior mobility is essential in counterguerrilla operations," the army's field manual noted, "to achieve surprise and to successfully counter the mobility of the enemy force. The extensive use of airmobile forces, if used with imagination, will ensure the military commander superior mobility."[68] Ia Drang thus served to confirm U.S. counterinsurgency doctrine as sound. The army's leadership never considered that the conventional three-brigade organization of divisions like the 1st Cavalry might, in fact, be ill suited for small-scale counterinsurgent operations. Officers flushed with success discounted problems with their innovative organization. Under battlefield conditions, the airmobile division proved to MACV that traditional concepts of mobility and firepower could successfully defeat the enemy in South Vietnam.[69]

By using new airmobile techniques, the 1st Cavalry seemed to achieve victory in the Ia Drang using standard, conventional operations. Moore had attacked and defended, terms that any World War II or Korean War veteran could comprehend. Thus, the metrics determining effectiveness of such operations did not require alteration. For the military component of Westmoreland's strategy, Moore's troopers had established the benchmark. If terrain could not serve as a scorecard, the body count would help keep tally. Kinnard's official after-action report noted that "when results of any action or campaign are assessed, statistics must be utilized. In many cases it is the only way results can be shown in a tangible manner and, therefore, readily grasped."[70] The report then proceeded to discuss its breakdown of enemy casualties, weapons captured, and friendly losses. Statistical analysis came through the Ia Drang battle as unscathed as MACV's faith in helicopters. Among those statistics, however, the body count rose to become the dominant indicator for success in the minds of many officers. Lieutenant Colonel Hal Moore had set the standard for the army, killing an "estimated" 1,849 enemy soldiers in only a few days of fighting. Surely other officers would want to follow in his footsteps.

The Price of Victory

By the end of 1965, most observers of the war in Vietnam concluded that Westmoreland had staved off defeat. Phase I of his strategy, intended to "halt the losing trend," had yielded favorable results. The American buildup continued, civic action programs proceeded, and combat patrols increasingly plunged into the countryside. "Military events," MACV reported near the end of the year, "reflected a continuing, aggressive effort on the part of GVN and Free World Military Assistance Forces (FWMAF) to search out and destroy the enemy, his materiel and previously secure strongholds."[71] Westmoreland began readying his forces for Phase II and a resumption of the offensive, confident that his soldiers could defeat NVA regulars on the conventional field of battle. All that remained was linking up the political aspect of his strategy to military events. The 1st Cavalry seemingly confirmed that the Americans could provide an effective shield behind which ARVN training and pacification could progress. A spirit of optimism undeniably had replaced the defeatism so palpable at the beginning of the year.[72]

The way in which the American mission defined success at the end of 1965, however, set an unfortunate precedent for future army operations in South Vietnam. When Westmoreland told reporters he considered Ia Drang an "unprecedented victory" he did so using metrics congenial to combat arms officers arriving into theater. "More enemy were killed and captured in this engagement than in any thus far."[73] The award of the Presidential Unit Citation to the 1st Cavalry for its efforts in the Pleiku province demonstrated to other units what MACV deemed central to winning the counterinsurgency fight. Nonmilitary measures mattered, but perhaps less than killing the enemy. If the Pleiku campaign did not cause MACV to alter any of its measurements of effectiveness, it certainly established a hierarchy among metrics most important to the chain of command. Unit commanders attempting to gauge progress through a host of measurements—percentage of village militia trained, numbers of roads open for movement, average days of employment in offensive operations—increasingly set their own benchmarks against the number of enemy killed. Even as the Defense Department began questioning the validity of MACV's casualty reporting, body counts became a dominant indicator of success for units in the field.[74]

U.S. Army officers were not alone in their narrow perceptions of how to measure victory against the NVA or Vietcong. One reporter at the end of 1965 offered his advice to "civilians here at home who want to keep their own score on the war." (Apparently this correspondent was not happy with MACV's scoring procedures.) Concentrating on the military aspects of counterinsurgency, the journalist, recently returned from Vietnam, recommended watching such indicators as: "Who initiates the major attacks (involving more than 500 men)? Who wins the big ones? Who lays the ambushes and combs the countryside at night? Who secures the countryside?"[75] Nowhere in this perspective could one find the intangibles of politics, popular attitudes, or motivations for resisting the insurgency.

Still, the army in Vietnam did not blindly commit itself solely to killing and counting the enemy. MACV continued to stress psychological operations and civic action, even in the aftermath of Ia Drang. Westmoreland wrote the 1st Infantry Division's commander in December about how the buildup of forces should allow for an increased emphasis on rural construction and pacification. "I am inviting this matter to your personal attention since I feel that an effective rural construction program is essential to the success of our mission."[76] Unfortunately, progress in rural construction offered few tangible incentives compared to the fighting in Pleiku province. No battalion commander concentrating on pacification could ever hope to achieve the same amount of glory, the same national attention that Moore had received in the wake of Ia Drang. No laurels came with methodical, year-long efforts at pacifying a village or district. Fighting and body counts offered one of the few avenues to demonstrating immediate progress and effectiveness. Throughout his tour as MACV's commander, Westmoreland thus would contend with, and often promote, these organizational preferences for displaying progress through aggressive, offensive action.

As the army looked to 1966, few officers realized the price they had paid for victory in the Ia Drang Valley. Internal, organizational measurements aimed at validating the airmobile concept took precedence over substantiating relevant measurements for the unique problems of counterinsurgency in Vietnam. A victory of firepower and mobility, however, did not create success in other areas of Westmoreland's strategy. MACV's command history reported "no indications that the VC political organization changed during 1965." American advisors in the field saw only trivial improvements among South Vietnamese units.[77] According to MACV's own estimates, GVN had made scant progress in securing areas under VC control. The firepower provided by airmobility had not translated into political power. Westmoreland and MACV realized the challenges still facing them, yet little could dampen the optimism generated by the "victory" at Ia Drang. As 1965 drew to a close it little mattered that body counts, now gaining prominence as *the* index of effectiveness, might be immaterial to Vietnam's political problems.[78]

As the dust settled in Pleiku province, Secretary of Defense Robert McNamara visited Saigon for briefings on the recent battles. Despite the 1st Cavalry Division's overwhelming success, Westmoreland highlighted Hanoi's continuing infiltration of forces. An evaluation of U.S. operations in early December underscored his concerns that "our attrition of their forces in South Vietnam is insufficient to offset this buildup."[79] Accordingly, Westmoreland requested an additional 41,500 troops. Further deployments might be needed based on Hanoi's reaction. The request staggered McNamara, who now realized there would be no rapid conclusion to the war. The secretary believed the odds were even that there would still be no decision by early 1967. "There has been no substantial change," McNamara wrote the president, "in the economic, political or pacification situations."[80] McNamara's doubts, however, were hardly forceful enough to disturb Johnson's commitment to a secure, stable, and non-communist South Vietnam. Nor were such doubts able to dissuade MACV from its belief that aggressively pursued military operations would positively influence all other areas of fighting the insurgency.

Victory in the Ia Drang thus established a precedent congenial to army culture and one seemingly, if ever so narrowly, in line with Westmoreland's strategy. For the next year, U.S. Army officers in South Vietnam would increasingly turn to body counts as the preferred metric for measuring their progress in achieving President Johnson's aims. In the process, they failed to translate the political-military precepts of their doctrine into effective operational concepts. The path upon which they were embarking obscured an important caveat in fighting revolutionary warfare. When military means do not support the political objectives of a comprehensive counterinsurgency strategy, measurements used to evaluate the effectiveness of those means soon become irrelevant.

"Godzilla never drew that kind of fire."
—MICHAEL HERR, *Dispatches*

4   Metrics in the Year of American Firepower

TO HARRY KINNARD, only one mission warranted consideration after the Ia Drang battles. The 1st Cavalry Division had to pursue the enemy, find him, and destroy him. Historically, pursuits ranked among the most coveted of all cavalry missions and Kinnard strained to further test the mobility and striking power of his new airmobile division. He did not have to wait long. As 1966 opened, Westmoreland ordered the 1st Cavalry toward the Bong Son Plain in Binh Dinh province. Bong Son long had been a Vietcong stronghold and the U.S. Military Assistance Command, Vietnam (MACV) wanted to break up guerrilla bases near the local villages. MACV's orders for the operation, code-named Masher, directed Kinnard to "locate and destroy VC/NVA units; enhance the security of GVN installations in Bong Son; and to lay the ground work for restoration of GVN control of the population and resources of the rich coastal plain area."[1] Like so many missions in 1966, however, the American units participating in Masher focused narrowly on locating and destroying the enemy. Even the code name seemed likely to yield an aggressive mind-set among U.S. soldiers. (President Johnson bristled at the choice, forcing Westmoreland to rename the operation White Wing.) Kinnard concerned himself little with political niceties. On January 25, the 1st Cavalry launched out of its base at An Khe and flew toward Binh Dinh province.[2]

For the next six weeks, the 1st Cavalry Division fought intense skirmishes and firefights with local VC units and regiments from the North Vietnam Army's 3rd Division. By the metrics established at Ia Drang only two months prior, Masher/White Wing was a huge success. The airmobile division had operated continuously for 41 consecutive days and had killed 1,342 of the enemy. The 3rd Brigade, now commanded by Colonel Hal Moore, achieved an astonishing kill ratio of 40:1. The numbers, though, hid some now familiar problems. Moore noted in his after-action report that throughout the operation "significant portions of the enemy forces made good their escape from the area of contact during hours of darkness."[3] Kinnard's superior, Major General Stanley Larsen, told an astonished news correspondent that neither he nor the local ARVN commander had enough troops to spare for follow-on pacification efforts. No one in the American command seemed fazed by the fifteen hamlets destroyed in the fighting or by the high number of civilian casualties. Asked if the Vietcong might infiltrate into the area as soon as U.S. troops left, Moore responded "It's possible, if the government doesn't really succeed in taking over the valley." Perhaps unsurprisingly, the government never did succeed, and when the 1st Cavalry moved on from Binh Dinh, the VC moved back in.[4]

The planning, conduct, and assessment of Operation Masher/White Wing typified U.S. Army operations in 1966. Search-and-destroy operations dominated MACV thinking throughout the year. From Westmoreland's perspective, there was good reason for this approach. The political-military problem of countering the southern insurgency fell into a logical, sequential pattern. U.S. forces first had to secure the population before local villagers would begin siding with the government. In the final days of 1965, Westmoreland explained to both the press and his commanders the importance of the South Vietnamese people in deciding which side they wanted to support. "When they chose to support the government this would be the most significant development and would probably designate the turn of the tide."[5] By launching sustained attacks against Vietcong strongholds, the Americans would provide the necessary security behind which Saigon could pursue pacification. Through these "spoiling attacks" Westmoreland hoped to keep the enemy off balance and provide time for the GVN to achieve an acceptable level of political stability.[6] Only then would the South Vietnamese turn their backs on the Vietcong insurgents.

With a total military strength now over 180,000 troops, Westmoreland felt he possessed the tools necessary to launch these large-scale attacks. During 1966 alone, MACV conducted eighteen major operations, each producing at least 500 enemy dead. Counting enemy killed in action served as an increasingly dominant indicator for measuring progress toward Westmoreland's strategic objectives. While MACV concentrated on military operations to entice the enemy to battle, commanders in the field evaluated their progress and effectiveness using body counts. It seemed a highly rational means of meeting Westmoreland's guidance. *U.S. News and World Report* found that many officers shared their commander's belief that security preceded pacification. "The feeling of U.S. officers," it reported in early March, "is that Red guerrilla action at village level can be brought under control if main-force units of the Communists are eliminated in operations such as White Wing."[7] Search-and-destroy operations thus would dominate U.S. actions in 1966, causing body counts, at least for a time, to dominate MACV's evaluation and reporting systems.

Perhaps inevitably, problems arose in using body counts as a measure of army effectiveness. Soldiers trained in conventional tactics, attracted by laurels won in defeating a battlefield enemy, concentrated on the military aspects of counterinsurgency. The political fight fell increasingly to the wayside. While army officers professed their commitment to the "other war" of pacification, they still felt a need to show tangible results in security operations by killing the enemy. Pressures to demonstrate progress created incentives for commanders to overestimate enemy kills. Worse, few officers in MACV related the body count metric to the larger goals of political stability and governmental control. In such a complex environment as South Vietnam, simple statistics of enemy dead were meaningless unless placed in some larger political-military context. Westmoreland, however, remained certain that defeating enemy main force units ranked as MACV's highest priority for 1966. Others were not so sure.

A Debate on Strategy

The week before Kinnard launched Operation Masher, a committee of staff members from MACV, Pacific Command, and the Joint Chiefs of Staff met in Honolulu to discuss planning for the coming year. The conference of over 400 staff officers preceded presidential sessions, which began on February 7. Lyndon Johnson, eager to stress the non-military aspects of the war while in Hawaii, intended to mobilize support for social reconstruction programs for the South Vietnamese people. Popular apathy toward the GVN persisted in the countryside, and the American mission felt Nguyen Cao Ky's government was making little progress in pacification. While Johnson emphasized that he would not relax the American military effort, during the conference he concentrated on social, political, and economic reforms.[8] Such a focus seemed appropriate for countering the insurgency in South Vietnam, as well as for silencing critics back home who felt the United States was committing too much attention to the military side of the struggle. For three days, the American and South Vietnamese delegations discussed the "other war" of pacification. As the

FIGURE 4.1 President Lyndon B. Johnson and General William Westmoreland meet with South Vietnamese leaders Nguyen Van Thieu and Nguyen Cao Ky at Cam Ranh Bay, October 1966.
Source RG409S, Scudder Collection, Folder 47

conference concluded, Johnson and Ky declared jointly "their determination in defense against aggression, their dedication to the hopes of all the people of South Vietnam, and their commitment to the search for just and stable peace."[9]

Despite the president's commitment to the pacification effort, Westmoreland concerned himself mostly with the military planning sessions. COMUSMACV regarded protection of the government, people, and his own growing logistics bases as the most important tasks for early 1966. At Honolulu, he hoped to validate his strategic concept with Secretary of Defense McNamara while receiving further guidance for the coming year. Westmoreland also believed pacification efforts important, but they could only come after achieving security. As he told the press corps at Honolulu, "Essential to any pacification campaign is destruction or at least nullification of the well armed main force troop formations."[10] The Joint Chiefs and Pacific Command shared this sequential view of counterinsurgency, as did a number of contemporary writings on insurgency warfare. Even the army's doctrine stressed the primary importance of ensuring internal security. So while Johnson pushed the "other war" at Honolulu, Westmoreland remained steadfast to his three-phased strategy developed in late 1965. McNamara and Secretary of State Dean Rusk endorsed MACV's position, and American strategy for the coming year solidified as the conference came to a close. The subsequent strategic document would have a lasting impact for the course and conduct of the Vietnam War.[11]

On February 8, Westmoreland received a formal memorandum titled "1966 Program to Increase the Effectiveness of Military Operations and Anticipated Results Thereof." The document laid out troop increases for the year—one of Westmoreland's goals in the early Honolulu sessions—before discussing an expansion of American offensive actions. Relying on statistical data that had become a mainstay in MACV reporting, McNamara and Rusk's memorandum outlined Westmoreland's goals for 1966. He would increase the population living in secure areas by 10 percent, increase critical roads and railroads for use by 20 percent, and increase the destruction of VC and PAVN base areas by 30 percent. Ensuring that the president's directives were not ignored, MACV was to increase the pacified population by 235,000 and ensure the defense of political and population centers under government control. To Westmoreland, the final goal ranked of highest priority. It directed MACV to "attrite, by year's end, VC/PAVN forces at a rate as high as their capability to put men in the field."[12]

Westmoreland thus arrived at and departed from the February Honolulu Conference convinced his first mission was to defeat North Vietnamese and Vietcong units in the field. Only then could pacification missions begin in earnest. MACV spent most of its attention and resources in 1966 on military operations not because it was snubbing presidential guidance. Rather, Westmoreland believed the war would be long and that rural reconstruction programs had to be established on a stable, secure foundation. (Few policy makers in Washington disagreed that military and pacification efforts went hand in hand in South Vietnam.) As Westmoreland began operations aimed at enemy attrition, the body count gained prominence in MACV's progress reports, minimizing the president's emphasis on rural development. Measurements on roads, secured population centers, and civic action programs seemed of secondary importance. MACV continued computing statistics in these areas as before, but an informal hierarchy began to develop among the army's metrics. Only body counts could ascertain when MACV had reached the rate when U.S. forces were killing more enemy than could be put into the field. Reaching this "crossover point" became the principal military goal for the next two years.[13]

For Westmoreland, measuring attrition of the enemy through body counts was not an end unto itself but a means of providing for population security. Believing the communists had moved to the final, conventional phase of revolutionary warfare, COMUSMACV argued later he could not ignore regular NVA units by concentrating solely on Vietcong guerrillas. Westmoreland employed a simple analogy to explain this dual threat. Political subversives and guerrillas, "termites," had been persistently eating away at the foundation of South Vietnam's house. At a distance hid main force units, "bully boys," waiting to pounce with crowbars to tear down the weakened building. Only by keeping the bully boys away could allied forces eliminate the termites. In essence, Westmoreland expected to build a screen of American forces behind which ARVN could undertake pacification missions. Much of this rationale relied upon appraisals of ARVN's limited effectiveness against enemy main force units. Americans could use their advantages in mobility and firepower to clear and secure. ARVN and regional and popular forces then gradually would assume responsibility for holding cleared areas. Successful operations like Masher/White Wing, which produced high body counts among the bully boys, appeared to confirm Westmoreland's logic.[14]

Not everyone in Johnson's administration agreed with MACV's commitment to reaching the attrition crossover point. Throughout 1966, numerous advisors encouraged higher prioritization on pacification efforts. Deputy Secretary of Defense Cyrus Vance reported in April that "the civil reconstruction program is lagging [behind] the military effort." In May, Robert Komer, a special assistant to the President on pacification, argued forcefully that Ambassador Lodge "must be told to insist on a better balance between military and civil needs." Even McNamara reported to Johnson in September that "progress in pacification has been negligible."[15] Yet not until mid-October did Westmoreland receive any indication from either McNamara or the Joint Chiefs that the administration held reservations about MACV's prioritization of effort. It was a monumental failure in communication. At Honolulu, Johnson had failed to provide clear strategic guidance to one of his principal field commanders. Despite reports of MACV minimizing pacification efforts, the president never voiced his concerns with Westmoreland. In the process, MACV, believing it was following official guidance from both State and Defense departments, persisted in concentrating on the bully boys.[16]

While official reports based on body counts filtered into the press, opposition to Westmoreland's attrition strategy grew both within and outside the administration. The first challenge materialized in a study commissioned by the Army Chief of Staff in 1965. "A Program for the Pacification and Long-Term Development of South Vietnam" (PROVN) appeared in March 1966 and confronted directly MACV's big-unit war approach and reliance on high body counts. "The critical actions are those that occur at the village, the district and provincial levels," read the study's summary statement. "This is where the war must be fought; this is where the war and the object which lies beyond it must be won." The study also concluded that both military and pacification efforts depended upon achieving a "viable government."[17] Westmoreland received a briefing on PROVN in May and recommended that it be reduced in status from study to conceptual document. To MACV, the report concentrated too heavily on the early phases of revolutionary warfare, when it seemed obvious that the war in Vietnam already had moved to a more conventional stage. In August, the Joint Chiefs sent a pointed memorandum to McNamara stating that they did not endorse the document and recommended its distribution be limited to a "need-to-know" audience. For all its insights, PROVN's challenge to American strategy in 1966 never produced any major transformation of U.S. military operations. The study did, however, begin to lay the foundations for a greater emphasis on pacification in 1967.[18]

One month after PROVN's release, the army's adjutant general office completed a comprehensive review of army units in Vietnam. Titled "United States Army Combat Operations in Vietnam" (ARCOV), the report concentrated on doctrinal and organizational issues of brigades and battalions fighting in a mid- to low-intensity war. Westmoreland concurred with much of the report's findings for it found current army doctrine to be sound. Unlike PROVN, "Army Combat Operations" offered no critiques of American strategy in Vietnam. ARCOV recommended that a fourth company be added to standard infantry battalions to better assist in search-and-destroy operations and provided positive survey responses from division and brigade commanders on U.S. "firepower doctrine."[19] The report did, though, demonstrate the inadequacies of the intelligence sections of brigade level staffs. "The flow of intelligence from higher headquarters to the maneuver battalion level in Vietnam today does not provide the commander with timely data on the enemy elements in his area of interest." Nowhere did ARCOV make the connection that faulty intelligence systems within MACV might be creating a need for additional infantrymen. The report made no mention of pacification.[20]

Those U.S. Marines serving in South Vietnam had much to say about pacification in 1966. Besides the PROVN study, the Marines presented the most critical assessment of Westmoreland's strategy within the U.S. government. Lieutenant General Lewis W. Walt, commander of the 3rd Marine Amphibious Force in Vietnam, and General Victor "Brute" Krulak, commander of the Fleet Marine Force, Pacific, led the opposition. Walt agreed that he could not ignore main force units, but he believed allegiance and control of the people were paramount. As he recalled, "I think the guerrilla—the one down among the people, the one that had got the stranglehold on the people—he is the one that had to be destroyed and eliminated. He and his infrastructure—his political infrastructure—had to be eliminated."[21] Concentrating on the village level, the Marines implemented a "combined action program" in which platoons and companies lived among the villagers and worked side by side with regional and popular militia forces. As Krulak wrote to McNamara, the signs of progress in such an approach might be "harder to quantify" but they were more meaningful than body counts. "The raw figure of VC killed," Krulak maintained, "can be a dubious index of success, since if their killing is accompanied by devastation of friendly areas, we may end up having done more harm than good." Westmoreland replied that the Marines' style of counterinsurgency required too many troops for countrywide application and left the enemy's main force units open to strike at will.[22]

While MACV and the Joint Chiefs discounted internal dissent, they met opposition from outside their ranks with downright contempt. Retired Lieutenant General James M. Gavin, who so vigorously had championed airmobility in the 1950s, brought similar energy to opposing the administration's Vietnam policy. Gavin testified to Congress in February that the U.S. presence in Southeast Asia was escalating without any understanding of the conflict's political nature. That same month Gavin advocated in *Harper's* magazine a reconsideration of the enclave strategy that MACV earlier had abandoned. The head of the British Advisory Mission to South Vietnam equally condemned the Americans for ignoring the first principle of counterinsurgency. Robert Thompson wrote in February that U.S. forces failed to see "that the insurgent political subversive organization should be the primary target." Later in the year, Thompson further denounced MACV's search-and-destroy missions in an article titled "America Fights the Wrong War."[23] The Joint Chiefs counterattacked by denouncing to the Secretary of Defense the many flaws in Gavin's proposals. Chairman Earle G. Wheeler told the House Armed Services Committee that the "Gavin theory, if carried out, would be an absolutely interminable stalemate." The MACV staff described the enclave approach as "an inglorious, static use of U.S. forces in overpopulated areas." For now, McNamara backed off. MACV and the Joint Chiefs had met their critics head on and had won. For the remainder of the year, U.S. forces in Vietnam would implement Westmoreland's strategy of defeating the military threat first, and only then increasing pacification efforts.[24]

These strategic debates had enormous implications for the ways in which MACV attempted to evaluate U.S. effort in 1966. Because Westmoreland waged war in 1966 without oversight from the Washington high command, MACV chose how best to report progress. The diffuse missions of fighting, pacifying, and training the ARVN continued to demand multiple metric systems and standards for effectiveness. However, since the administration failed to synchronize military and political efforts in Vietnam, MACV determined which indicators put Westmoreland's strategy in the best light. The staff continued tracking the myriad statistics that helped assess progress toward the goals established at Honolulu. Nevertheless, metrics relating to enemy killed mattered most in 1966.[25] MACV's March Monthly Evaluation Report represented the new hierarchy among measurements of progress. Despite the political unrest and corruption affecting South Vietnam's government, the report proclaimed progress by relying on hard, military-related statistics—a 27 percent increase in battalion size operations, a 17 percent increase in the number of VC killed, and a 16 percent increase in the number of in-country air strike sorties. Whether such markers were gauging true progress remained doubtful. Even the report admitted, "It is apparent that, in spite of the severe punishment he has absorbed, the enemy's strength is largely undiminished, his will to continue essentially unshaken." Of course, Westmoreland knew it would be a long process. At least, he believed, operations like Masher/White Wing got American forces off to a good start.[26]

The Body Count, Part I: The Human Dimension

Since 1961, the South Vietnamese armed forces had divided the country into tactical zones for administering the war effort. Organized along conventional American lines, ARVN divisions served under four corps headquarters, each corps holding responsibility for one of these military areas. American units operated as well within these four Corps Tactical Zones (CTZs), the Marines mostly in I CTZ at Da Nang in the north. Army brigades and divisions covered the remaining sectors—II CTZ in the western highlands, III CTZ surrounding Saigon, and IV CTZ in the Mekong Delta.[27] Much of the fighting in these military zones consisted of small-unit clashes, often nullifying American advantages in heavy firepower. Of the more than 900 communist ground assaults in 1966, only 44 were made by battalion-sized or larger units. American troops participated in few set-piece battles. Simply locating the enemy in the villages, rice paddies, and jungles became a major undertaking. As one correspondent noted, "Ground warfare, in these circumstances, frequently is a game of hide-and-seek."[28]

Commanders and staffs badgered units to maintain contact with an elusive enemy. Major General William E. DePuy, now commanding the 1st Infantry Division, illustrated how far commanders would go in attempting to bring the enemy to battle. "The game in the jungle is to send in a small force as bait, let the enemy attack, and be able to react with a larger force in reserve nearby. But if the enemy doesn't want to fight, then the jungle goes off in 360 directions."[29] In this environment, highly disciplined Vietcong and NVA units controlled the tempo of battlefield engagements. One army operational report found that the enemy had initiated 88 percent of the fighting against U.S. forces, nearly half of those beginning as ambushes. For the individual soldier serving as "bait," the unpredictable nature of search-and-destroy missions took a heavy psychological toll. Constant fear and tension pervaded American patrols with potential threats lurking in every hamlet or rice paddy.[30]

Despite Westmoreland's emphasis on finding and killing the enemy, these patrols often consisted of long marches, a great deal of searching, and little fighting. One soldier described a normal operation as a "slow anabasis through the mountains in search of a slippery phantom who was seldom overtaken by the chasing bloodhound packs of the 101st infantrymen." Glory, he recalled, "would prove an elusive and ultimately disappointing prize."[31] With pressure from above to make contact and most days filled with nothing tangible to justify their efforts, soldiers who did find the enemy reveled in the triumph. "One body! Everybody was elated!" remembered Donald Putnam. "They felt like they had done their job, that things had happened like they were supposed to. It was great, something to show for all the effort." Official reports echoed the euphoria of successful contact. The 1st Infantry Division's official synopsis of the battle of Lo Khe in March, a battalion search-and-destroy mission west of Lai Khe, celebrated the 199 VC killed in action. The report also estimated another 300 VC killed, though the number came from air observation, not from actual body counts.[32]

As search-and-destroy missions formed the centerpiece of MACV operations in 1966, elation in achieving an enemy body count inevitably blossomed. One company commander explained the emotions. "It was not that we were jubilant about the sudden violent demise of . . . fellow human beings. It was simply that we had scored. . . . The death of enemy soldiers at our hands quite simply produced a good feeling, a feeling of exhilaration like that experienced when one's football team scores a touchdown."[33] Another soldier relied on a similar analogy. "There's nothing like a confirmed kill either. They make you crazy. You want more. You know everybody back at battalion will look at you with envy when you get back in. You scored a touchdown in front of the hometown fans." This respect from peers served as a powerful incentive for high body counts. Even general officers were not immune to the exhilaration of killing. An assistant division commander in the 1st Infantry recalled generals shooting from helicopters and bragging about it back at base camp.[34]

As with football touchdowns, specific rules defined what constituted a body count. In 1966, MACV classified a confirmed killed in action (KIA) as one "based on actual body count of males of fighting age and other, male or female, known to have carried arms." Probable KIAs were not to be reported. Of course, not every enemy body could be viewed by a foot patrol and recorded. Counts made from aerial observations were supposed to meet the same criteria as those done on the ground. Even at close range, the system proved inaccurate. (No instant-replay guided calls in this game.) Soldiers rarely marked enemy corpses to prevent double-counting.[35] Perhaps more importantly, the Department of Defense's Systems Analysis office identified concrete incentives to claim a high body count. "Padded claims kept everyone happy; there were no penalties for overstating enemy losses, but an understatement could lead to sharp questions as to why U.S. casualties were so high with the results achieved." Commanders relied increasingly on firepower as expectations for higher body counts rose among MACV's senior leadership.[36]

If respect from peers provided insufficient motivation for infantrymen slogging daily through the jungles and mountains of South Vietnam, units themselves offered inducements for producing high body counts. The 25th Infantry sponsored a "Best of the Pack" contest for all of platoons in the division. The command awarded platoons ten points for each "possible body count," one hundred points for each enemy crew served weapon captured, and two hundred points for each tactical radio captured. For every U.S. soldier killed in action, the platoon lost five hundred points. After reconciling the credits and debits, the unit's "index of efficiency" allowed higher level commanders to assess the effectiveness of all the division's platoons. "Productive" companies and platoons became easily identifiable for the chain of command on a monthly basis. Glory might prove elusive for soldiers on search-and-destroy missions but official recognition could be won through favorable kill ratios.[37]

Certainly not all U.S. soldiers defined their actions based on official recognition or momentary notoriety among peers. Self-preservation was too important in such an unpredictable ground war. Combat could explode at any moment. Because most infantrymen were "walking arsenals," enemy casualties seemed predictable once American units finally made contact. Given such a talented adversary, however, American casualties seemed equally expected. In the first half of 1966 alone, the VC

FIGURE 4.2 A measure of success. Soldiers line up enemy dead and weapons at an American firebase.
Source RG124S, SLA Marshall Collection, Box 4, Folder 442

and NVA inflicted 15,000 U.S. casualties, more than 2,000 of those being killed. Doctrine stressed aggressiveness against insurgents and, as one rifleman with the 1st Cavalry Division indicated, the loss of friends in combat provoked only greater levels of hostility and aggression. "The casualties taken in the fighting really got to us and uprooted us. That also incited fighting in a way that when somebody was hit or killed, it made the others that much angrier, wanting revenge."[38] Body counts could satisfy on a deeply personal level while also meeting organizational requirements for reaching a casualty crossover point. Another veteran, however, revealed the drawbacks when personal revenge went too far. "After [a close friend] died, I was hurting, hurting bad. Then I went on a fucking vendetta. All I wanted to do was rain fucking destruction on that fucking country. If it fucking burned, I burnt it. I used more fucking ammo in the next three months than the whole fucking time I was there."[39] Body counts might be crucial in assessing enemy attrition, but tempering the use of force in the political-military environment of South Vietnam was equally important. As MACV found, wholesale destruction among the country's hamlets and villages could be counterproductive.

Balancing the weight of American firepower with the political aspects of fighting a war among a rural population confounded MACV for much of 1966. While soldiers on the ground often saw killing as an end unto itself, Westmoreland still required an indicator for measuring progress of the attrition phase of his strategy. Truthfully, there was nothing unique in MACV searching for metrics to help impose order on the chaos of counterinsurgency warfare in Vietnam. As one M.I.T. professor suggested that year, there "is the persistent human temptation to make life more explicable by making it more calculable."[40] With the Secretary of Defense insisting that MACV measure and report progress, counting enemy dead appeared to satisfy all parties. The notion of body count thus entered the American lexicon, both at home and in Southeast Asia. As McNamara later noted, "We undertook it [the body count] because one of Westy's objectives was to reach a so-called crossover point.... To reach such a point, we needed to have some idea what they could sustain and what their losses were."[41] McNamara's insistence on measuring progress implied, of course, that progress was in fact being made.

The Body Count, Part II: The Pressure to Perform

While President Johnson's top advisors debated the need for increasing pacification efforts in 1966, Westmoreland forged ahead with his war against enemy main force units. COMUSMACV's operational focus, coupled with McNamara's determination to evaluate statistically the war's progress, placed intense pressures on field commanders. When the Secretary of Defense visited one division in October and expressed displeasure at its low body count compared to another unit, the message was clear. Body counts demonstrated progress and thus unit effectiveness. Pacification might be important, as many officers knew it to be, but MACV's reporting system offered no transparent way for units to display improvement in their operational areas. Edward Lansdale found this "bookkeeper's mentality" disturbing. Working in the U.S. Embassy in 1966, the civic action advocate suggested afterward that the profusion of arithmetical reports shaped MACV's conduct of the war. To Lansdale, body counts pulled attention away from pacification, "their very profusion a constant influence on military leaders to upgrade the importance of 'attriting' the enemy."[42]

With body counts serving as both an indicator of military progress and as a criterion for professional success, commanders and staffs pursued them actively. Charles Mohr of the *New York Times* found demands for casualty reports already well established by early 1966. As the nine-day siege of the Pleiku Special Forces camp finally lifted in late 1965, MACV's chief of staff insisted on an immediate body count for an upcoming briefing. Major Charles Beckwith, the camp's commanding officer, snapped to his radio operator, "We haven't even been outside the wire yet. Tell him I'm not going to give any figure until I can count." By the time Beckwith reported 40 enemy casualties, the figure announced in Saigon was already five times that large.[43] Such pressures for immediate information on enemy casualties brought into question whether commanders could estimate their units' body counts objectively.

As McNamara's October visit implied, field commanders contended not only with the enemy, but also competed against each other for recognition and professional advancement. MACV's evaluation report that month continued to equate high body counts with favorable trends in the war effort. Ambitious officers in the field followed suit. With few other indicators allowing units to stand out among their peers, the body count served as *the* visible yardstick for performance. One general staff officer believed that all tactical commanders were "judged on how many enemy they kill and how many operations they launch and how successful they are."[44] Pressures to perform permeated the chain of command. After a nearly two-week long battle in Phuoc Long province, Brigadier General Willard Pearson, a brigade commander in the 101st Airborne Division, congratulated one of his infantry battalion commanders based solely on favorable kill ratios. As Pearson told his subordinate, "The comparison of 8 friendly KIA as to 97 NVA KIA (BC) reflects the effectiveness of US forces and the determination of the Airborne soldier to fight and win." To officers waging a strategy of attrition, body counts measured both progress and effectiveness. Unfortunately, to officers concerned with career advancement, body counts also meant demonstrating personal expertise and potential for promotion.[45]

For those units like Pearson's brigade, conducting spoiling attacks against NVA regular units, the body count likely functioned as an appropriate metric. Counterinsurgency in Vietnam, however, encompassed more than just destroying enemy main force units. Lansdale judged correctly how body counts affected American commanders' conduct of the war. Pressure to produce high numbers resulted in a prodigious use of firepower that tended to alienate the population and ignored the problem of countering the Vietcong's political infrastructure. Even without overt command emphasis, the body count influenced perceptions of progress and effectiveness. Colonel Donald A. Siebert, who commanded the 1st Brigade in the 9th Infantry Division, recalled how casualty figures shaped leaders' assessments of the war. Though his division commander did not place undue emphasis on body counts, Siebert questioned his own approach when his unit produced low numbers. "Since the 1st Brigade had had no major contacts or great body counts, I looked over our operations carefully. Were we too cautious? Were our tactics sound? Was our intelligence reliable? Were operations compromised during coordination with the Vietnamese? What was the problem?" After a thorough review, Siebert concluded that his battalions were being aggressive and effectively carrying out their mission of providing local security. The enemy simply had been avoiding contact.[46]

Siebert's doubts revealed the subtle ways in which body counts persuaded commanders to validate their operational effectiveness through statistical means. The very nature of fighting in South Vietnam frustrated officers' conventional understanding of warfare. While one "lessons learned" report from the Bong Son campaign emphasized the continuing validity of the doctrine of "Find, Fix, Fight and Finish," American combat actions rarely succeeded in annihilating the enemy. Difficulties in distinguishing regular and irregular forces from noncombatant civilians further complicated the battle area. Fourth Infantry Division Commander Major General Arthur S. Collins, Jr., commented correctly that the "tactical problem is determined by the attitude of the population."[47] However, assessing popular attitudes remained outside of MACV's reporting system in 1966. Changing Vietnamese opinions appeared even more difficult. Early in the year, MACV assigned the 173rd Airborne Brigade the mission of destroying the Vietcong's political-military headquarters in Binh Duoug province. The commander reported his task accomplished yet surmised that more work remained. "The civilians in this area were thoroughly indoctrinated," Brigadier Ellis W. Williamson noted. "It will take a long term civic action program to win them over."[48]

Here lay one of the central incentives for relying on body counts. Numerous field commanders in MACV believed that no indicator except body counts could substantiate progress during their short tours of duty. The army's one-year tour policy not only caused unit instability, but helped increase pressures to demonstrate improvement quickly. As one officer explained, "A lot of careers were made or ruined on short duty assignments."[49] According to French theorists like Galula and Trinquier, for counterinsurgencies to be effective, military forces had to be patient and methodical. In such an approach there might be few tangible indications to exhibit progress over a six- to twelve-month tour. Supporting revolutionary development and civic action programs, while crucial to the political fight, offered few quantitative markers to measure effectiveness at the company and battalion level. Nonetheless, the pressure on tactical troop leaders persisted. MACV, the Joint Chiefs, the Defense Department, and the White House all pressed for indications of progress, as did the American rural public. A brigadier general in the 1st Infantry Division described the ramifications for leaders who believed they had a limited chance to make a reputation in combat. "The business of getting mixed up with the Vietnamese was something that could get in their way of performing in a spectacular fashion. Many of them were absolutely and completely insensitive to . . . the local population, to the Vietnamese soldiers, and to the regional and popular forces. They were just an obstruction." The population no longer became the purpose of security, but too often an object of scorn.[50]

Thus, while officers professed their commitment to the "other war," they still felt a need to show results by killing the enemy. With few metrics to measure how battalions and brigades might contribute to a viable national life, unit commanders stressed, almost naturally, the military virtues of internal defense and security. Westmoreland's own emphasis on search-and-destroy operations preceding pacification meshed well with officers' conceptions of military force in a counterinsurgency environment. To those with experience in Korea and World War II, war meant killing your opponent; success meant gaining ground. Battles like Ia Drang served only to validate these preferences. Effective units thus were aggressive units which killed the enemy. One infantry division commander epitomized the American approach when he explained to his principal subordinates, "As a rule when an outfit has a fight—and it does not get a body count—it is not pushing in the way it should."[51] Unfortunately, few officers in MACV questioned whether high body counts denoted actual progress.

The Body Count, Part III: A Problem of Metrics

On June 27, 1966, the *New York Times* correspondent Charles Mohr published the first of three articles appraising the military situation in South Vietnam. Mohr discussed the importance of gaining the allegiance of both the hostile and indifferent portions of the rural population before turning his attention to measurements of success. "The most important thing to realize," he noted, "is not that statistics are unreliable but that they are meaningless in themselves.... Statistically, the war has been won several times already."[52] To Mohr, the fact that 200,000 enemy troops still were fighting seemed much more important than figures like body counts. MACV tended to overlook such insightful commentary in 1966. The 57,000 VC and NVA deaths in the first half of the year seemed proof that American forces had dealt powerful blows to the communists. Indeed, Westmoreland had kept the enemy off balance militarily. But body counts, as Mohr conveyed, proved to be an imprecise tool for measuring how much pain MACV was inflicting on the enemy and whether these high casualties led to increased security of the South Vietnamese population. According to the Honolulu Conference agenda, Westmoreland was to raise the pacified population by 235,000. However, the same month that Mohr's articles appeared, MACV's evaluation report noted that search-and-destroy operations "predominated allied military activities" and registered only a .1 percent gain in secured population.[53]

The pressures to demonstrate battlefield effectiveness not only diminished the role of pacification efforts but helped to distort the accuracy of body counts as a reliable metric for progress. Inaccurate statements plagued MACV's reporting of enemy casualties. Problems in differentiating innocent civilians from Vietcong led many units to classify all dead from an engagement as enemy VC. After the war, a majority of surveyed general officers considered body counts inflated, one judging them "often blatant lies." McNamara, however, continued to press MACV for signs of progress that could be briefed to the White House and to the American public. Westmoreland remarked later that he "abhorred the term" though several detailed studies concluded that body counts "probably erred on the side of caution."[54] Analysts working in the Defense Department's Systems Analysis office disagreed. Their estimates of enemy killed in action offered numbers 29 percent lower than MACV's count for 1966 and 34 percent lower for 1967. The analysts could not determine if the difference arose from double-counting, disingenuous reporting, or the inclusion of civilians in body counts. This lack of consistency held enormous implications for officials attempting to determine progress toward a crossover point. How could the White House make informed strategic decisions when the facts emanating from MACV's reporting system remained so contentious?[55]

If high-level officials struggled with unearthing the truth on enemy casualties, efforts in the field proved equally troublesome. The American reliance on artillery high explosives and air-delivered napalm complicated attempts to count bodies accurately. S. L. A. Marshall, reporting on the war effort in the Central Highlands in 1966, recounted one officer's difficulties in supervising enemy body counts after an artillery strike. "It was hard to do. Most of these bodies had been brayed apart by the blast, and arms, legs and heads had been scattered over a wide space."[56] Estimated body counts solidified quickly in MACV's reporting system, taken at face value with few further inquiries to distinguish them from physical body counts. At times, visual counts and estimates became conflated when assessing enemy casualties. If bodies were too dismembered to assess properly, individual canteens might be accepted as authorized substitutes. Other times, officers, feeling the pressure to report favorable figures, relied knowingly on estimations. As one cavalry troop commander recalled, "Occasionally, we were asked for an estimate of casualties that we couldn't count and all I can say is that that was by guess and by golly and it just couldn't possibly have been right. I mean, it couldn't possibly have been accurate."[57]

Estimated body counts, whether from ground or air reports, led invariably to questions by the press and even within MACV. Correspondents marveled at the effects of U.S. firepower yet wondered aloud if military successes as reported by body counts were leading to necessary political action. Study groups contracted by the Department of Defense reached similar conclusions. After eight days of briefings on the war effort in mid-June, the Vice President of the National Academy of Sciences reported to McNamara that the suppression and liquidation of main enemy forces mattered little to pacification of the countryside. "In fact, the emphasis on the war of the big battalions and the attendant buildup of U.S. forces is apparently having harmful effects on the war in the villages because of its economic impact on South Vietnam [and] gradual disintegration of the fabric of Vietnamese society."[58] Given such an assessment, body counts seemed unsuitable for measuring progress toward the administration's ultimate objectives. Even if the attrition numbers were accurate, McNamara argued late in the year, it appeared increasingly unlikely that MACV could break the enemy's morale. Westmoreland himself questioned the data on enemy attrition from his staff but never took any prescriptive action. Throughout 1966 he remained committed to his sequential view of counterinsurgency. MACV's reporting system remained unchanged.[59]

Neither Westmoreland nor the Department of Defense could complain about a lack of resources in examining their counterinsurgency indicators. Numerous agencies conducted studies on measuring effectiveness and progress outside the parameters of simple body counts. In May, the Advanced Research Projects Agency (ARPA) prepared a memorandum on indicators for Vietnam progress that questioned the focus on "military things that are measureable (KIA, MIA, WIA, weapons, etc.). Unfortunately, these as a general rule, only seem to measure escalation and effort." Acknowledging differences between Vietnamese provinces, ARPA recommended establishing interdisciplinary teams to link military and non-military measurements into meaningful "area specific indicators" that could better gauge pacification progress. That summer, the Planning Research Corporation advanced a similar theme. Its study on counterinsurgency indicators argued "the clues as to the enemy's condition can best be found in the economic and political impact of his military actions." Recommending indicators that measured the enemy's military-economic stability, the report maintained that trade patterns, taxation success, and labor structure provided insights into the insurgents' status within a local area.[60] In September, the Office of National Security Studies in Ann Arbor, Michigan, proposed a study project on indicators of political success in South Vietnam. As with ARPA's study, the proposal believed indicators like body counts and captured weapons provided "few insights into the question which may most significantly affect the outcome of an intra-state war: the attitude of the people toward their government." Instead, it suggested two broad categories for measuring political progress: governmental effectiveness and popular support or acceptance. Under each of these headings, the report proposed various indicators like public health, tax collection, purchases of rice land, and strength of overt political opposition.[61]

Despite the thoughtful questioning of body counts as a suitable metric for assessing counterinsurgency progress, MACV failed to dissect its internal evaluation and reporting procedures. The measurement system remained unexamined. By year's end, MACV's monthly evaluation reports continued to praise the favorable statistics of enemy casualties, kill ratios, and battalion-sized operations. Assessment methods for pacification and revolutionary development remained mired in ambiguity. At the end of 1966, Westmoreland's staff indicated chronic problems in the accuracy of measurement criteria for hamlet statuses and census figures. Even precise estimates for South Vietnam's population eluded the military command and the U.S. Embassy. Without accurate figures, any progress MACV reported toward the Honolulu Conference's goal of increasing the percentage of pacified areas remained dubious. (In December, MACV considered 59.6 percent of the population secure.) The Commander's Conference held on November 20 illustrated MACV's now typical approach to measuring progress and effectiveness—huge efforts in quantification with marginal attempts at analysis. The conference's "Measurement of Progress" briefing detailed the familiar statistics on enemy personnel, VC/NVA incidents, and population security. As in the past, no dominant indicators emerged. While kill ratios and body counts received attention, no one linked the myriad statistics to MACV's larger strategic goals. Factoids like 40,660 rounds of naval gunfire used and 167 million leaflets dropped in South Vietnam meant little if no staff officer analyzed their effects.[62]

This dearth of analysis underscored the drawbacks of using metrics like body counts to measure progress and effectiveness. In essence, the MACV staff never applied any collective judgment to ensure that such metrics connected to the operational environment. Westmoreland relied on body counts because they served to measure progress toward reaching the crossover point. This notion, however, rested on flawed data. MACV achieved little consensus on enemy combat strength and whether part-time guerrillas, local militias, or political cadre should be included in the enemy's order of battle.[63] The August 1966 estimate of 282,000 enemy troops in South Vietnam appeared to some analysts misleadingly low. One CIA intelligence analyst contended afterward that MACV purposefully had falsified Vietcong strength estimates to demonstrate progress in enemy attrition. Even discounting deceitful reporting, MACV's August estimate registered 52,000 more enemy troops than reported in January. Westmoreland was no closer to reaching his crossover point. Despite these increases, after nearly a full year of U.S. search-and-destroy operations, MACV's chief intelligence officer concluded that the attrition strategy would show decisive results by mid-1967.[64]

With optimism replacing critical analysis, MACV's staff officers failed to explore the correlation between body counts and progress in the larger U.S. mission. They were not alone. At the time, few uniformed leaders considered if such a metric might not be measuring progress toward higher objectives. A mid-year conference between Admiral U. S. Grant Sharp, head of Pacific Command, and the Secretary of Defense revealed that MACV had not achieved any of the six goals established at the Honolulu Conference. According to MACV's command history, Sharp felt the goal of attriting enemy forces as high as their capability for putting men into the field would not be reached by year's end. The enemy had demonstrated the ability to increase forces in South Vietnam despite its losses. Similarly, a Defense Department Systems Analysis study found the enemy successful in controlling its losses within a sustainable range. As the survey discovered, "regardless of the level of enemy allied activity, the VC/NVA lost significant numbers of men only when they decided to stand and fight." It seemed unlikely, given these circumstances, that the U.S. armed forces could neutralize the enemy's military and political influence among the South Vietnamese population or undermine Hanoi's will to fight.[65]

MACV never questioned its analytical framework for measuring progress or effectiveness. Gaps existed between means and ends and the metrics used to assess the relationship between the two. Simple body counts did not account for the enemy controlling the tempo of fighting or choosing the time and place in which to battle U.S. forces. Nor could such metrics assess fully the security of a local area. MACV may have missed this point; others did not. On the same day that Sharp briefed McNamara on the Honolulu Conference goals, Robert Komer sent President Johnson a memorandum outlining his observations from a recent trip to South Vietnam. Komer returned "both an optimist and a realist." Westmoreland's spoiling attacks appeared to be going well, yet the military effort had not been matched by pacification or civil affairs operations. As Komer noted, "The more I learn the more I'm sobered by the realization of how much further we may have to go." Komer implored the President to step up support of pacification and pressure the GVN and ARVN for increased efforts. To date, no one in the administration or the Pentagon had forced Westmoreland to reassess his strategy or methods for evaluating progress. As 1966 drew to a close, Johnson and McNamara decided finally to intervene on the question of strategy. The problem of metrics they left alone.[66]

A Question of Relevance

In December 1966, the RAND Corporation published its findings from a mid-year symposium on province operations in South Vietnam. Participants discussed at length the effectiveness of several programs undertaken in the war-torn country and of indicators for success and failure. U.S. Army Major Robert B. Osborn, who had served in Quang Nai province in I CTZ, offered insightful commentary. "If you go into a battle area and a villager comes along and warns you about mines along the road, to me this is an indicator of success. Or, if the villager does not warn the military, that's an indication of failure. The mere fact that ground is occupied is not an indicator of success or failure." John Paul Vann, the former army officer who had advised ARVN troops at the battle of Ap Bac, attended the symposium as well, arguing that security considerations continued to merit attention. Now working with the Department of State's Agency for International Development (USAID), Vann maintained that the ability to exclude the VC from an area served as a military indicator but only a temporary one. Military successes alone did not guarantee lasting effects. As he informed the symposium, "we Americans who are serving a one-year or two-year tour in Vietnam generally look for factors that will reflect our own contributions during this short period of time." Vann then cut to the heart of MACV's faulty metric system. "So many of these short-range, short-term factors we report on are almost meaningless, because we're in an environment where the attitudes have been influenced over several decades." For Vann, the Americans' inability to reflect the conflict's true nature ranked as one of the greatest failures in Vietnam.[67]

Westmoreland, of course, believed that he understood the true nature of the war. Changing attitudes through pacification programs would flourish only after the defeat of enemy main force units. Even with an increased U.S. troop strength, he simply lacked the manpower necessary to focus on both problems simultaneously. "The threat of enemy main forces (VC/NVA) has been of such magnitude," Westmoreland maintained, "that fewer friendly troops could be diverted to general area security and support of revolutionary development." Given this concept of operations, there seemed no other way to track progress except through body counts. In the process, body counting led to a vicious cycle of concentrating on the military aspect of counterinsurgency in 1966. If there existed no way to demonstrate progress except through a high body count, then commanders in the field purposefully sought a high body count. The advice from Major Osborn and John Vann required patience and a discerning eye, attributes deemed not especially important for attrition warfare. As one division commander recalled of body counts, "It is a gruesome way of accounting, but there didn't seem to be any other way to keep track of the progress being made."[68]

Such attitudes suggested that many senior U.S. Army officers serving in Vietnam in 1966 did not fully recognize a distinction between measuring progress and effectiveness. Favorable kill ratios and high body counts implied a high level of combat effectiveness, at least in conventional terms. On the whole, American troops managed proficiently a wide array of firepower. Commanders took this as evidence of their units' proficiency in battle and, within strict military parameters, equated body counts with progress. The ramifications to the political side of the war were immense. The abundant firepower that resulted in high body counts also destroyed the countryside, created thousands of refugees, and weakened an already fragile economic and political system. From a strategic standpoint, MACV had made little progress toward attriting the enemy. Hanoi quickly replaced its losses from within, and the destruction of the South Vietnamese countryside served as a valuable recruiting tool for the Vietcong. By the end of 1966, the American armed forces might have been "immune to military defeat" in Vietnam but they were no closer to achieving their long-term strategic goals.[69]

However, dismissing Westmoreland's strategy as wholly inappropriate to the political and military landscape of South Vietnam would be simplistic. Understanding the multifaceted nature of the conflict, Westmoreland advocated addressing the political, economic, and psychological dimensions of the war as well as the military. As he remarked to correspondents in late fall, "The situation is so complex that it is very difficult to understand, even if one is on the scene."[70] Westmoreland was no fool. There existed areas worthy of praise in MACV's concept of operations. In portions of Vietnam, the "bully boys" in fact comprised the greatest threat to South Vietnam's government. But Westmoreland's vision for success apparently misinterpreted the mosaic nature of revolutionary warfare in South Vietnam. Counterinsurgencies did not proceed along logical, sequential lines. Insurgents and main force units acted in tandem, balancing the military and political struggle, depending on local conditions. NVA and VC units concentrated on eroding the allies' willpower through costly encounters. Attrition worked both ways. Conversely, political insurgents intended only to foster GVN instability, not needing to defeat governmental forces in decisive battles. Thus, in some provinces and districts, body counting might have made sense; in others, it could be irrelevant, even counterproductive.[71]

If body counts proved insufficient for evaluating progress, Westmoreland required some marker to demonstrate forward movement. By the close of 1966, the war was unfolding in a highly charged and increasingly politicized environment at home. A host of actors and agencies applied pressure on MACV to demonstrate advances in the war effort—the press corps, the Joint Chiefs of Staff, the U.S. Embassy in Saigon, the Secretary of Defense, and the President. Rising American casualties demanded justification. Johnson, knowing the war's costs were affecting his Great Society programs, pressed for evidence of progress to silence the growing number of critics. Representing many Americans' expectations, Ambassador Henry Cabot Lodge wrote the president, "I have been hoping that we could get decisive military results within a year."[72] As prospects for such results evaporated in 1966, Secretary of Defense McNamara turned his attention progressively toward pacification efforts. After visiting South Vietnam in late autumn, McNamara reported to Johnson that he saw "no reasonable way to bring the war to an end soon." There appeared no signs of an impending break in the enemy's morale or will. The military effort would have to continue, at a sustainable level, but McNamara argued that MACV needed to place more attention on pacification.[73] Westmoreland had yet to discover how best to measure progress in the attrition phase of his strategy. The increasing emphasis on pacification would complicate further MACV's attempts to develop useful indicators for such a confusing war.

> "When we don't know how long it takes to pacify a village, how do officials in Washington know how long it will take to clean up the whole country?"
> —American officer, quoted in *U.S. News & World Report*

5   "We Are Winning Slowly but Steadily"

AS 1967 OPENED, William Westmoreland's assessment of the war in South Vietnam had changed little. Though U.S. forces had punished enemy main force units in 1966, MACV's commander believed that North Vietnamese regiments and divisions still were capable of attacking selected targets throughout all four corps tactical zones. Moreover, the dual threat to the GVN remained. Despite the North's capacity for large-scale attacks, Westmoreland surmised that U.S. military pressure had forced the enemy to revert, at least partially, to guerrilla operations aimed at destroying governmental effectiveness in the South Vietnamese hamlets and village. In short, both bully boys and termites warranted continued attention. The 1967 Combined Campaign Plan thus upheld Westmoreland's earlier views on the war. South Vietnamese units would maintain their focus on pacification efforts, while the Americans would engage in assault operations to destroy major enemy base areas and deny enemy access to the people. Neither of these efforts, Westmoreland judged, would result in a decisive victory during the coming year. MACV's objective simply was to extend government controlled areas while pummeling Vietcong and NVA units. As COMUSMACV concluded to his superiors, the enemy "is waging against us a conflict of strategic political attrition in which, according to his equation, victory equals time plus pressure."[1]

This continuity of strategic thought found expression on the battlefield. On January 8, U.S. and ARVN forces launched Operation Cedar Falls. The first corps-sized operation of the war, Cedar Falls targeted the "Iron Triangle," a Vietcong refuge northwest of Saigon. Planners intended to evacuate the entire population within the triangle's sixty square miles to facilitate U.S. advantages in mobility and firepower. After relocating the civilians, the Americans would designate the area a "specified strike zone," destroying residual enemy forces and infrastructure while denuding the jungle of its protective cover.[2] Four days of intensive B-52 bombing preceded the ground assault. On the 8th, twenty-three battalions jumped off in a classic hammer and anvil attack. Two brigades established blocking positions west of the Saigon River, while units from the 1st Infantry Division, 11th Armored Cavalry Regiment, and 173rd Airborne Brigade assaulted from various points around the triangle to close the trap. It was a masterpiece of conventional military planning and execution. After nineteen days, the allies seemingly had cleared the Iron Triangle. Westmoreland, cognizant that such operations could not be undertaken as ends unto themselves, reported Cedar Falls had "permitted a speedup in the pacification area close to Saigon."[3]

MACV's assessment proved misleading. Cedar Falls had not advanced the larger goals of pacification. Villages deemed insurgent strongholds, like Ben Suc in the center of the Iron Triangle, were conceded to the enemy and became targets for wholesale destruction. One correspondent believed that the army had "reversed the search-and-destroy method. This time, they would destroy first and search later." Nineteen-year-old David Ross, a medic in the 1st Infantry Division, found the American approach equally disturbing. "So what we were trying to do was either win the village over or, if we couldn't do that, move the people out, burn the village, put the people in concentration camps and designate the area a free-fire zone."[4] As had been the case throughout 1966, military needs trumped problems associated with forced relocations. American officers presumed all civilian males in the triangle were VC. MACV concluded that the military necessity of destroying enemy sanctuaries during Cedar Falls far outweighed popular resentment caused by the creation of thousands of refugees. Staff officers and commanders instead took solace in their traditional metrics of progress: 720 enemy killed, 1,100 bunkers and 400 tunnels destroyed, and 495,610 pages of enemy documents captured. So sure of its approach—one senior officer called Cedar Falls a "decisive *turning point* . . . and a blow from which the VC in this area may never recover"—MACV followed its foray into the Iron Triangle with its largest operation of the war to date.[5]

In February, Westmoreland struck into War Zone C with aspirations of locating and destroying the 9th Vietcong Division, that troublesome unit which had eluded annihilation during Operation Attleboro in November 1966. MACV hoped also to unearth and dismantle the Central Office of South Vietnam (COSVN), the leadership agency Hanoi relied upon to control and direct insurgent activities in the south.

Code-named Junction City, the operation kicked off on February 22 and lasted for more than eighty days. Thirty thousand U.S. troops swept into a combat zone leveled by air force high explosives in hopes of pinning down their elusive foes. Initial MACV assessments of Junction City, mostly emphasizing high enemy body counts, overlooked the operation's larger failures. Instead of destroying COSVN, American forces only drove VC headquarters and supply depots into bordering Cambodian sanctuaries. As in the past, the 9th PLAF Division, though bloodied, decided when to avoid battle and conserve manpower. Additionally, Vietcong in War Zone C quietly returned when American units departed to other missions. Perhaps most importantly, Saigon made few political inroads with the local population after Junction City. Westmoreland might find satisfaction in the enemy's reversion to small unit tactics, a fact which ostensibly helped Americans cover pacification missions, but hard truths remained. After three months of difficult fighting in early 1967, it appeared to many observers at home that the American mission in Vietnam was drawing no closer to its overall objectives.[6]

MACV's positive assessments notwithstanding, evident shortcomings in operations like Cedar Falls and Junction City led to mounting criticism of Westmoreland's strategy. Presidential advisors Robert Komer and Robert McNamara argued increasingly that enemy attrition alone was not enough to produce victory. With Cedar Falls winding down, Komer warned the president of a "grievous lack of integrated, detailed civil/military pacification planning in Vietnam." The typically blunt Komer wondered aloud if Westmoreland was moving fast enough to keep up with the enemy's shift to a "more guerrilla-type strategy." Successful pacification depended on clearing and holding an area, yet two weeks after Cedar Falls a senior officer in the 1st Infantry Division found "the Iron Triangle was again literally crawling with what appeared to be Viet Cong." Such discrepancies between reality and MACV's optimistic evaluations highlighted the American staff's chronic difficulties in measuring battlefield progress in South Vietnam. In fact, MACV's unpreparedness to assess progress in the "other war" would become one of the most important aspects of the conflict in 1967.[7]

As Westmoreland dutifully placed increased emphasis on revolutionary development (RD) in 1967, MACV struggled to implement a new system for measuring pacification progress and effectiveness. Unfortunately, U.S. Army staff officers and commanders had not yet resolved their issues with assessing the war of attrition before this change in strategic emphasis took hold.[8] Believing that he was fighting two complementary wars, Westmoreland possessed flawed measurement tools for evaluating both, and time was not on his side. A growing chorus of Americans, both at home and abroad, shared Komer's concerns that MACV was not moving fast enough. More and more, a perception of stalemate hung over the war. A throng of vocal critics began to question openly the path that Americans had taken in Southeast Asia. With the war seemingly drifting, MACV's inability to demonstrate tangible and reliable progress in 1967 prompted a White House–led media campaign to shore up American popular support at year's end. Unfortunately, the president's aggressive marketing activities would hold disastrous implications when the enemy's Tet offensive commenced in early 1968.

Questioning Westmoreland's Approach

Momentum: the word never strayed far from William Westmoreland's central thoughts on the war in South Vietnam. After nearly two full years of fighting, MACV's commanding general could reason confidently that his forces had wrested momentum away from the enemy. U.S. and allied forces had fought to gain the initiative on South Vietnam's multiple battlefields since the Ia Drang battles in late 1965. Throughout 1966, North Vietnamese and Vietcong units had endured an onslaught of U.S. firepower while increasing numbers of American troops and support assets flooded into Southeast Asia. Westmoreland knew the fighting extended to the political, economic, and even psychological fronts, yet in nearly all these areas indicators of progress existed if one examined the right numbers. Even President Johnson recalled that by "early 1967 most of my advisers and I felt confident that the tide of war was moving strongly in favor of the South Vietnamese and their allies, and against the Communists."[9] Not all, however, shared the convictions of Westmoreland or his commander in chief. On the ground, momentum seemed less certain. One senior American advisor in I CTZ reported that the population "remains to an undetermined degree infected with the same causative factors for insurgency as they were prior to 1954." The people lacked political identification with the Saigon government and desired to be rid of foreign domination, while ARVN continued to be wracked by corruption and a shallow pool of effective military leaders.[10] Clearly, not all South Vietnamese provinces experienced the same level of momentum to which Westmoreland aspired.

This uneven pace of progress weighed heavily on a growing number of officials within Johnson's administration, perhaps most significantly on Robert S. McNamara. During an October 1966 trip to South Vietnam, the increasingly disillusioned Secretary of Defense expressed to U.S. and GVN officials in Saigon his disappointment with pacification. Challenging directly MACV's strategic concept, McNamara contended that the large-unit war "is largely irrelevant to pacification as long as we do not lose it."[11] The Defense Department's Office of Systems Analysis further condemned Westmoreland's strategy by suggesting that VC and NVA units were recovering their large losses incurred from American operations. The RAND Corporation followed suit. After a visit to Vietnam in early 1967, RAND's Richard Moorsteen reported to the White House that "chasing after victory through attrition is a will-o'-the wisp" and that sending additional U.S. forces might even be counterproductive. Westmoreland and his superiors in Pacific Command concurred with their critics that success in the attrition war would not lead automatically to the insurgency's defeat.[12] Despite the questioning of his sequential strategy, in which destruction of communist forces preceded successful pacification, the general plan for victory remained largely unaltered. The shift in strategy during 1967 would be one of degree, not form.

Westmoreland did not ignore the growing chorus of presidential advisors urging a greater emphasis on pacification. After reviewing MACV's command guidance for 1967, National Security Advisor Walt Rostow wrote President Johnson in January that Westmoreland's vision was "cheering" because it assigned forces to both offensive operations and pacification. Even *Time* reported that during the coming year "the emphasis will shift more and more away from killing Communists to the less spectacular—but equally demanding—tasks of land control, population security and nation building."[13] Since no official in Johnson's administration or in the Joint Chiefs of Staff provided COMUSMACV with any guidance on how to achieve these objectives, Westmoreland assumed confidently that he was meeting the intent of his civilian superiors. As in 1966, U.S. forces would concentrate on maintaining their shield against enemy main force units. Westmoreland's charge for 1967 would be to work out the details of provincial level pacification while assigning ARVN the main task of supporting revolutionary development activities. Here, little had changed from previous years. The strategic dialogue between Washington, D.C., and Saigon remained inadequate for either grasping the war's complexities or for developing a concerted national plan of action.[14] What did change in early 1967, thanks to increased pressures for pacification efforts, was the sequential aspect of MACV's strategic concept. No longer could Westmoreland view counterinsurgency in strictly linear terms. Pacification and the big-unit war would occur simultaneously and on increasingly equal footing.

Perhaps more than any other presidential advisor, Robert Komer stood responsible for this subtle shift in American strategy. At a time when McNamara was falling gradually out of favor within the administration, Komer pressed hard in late 1966 and early 1967 for a change in Johnson's Vietnam policy. An aggressive and abrasive bureaucratic infighter, the "Blowtorch" knew how to press hard, even if he lacked expertise in Southeast Asia. Komer had served in army intelligence in Italy during World War II and afterward began a long career as a CIA analyst. He headed staffs on Europe and the Middle East and served on the National Security Council staff in the Kennedy administration.¹⁵ Johnson, admiring Komer's drive and ambition, retained the Harvard Business School alum and in 1966 assigned Komer the task of developing an organizational concept for pacification efforts in South Vietnam. The resulting staff paper divided the revolutionary development problem into three parts—ensuring population security, breaking the communists' political infrastructure, and committing MACV to large-scale pacification operations. Komer recalled that "it was a question of balance." Johnson concurred, and in his 1967 State of the Union address he reported to Congress that South Vietnam was turning to pacification tasks "with a new sense of urgency."¹⁶

Komer's influence on LBJ and his views on pacification progress solidified during the Guam Conference in late March. Johnson held several goals for bringing together the allied war managers. Besides introducing Ellsworth Bunker as the new ambassador to South Vietnam, the president, following Komer's advice, pressed for further emphasis on GVN pacification and political development. President Thieu's presentation of a new Vietnamese constitution seemed encouraging; however, a frank assessment by Westmoreland belied earlier optimistic treatments of the war's progress. COMUSMACV reported that the enemy had made gains during recent pauses in the bombing of North Vietnam. Recalling his concluding remarks to a now silent audience, the general noted that "if the Viet Cong organization failed to disintegrate, which I saw as unlikely, and we were unable to find a way to halt North Vietnamese infiltration, the war would go on indefinitely."¹⁷ Johnson considered the report a petition for renewed bombing of the North and additional ground troops in the South. Discussion returned abruptly to MACV's organizational construct for supporting pacification. As the conference ended, few doubted the president's commitment to making pacification work. Westmoreland headed back to Saigon with the prospect of a new civilian deputy directing his Revolutionary Development Support Directorate.

Not surprisingly, Komer emerged as the clear choice for the civilian deputy supervising all of MACV's pacification efforts. His first task was to coordinate the loose collection of agencies involved in revolutionary development. As Komer recalled, "Everybody and nobody was responsible for pacification until I came along, so as a result nobody was in charge."¹⁸ The U.S. Agency for International Development, the CIA, and the South Vietnamese Ministry of Rural Construction frequently had been working at cross-purposes since the demise of the Strategic Hamlet Program. Additionally, MACV, which controlled most of the in-country resources, concerned itself with the big-unit war, leaving pacification to the civilian agencies. Coordinating military operations with the revolutionary development program foundered throughout much of 1966. An inaccurate measurement system to assess hamlet security and population control exacerbated these difficulties of pacification implementation. By mid-1966, MACV could report only "a rough approximation" of population area control. Nor could MACV identify the location of boundaries between areas controlled by the GVN and the Vietcong. Arriving in May, Komer faced a monumental bureaucratic, if not conceptual, challenge.[19]

Carrying ambassadorial rank, Komer became Westmoreland's chief agent for CORDS—Civil Operations and Revolutionary Development Support. While pacification was to remain an essentially South Vietnamese program, CORDS reached from Saigon down to the district level. MACV took control of both civilian and military personnel and resources and assigned each U.S. corps senior advisor a civilian deputy for CORDS. Komer detailed the sheer breadth of responsibilities under this new organization. MACV now provided oversight for all of GVN's pacification-related programs: "territorial security forces, the whole RD effort, care and resettlement of refugees, the Chieu Hoi ('Open Arms,' or amnesty) program to bring VC to the GVN side, the police program, the attempts to stimulate rural economic revival, hamlet schools, and so on."[20] In short, CORDS assumed full responsibility for pacification. Not everyone was enamored of this civil-military unification. One civilian field official believed the new chain of command held gloomy implications for reporting pacification progress. "We are going to be unable to give factual reports, if they are critical."[21] Komer remained confident, however, that he could retain independence in MACV and positively influence the course of America's war effort.

On May 13, the new CORDS chief attended his first MACV Commander's Conference. Despite the massive reorganization entailed by the establishment of CORDS and Komer's comprehensive plan of action, little changed in MACV's strategic approach. Komer assured the assembly of senior officers that "pacification is a GVN responsibility, with the U.S. providing advice and resources." Such assurances fit well with Westmoreland's own vision of the war.[22] The MACV commander could accept the responsibilities of pacification without having to run the myriad programs associated with CORDS. As before, MACV concerned itself with internal security, political and economic stability, and the destruction of external belligerent forces. The consolidation and centralization of pacification efforts, however, allowed Westmoreland to maintain his focus on VC and NVA main force units.[23]

Thus, despite critiques of his strategic approach and an organizational overhaul of MACV, Westmoreland's views on pacification and the war in general remained constant. He continued arguing for more troops to accomplish both attrition and pacification, believing that American victories in 1965 and 1966 had robbed the enemy of his momentum and provided the shield behind which pacification could expand. He persisted in judging U.S. forces most qualified for military operations against NVA main force units. South Vietnamese troops, with additional training, would conduct revolutionary development tasks while GVN civil officials assisted with nation building.[24] The three pillars of American strategy in South Vietnam remained essentially unchanged: defeating communist insurgents and aggressors from the North, expanding population security, and supporting nation building. As Westmoreland recalled, "pacification was an important program in the south. But it was not necessarily the decisive element."[25]

Westmoreland's reservations about pacification as a counterinsurgency panacea were not unfounded. The implementation of CORDS throughout MACV's area of responsibility encountered a host of problems, many of which had bedeviled anti-communist efforts since the days of French occupation. Physically controlling the population did not guarantee that U.S. or ARVN forces were making inroads against the VC political infrastructure. Improved security conditions did not necessarily win civilian hearts and minds. Revolutionary development tasks competed with other urgent operational and planning commitments, which further strained American commanders and their staffs. More importantly, pacification required perceptive judgment on a daily basis and a deeper understanding of Vietnamese culture than most Americans possessed. Senior officers labored to balance the often competing requirements of attacking the Vietcong infrastructure with performing civic action programs in the hamlets and villages. Many American soldiers made few distinctions between friend and foe when operating in the countryside. The army's individual rotation policy only exacerbated RD problems. With some units experiencing a 90 percent turnover in personnel within a three-month period, the implementation of CORDS commenced only fitfully.[26]

Komer claimed pacification to be a GVN mission, but problems abounded with its local execution. In theory, once U.S. troops destroyed enemy main force units, ARVN forces assumed the task of clearing the contested area so that local Regional Forces and Popular Forces (RF/PF) could undertake security operations. Like many of MACV's plans, expectations outdistanced capabilities. The inclusion of pacification tasks overburdened an already strained South Vietnamese army, while leadership deficiencies and corruption continued to hobble ARVN. Westmoreland even had to intervene to discourage ARVN troops "from taking food from the people and thereby antagonizing them."[27] The performance of RF/PFs (called "ruff-puffs" by Americans) varied so widely that MACV staff officers had difficulty establishing trends for population security and area control. The civil side of nation building was equally unsettled. Ambassador Bunker reported in early summer that a "lack of involvement and motivation are evident in the apathy, inertia, widespread corruption and incompetence one finds in many areas of the civil administration."[28] At nearly all levels, Americans fumed over the South Vietnamese inability to foster local initiative.

FIGURE 5.1 An alternative to attrition? Captain Charles Herron of the 101st Airborne Division's 326th Medical Battalion examines villagers during a medical civil affairs operation near Hue, South Vietnam.

Source RG124S, SLA Marshall Collection, Box 5, Folder 532

These problems with CORDS implementation illustrated not only the complexity of counterinsurgency warfare, but helped explain why changes in American strategy went unnoticed by so many observers. The desire of administration officials to place more emphasis on pacification had not altered battlefield conditions in South Vietnam. A Research Analysis Corporation report on pacification well described the complexities. "Three levels of violence or armed conflict exist in Vietnam: terrorism, paramilitary or guerrilla actions, and limited conventional warfare. Simultaneously, and closely integrated, there is the 'other war,' involving political, economic, psychological, and sociological activities."[29] To be successful, Westmoreland had to contend with all of these factors. Pacification alone was not the answer. The new CORDS programs did, though, add yet another challenge to the military command's already questionable reporting system. How could MACV measure pacification progress when it had yet to establish an effective system for measuring progress in the big-unit war?

Measuring the Progress of Pacification

Obtaining accurate information from the provinces was essential to the success of CORDS. As in other areas of MACV's data collection effort, however, establishing clear indicators for measuring pacification progress remained challenging. Area and population control was an undisputed element of revolutionary development, but how to define control in the more than 2,000 villages and 13,000 hamlets was less obvious. One contemporary study defined control as the "degree of security established as well as the degree of influence exercised over the populace" but neither of these dimensions lent itself to measurement.[30] Additionally, MACV's staff in 1967 continued to wrestle with estimations on the enemy's order of battle and on the number of northern troops infiltrating into South Vietnam. With different numbers from different intelligence sources, both in Washington and Saigon, correspondents began to view MACV's statistics with increasing suspicion. One senior officer maintained that the problem lay with Westmoreland's staff, which had not "developed a cohesive effective [intelligence] system in this theater against this kind of enemy and this kind of an environment."[31] How to measure contested or controlled areas would be difficult if MACV lacked confidence in its intelligence estimates on enemy strength.

In the autumn of 1966, the Secretary of Defense, pushing for a greater emphasis on revolutionary development, instructed the CIA to develop new procedures for measuring pacification progress. McNamara realized that the reporting system for population control had become insufficient to meet administration needs. So inaccurate were population statistics that villages moved from secured or uncontested to VC-controlled categories simply because of "administrative reevaluations." Prepared manually, the narrative reports concentrated primarily on measuring security and GVN presence at the provincial level. The CIA, working from a matrix developed by the Marines in I Corps, focused instead on hamlet activity and sought a fully automated system to ease the advisors' paperwork burdens and lend itself to tabulation and analysis. Though the Joint Chiefs bristled at the CIA operating in military areas, the intelligence agency conducted several field tests and made revisions based on MACV commentary. The resulting Hamlet Evaluation System (HES) became operational in January 1967.[32]

To keep track of pacification in South Vietnam's forty-four diverse provinces and 13,000 hamlets, HES relied on simple quantitative techniques. The new system expected U.S. advisors to assess their hamlets on a monthly basis, while keeping their South Vietnamese counterparts abreast of their evaluations. (Those developing HES apparently never considered that pacification was supposed to be a GVN program.) Despite its goal of simplicity, evaluating hamlets using HES required advisors to become familiar with a wide range of issues in their districts. As one senior CORDS officer explained, "HES is primarily concerned with evaluating, measuring, and reporting progress of the GVN toward the goal of restoring and maintaining security, extending firm government control, improving the living conditions and advancing the economic development of its people."[33] Komer realized the essentials of pacification remained difficult to quantify, regardless of the measurement system. At a news conference on the HES, the ambassador noted that, in addition to providing security, pacification "is essentially a process of converting people who are either on the fence or oriented toward the VC to the Government of Vietnam side."[34] Here lay one of the central dilemmas for any evaluative approach. How could advisors assess progress in local Vietnamese supporting the GVN side?

Aiming to achieve a greater degree of objectivity in answering such a question, the HES worksheet relied on a matrix of eighteen indicators in which to assess a hamlet's security and development. Factors relating to security included VC military activities, VC political and subversive activities, and friendly security capabilities. Advisors rated development factors by assessing administrative and political activities, health, education and welfare, and economic development. Each of the eighteen indicators were scored "E" (worst) through "A" (best). MACV then processed these scores electronically to produce a hamlet's comprehensive rating. In an "A" hamlet, Vietcong military and political remnants had been driven out, GVN officials resided in the hamlet or village, and all welfare needs were being satisfied. In "E" hamlets, ineffective governmental officials spent their nights elsewhere and U.S. advisors could ascertain no economic development. The tendency of hamlets to shift from one side to another and even to collaborate with both sides simultaneously required advisors to make subjective judgment calls when completing their evaluations. Not all aspects of hamlet life could be quantified. Concentrating almost exclusively on programs and activities, the HES worksheet offered little opportunity for advisors to evaluate what Komer deemed most important in pacification—the process of people converting to the GVN side.[35]

The Hamlet Evaluation System's usefulness to MACV in assessing pacification progress proved a double-edged sword. William A. Knowlton, who served in MACV's Revolutionary Development Support Directorate, considered previous ratings under the Strategic Hamlet Program "far too gross an estimation." While HES might not answer the critical question of "What did those in the hamlets *really* want?" the new evaluation system did allow CORDS to monitor the effectiveness of its numerous programs.[36] One of Knowlton's principal subordinates believed HES "to be a reasonably reliable technique for measuring those key aspects of pacification that are measurable—hamlet population, security, and development." This faith in the credibility of HES reporting came with a heavy price. Driven by its belief that statistics actually measured progress rather than just activity, MACV publicized HES statistics to the press before confirming the data. While internal documents cautioned that evaluation results might not be reliable until midsummer, MACV headquarters used HES as a way to publicly illustrate progress before it was sure of the system's accuracy.[37]

Unsurprisingly, the reporting system contained a number of deficiencies. As much as HES attempted to rely on quantitative input, the judgment of more than 250 district advisors (most with different standards and perspectives) still determined the results of each monthly report. These advisors collected data on an average of thirty-seven hamlets each month; by June, MACV still had not attained a complete inventory of hamlets in South Vietnam.[38] Advisors faced additional challenges with HES. For accurate evaluations, they needed to be well versed in a wide spectrum of political, economic, and military matters—tax collections, agricultural and manufacturing productivity, cost of living, population distribution and densities, and VC defections and desertions. The advisors' conventional backgrounds hampered their efforts. One contemporary observer estimated that "99 percent of the U.S. Army advisers have neither language facility nor the knowledge of Vietnamese culture to know what is happening in their own district." Relying on interpreters, Americans too often gathered only what local officials wanted them to hear. A village or hamlet chief, believing the Vietcong would remain long after the Americans departed, easily could provide inaccurate data to an unwary advisor.[39]

American data could be as unreliable as Vietnamese. As with body counts in field units, officers serving as district advisors confronted pressures to demonstrate tangible progress. One officer in CORDS recalled "there was a bit of grade creep even if the situation had not changed that much." The reasons were clear. Advisors who downgraded evaluations met a flurry of harsh questioning. Another first lieutenant arrived to his assignment within a month of an entire ARVN platoon being destroyed nearby. He downgraded his hamlets' security rating and was summoned immediately to district headquarters to meet with several colonels from corps headquarters. The young officer recalled the "meeting was fairly tense.... They wanted to know the whole nine yards of why I had thought it necessary to downgrade the security of these hamlets, because this was definitely running counter to what it was that we were supposed to be reporting."[40] Yet another officer met a similar response when he reported retrogression in his hamlets. "I believe I am an honest man, and although I hate to admit it, it may be a long time in hell before I downgrade another hamlet." Even Westmoreland acknowledged the lack of candor. After a May briefing on HES, the general noted in his journal, "It appears that again facts will reveal that there has been distortion of reports on the optimistic side. It seems to be one of the things that has plagued this war from the beginning."[41]

MACV optimism aside, it never was clear whether HES measured what McNamara intended it to measure. No one reporting system could have evaluated accurately a program as complex as CORDS. Indeed, revolutionary development precluded clear measurement. McNamara and Komer expected HES to quantify elements of South Vietnamese society that simply could not be enumerated on a matrix—control, security, and conversion of the people to the GVN side.[42] Advisors might assess a hamlet as VC- or GVN-controlled, but their evaluations could never identify let alone quantify the causal relationships between allied operations and population control. The term "security" remained a relative term. One perceptive correspondent asked "How Secure is 'Secure'?" when U.S. officers bragged that they could move anywhere in their province by day, but were reluctant to drive outside the capital after dark. Nor could the HES measure adequately attitudes, aspirations, and loyalties. Cultural divides prevented Americans from appreciating fully South Vietnam's social and political landscape and thus reporting accurately on pacification's progress. Still, 75 percent of general officers surveyed after the war responded that HES "had weaknesses but was about as good as could be devised."[43]

The very construct of HES reflected the now perennial problem with MACV's metrics for effectiveness and progress. Concentrating on data collection rather than on trend analysis, officers continued to highlight the quantitative aspects of their reporting systems. Komer argued that the Hamlet Evaluation System "was designed for management, not just progress reporting." But data management proved overwhelming. HES generated a monthly average of 90,000 pages of reports. When added to MACV's other analysis documents, the U.S. Army alone in Vietnam was producing 14,000 *pounds* of reports *daily*. Even Alain Enthoven, one of the Defense Department's staunchest systems analysis advocates, warned: "We ought to be careful not to overload the system with excessive [pacification] reporting requirements."[44] Still, MACV persisted in amassing and tabulating numbers to measure absolute levels of control and violence without spending time, effort, or resources ascertaining their meaning. The CORDS Chieu Hoi ("Open Arms") program was one example. Initiated in 1963 to encourage Vietcong followers to return to the government, the program foundered on Saigon's inability to create long-range rehabilitation programs geared to the country's social and economic reconstruction after the war. CORDS charted the numbers of "ralliers" returning to the GVN fold, but left analysis of their motivation, morale, and quality to outside civilian agencies. As in other pacification areas, causal relationships between allied operations and enemy activity remained largely unexamined.[45]

Ideologically and culturally unequipped to manage revolutionary development, American officers substituted statistics for a genuine understanding of the "other war." Unit commanders tended to define pacification progress using such quantifiable metrics as increased security to provide clarity in an otherwise confusing war. Such attitudes confronted sharply with the enemy's view of revolution as a long-term social process. One U.S. Army officer illustrated both the frustration and intellectual limitations bred by MACV's reliance on administrative numbers. "I wish people's ears would light up or something when we have won their heart or their mind." Or, as another officer put it, "What we need is some... kind of litmus paper that turns red when it's near a communist."[46] In the process, as MACV reported slow but steady gains in their pacification programs throughout 1967, the bulk of Vietnamese in the countryside remained uncommitted to the Saigon government. Nor had the U.S. or GVN made serious inroads against the Vietcong's political infrastructure. A *CBS News* survey of South Vietnamese public opinion conducted in March found that 48 percent of respondents believed their lives to be worse than they had been a year earlier. Despite the mounds of pacification data collected and MACV's resolve in placing values on intangibles, Vietnamese society remained as impenetrable as ever.[47]

All the while, the U.S. mission in South Vietnam tempered any signs of failure with a blizzard of statistics suggesting progress. In the six month period between May and October, MACV reported steady gains of hamlets moving into the HES "A" category, well before it was certain of the data's accuracy. By late 1967, the sheer weight of statistics had become crushing. Enthoven's warning not to overburden the system had gone unheeded. At MACV commander conferences, staff officers deluged Westmoreland with sixty-five charts during the Measurement of Progress briefing alone. According to the briefing officer, no senior general expressed any interest in one indicator over another. To the White House, Komer complained that the war was "so fragmented—so much a matter of little things happening everywhere—that the results are barely visible to the untrained eye."[48] Even the establishment of an operations research and systems analysis office in MACV (MACEVAL) and an increasing reliance on automation did little to facilitate analysis of the war's trends. Obsessed with statistics and measurement, the war's complexity simply had overwhelmed MACV's capacity for understanding.[49]

Pacification versus the "Big-Unit War"

One of the reasons that MACV could not deal with the war's intricate nature rested in the uncertain relationship between pacification and the big unit war. Revolutionary development did not occur in a vacuum. While CORDS took hold within the U.S. mission in mid-summer, Westmoreland concentrated his forces in the northern provinces for a major enemy offensive in I CTZ. Since January MACV's commander concerned himself with northern infiltration across the demilitarized zone and the possibility of a large-scale NVA assault. Marines fought off guerrilla and terrorist attacks throughout June and July, yet the major confrontation that Westmoreland predicted never materialized.[50] Fighting certainly remained high. During Secretary McNamara's visit to Saigon in early July, Con Thien, just two miles south of the Vietnam border, endured a barrage of more than 800 rocket, artillery, and mortar rounds in a twenty-four-hour period. Still worried about high infiltration rates, Westmoreland pressed the Defense Secretary for more troops to perform both attrition and pacification tasks. McNamara, on his ninth visit to Vietnam, demurred. Despite the president's increasing anxiety over the war's slow pace and mounting American casualties, McNamara "remained skeptical about . . . military requests to expand it."[51]

The Marines' experience in I CTZ that summer typified the enemy's approach to battle in 1967. North Vietnamese and Vietcong units avoided contact with American forces unless it was to their utmost advantage. While incidents of assassinations, propaganda, and kidnappings mounted throughout late spring and early summer, frustrated MACV officers chaffed at their inability to induce the enemy to battle. One division commander recalled the difficulties in simply finding the enemy. "They metered out their casualties, and when the casualties were getting too high . . . they just backed off and waited. . . . They were more elusive. They controlled the battle better. They were the ones who decided whether there would be a fight."[52] By 1967, over 96 percent of enemy engagements occurred at or below company level. In a telling appraisal of MACV strategy, the Defense Department's Systems Analysis Office noted in late spring that "the enemy's degree of control over the pace of the action determines how well he can control his attrition." Westmoreland, reversing his Guam opinion, remained optimistic. "The war is not a stalemate," he assured McNamara during the secretary's July visit. "We are winning slowly but steadily. . . . North Vietnam is paying a tremendous price with nothing to show for it in return."[53]

Certainly, North Vietnam was paying a high price for continuing the war. Even company-level engagements came with a cost. Because of this reality, American military commanders persisted in relying on body counts as a tool for assessing progress, despite MACV's renewed emphasis on revolutionary development. Such proclivities made sense given the responsibility of U.S. forces in Westmoreland's 1967 campaign plan. Unit commanders believed correctly that their first mission was to initiate contact with the enemy and provide security for ARVN to commence pacification efforts. In the process, officers could continue to define the war using comfortable labels without worrying about coordination between military operations and civil programs. As William R. Peers, commander of the 4th Infantry Division in

1967, recalled, "I paid a hell of a lot of attention to body count. I think body count has its place because you never know whether you are winning or losing if you don't have some means of measuring."[54] By late 1967, though, MACV had yet to solve its problems with "administrative errors" in body counting. Several in-house studies investigated suspected inaccuracies over VC and NVA losses but could recommend only that commanders emphasize more care in their reporting procedures.[55]

The body count endured as a useful metric for MACV because pressures to report progress in the attrition portion of Westmoreland's strategy remained so strong. In fact, after the "mounting successes" of 1966 and early 1967, demands on MACV to demonstrate forward momentum increased dramatically. McNamara and President Johnson badgered Westmoreland over when he would reach the elusive "crossover point," yet the enemy visibly maintained the ability to replace his losses. North Vietnamese infiltration and southern recruitment drives compensated for heavy battlefield casualties.[56] In early August, *The Christian Science Monitor* reported that despite Westmoreland having roughly eighty maneuver battalions at his disposal, "Viet Cong troop strength has steadily risen . . . to an estimated 297,000 today." One RAND analyst likened the VC and NVA to a spring which gave under pressure yet retained its ability to push back, since American attrition efforts thus far had not produced metal fatigue. In the process, the United States was now spending $2 billion a month on the war in Southeast Asia.[57]

This apparent impasse in the big-unit war, at least in the eyes of those outside MACV headquarters, corresponded with a demonstrable lack of progress in revolutionary development. Foreign Service officer Richard Holbrooke reported to the White House in June that the "1967 pacification program is in deep trouble almost everywhere in Vietnam." Holbrooke lamented the South Vietnamese people's unwillingness to provide allied troops with intelligence or to form volunteer militia units, yet, in typical American fashion, never sought any explanation for their reluctance in supporting the GVN. Echoing earlier testimony by the Joint Chiefs, he warned against placing U.S. troops in a defensive posture that eased pressure on the Vietcong. Holbrooke concluded that the best use of troops lay in attacking VC main force units near areas being pacified.[58] MACV reacted by increasing its operations against Vietcong strongholds while encouraging ARVN to step up its efforts in the villages and hamlets. The American military chain of command exhorted subordinate unit commanders to exploit contact with all their resources. "Killing the enemy," one senior officer declared "is the name of the game."[59]

The premium MACV placed on aggressiveness illustrated not only the unshakable allure of conventional operations on the military's organizational culture, but the army's resistance to embrace pacification. Throughout 1967, the American mission focused almost exclusively on population security. Military and civilian advisors from the White House through the Department of Defense to MACV reasoned with unquestioning faith that security ranked as *the* central problem of pacification.[60] Army officers insisted in their professional journals that the "primary means of supporting revolutionary development would be through security, and security would be gained by search and clear operations in each province followed by constant and aggressive patrolling and night ambushes." Obsessed with the tactical aspects of security, these officers largely discounted the importance of social policies that might sway the population away from the VC.[61] Westmoreland's sequential view of counterinsurgency strategy still attracted a wide range of supporters. Security remained the vital precondition to pacification.

While Komer struggled with the massive bureaucratic challenge of CORDS, MACV's insistence on security had the unfortunate consequence of pitting civil and military programs against each other. More than a few American officers regarded civic action as "political" and thus falling outside their purview. Combat maneuvers thus received greater attention than did pacification programs. One battalion commander displayed the conventional reluctance with, if not disdain for, the army's supposed new role. "Remember, we're watchdogs you unchain to eat up the burglar. Don't ask us to be mayors or sociologists worrying about hearts and minds."[62] Doctrine counseled otherwise, encouraging units and staffs to incorporate political considerations into military operations. CORDS, though, remained in organizational conflict with U.S. and ARVN forces, which eschewed civic action programs for firepower and maneuver. Contradictory policies thus created friction between divisional combat units and provincial advisors. While Komer urged U.S. advisors to expand pacification efforts in their hamlets—and potentially tie down forces in an area security role—Westmoreland pressed unit commanders to pursue mainforce VC and NVA, leaving local provincial security forces with little to no support. Not only was the war fragmented, but so too was the U.S. response to it.[63]

The South Vietnamese population suffered most from this interagency conflict. By 1967, search-and-destroy missions and bombing raids had left homeless roughly three million South Vietnamese. American operations generated scores of refugees, unraveling the countryside's social and political fabric and destabilizing any foundation on which pacification programs could build.[64] Even well-meaning civic action plans exacted a toll on South Vietnamese villagers. One RAND provincial study discovered that revolutionary development had placed inhabitants in a dilemma. "An effect of pacification operations in Dinh Tuong of particular note was the burden of cross-pressure on the Viet Cong controlled population. They were under pressure to respond to two authorities, the GVN and the Viet Cong, arousing deep fears of becoming 'illegals.'" Caught in this vice between two "governmental authorities," villagers remained suspicious of U.S. soldiers, who rarely stayed long. For their part, exasperated Americans wondered why the population was taking so long in its decision to support the Saigon government.[65]

As the year wore on, Americans concerned themselves less with pacification's impact on the civilian population than in finding ways to dramatize progress. Though HES reports indicated improvements in area security and rural welfare, domestic political pressures compelled administration officials to emphasize dramatic battlefield accomplishments. Insightful army officers and defense analysts knew, however, that GVN sociopolitical developments took time. Building a political community able to withstand the Vietcong's revolutionary demands required a patience that Johnson's presidency no longer possessed. In August, Walt Rostow conveyed to the president a "general feeling that we are on a treadmill in Viet Nam." In spite of efforts to display signs of momentum in both the big unit war and CORDS's pacification program, the word "stalemate" gradually crept into public newspapers and official communiqués.[66]

Selling Progress

With American ground troops entering their second full year of fighting, newspapers across the country began expressing a growing uneasiness with the war in South Vietnam. Doubt surfaced over whether military operations that devastated the countryside could lead to a stable and prosperous Vietnam and even whether U.S. vital interests were at stake in Southeast Asia. Statistics flowing from Saigon clarified little for an increasingly impatient American public. One bewildered correspondent, seeking "benchmarks" that might offer some perspective, argued persuasively that the "public yearns for certainties but in Vietnam there are no certainties." This "absence of reliable standards" weighed heavily on President Johnson, and in April he summoned Westmoreland home to brief a joint session of Congress on the war's progress.[67] The general, aiming not to oversell the war, inadvertently helped perpetuate the impression of stalemate. Despite an upbeat prognosis to Congress, at an Associated Press meeting Westmoreland stated he did "not see any end to the war in sight" and suggested that anti-war demonstrations at home only encouraged the enemy abroad. Critics accused Johnson of attempting to stifle dissent and drum up political support for the war.[68]

Media critiques questioned not only the administration's stalled military strategy but MACV's system for assessing and reporting progress. Journalists charged that Westmoreland was covering up ARVN failures in prosecuting revolutionary development. Similarly, MACV failed to mention the "side effects" of the big unit war. Jonathan Schell, who reported on the destruction of Ben Suc during Operation

Cedar Falls, believed it "not very surprising that Bomb Damage Assessment Reports supplied no blanks for 'Homes Destroyed' or 'Civilians Killed.'"[69] Even if MACV had not been suppressing bad news—in fact, it was—reporters claimed that the U.S. mission had chosen flawed metrics for gauging its success. Ward Just of the *Washington Post* maintained that by professing to find significance in the body count, the army was "mistaking valor for progress." With late-summer news stories running under such headlines as "Vietnam: The Signs of Stalemate" and "This War May Be Unwinnable," senior officers, including Westmoreland, shot back by condemning the news media's incompetence and biases. As the summer dragged on with still no end in sight, Johnson's greatest fears began to materialize. Domestic resolve appeared to be faltering. A September public opinion poll showed for the first time that more Americans opposed than supported the war.[70]

Johnson responded to the mounting public skepticism by dispatching a presidential fact-finding mission to the Far East. Led by personal friend and advisor Clark Clifford and General Maxwell Taylor, the small task force visited several Asian governments to discuss the possibility of increasing their troop commitments to the ongoing American war effort. Clifford, supportive of Johnson's goals in Vietnam, returned full of doubt. On August 5, he and Taylor briefed the president. The trip convinced Clifford that the foundation of American foreign policy rested on shaky ground. None of the countries he visited subscribed to "Washington's treasured domino theory." In regard to strategy, there seemed little cause for optimism. Westmoreland provided Clifford and Taylor with a memorandum titled "Achievement of Objectives" that measured progress in a number of significant areas: enemy losses, the securing of major food producing areas, increased ARVN effectiveness, and improvement in revolutionary development support. Clifford remained unconvinced. As he told the president, "If we continue the war at the same level of ground and air effort I am unable to see that it will bring us any nearer to our goal."[71]

For Johnson, the problem lay not in strategy or objectives but in communication. By nearly every measurement emanating from MACV headquarters, progress existed. Slow to be sure, but progress nonetheless. In spite of positive reports from Westmoreland and Komer, both the media and even some trusted advisors returned from Vietnam expressing reservations about U.S. military strategy. The White House countered these doubts by launching what Clifford called a "multimedia public-relations campaign . . . to persuade the American public that the war was being won."[72] It proved to be one of the most fateful decisions of 1967. For the last quarter of the year the Johnson administration commenced on an elaborate public relations campaign to prove that no stalemate existed in Vietnam. (Ironically, the Joint Chiefs of Staff had denounced Gavin's enclave strategy in 1966 as one leading inevitably to stalemate.) In late September, the president ordered MACV and the embassy in Saigon to "search urgently for occasions to present sound evidence of progress in Viet Nam." Officials replied with cheery assessments on the recent nationwide elections, on increases made in population security, and on improvements in the morale and aggressiveness of ARVN forces.[73]

With the media campaign under way, Johnson gathered a group of retired senior foreign policy and military advisors—dubbed the "Wise Men"—to review the war in Southeast Asia. The cast included such dignitaries as Dean Acheson, Omar Bradley, and Henry Cabot Lodge, as well as serving officials like McNamara and Rusk. Rusk opened the November 2 meeting by reading Ambassador Bunker's upbeat review of his first six months in Saigon. After a day of discussions, nearly all of the Wise Men recommended staying on the current course in Vietnam. McGeorge Bundy urged Johnson, "Don't let communications people in New York set the tone of the debate. Emphasize the 'light at the end of the tunnel' instead of battles, deaths and danger."[74] By now, nearly all agencies involved in the war effort were doing just that. Westmoreland even advised his chief deputy, General Creighton Abrams, to encourage the GVN to undertake its own publicity campaign. When the president summoned Bunker and Westmoreland home in mid-November to report on their progress, the administration's salesmanship of the war became glaringly obvious.[75]

The night before the Wise Men meeting, Robert McNamara broke ranks with the propaganda machine and provided Johnson with a stark assessment of the war. Echoing a similar memorandum in May that expressed doubt as to whether the United States could prevail in Vietnam, McNamara's new evaluation reasoned that "continuation of our present course of action in Southeast Asia would be dangerous, costly in lives, and unsatisfactory to the American people." The troubled Defense Secretary argued against military proposals for an expansion of the ground war, recommended a cessation to the bombing of North Vietnam, and advocated transferring greater responsibility to the South Vietnamese. Discouraged by his inability to solve the war through personal drive and managerial expertise, McNamara had run out of options to break the North's will to fight. Comparatively, "the American public, frustrated by the slow rate of progress, fearing continued escalation, and doubting all approaches to peace have been sincerely probed, does not give the appearance of having the will to persist." To McNamara, only a radical change in policy could lead to some favorable outcome in the war. Johnson instead opted for a change in his Defense secretary and announced at month's end that McNamara had been selected to be president of the World Bank.[76]

McNamara's dissent stunned Johnson, but not enough to derail the administration's public relations campaign. When Bunker and Westmoreland arrived home in mid-November, the media blitz accelerated to full throttle. On November 17, Steve Rowan of CBS interviewed Westmoreland and asked about evidence of stalemate in

South Vietnam. "Well," the general responded, "stalemate implies a lack of progress and such is not the case in Vietnam. We are making steady and real progress on all fronts—political progress, economic progress, and military progress."[77] Three days later, he and Bunker reiterated their message on NBC's "Meet the Press." Westmoreland said he found "an attitude of confidence and growing optimism" which prevailed across the countryside. (Interestingly, none of MACV's statistical reports assessed popular attitudes at this time.) Then, on November 21, Westmoreland gave the most important speech of his trip at the National Press Club. Acknowledging that the war "eludes any precise numerical system of measurement or any easy portrayal of progress on battle maps," the general went on to present "the most optimistic appraisal of the way the war was going that I had yet made." Given past upbeat evaluations, Washington officials and seasoned war correspondents received the new estimate with skepticism.[78]

Lack of enthusiasm over the White House–directed media campaign rested on justifiable reservations over the quality of information received from Saigon. Despite Westmoreland's emphasis on popular attitudes, MACV's reporting system still relied, almost exclusively, on hard statistics. Senior officer debriefs from the field measured progress based entirely on percentages and often contained glaring inconsistencies. One report trumpeted an increased number of enemy kills and comparative decrease in friendly losses yet noted an incredible 215 percent rise in friendly wounded in action. Pacific Command's end of year assessment contained similarly contradictory data. The report conceded discrepancies between the HES and GVN estimates over population security; still, it used the higher American numbers to demonstrate success in moving 66 percent of the population into secured areas. Discounting problems with body counts, the report also noted that MACV had inflicted losses on the VC and NVA at a rate exceeding their input. Goals not attained in 1967 went unmentioned during the public relations campaign. U.S. and allied forces fell short in opening and securing South Vietnam's rail and waterways and, perhaps more importantly, had failed to neutralize VC and NVA base areas.[79]

The self-assurance expressed in public statements and internal assessments concealed what McNamara deemed "rot in the fabric." Improvements in the Hamlet Evaluation System notwithstanding, MACV's reporting system remained broken in 1967. Staff officers and commanders simply believed what they wanted to hear. Under pressure from the White House to report progress, they turned to those statistics that best reflected positive trends and momentum. No one in Saigon questioned the data's accuracy; what mattered was that officials could use the reams of figures produced by MACV as evidence of progress. The administration's burning desire for positive reports outweighed any concerns over reliable information. As one correspondent quipped, "there were people leaning so far out to hear good news that a lot of them slipped over the edge and said they could see it too."[80] Westmoreland's year-end report illustrated the levels to which this self-deception had reached. COMUSMACV relied on dubious numbers to claim gains in both pacification and the big unit war, highlighting progress in nearly every measurable category within MACV's colossal metric system. Of note, Westmoreland boasted that the enemy had not won a major battle in Vietnam in 1967. The enemy, of course, had avoided battle intentionally, making such declarations irrelevant and underscoring the continued problems in finding pertinent metrics of progress. By December, however, the enemy readied itself for a return to the battlefield in large numbers, a fact which the White House's public relations campaign never fully contemplated.[81]

On the Eve of Tet

More than two years had passed since the 1st Cavalry Division's "unprecedented victory" in the Ia Drang Valley. Since that time, MACV had churned out positive assessments of the war using a host of measurements and statistics that covered nearly every aspect of the fighting. The military command's December evaluation report hailed 1967 as a "Year of Progress," citing improvements in the rate of enemy losses, percentages of the population under GVN control, and in the motivation, training, and leadership of ARVN forces. After two years of fighting, though, "slow and steady" progress satisfied neither those running the war nor an increasingly war-weary American public. The Joint Chiefs claimed administration-imposed restrictions limited military effectiveness and slowed the rate of progress. A year-end CIA assessment found that the communists still retained the will and capability to continue pursuing a protracted war of attrition for at least another year.[82] Even Robert Komer, normally one of MACV's most optimistic deputies, found little comfort in the sluggish pace of pacification. One senior advisor captured the mood by noting in his debriefing report that "day to day progress is like watching the hour hand of a clock." On the domestic front, those Americans reading David Halberstam's "Return to Vietnam" in the December issue of *Harper's* magazine wondered why so much effort was being expended for a Vietnamese society that was "rotten, tired, and numb."[83]

MACV could not refute Halberstam's appraisal of Vietnamese society because political loyalty to Saigon and popular confidence in the GVN fell outside of its evaluation system. HES could not measure individual or collective morale. MACV's byzantine reporting procedures continued to rely on statistics and data collection that left popular attitudes largely unexamined. In the process, the army's measurement system failed to capture what two RAND analysts deemed the "inextricable connections between the 'search and destroy' and the 'pacification' tasks." Their report emphasized a crucial point not accounted for in MACV's massive reporting structure. "If U.S. troops were successful in searching out and destroying the larger Viet Cong units, but did not succeed in 'pacification,' their successes in the more conventional type of military operation would be undermined."[84] Body counts and HES reports thus remained separated in computer-tabulated groupings that few officers bothered to compare. In 1967, it was important only to show progress in both categories. Only occasionally did senior CORDS advisors meet with field commanders and relate HES data to unit operations.[85] In short, MACV both fought and assessed two simultaneous yet disconnected ground wars.

The enemy made no such distinctions. Despite the pressures of massive American firepower and increased GVN efforts in pacification, the Vietcong maintained its balancing act of political and military activity in the countryside. Responding to operations like Cedar Falls and Junction City, the enemy simply refused large-scale battles, instead striking into undefended areas that forced allied troops to spread themselves thin. The communists also adapted to MACV's latest emphasis on pacification. Incidents against revolutionary development workers rose sharply throughout 1967. In September, the Defense Department's Systems Analysis Office estimated that 16 percent of the RD cadre would desert that year.[86] Additionally, the VC's tax system and proselytizing effort remained intact in most areas. One Foreign Service officer working in intelligence found "the Viet Cong infrastructure are usually very articulate and very well informed about not only the GVN, but also their own organization, and communicate perhaps more effectively." Though not featured in the White House's end-of-year public relations campaign, the enemy had acclimated itself to MACV's change in strategic emphasis.[87]

Americans appeared more unsettled than their adversaries in adjusting to the new military situation. A lack of dramatic developments coincided with conflicting evidence of progress that confounded people at home and left officers scrambling for yardsticks to measure a constantly changing military environment. White House advisor Chester Cooper believed that the "compulsive need for a daily temperature reading was not simply a fetish for charts and graphs but reflected instead a deep sense of anxiety and self-doubt in Washington."[88] Cooper, though, missed an important point. Anxiety in Washington developed because after two years of fighting, MACV had not figured out how to determine if it was winning or losing. Useful indicators continued to elude the American military staff. At a December command briefing, Westmoreland provided guidance for the coming year that included familiar concepts. Operations would involve weakening the enemy while strengthening ARVN forces. The MACV commander then noted a staggering requirement. "Measurements of these two major projects must be developed."[89]

This failure to build a functional measurement system not only reflected the complexity of counterinsurgency warfare in South Vietnam, but undermined the solid efforts of American and ARVN troops in the field. The optimistic reporting emanating from Saigon, while yielding improved public opinion poll results at home, nonetheless created false expectations. Selling progress became more important than accurately measuring progress. MACV touted accomplishments in both its ground wars when in fact it had failed to break the morale and willpower of either the NVA or VC. Even in a war without fronts, Americans expected progress to be linear. In short, effort should equal progress. Reporters wary of the army's "statistical urges," however, speculated that MACV had been leaving out some of the fine print in its statements to the public.[90] White House officials surveyed the shifting political landscape with equal suspicion. As Undersecretary of State Nicholas Katzenbach wrote the president near the end of the year, "Time is the crucial element at this stage of our involvement in Viet-Nam. Can the tortoise of progress in Viet-Nam stay ahead of the hare of dissent at home?"[91] Johnson soon would have his answer. The North's decision to launch Tet was about to undermine all of MACV's progress reporting thus far and to help solidify a credibility gap that Johnson would endure for the remainder of his presidency.

"We have been too often disappointed by the optimism of the American leaders, both in Vietnam and Washington, to have faith any longer in the silver linings they find in the darkest clouds."
—WALTER CRONKITE, 27 February 1968

6 The Year of Tet: Victory, Defeat, or Stalemate?

AS 1967 ENDED with MACV optimism, U.S. military strength in Vietnam stood at 485,600 total military personnel. Though Westmoreland had pressed unsuccessfully in the year's closing months for more men to expand his offensive operations, he reported in December that the U.S. Military Assistance Command, Vietnam, "at all levels is rapidly gaining momentum." Westmoreland planned to exploit this momentum in 1968 by continuing to pursue a strategy based on two objectives: seeking out and destroying communist forces and infrastructure "across the entire spectrum of the enemy threat" and assisting the Saigon government in a major pacification and nation-building program. MACV's goals for the coming year ranged from increasing intelligence efforts to improving ARVN morale and effectiveness.[1] Westmoreland believed the time finally had come for an "all-out offensive on all fronts"—political, military, economic, and psychological—and his optimism permeated throughout the American camp. One senior officer serving in the Mekong Delta told reporters in early January 1968 that "I think we have the force to win. We have gained the upper hand." Even White House officials shared MACV's confidence. National Security Advisor Walt Rostow perceived Hanoi might be inclined to negotiating an end to the war before the November presidential election.[2]

This confidence in late 1967 and early 1968 rested largely on MACV's interpretation of its own metrics. In November, North Vietnamese regiments assaulted allied forces near Dak To, an outpost in northern Kontum province close to the Cambodian–Laotian–South Vietnamese border. As in earlier attacks at Song Be and Loc Ninh, the enemy suffered heavily at Dak To. American troops reported 1,644 enemy dead. Westmoreland, still uncertain of Hanoi's motives, welcomed these "border battles" in which he could maximize U.S. firepower away from population centers. (At one battle alone, nearly 800 B-52 bombers dropped 22,000 tons of bombs.)[3] Whether these enemy assaults on the periphery and buildup of forces in the Laotian panhandle revealed a change in North Vietnamese strategy remained to be seen. In one sense, it seemed not to matter. By January 1968, demonstrating friendly progress counted more than ascertaining enemy intentions. Lyndon Johnson's State of the Union address hailed the progress of South Vietnam's elections, the enemy's numerous defeats in battle, and the increased number of South Vietnamese living in areas under government protection.[4]

The optimism radiating from the White House and MACV headquarters aimed at lifting domestic confidence in an eventual U.S. victory. As 1968 opened, public opinion polls revealed that while the majority of Americans disapproved Johnson's handling of the war, over 60 percent favored escalation over military curtailments. MACV, however, had yet to establish the relationship between escalation and progress. For the American public, victory was no closer in early 1968, with nearly half a million U.S. troops in South Vietnam, than it was in early 1967. Many speculated whether victory was even attainable. *Newsweek* reported in January that "more Americans than not are still determined to see the U.S. 'win' the Vietnamese war. But winning in Vietnam does not appear to mean to them what it meant in World War II." American correspondents in Vietnam found it increasingly difficult to reconcile the upbeat military briefings in air-conditioned headquarters buildings with the bloody and destructive battles that seemed only to produce meaningless statistics. *Newsweek* asked the question most prevalent on American minds and the one most difficult to answer in the political-military quagmire of Vietnam. "In short, how goes the war?"[5]

The enemy's Tet holiday offensive, which engulfed South Vietnam in late January, helped answer that question for a wide array of American observers. The attack created a nearly insurmountable credibility gap between MACV and media correspondents and between the Johnson administration and the American people. Tet also exposed virtually all of MACV's difficulties in measuring progress since the Harkins era. Within one week of the start of the offensive, Americans at home began questioning MACV's metrics for gauging progress in intelligence gathering, in determining enemy strength, capabilities, and willpower, and in assessing population security. Tet also bared MACV's inability to connect battlefield progress to a larger public understanding of strategic progress. American units pounded NVA and VC units during Tet and throughout the spring and summer months of 1968. Still, after all the effort and casualties—1968 marked the deadliest year for U.S. military forces—it seemed that allied troops had fought only to recapture pre-Tet levels of population security and government stability. MACV stressed its tactical and operational accomplishments on the battlefield, yet the fundamental strategic level problems of the Vietnamese war remained unresolved.[6]

Despite its obvious significance, Tet did not alter MACV's strategy or metrics in 1968. The twofold strategy submitted by Westmoreland in late 1967 persisted under his successor, Creighton W. Abrams. Certainly, Abrams reacted wisely to the enemy's battlefield adjustments and to domestic political pressures for increasing ARVN effectiveness. His "one-war" approach aimed to reverse the sequential view of counterinsurgency as expressed so often under Westmoreland. Yet the new MACV commander confronted a war as decentralized as in earlier years, pulled in often opposing directions by the CIA, the State Department, and the Saigon government. The enemy, of course, still had his say in how the war progressed. The political-military nature of the conflict still required MACV to measure the same areas it had evaluated in the past. Defeating enemy units, increasing population security, and encouraging ARVN still ranked at the top of the American mission's numerous goals, while determining what constituted political progress remained as confusing as ever. So too did demonstrating progress against an enemy whose pain threshold appeared beyond influence, despite years' worth of bloodletting.[7]

Measuring Progress in the Intelligence War

Debates on strategy and progress occurred not only in Washington and Saigon. In Hanoi, political and military leaders deliberated throughout 1967 over the war's course and the best response to U.S. military escalation. Because of the American imperialists' "aggressive nature and their confidence in their own strength," the Communist Party's Central Committee acknowledged that the southern insurgency campaign had stalemated in the countryside. Still, an opportunity existed. A strategic offensive might break the stalemate by instigating a popular uprising in the South, thus weakening the South Vietnamese–American alliance and forcing the enemy to the negotiating table. As in all aspects of their war, the communists synchronized military aims with their ultimate political objectives. Even if this "policy for achieving a decisive victory" failed, Hanoi could improve its position by circumscribing U.S. political commitment to Saigon. A southern uprising might very well convince the international community that the United States was fighting as an external aggressor to subdue an internally led popular revolution. Perhaps more importantly, a military defeat of the Americans, real or perceived, could change the political context of the conflict in South Vietnam.[8]

Communist Party Secretary Lê Duẩn and General Văn Tiến Dũng emerged from Hanoi's strategic debates to map out the final plans for a "General Offensive-General Uprising" (*Tong Cong Kich–Tong Khoi Nghia*, or TCK-TKN). The success of TCK-TKN would rely on surprise and a daunting level of coordination to achieve its numerous ends. As Vo Nguyen Giap, the North Vietnamese general who had engineered the French defeat at Dien Bien Phu in 1954, recalled, "For us, you know, there is no such thing as a single strategy. Ours is always a synthesis, simultaneously military, political, and diplomatic—which is why the Tet offensive had multiple objectives."[9] During the plan's first phase, to be executed at the end of 1967, NVA units would conduct conventional operations along the demilitarized zone and in the Central Highlands to draw American forces away from urban areas and to facilitate Vietcong infiltration into the cities. Lê Duẩn and Văn Tiến Dũng planned the second phase for early 1968, a coordinated offensive by VC and North Vietnamese troops to attack enemy units and support popular uprisings in the cities and surrounding areas. Additional NVA units would reinforce the uprising in the plan's final phase by assaulting American forces and attriting U.S. military strength in South Vietnam. If successful, Hanoi's leaders would be in an advantageous position as they entered the "fighting while negotiating" phase of the war.[10]

The autumn 1967 "border battles" in which MACV took such delight marked the first phase of Hanoi's plan. Though suffering terribly under the onslaught of U.S. firepower, NVA leaders gained additional experience for TCK-TKN's upcoming battles while confirming that Westmoreland would not attack into North Vietnam even if the DMZ came under considerable military threat. The Americans, however, found ascertaining Hanoi's true intentions beyond their means. In December, the Defense Department's Office of Systems Analysis asserted that Giap, who in fact was not involved in the final Tet planning, was purposefully luring U.S. forces away from populated areas. "He believes that the vacuum left by US forces moving outward to fight VC/NVA main force units . . . presents significant tactical opportunities to local and regional forces operating in the populated areas of SVN."[11] When the communists shifted from Dak To to the Marine garrison at Khe Sanh in early January, intelligence analysts and commanders revisited the meaning of the North Vietnamese incursions. Chairman of the Joint Chiefs of Staff Earle G. Wheeler considered Khe Sanh "the western anchor of our defense of the DMZ area" and a position that could not be abandoned without serious impact to allied morale. Was Hanoi hoping to score a major propaganda victory at Khe Sanh, or did this attack serve other purposes? By mid-January the CIA could only offer that in "present circumstances it is true that any multitude of things *could* happen, at almost any time."[12]

American intelligence analysts were not operating blindly on the eve of Tet. MACV initiated a comprehensive information collection effort in early January, code-named Operation Niagara, which flooded the I Corps Tactical Zone with aerial and ground searches. Yet as with its other measurement systems, MACV had trouble gauging the effectiveness of its intelligence-gathering network. The sheer breadth of intelligence sources confounded MACV's attempts at determining the accuracy of its data. Information coursed in from prisoner interrogations, captured documents, defectors, Regional and Popular Force units, U.S. advisors and Special Forces personnel, ARVN troops, and even private citizens. The "noise" of so much data overwhelmed MACV analysts, who tended anyway to concentrate their efforts on battlefield events. (Officers often left political, economic, and social considerations to the CIA.)[13] Westmoreland's chief intelligence officer recalled that "hundreds of reports on upcoming enemy attacks poured through the MACV intelligence system. As usual, many were largely or totally false, some contained partial truths (had one known which parts were true), and a few even turned out to be accurate." Staff officers searched for any clues that might reveal Hanoi's intentions as they examined the enemy's military and political strength. However, as had become a normal condition within Westmoreland's headquarters, data collection overwhelmed MACV's capacity for analysis.[14]

MACV's chief of intelligence production surmised correctly that "intelligence is an inexact science, and so often when we make mistakes it's because we put ourself [sic] in the position of the enemy." Looking to place themselves in an absent Giap's shoes, MACV staff officers believed that the enemy's best chance for success lay in striking the two northern provinces of Quang Tri and Thua Thien. In doing so, the NVA could concentrate its forces and, in overrunning Khe Sanh or Hue, replicate its victory at Dien Bien Phu. At the time, Westmoreland remembered, "the most logical course for the enemy" was to overrun the northern provinces "coupled with lesser attacks throughout the rest of the country to tie down American forces that might be moved to reinforce the north."[15] Anything more ambitious, such as inciting a popular uprising in South Vietnam, seemed unrealistic to U.S. Army officers. After two years of attrition warfare, the enemy could not possibly have the capability or willpower to undertake a nationwide strategic offensive. As one U.S. intelligence officer admitted, "If we'd gotten the whole battle plan, it wouldn't have been credible to us."[16]

In fact, MACV did possess much of the enemy's battle plans. American soldiers had captured a key document during the battle of Dak To that listed the communists' objectives for the impending winter-spring campaign. By mid-January, the CIA had identified specific targets and, after deciphering enemy messages, had proof that NVA attacks might be conducted in the Central Highlands during the

Tet holiday. As one CIA report concluded, "Despite enemy security measures, communications intelligence was able to provide clear warning that attacks, probably on a larger scale than ever before, were in the offing."[17] American officials, though, simply could not trust the evidence. Their indicators did not match their expectations and, as had happened so often in the past, political and military leaders tailored the data to fit their own concept of operations. Whether due to biases bred from ethnocentrism or a refusal to believe in the possibility of a popular uprising, MACV's senior officers concluded that Hanoi's offensive, while menacing, could never be as extensive as the intelligence indicators portended. American field commanders realized the importance of effective intelligence operations, especially in a counterinsurgency environment. Predicting enemy intentions in the days before Tet, however, proved more difficult than gathering facts.[18]

Westmoreland's intelligence setback in early 1968 emerged out of MACV's customary approach to data—massive collection coupled with imperfect attempts at analysis. With more than ten thousand officers and civilians employed in intelligence work in South Vietnam, the sheer amount of information left MACV little time for properly evaluating, responding to, or disseminating warnings. Even with all this data, the picture was hardly complete. One battalion intelligence officer in the 1st Cavalry Division recalled that "as hard as we tried, we couldn't locate any signs of significant buildup.... I was puzzled, and so was everyone."[19] With Westmoreland's attention fixed on South Vietnam's borders, the U.S. field commander in charge of Saigon's defenses felt uneasy over all this "sketchy intelligence." In an impressive example of battlefield initiative, Lieutenant General Frederick C. Weyand, the II Field Force commander, convinced Westmoreland in mid-January to reposition units into blocking positions covering the Saigon approaches. As Weyand recalled, "That really proved to be a stroke of good fortune, for if those units had gone north, the VC would have had a field day in Saigon."[20]

Nonetheless, the American public soon would reckon the Vietcong had enjoyed a "field day" in Saigon. Miscommunication played a central role. The ways in which the military command conveyed intelligence information to White House officials and the American public failed to square potential enemy actions with domestic expectations for allied progress. In short, MACV never reconciled the positive media campaign in late 1967 with its own estimates of an impending enemy offensive in early 1968. Few asked how there could be a looming crisis, even if limited to the northern provinces, after months of reassuring progress reports. Westmoreland and his chief intelligence officer would later blame the president for not alerting the American public to a potential Tet offensive.[21] Yet these same officers never thought through the consequences of a "we are winning" media campaign, coupled with internal reports that the enemy still possessed the potential for a countrywide attack. MACV's head intelligence officer, Phillip B. Davidson, admitted later that Hanoi had achieved a "mild surprise" with Tet. While debatable, Davidson and other MACV officers overlooked how Americans watching the war at home might consider any attack proof that the U.S. had lost control of the war. MACV might not have been shocked by the intensity of the enemy's offensive. Viewers at home certainly were.[22]

Tactical Success, Strategic Questions

Shortly after midnight on January 30, 1968, Vietcong and NVA forces opened the second phase of TCK-TKN with a nationwide assault on South Vietnam during its most sacred of holidays. In coordinated attacks, some 84,000 insurgents and NVA troops struck thirty-six of the forty-four provincial capitals, the U.S. embassy in Saigon, and the six largest cities in South Vietnam.[23] At the embassy, VC sappers broke through the outer wall and survived for six hours inside the compound during a running battle with military police and Marine guards. In the Mekong Delta, Vietcong troops, under the noses of unaware American advisors, infiltrated the supposedly friendly hamlets of Can Tho and Vinh Long four days before Tet. Giap's legions held on to their objectives for hours in some areas, days in others, and up to three weeks in the ancient imperial city of Hue. With many ARVN soldiers on leave for the Tet holiday, the offensive shattered any sense of security previously held in Saigon. The psychological impact ran deep. As one U.S. official explained, "The people are in a vacuum of shock. They don't know which way to turn now."[24]

Amid fear and confusion, Westmoreland sensed a rare opportunity. As early as February 3, MACV's commander believed he had weathered the storm. The VC had paid heavily for their open attacks on South Vietnam's cities and Westmoreland, still believing Hanoi's leaders held their eyes on Khe Sanh, reasoned he could "inflict the same disastrous defeats on his NVA troops as we have on his VC troops."[25] If the allies could recover quickly from the shock of Tet, COMUSMACV hoped to capitalize on the enemy's mounting coordination problems between NVA regulars and VC guerrillas. Westmoreland estimated communist casualties at nearly 34,000 killed in action during the first two weeks of Tet. Though U.S. forces suffered some 1,100 casualties and ARVN over 2,000 during the same time period, the prospect of regaining the initiative tantalized the American commanding general. Putting an end to the "bully boy" threat seemed finally within arm's reach. Westmoreland took heart in the solid performance of several ARVN units during Tet, and by mid-February and early March he pressed all subordinate commands to resume offensive operations to locate and destroy the enemy.[26]

Not surprisingly, body counts returned to the forefront of MACV's reporting system as U.S. forces expended munitions in unprecedented amounts. Units reportedly were granting soldiers three-day passes for killing one or more Vietcong. One 9th Infantry Division platoon leader wrote home of the surreal way in which his chain of command linked old metrics to the chaotic post-Tet atmosphere. "Our new battalion CO said, 'Maybe we'll run into some VC soon and get a good body count and the morale will go up again.'" Journalists' queries about how kill ratios could jump so dramatically if fighting was occurring in urban areas instead of the countryside caused Westmoreland once more to publicly defend his accounting system.[27] While military officers scored impressive body count numbers, CORDS civilians lamented that MACV was ignoring governmental inaction in rural areas. In II Corps, John Paul Vann marveled at unit commanders who failed to tell Westmoreland the Vietcong were "being given more freedom to intimidate the rural population than ever before in the past two-and-a-half years." All the while, South Vietnamese cities suffered under the weight of U.S. firepower. At Ben Tre in the Mekong Delta, one air force major symbolized the war's absurdity for many Americans when he allegedly told an A.P. correspondent that "it became necessary to destroy the town to save it." Westmoreland was making clear inroads in killing the enemy—by early March enemy losses surpassed 58,000—yet their destruction came at a high cost for the Americans.[28]

Tet's impact on the pacification program constituted the most disconcerting news flowing into MACV headquarters. The enemy's general offensive exposed both the fragility of CORDS's revolutionary development efforts and the limitations of the hamlet evaluation reporting system. Westmoreland had predicated the success of pacification on security, yet the Vietcong plainly had shown that hamlets rated as "secure" turned a blind eye to the enemy's final preparations for Tet. HES figures indicated that the population under GVN control dropped from over 67 percent in January to less than 60 percent in February.[29] The percentage of contested hamlets also rose appreciably. One province official noted that years of hard work were "destroyed in 30 minutes of military action, not to mention the propaganda value such destruction gives to the VC." Other U.S. district advisors reported a "loss of momentum" in pacification and a security situation that had "deteriorated badly." While American correspondents questioned the future of pacification in the aftermath of Tet, Robert Komer emphasized the temporary nature of these setbacks. By mid-April he reported cheerfully that revolutionary development was "back on track" and CORDS was making up its losses. "We are definitely on a recovery curve," remarked Komer. The HES figures, though, masked the reality that the enemy still controlled much of the countryside, even if urban population centers had remained largely in government hands.[30]

The imprecision of HES data typified larger challenges in measuring enemy intentions and dispositions in the months following Tet. American officials disputed Tet's broader meaning because they lacked confidence in their reporting systems' statistics. One correspondent recalled that interpretations of Hanoi's inclinations "ranged widely; some people took literally the stated objectives, which were to win the war. Others felt that it was done for American public opinion, still others felt that it was done to affect the political situation in the South. Then there was a feeling that it might be a prelude to negotiations."[31] Military officials wondered if the war was entering a new phase that required a fresh strategic approach or if Tet represented a "last gasp action" that would lead to the war's swift conclusion. The communists certainly paid a high price for their offensive, but why? After visiting South Vietnam in late February, JCS Chairman Wheeler believed the enemy was seeking to expand territorial control in hopes of quickly establishing an NLF-dominated government. Wheeler surmised correctly that the enemy's military plans rested on concrete political objectives. Nevertheless, determining if Tet's high casualty figures were affecting enemy willpower and capabilities eluded the Americans.[32]

Finding it difficult to assess the enemy's strategic intentions, MACV committed itself to demonstrating tactical progress on the battlefield. Like Komer, Westmoreland argued that Tet was only a temporary setback. Officers compared Tet to the Battle of the Bulge, "a desperate effort" that had failed as miserably as Hitler's World War II offensive in the Ardennes. Others likened the enemy's plan to Pearl Harbor arguing that Tet had "crystallized support" for the Saigon government and united the countryside against the Vietcong.[33] Besides the high body counts, MACV highlighted reports of a new self-confidence in the South Vietnamese army, the national mobilization program instituted by President Thieu, and the high number of enemy rallying to the government's side. Most significantly, officers argued, the absence of a massive popular uprising proved that the VC had no support in the countryside. As General Weyand commented later, "There was a great general uprising all right, but it was against them rather than for them." Weyand and other officers overlooked a central point—in some areas, such as in Dinh Tuong province, a rural uprising did in fact take place. MACV also downplayed the social upheaval caused by the nearly 900,000 refugees displaced in the Tet offensive's wake. Westmoreland might be claiming victory, but inconsistencies plagued reports coming out of Saigon.[34]

For many administration officials, these inconsistencies turned into blatant contradictions when Wheeler returned from a Saigon inspection trip in late February and revealed that Westmoreland had requested more than 200,000 additional troops. Since early in the month, MACV's commander had urged a change in strategy. "If the enemy has changed his strategy, we must change ours," he reported to Wheeler on February 12. Westmoreland saw an opportunity to break the long war of attrition, but to do so would require reinforcements. Outwardly, the general spoke of continuity so as not to challenge publicly administration policies. On the 25th he remarked to the press that "I see no requirement to change our strategy. Friendly forces still must find, fix, fight, and destroy the enemy, and concurrently provide the necessary security for the population." To Wheeler, however, Westmoreland pushed for an expansion of the war into the Cambodian and Laotian sanctuaries and even into North Vietnam proper. This revised strategy would come with a price, namely a call-up of reserve forces in the United States. For years, Johnson had balked at such proposals, yet Wheeler believed that the time had come to force the president into doing so. Uniformed leaders placed immense faith in the power of "seizing the initiative," and in the aftermath of Tet, Westmoreland argued forcefully for a chance to crush the enemy once and for all. "Exploiting this opportunity could materially shorten the war."[35]

As in the 1965 debates over U.S. troop commitments to Vietnam, after the Tet offensive White House officials concerned themselves more with force levels than general strategy. The sheer size of Westmoreland's request astonished most of Johnson's advisors. McNamara saw the problem as one of GVN political stability rather than a shortage of U.S. battalions. Clark Clifford, scheduled to replace McNamara as Secretary of Defense on March 1, questioned outright the contradictions in MACV's troop request. "I think we should give some very serious thought," Clifford stated in a White House meeting, "to how we explain saying on one hand the enemy did not take a victory and yet we are in need of many more troops and possibly an emergency call up."[36] When the *New York Times* broke the story on March 10 that Westmoreland had requested 206,000 more men, the administration's Vietnam policy seemed mired irretrievably in doubt and uncertainty. Westmoreland had made a habit in press briefings of relying on statistics to demonstrate progress and implying that more men would mean more progress. By early March, the inconsistencies were too much for either the White House or the American public to accept any further. As one senior officer recalled, the troop request "gave the impression that it was an emergency situation, that we were going to be defeated if we didn't get more troops." Westmoreland's quest for a new strategy thus foundered on a paradoxical message that left Americans more uncertain of U.S. aims in South Vietnam than ever before.[37]

The debate within Johnson's cabinet spilled over into the legislative branch and, notably, into the domestic media. In a meeting with the Democratic congressional leadership on February 6, Johnson faced harsh questioning from Senator Robert Byrd, heretofore a loyal supporter of the president's war policies. Byrd accused the administration of poor intelligence and preparation for Tet, of underestimating the strength of the Vietcong, and of overestimating the support of the South Vietnamese government. Two days later, Senator Robert Kennedy called Johnson's claims of progress "illusory" and maintained that "a military victory is not in sight, and that it probably will never come."[38] *Newsweek* reported in early March that officials could agree on neither communist capabilities nor the best course for American policy in Vietnam. Public opinion echoed growing doubt in the halls of government. A March 10 Gallup poll found only 33 percent of Americans believed the United States was making progress in the war. For an increasingly isolated president, the collapse of congressional and public support forced painful decisions on the war's future conduct. Johnson approved only 10,500 additional troops for Westmoreland and by late March conceded to a suspension of air attacks over North Vietnam. When Johnson spoke to the American public on March 31 about his decision to deescalate the war in a bid for peace, he concluded that "partisan causes" should not interfere with his management of the conflict and as such he would not seek or accept another term as president.[39]

Johnson's bombshell reverberated through the nation and opened up serious questions about claims of victory in the aftermath of Tet. If U.S. forces had been so successful, why was the United States bidding for peace and the president departing the oval office? U.S. Army officers expressed particular frustration with the contradictions between battlefield events and strategic outcomes. One senior staff officer epitomized the army's discontent by complaining about the "intensely hostile press" which had completely lost sight that the enemy "was being killed literally by the thousands and that entire units were being wiped out. This is something that is very hard for the military individual to accept."[40] Too few officers understood the importance of publicly relating the purpose of its counterinsurgency efforts to the attainment of national objectives. MACV had failed to convince Americans that its battlefield successes were leading to progress in the war. In truth, journalists accepted MACV's claims of a tactical victory during Tet. However, as one correspondent recalled, "this did not ultimately constitute a strategic victory for South Vietnam."[41] Tet illustrated, better than any battle during the long conflict, MACV's difficulties in defining progress at different levels of war. Progress on the battlefield did not translate into progress in defeating the insurgency, or if it did, the connection was clear neither to opinion leaders in the United States nor to the American public.

The Media's Role in Questioning Progress

Blaming the media for their failures in Vietnam became a common postwar fixation for many U.S. civil and military officials. Even during the war, officers accused reporters of willful misrepresentation and of being used unwittingly as communist propaganda tools. These accusations ignored not only the Johnson administration's campaign to manipulate American public opinion in late 1967 but also MACV's inability to communicate its progress in a clear or persuasive manner.[42] The media floodgates opened on February 27, 1968, when veteran CBS correspondent Walter Cronkite, reported on his recent trip to South Vietnam. The American public revered Cronkite and his objective reporting on Vietnam had earned him an unrivaled level of trust. In mid-February, Cronkite toured the war-damaged country in Tet's aftermath, visiting Hue and gathering reports from Abrams and other senior MACV officers. "It was sickening to me," Cronkite recalled. "They were talking strategy and tactics with no consideration of the bigger job of pacifying and restoring the country." His evening telecast on the 27th detailed how the enemy had mounted its offensive "with such complete surprise." Then, in a blow to Johnson and his loyal supporters, Cronkite concluded with a personal analysis that the Vietnam War was "mired in stalemate."[43]

Cronkite's editorial reportedly devastated the president. Even so, the inconsistencies in MACV's claims of progress after Tet validated such questioning by the press corps. The Tet offensive, quite simply, made the war a legitimate subject for debate as a political issue. For years the United States government had been escalating hostilities in Southeast Asia, reporting progress via a host of statistical evidence. Still, Americans saw no end in sight. Barry Zorthian, head of the American mission's media relations, found the idea that the press "lost the war" meritless. "Despite the controversy over whether the Tet offensive was anticipated or not, the fact that the VC were able to undertake such a major effort, even though they were beaten back, nevertheless indicated that they still had enormous strength and lasting power."[44] Likewise, accusations of media bias causing dramatic shifts in public opinion rested on faulty evidence. Polls suggested that public approval of Johnson's handling of the war had been in steady decline since well before Tet and had rebounded only slightly during the late 1967 media relations campaign. Cronkite's editorial and other television reports showing the brutality of fighting during the Tet campaign actually had done little to change overall public opinion on the war.[45]

Certainly, reporting in the aftermath of Tet was far from perfect. Given the military's condemnation of the media, it is worth noting that the press corps experienced problems comparable to those of the army while operating in Vietnam. American journalists confronted similar linguistic and cultural barriers and, like many ground combat units, faced pressures to perform—in their case, to file stories faster than competitors at AP, UPI, or Reuters. The media found the politically complex and fragmented nature of the war as perplexing as the army staff. With MACV having difficulties linking military actions on the battlefield to progress in the war generally, correspondents struggled to explain a vague war that looked nothing like World War

II or Korea. "Conventional journalism could no more reveal this war than conventional firepower could win it," observed columnist Michael Herr.[46] Tet only compounded the ambiguities. The fighting in Saigon undeniably made a dramatic story easily accessible; however, the media's inclination to focus on battles like Saigon, Hue, and Khe Sanh (much like the army's) hindered broader assessments of Tet's strategic meaning. The American press corps in South Vietnam was no better placed than the army to determine who was winning.[47]

Contradictory information from MACV headquarters and the U.S. embassy exacerbated the media's reporting difficulties. Journalists learned of "steady progress" from top officials yet heard openly from lower echelons about a "lost cause." Westmoreland unintentionally added to the growing credibility gap. Standing in the shadow of a damaged American embassy on the first day of Tet, COMUSMACV spoke confidently of going on the offensive and inflicting great casualties on the enemy. One astonished reporter recalled the vacant optimism of Westmoreland's predecessor, General Paul D. Harkins, after the disastrous battle of Ap Bac.[48] In the weeks and months following Tet, MACV's commander inundated the media with positive reports in an attempt to bolster morale at home. Despite warnings from the Joint Chiefs to minimize overstatements of progress, Westmoreland declared in April that "we have never been in better relative position in South Viet Nam." In May, the general noted that Hanoi had failed to attain any of its objectives and was "motivated by an attitude which may reflect desperation." At the daily command press conferences in Saigon—known among journalists as the "Five O'clock Follies"—the press corps received equally optimistic progress reports from senior military officials. None of these sanguine announcements, however, explained the American command's inability to prevent the Tet offensive from happening in the first place.[49]

Confronted by unfavorable press reports about the U.S. losing the initiative, MACV turned to its reporting system for substantiating its claims of victory. The traditional metrics of progress, though, proved insufficient in countering the media's claims of stalemate. Improved kill ratios meant little when American forces had done nothing more than contain the Tet offensive. In the process, soaring American casualty rates mollified few critics. U.S. Army officers spoke of a new confidence among GVN officials and ARVN soldiers, yet nothing in their vast array of statistics could demonstrate that such claims mattered when Hanoi's will appeared unbreakable.[50] On the pacification front, CORDS officials judged the declining percentages in population security temporary. Westmoreland, sensing the pressure, concentrated on "quick-fix solutions" that would demonstrate immediate positive trends in the restoration of governmental control in rural areas. Still, pessimism lingered. As the *New York Times* reported in late spring, "even if the optimists are correct in all their claims, the advantages are not sufficient to turn the tide this year, next year or even the year after."[51]

White House officials and especially U.S. Army officers accused the media of sowing this domestic doubt and despair. Johnson found the post-Tet newsmagazine coverage particularly disturbing and, according to his press secretary, became distracted by negative press reports. As the president recollected, "The media seemed to be in competition as to who could provide the most lurid and depressing accounts."[52] None, however, could match the intensity of uniformed leaders in their scorn for the press. From the Chairman of the Joint Chiefs to commanders in the field, vilification of the media reached epic proportions. Earle Wheeler impugned the press corps for turning Tet into a "propaganda victory for the North Vietnamese here in the United States." In the immediate aftermath of Tet, Westmoreland believed "the press were gleeful that the VC had finally accomplished something significant and the US and South Vietnamese were in an awkward position." One division commander reported that the "press would have us believe that the enemy is 'ten feet tall'" while another officer remembered the media's "sensationalized reporting outweighed stories about the progress we were making and put unnecessary fear in the hearts of soldiers' families back home."[53] In all these attacks the "media" remained a nebulous entity guided by an unseen, yet surely liberal—or even communist—hand.

Despite MACV's claims of progress and the media's increasing criticism of the war effort, Johnson's advisors were in fact coming to their own conclusions in the weeks and months following Tet. The media did not conspire to lose Vietnam and in truth mimicked much of the administration's official position on the war. Tet simply afforded the occasion for a fresh assessment of the conflict and the new Secretary of Defense, prodded by a growing number of governmental officials, seized the opportunity.

Clark Clifford brought to the Pentagon years of experience as a Washington lawyer and an advisor to presidents since Truman. A close confidante of Johnson, Clifford earned a reputation as a hawk who supported U.S. commitments in Southeast Asia. Upon succeeding McNamara on March 1, Clifford was asked by the president to establish a "task force" to "reconcile the military, diplomatic, economic, congressional, and public opinion problems involved" in the war.[54] The new defense chief emerged from his fact-finding exercise utterly disheartened. The Joint Chiefs could give him no assurances that additional troops would help win the war or if the U.S. mission in Vietnam was making progress toward ultimate victory. Concurrently, the Pentagon's civilian advisors backed a strategic shift, placing increased emphasis on pacification and affording ARVN greater responsibilities as a precursor for negotiations. The unlikelihood of military victory in Vietnam, Under Secretary of the Air Force Townsend Hoopes argued, demanded a change in objectives that would lead to an "honorable political settlement." When the Wise Men reconvened in late March and advocated similar course changes to Johnson, the infuriated president alleged that someone had "poisoned the well."[55]

The recommendations of the Clifford task force and the Wise Men came not from public opinion pressure inflamed by an irresponsible, biased press corps but rather from a long-overdue, objective appraisal of U.S. foreign policy in Southeast Asia. For years, Westmoreland had promoted tactical progress based on mountainous statistics. Still, strategic momentum eluded the Americans. The shock of Tet not only exposed imperfections in MACV's policies for measuring and publicizing progress but occasioned modifications to the United States' Vietnam strategy. Johnson's decision to limit American reinforcements to Southeast Asia meant that the U.S. mission would have to boost its plans for improving the quality and strength of South Vietnam's armed forces. While media reports pondered timetables for American withdrawal, these changes in strategic emphasis necessitated a new set of metrics for measuring progress and effectiveness. In the wake of Tet, the enemy would also alter his tactics, eschewing large-scale engagements while he recovered from the bloody battles of TCK-TKN. MACV's reporting system would be hard-pressed, as always, to determine progress accurately given the conflict's changing nature.[56]

Abrams's "One War": Continuity in Change

In March, MACV's Deputy Commander, Creighton W. Abrams, returned to Washington for discussions with administration officials. Asked by the president if "there is anything we should be doing that we aren't doing," General Wheeler responded that American strategy was sound. Abrams concurred. "I don't feel we need a change in strategy," the fifty-three-year-old Massachusetts native replied. "We need to be more flexible tactically inside South Vietnam."[57] Abrams returned to Vietnam in time to survey the results of a new enemy offensive launched on May 5. Dubbed "mini-Tet" by Americans, the attacks, relying mostly on rockets and mortars, fizzled out in less than two weeks but created another 125,000 South Vietnamese refugees. The following month Westmoreland assumed duties as the army chief of staff after four years as MACV's commander. Abrams replaced his former boss and West Point classmate while the enemy still was shelling Saigon. An armor officer, the new COMUSMACV had gained fame spearheading Patton's drive to relieve Bastogne in World War II. He had served as a corps chief of staff in Korea and, prior to Vietnam, as the army's vice chief of staff. Bright, well-read, and commonsensical, "Abe"

FIGURE 6.1 A new MACV commander, but a new war? General Creighton W. Abrams talks with Major General Harris W. Hollis, commanding general of the 25th Infantry Division, October 9, 1969.

possessed a volatile temper famous among the army's officer ranks. Like Westmoreland, he lacked any prior experience in counterinsurgency operations.[58]

Reporters were quick to highlight the differences between the outgoing and incoming commanders (the two had maintained a cool relationship at best), and press reports intimated that Westmoreland's reassignment marked official recognition of a change, if not failure, in Vietnam strategy. Abrams, however, differed from his predecessor "more in emphasis than in substance." Stressing a "one war" concept that viewed the enemy as an interlocking "system," the new COMUSMACV confronted problems similar to Westmoreland. As one officer recalled, "By the time Abrams arrived on the scene, there were few options left for changing the character of the war."[59] Enemy main force units, local Vietcong, and political cadre continued to challenge U.S. pacification efforts, rural security missions, and the training of ARVN forces. Certainly, Abrams concerned himself more with pacification and ARVN training than did Westmoreland. These programs rose in importance, though, not because of a new strategic concept devised by Abrams, but rather because Johnson's administration had decided the Americanization phase of the war had run its course. While the president remained committed to an independent, non-communist Vietnam, peace had replaced military victory as the principal national objective.[60]

As during Westmoreland's tenure, the enemy continued to influence American tactical and strategic options. Though suffering 12,000 additional casualties during mini-Tet, NVA units and battered VC forces maintained their pressure on South Vietnam's cities, leaving Abrams little choice but to join battle. Pacification remained inexorably tied to security. Committed to protecting Saigon against further attacks, Abrams flooded the countryside with small patrols to keep the enemy off balance. Reporters hailed the reduction in battalion-level search-and-destroy operations under Abrams as proof of a different war. Abrams, however, simply was reacting to his opponent's own tactical changes. In the wake of Tet, the threat of enemy main force units invading South Vietnam's northern provinces had diminished considerably. High casualty figures were forcing Hanoi to increase its flow of troops infiltrating into South Vietnam to replace losses in the Vietcong's ranks. In spite of these battlefield adjustments, MACV still confronted the problem of finding and fixing an enemy who avoided U.S. troops and reverted to small-unit actions while recuperating from the bloodbaths of two costly offensives.[61]

The Tet offensives took an undeniable toll on both Giap's NVA units and local Vietcong forces. American officers sensed the decreasing quality of replacement troops filling the depleted VC ranks. While the "lull" created by the enemy's reconsolidation efforts allowed Abrams to alter his tactical approach, the new commander continued to rely on MACV's traditional metrics for assessing progress and effectiveness. Though publicly shunning body counts, Abrams gauged the aggressiveness of ARVN units by favorable kill ratios during internal staff meetings. MACV's quarterly evaluation reports persisted in following established formats for measuring progress—weapons captured, roads opened, and population secured.[62] HES procedures remained unaltered, although, on a positive note, some advisors reported feeling less pressure to report progress. As one officer quipped, "Occasionally we are allowed to state frankly that we didn't do a damn thing this month." Mindful of heightened expectations caused by his predecessors' overstated optimism, Abrams trod lightly when reporting signs of improvement to the press.[63]

Abrams proceeded cautiously with the media for good reason. The American mission's various intelligence-gathering agencies still could not agree on enemy infiltration figures. Nor could MACV ascertain how much damage it had inflicted on VC units or political infrastructure during the Tet campaign. Additionally, high desertion rates continued to undermine general improvements in ARVN effectiveness. In mid-May, the opening of preliminary negotiations in Paris further complicated MACV's attempts at measuring progress. Ambassador Ellsworth Bunker noted that all actors were "well aware that success in the pacification and military sphere will have a direct effect on the negotiations."[64] U.S. officials rushed to boost ARVN strength in case negotiations led to a freeze on force levels inside South Vietnam. Each side claimed gains in representing the population—a difficult task, given so many refugees—with hopes of obtaining an upper hand during peace talks. MACV, responding to the prospect of looming negotiations, hastened to establish "minimal presence" throughout the countryside. One U.S. advisor noted that the "name of the game is planting the government flag."[65] In the process, HES statistics lost much of their reliability in determining genuine population security levels.

The relationship between population security and negotiations highlighted the military command's shifting emphasis in South Vietnam. While MACV fended off yet another enemy offensive in August, the third of the year, Abrams turned increasing attention to pacification. Revealing progress, however, remained as obscure for the new commander as for the old. Komer likened the HES map in mid-summer to a "checkerboard" with the enemy controlling nearly 45 percent of the rural population, a sign that CORDS faced ongoing obstacles in establishing trends within its data collection efforts. Abrams could view the hamlet evaluation statistics only with wary skepticism. (He treated Komer with equal suspicion and lobbied for a new CORDS chief after taking command.)[66] Research studies cautioned that the HES provided no indication of VC taxation methods inside Vietnamese hamlets or if the Vietcong were successfully recruiting replacements after Tet. Furthermore, HES offered no index of villagers' willingness to voice publicly their dismay with local governmental policies and practices. One study stressed the innate limitations of HES. "There is no independent absolute criterion of truth about pacification. All we can measure is how the degree of pacification as it appears to advisors corresponds to the degree of pacification as it appears to other observers such as the villagers themselves … [and] their Vietnamese officials." The system in place now for more than a year, researchers confirmed a number of deficiencies in HES yet judged the reporting system "basically sound."[67]

The president appointed Komer ambassador to Turkey on October 28, leaving William Colby to contend with the problems of gauging pacification progress under Abrams's "one war" concept. Abrams already had commissioned a late-summer study on prioritizing pacification efforts and, under the auspices of Colby, the GVN initiated an Accelerated Pacification Campaign (APC) at year's end. The campaign endeavored to upgrade at least 1,000 contested hamlets to relatively secure ratings by January 31, 1969. U.S. military operations increased dramatically to keep the VC off balance, further depopulating the countryside. Measured by HES, the population living in secure areas rose by 1.7 million people in the last quarter of 1968, but critics doubted the statistics.[68] A militarily weakened enemy resorted increasingly to terrorism to disrupt GVN efforts in the countryside, making debatable the definition of "secure." President Thieu directed that the HES category of "contested" hamlets be stricken from official lexicon to help GVN negotiators in Paris. As with past body count efforts, pressures to demonstrate progress quickly resurfaced. One U.S. division commander told his officers he would not tolerate any "red hamlets" controlled by the Vietcong in his province by the end of the APC. In the process, the very meaning of pacification became lost in ambiguity. As an American civilian official lamented, the "plan goes forward, but it is only occupation, not pacification."[69]

Increasing the percentage of the population in secure areas ranked as only one objective of the Accelerated Pacification Campaign. MACV also aimed to increase the number of ralliers under the Chieu Hoi program, to expand local defense forces, and to neutralize monthly at least 3,000 of the Vietcong's political cadre. This last goal fell largely to "Phoenix," an intelligence coordination program that targeted the VC political organization for destruction by police and local militia forces. MACV believed the defeat of the Vietcong infrastructure (or VCI) "essential to preclude re-establishment of an operational or support base to which the VC can return."[70] CORDS had been formally attempting to neutralize the enemy's shadow government since mid-1967, yet under the APC provided expanded resources and greater emphasis to the program. Aided by American advisors, Phoenix operations ran the gamut from determining VC patterns of activity to assigning case officers to terrorist activities and suspected VC political cadre. While detractors alleged that Phoenix was nothing more than an assassination agency, U.S. officials replied that more than two-thirds of the some 81,740 Vietcong neutralized between 1968 and 1972 were captured rather than killed.[71]

Accurately measuring the effectiveness of Phoenix proved nearly impossible for U.S. advisors. Despite the colossal amount of data—the senior U.S. officer in Bien Hoa was filing sixty-three recurring monthly reports at the end of his tour in 1968—district advisors still could not assess popular attitudes with much confidence. HES overlooked the insurgency's political structure inside South Vietnamese hamlets and offered no insights into gauging villagers' passive resistance efforts that so often frustrated allied intelligence programs.[72] Worse, the U.S. mission set quotas for neutralizing the VC infrastructure. The results were predictable. VCI losses rose dramatically as South Vietnamese officials padded their reports with questionable neutralization figures. One Phoenix advisor recalled that the "statistics were so inflated that they lost their meaning." The CIA's year-end field assessment of Phoenix contended that the attack on the VCI had made "encouraging progress" though had not produced any considerable reductions in the communists' ability to perform their essential duties.[73]

The Accelerated Pacification Campaign, of which Phoenix was a part, coincided with a presidential decision in early November to halt the American bombing offensive in North Vietnam to help revive stalled peace negotiations in Paris. Thieu criticized both the announcement and an American move to include the NLF in the negotiations. The critique created a stir ahead of the presidential election pitting Vice President Hubert Humphrey against Republican challenger Richard Nixon.

Despite the commotion it caused within the allied camp, Thieu's independent stance further encouraged an already upbeat Ambassador Bunker. In late October, Bunker reported on Thieu's rising confidence, a trend toward national unity, and an improving military situation. Acknowledging that the GVN required much more popular support and that the enemy still retained the capacity for further offensives, Bunker turned to the question of whether the U.S. mission was gaining or losing ground. He wrote Johnson that he felt "optimistic" that the "steady, though not spectacular progress I have previously noted has continued and accelerated." Bunker's assessment relied on a wide range of metrics: an increase in performance and confidence among ARVN units, an increase of population living in relatively secure areas, and improvements in the strength and numbers of regional and popular forces. While Bunker conceded difficulties in quantifying many of the intangibles in his report, he concluded nonetheless that the "tide of history now seems to be moving with us and not against us."[74]

Despite Bunker's optimism and the virtues of Abrams's "one war" concept, disconnects remained between the military and political campaigns. Thieu's regime still faced many challenges, even though it had made considerable strides in the wake of Tet. As *Time* reported in late summer, "So complex and overwhelming are the problems confronting South Viet Nam that the nation's progress must be judged in terms of effort rather than achievement."[75] While aspects of pacification expanded under Abrams, military operations accelerated into overdrive. Abrams's summer and autumn operational guidance to field commanders demonstrated that the new MACV commander placed just as much importance on finding and destroying the enemy as did Westmoreland. Abrams told his principal subordinates that they must anticipate the enemy, "fix his major forces as far away as possible from our vital areas, and defeat him decisively." The former tank commander spoke of counteroffensives "to exploit enemy losses" and of all types of operations proceeding "simultaneously, aggressively, persistently, and intelligently." Abrams found the "manner in which all commanders have captured and demonstrated the spirit of the offensive" to be "extremely pleasing." Words like tempo, initiative, and results infused Abrams's guidance. His "one war" concept might elevate the importance of pacification and political efforts, but it was hardly a passive approach to counterinsurgency.[76]

Try as he might, Abrams could not change the nature of the war. MACV's staff, described by one correspondent as "short on initiative and long on efficiency," remained mired in a reactionary mode as the enemy maintained its pressure throughout 1968. Commanders in the field found it equally hard to embrace Abrams's "one war" concept. Conventional-minded army officers undertook pacification missions reluctantly, while continuing to rely on gunships, airstrikes, and heavy artillery.

Unable to break the grip of statistical mania, the 101st Airborne Division Commander kept a stack of three-by-five cards in his pocket denoting enemy casualty ratios, weapons losses, and breakdowns of ambush operations.[77] Senior officers saw little improvement in intelligence operations and the Vietcong, beaten but not annihilated after Tet, continued to evade American patrols. Perhaps most importantly, clear-cut, meaningful objectives escaped U.S. field commanders. Lieutenant General Weyand noted a problem neither Abrams could solve nor MACV's statistics could measure. "In a counter-insurgency, the objectives tend to be nebulous and more often than not they tend to be psychological or political in nature."[78] As 1968 came to an inconclusive close, Creighton Abrams and the MACV staff found themselves in an all too familiar strategic position.

A Turning Point?

Tet marked only one shock Americans experienced in a turbulent year both at home and abroad. In late January, North Korea seized the *USS Pueblo* and its eighty-three crew members, raising concerns of a coordinated global design between Korean and Vietnamese communists to spread thin U.S. resources. President Johnson received concurrent reports of a potential crisis developing near West Berlin. In August, the Soviet Union and Warsaw Pact allies invaded Czechoslovakia. The home front appeared no less chaotic. The dollar's strength abroad fell precipitously, triggering a gold crisis in Washington and Western capitals. The country mourned the loss of two prominent leaders to assassins' bullets—Martin Luther King, Jr., in April and Robert F. Kennedy in June. Racial tensions coursed through American society. At the Olympics in October, African American athletes Tommie Smith and John Carlos angered the nation with their "Black Power" salute while accepting track and field medals. Anti-war and inner-city riots broke out across the country, the violence culminating in August at the Democratic National Convention in Chicago. As one correspondent recalled, "the country seemed more than ever divided across gulfs of ignorance, mistrust and antipathy."[79]

Among all this turmoil, however, the Tet offensive coming at the beginning of the year astounded Americans in a special way. Their expectations elevated by months of positive progress reports, few understood how the enemy could launch such an unexpected attack across nearly all of South Vietnam. Nor could the public comprehend how MACV defined Tet as a great military victory when the war seemed no closer to ending. MACV broadcasted its tactical progress using a host of statistical data but it could not convey that data in such a way that led to perceptions of strategic momentum. In the larger picture, body counts and population security figures appeared meaningless when the enemy staged some of his attacks from villages considered among the most pacified in Vietnam. The offensive illustrated more than any other event in 1968 the problems of relying on and propagating flawed metrics as a public relations tool for declaring progress. Despite all of MACV's statistics, the American public still had no idea how or where the war was going. It appeared only that the army had been ineffective in suppressing violence to allow resumption of normal political and economic activities.[80]

While Americans at home viewed the war as one of enduring stalemate, in Vietnam, Tet prodded fresh assessments of the war. Correspondent Ward Just reported near year's end that "the best indicator of progress was that Americans saw more clearly how bad things were." On the MACV staff, officers including Abrams backed away from the public "statistical war . . . that the American press just *loves*." Expectations among the officer corps leveled off. A battalion commander in the 1st Cavalry Regiment noted in mid-summer that to "come over here and expect to make gigantic strides in a year is foolish."[81] Tet may not have been the decisive turning point for which Hanoi had hoped—though it did mark an end to U.S. escalation in Southeast Asia—but it did help to alter the U.S. mission's views on the nature of the conflict. Realizing the era of American escalation over, Abrams focused on improving South Vietnamese forces to counter rising NVA infiltration rates. Defense analysts suggested meanwhile that North Vietnam's manpower reserves could replace VC losses in the south while supporting even higher levels of mobilization. Furthermore, MACV recognized that ongoing negotiations in Paris complicated the coordination of efforts between the political and military campaigns. For now, the days of heady optimism emanating from MACV headquarters abated.[82]

This leveling of expectations was not accompanied by a clearer vision of how to measure success in South Vietnam. Beset by the army's one-year rotation policy, MACV could expect only five to six months of work from staff officers before they left to more valued duty with field units. Promotions relied on command assignments, not staff work. In the process, officers with little staff experience waiting for command spent minimal intellectual energy on the problems of identifying useful indicators for progress and effectiveness. Abrams, like Westmoreland before him, found no choice but to rely on statistics. Reports continued to stress figures relating to battalion days in the field, force ratios, personnel losses, weapons losses, population security, hamlet security, VCI neutralization, and incidents of enemy attacks. One MACV report even conceded the massive data collection efforts to be futile. "In conclusion, there appears to be no significant relationship among the data portrayed herein and therefore no firm conclusions can be drawn." The admission neared absurdity in a time of war. The MACV staff had been collecting information for the sake of collecting information.[83]

The lack of intellectual effort on MACV's staff meant that its system for measuring progress, even after a tumultuous 1968, would remain deficient for the rest of the war. At year's end, officers expressed cautious confidence in dubious HES results showing more than 76 percent of the population living in relatively secure hamlets. Others found encouragement in local civilians voluntarily taking American troops to hidden caches of enemy weapons and supplies, an indicator that should have received much more weight within MACV headquarters. The embassy mirrored the army's restrained optimism. "Adding up the plusses and minuses" in his final report to President Johnson, Ambassador Bunker stated "objectively that 1968 has been a year of very substantial progress."[84] Bunker's assessment, however, spoke nothing of substantiating such claims to the American public. To domestic observers, the loss of 16,511 U.S. military personnel in 1968 had achieved nothing. The U.S. mission in Vietnam, particularly MACV, had ignored the problem of reconciling battlefield victories with political expectations at home. U.S. Army officers simply could not comprehend the lack of public support. In general, they failed to appreciate the larger political framework of their "limited" war. Why Americans spoke of stalemate when all military indicators suggested progress confounded the MACV staff. In the context of measuring progress, 1968 ended not only with a stalemate in the war but a stalemate in thinking about the war.[85]

"Never has a military force had so many names of contempt for the people they were supposed to be trying to help."

—PHILIP D. BEIDLER, *Late Thoughts on an Old War*

7 "A Time for Testing"

IN A LARGE sense, 1969 began in a manner indistinguishable from previous years in South Vietnam. Optimistic reports flooded from Saigon while MACV carried out substantial military operations to maintain pressure on the enemy. In the wake of Giap's 1968 Tet offensive, confident analysts described the Vietcong military and political movement as broken. Their charts and figures reflected that enthusiasm. The number of civilians willingly supporting the VC had dropped sharply in recent months, and the South Vietnamese government appeared more stable than ever. At the same time, Creighton Abrams pursued his enemy with vigor. MACV's commander perceived a momentum shift and looked to exploit it. He exhorted his officers to "stay on top of them and smash every move they try to make."[1] As in the past, sweeping military offensives opened the new year. On January 22, the Marines carried out Operation Dewey Canyon, a two-month-long search-and-destroy mission aimed at enemy logistic bases in I CTZ. Other large-scale "preemptive operations" followed. Emphasizing high totals in enemy body counts and enemy-to-friendly kill ratios, the MACV staff concluded that these operations were successful. They had restricted enemy movement and denied him the initiative.[2]

Despite MACV's optimistic assessments and the devastating losses inflicted on the enemy, the war remained complex. Field commanders struggled to balance the competing demands of Abrams's "one war" strategy, attempting to coordinate combat actions and pacification programs with efforts to improve the effectiveness of South Vietnam's army. In the 1st Infantry Division, U.S. Army officers juggled countless tasks in early 1969. Companies and platoons provided logistical support to regional and popular forces, assigned "sponsors" to local hamlets, performed civic action operations, and conducted cordon and search missions.[3] The statistics keeping track of these disparate undertakings reached new heights as MACV altered some of its methods to support Abrams's "one war" approach. The enemy also modified his tactics. American commanders noticed a reversion to hit-and-run guerrilla and terrorist attacks as the VC looked to injure the allies while preventing their own heavy losses. In early February, the *New York Times* reported that Vietcong terrorism had increased nearly 30 percent during the prior month. MACV's officers realized the change in enemy tactics (to avoid large-scale clashes with American forces) but, as was so often the case, could only guess at the enemy's intentions. As one senior officer stated, "There are lots of theories that sound good, but who knows. The increase could mean almost anything."[4]

These changes, on both sides of the battlefield, coincided not only with the new year, but with the inauguration of a new administration. Two days before Dewey Canyon began, Chief Justice Earl Warren swore in Richard M. Nixon as the nation's thirty-seventh president. Nixon wanted an end to the war in Vietnam, in part to concentrate on his larger goals of improving relations with China and the Soviet Union. These foreign policy designs hinged on reversing the "Americanization" of the war while fortifying South Vietnam to withstand future communist aggression. As Nixon's national security advisor Henry Kissinger recalled, the basic challenge was to withdraw American forces "as an expression of policy and not as a collapse."[5] The new president's world views surely molded these desired ends. Despite hopes of restructuring global relations, Nixon, along with Kissinger, remained as committed as his predecessors to opposing global communism and winning the Cold War. Withdrawal from Vietnam required maintaining an image of strength during peace negotiations if the United States was to retain credibility as a world power and deterrent to communist expansion. To serve the new administration's geopolitical interests, the war's ending could not be construable as a U.S. defeat.[6]

The process of de-Americanizing the war, soon dubbed "Vietnamization" by Secretary of Defense Melvin Laird, would add yet another facet to MACV's already bloated system for measuring and reporting progress. MACV now had to determine and assess indicators of ARVN effectiveness in providing security for the South Vietnam nation. Finding metrics for evaluating Vietnamization proved to be no small problem. Measurements of success for search-and-destroy or pacification missions might not apply to the training of ARVN forces. Effectiveness against insurgents might not indicate effectiveness against conventional threats. MACV had to consider a host of political, military, economic, and social issues that would lead to the South Vietnamese assuming full responsibility for their country's defense and political viability. Ambassador Ellsworth Bunker maintained in January that his "yardstick for success here is what the Vietnamese can do for themselves, because that eventually is the ultimate test." Officials in the U.S. mission, however, found it difficult to reach consensus on the details of Bunker's personal yardstick. The CIA, for instance, reported that same month that it was "almost impossible to measure" efforts to gain the people's allegiance. Yet for Vietnamization to succeed, the GVN had to achieve demonstrable political reform and stability in the countryside.[7]

The Nixon administration's strategic revisions further complicated the process of Vietnamization. In shifting more of the war's burden to the South Vietnamese, the new president quietly was redefining success in Southeast Asia. Rather than winning a military victory, achieving an honorable peace emerged as the guiding strategic objective. (Both Nixon and Laird believed flagging domestic support by early 1969 had limited their options.) Abrams would preside over an American war effort increasingly concerned with limiting allied casualties while arranging for U.S. troop withdrawals. The impending American departure did little to ease MACV's problems. With flawed metrics for measuring progress in both counterinsurgency combat actions and pacification efforts, Abrams's staff now confronted the additional challenge of evaluating ARVN's progress for assuming control of the war. MACV claimed the "most valid measurement of success or failure in military training is demonstrated combat effectiveness."[8] Equating progress with effectiveness, though, had bedeviled earlier efforts in evaluating counterinsurgency operations. Killing the enemy had not led necessarily to political progress in Saigon. More problematic in 1969, U.S. military advisors remained divided over the most pressing threat to South Vietnam. Should ARVN be training to defeat conventional North Vietnamese forces or a battered yet resilient insurgency in the countryside?[9]

A New Administration, A New Strategy

To both Nixon and Kissinger, the stalemate in Vietnam dangerously exposed the limitations of American power abroad. This recognition did not come easy for a president intent on fighting the Cold War and containing communist expansion. Realizing, in Nixon's words, that "total military victory was no longer possible," the new administration sought a "fair negotiated settlement that would preserve the independence of South Vietnam."[10] In the process, Nixon meant also to preserve American honor and credibility as he withdrew from the conflict. The nation's position as a global leader would be damaged irreparably if world leaders viewed the

American withdrawal as a defeat. Maintaining credibility in negotiations with Hanoi and on the world stage with Peking and Moscow would drive Nixon's Vietnam policy for the remainder of the war. Unfortunately, the dynamics making the Vietnam War so unmanageable under Johnson hardly diminished in 1969. The North had no intention of surrendering its goal of national unification. The South remained dependent on American backing for survival. At home, public and congressional support for a seemingly open-ended war continued to diminish. Nixon wanted to uphold American commitments to the GVN, but his desire to end the war while achieving larger foreign policy goals portended a change to U.S. strategy in Southeast Asia.[11]

National Security Study Memorandum (NSSM) 1 served as the administration's first official steps toward rethinking strategy. Under the auspices of Kissinger, NSSM 1 requested all agencies involved in the war to review, evaluate, and even disagree on wide-ranging questions relating to South Vietnam. Kissinger knew the "criteria by which to measure progress have been hard to come by" and intended for the CIA, State Department, the Joint Chiefs of Staff, and MACV to provide honest assessments that might clarify the U.S. position in Vietnam.[12] NSSM 1 queried enemy strength and capabilities, differences of opinion on ARVN improvement, the security situation in South Vietnam, and the impact of changes to military tactics in the last six to twelve months. If Kissinger wanted to air disagreements, his respondents did not disappoint. The CIA and MACV continued to disagree over total VC strength in South Vietnam. (Relying on its customary statistical indicators, MACV provided some of the most optimistic prognoses while downplaying, if not suppressing, any of its own shortcomings.) Other discrepancies focused on the impact of negotiations on military operations, the rate of political progress in Saigon, and potential implications of U.S. force reductions. Most, however, did agree that ARVN could not stand alone against the enemy threat, now or in the foreseeable future. As Kissinger concluded, "There was no consensus as to facts, much less to policy."[13]

The NSSM 1 review exposed the difficulties of gaining a clear strategic picture in the counterinsurgency environment of Vietnam. Too many agencies reached too many different conclusions. The president, though, already had decided upon a new strategic approach before studying all the NSSM 1 responses. Kissinger's examination process had occurred concurrently with, not before, Nixon's formulation of a five-point strategy "to end the war and win the peace." The new Vietnam policy depended first on pacification, still defined as "meaningful continuing security for the Vietnamese people." Nixon also sought diplomatic isolation of North Vietnam and placed increasing weight on negotiations in Paris. Gradual withdrawal of U.S. forces comprised the fourth aspect of Nixon's strategy. As the president recalled,

"Americans needed tangible evidence that we were winding down the war, and the South Vietnamese needed to be given more responsibility for their defense." This final element of Nixon's plan, Vietnamization, aimed at training and equipping South Vietnam's armed forces so they could defend the country on their own. (Political reform in Saigon was to accompany the military side of Vietnamization.) "Our whole strategy," Nixon declared, "depended on whether this program succeeded."[14]

Vietnamization had its roots in MACV operational planning dating back to 1963. Westmoreland had held similar long-term ambitions and had stated publicly in 1967 that the final phases of his own strategy included upgrading ARVN equipment to allow the South Vietnamese to "take on an ever-increasing share of the war."[15] Although Tet had disrupted these plans, Nixon intended to withdraw U.S. forces once ARVN sufficiently developed its capabilities. In essence, Abrams would be realizing the goals of his predecessor. While serving as Westmoreland's deputy, Abrams had led American efforts at increasing ARVN effectiveness. Better than any senior officer, he knew the problems entailed in helping South Vietnam's military forces achieve self-sufficiency. Training while fighting was not easy. The Vietnamization program thus proceeded slowly. While news agencies pressed the administration on timetables for withdrawing American troops, senior officers maintained privately that U.S. advisory and security elements would have to remain in Vietnam "for some years to come."[16] Nixon meanwhile resolved not to be pressured by domestic opinion. The ability of GVN to assume responsibility for internal security and for self-government, not demands from anti-war critics, would determine the pace of U.S. withdrawals.

Predictably, the enemy decided to insert itself into the Vietnamization equation. On February 23, with Nixon visiting Europe, communist mortar and rocket attacks hit more than 200 cities, villages, and military installations across South Vietnam. The allies beat back the simultaneous ground attacks, though most enemy main force units avoided heavy contact. The goal of illustrating their capacity to conduct a country-wide attack had been met. The loss of more than 400 American troops infuriated Nixon. The president viewed the "savage offensive" as a "deliberate test" and immediately sought retaliation. Less than a month later, on March 17, Nixon ordered the secret bombing of enemy sanctuaries inside Cambodia. Nixon wanted not only to disrupt North Vietnamese supply lines along the Ho Chi Minh Trail but also signal to Hanoi that he would not be manipulated. If necessary, he would, and could, escalate the war.[17]

The bombing of Cambodia came on the heels of Secretary of Defense Laird's five-day visit to South Vietnam, which began on March 5. The former Wisconsin congressman received briefings from Abrams and Bunker, spoke with President

Thieu, and toured I, II, and IV corps tactical zones. He concentrated on U.S. troop withdrawals, informing MACV that its task was to "shift the combat burden 'promptly and methodically' to the South Vietnamese."[18] Abrams objected to establishing any withdrawal timetables while Wheeler, ever looking to expand the war outside of South Vietnam proper, recommended ground operations into the southern DMZ and Cambodia. Laird's report to Nixon contained the established range of both good and bad news. The United States had enough strength in Vietnam, Laird believed, to prevent the enemy from achieving a military victory. Moreover, nearly 80 percent of the population lived in "relatively secure" areas. Laird acknowledged, however, that "none of our officials, either military or civilian, is under any illusion that the battle in South Vietnam can be brought to a military conclusion within six months, a year or even several years." The defense secretary left Vietnam further disappointed by the slow rate of progress in increasing ARVN effectiveness. Nonetheless, he recommended to Nixon that conditions permitted the redeployment of 50,000 to 70,000 U.S. troops during the remainder of 1969. A keen observer of public opinion, Laird knew the administration had to demonstrate some progress that the war was winding down.[19]

Laird's sober testimony not only reemphasized the role of Vietnamization, but signaled impending changes to U.S. global and military strategies. Nixon visited Guam in late July to confer with Thieu. Meeting with reporters, the American president stated that unless threatened by nuclear powers, Asian nations should be responsible for defending themselves against internal and external aggression. While the "Guam Doctrine"—soon renamed the "Nixon Doctrine," according to the president's wishes—hardly influenced projected plans in Vietnam, it did serve as an official precursor for a change to MACV's mission statement.[20]

Formulated in early July, the revised mission for the American effort in Vietnam backed away from defeating the enemy and forcing his removal from South Vietnam. MACV would instead provide "maximum assistance" for strengthening ARVN forces while supporting pacification and targeting enemy supply areas. Abrams, however, insisted that he must continue offensive operations if he were to keep U.S. casualties to a minimum. A change in mission could not concede the initiative to the enemy. For Abrams, security remained a crucial element to counterinsurgency. The new U.S. objective defined success as assuring the South Vietnamese people's right "to determine their future without outside interference."[21] In late August, MACV received its new mission. Defeating the enemy was no longer an expressed goal for Abrams and his command. Kissinger later doubted if the changed orders "made any practical difference. Given the administration's commitment to withdrawal, they reflected capabilities, whatever the doctrine."[22] No public announcements accompanied the change.

The modification of MACV's mission statement held obvious implications for measuring progress. If the definition of success changed, MACV then would have to reconsider its metrics for determining that success. Hanoi's leaders complicated matters as they too reassessed their own strategy in 1969. MACV's increasing emphasis on pacification, coupled with military operations, was upsetting communist plans in South Vietnam's countryside. Cadre numbers diminished, as did popular support for the insurgency. Tax collections and recruiting numbers fell dramatically. Shifting their efforts to political training, the VC consolidated their local forces and avoided large engagements. "The Communists seem less interested in losing men in big frontal assaults against major targets," stated one analyst, "than strengthening themselves at the rural levels."[23] MACV planners heralded this reversion to guerrilla warfare as a sign of allied progress. If the enemy threat remained at current levels, U.S. troop withdrawals might be possible by year's end. Yet according to revolutionary warfare theory, flexibility between the political and military struggle served as a guiding strategic principle. Reversion to earlier stages of revolutionary war did not necessarily mean that the communists were losing. Defeated militarily in the aftermath of Tet, the enemy shifted, if somewhat belatedly, to attacking the allies' pacification program while reconstituting its political and military strength. With Nixon expressing interest in negotiations and a withdrawal of U.S. forces from Southeast Asia, a strategy of waiting seemed increasingly attractive to Hanoi's leaders.[24]

Abrams attempted to match the enemy's synchronization of political and military factors with his "one war" approach. The fluid strategic environment in 1969, however, made the assessment of progress and effectiveness exceedingly difficult. As Army Chief of Staff Westmoreland reported in April, five wars still were being waged in Vietnam—political, sociological, economic, psychological, and military. Abrams told his commanders that same month that their focus should be on pacification, ARVN expansion and improvement, and combat operations. "Each is to receive the highest priority."[25] Such guidance offered little direction to MACV's staff. Though Abrams sought to view the conflict as an integrated whole, he established no dominant indicators to tie his "one war" together. Thus, MACV continued to be overwhelmed by its voluminous statistical metrics for gauging progress and effectiveness. Changes in strategies, objectives, and definitions for success ultimately had made little impact on Abrams's reporting system. Even after MACV's mission statement changed, the measurement of progress briefings remained unaltered from Westmoreland's days in command.[26] Abrams regarded the enemy as a "total system" but, like his predecessor, he could not settle on metrics suitable for assessing the enemy's intentions, capabilities, or political resiliency.

In Defense of Body Counts

Strategic shifts aside, putting pressure on the enemy remained fundamental to Abrams's operational guidance and "one war" approach. To many Americans, firepower still governed the battlefield. Laird described U.S. military tactics in May as "maximum military pressure on the enemy consistent with the lowest possible casualties." Senior officers concurred with this apparent double-talk, arguing that aggressive, offensive operations were the only way to minimize U.S. casualties. Supporting this line, Kissinger believed that military pressure on the enemy would avert the kind of protracted negotiations that had ended the Korean War.[27] Abrams, a tanker with no penchant for the defensive, pushed his subordinates forward into battle. As he told a command briefing late in the year, combat operations "basically are designed to keep the bad men away from where the pacification's going on." The 1969 Combined Campaign Plan further illustrated an important aspect of MACV's tone that year. Among its numerous objectives, the goal to "inflict more losses on the enemy than he can replace" ranked fourth. (Defeating the VC and NVA forces ranked first.)[28] Despite changes to strategies and mission statements, the U.S. Army in Vietnam still was searching for Westmoreland's crossover point.

However flawed it was as assessment tool, the body count still appealed to some American officers. Inside the Mekong Delta, commanders in the 9th Infantry Division counted corpses to evaluate both unit effectiveness and progress against the VC threat. Operation Speedy Express, lasting from December 1, 1968 through May 31, 1969, revealed the controversial role that such metrics continued to play within MACV. Under Major General Julian J. Ewell, the 9th Division flooded the Mekong with small patrols for the sole purpose of finding the enemy. (Ironically, the operation coincided with the Accelerated Pacification Campaign.) Fellow officers considered Ewell a fine tactician, and his dispersed style of fighting initiated frequent engagements with the enemy. Ewell, however, also was an active proponent of the body count, earning him the sobriquet "the Butcher of the Mekong Delta." During Speedy Express, Ewell lived up to his nickname. His division reported 10,899 VC killed in action and an additional 2,579 captured. During the same six-month period, only 242 Americans were killed, generating an astonishing 40.8:1 kill ratio.[29] No other division in Vietnam had achieved such results.

The results, though, were suspect. In killing over 10,000 enemy soldiers, the 9th Division captured only 688 individual and 60 crew-served weapons. MACV offered a number of contributing factors for the relatively low weapons count—a high percentage of kills made at night and by aviation units, the ease by which the VC could dispose of weapons in the Delta's canals and paddies, and the rapid movement of

FIGURE 7.1 The fighting continues. 9th Infantry Division soldiers disembark from their helicopters during an offensive operation, March 29, 1969.
Source RG282S, Kerwin Collection, Box 1, 9th ID Photo Album

troops, which left little time for detailed searches. Reporters, however, inquired about the possible high number of unarmed and innocent civilians included in Ewell's body counts. The division's after-action report claimed implausibly that discrepancies resulted because "many individuals in the VC and guerrilla units are not armed with weapons."[30] CORDS officials further accused Ewell of heavy-handedness. John Paul Vann, the senior CORDS advisor in IV Corps, criticized the 9th Infantry for alienating civilians in the Delta and believed the division's presence counterproductive to pacification efforts. HES figures supported Vann's allegations. By the end of 1969, less than 50 percent of the hamlets in both Dinh Tuong and Kien Hoa provinces were under government control.[31]

Ewell remained unfazed by the criticism and defended robustly the use of kill ratios and statistical measurements. For Ewell, a unit's productivity mattered most. The division commander was not interested in activity that did not produce results, arguing that "contacts" with the enemy determined unit effectiveness. "A division that achieved 25 contacts each day will be very good, 50 outstanding, and 75 would be phenomenal." Subordinate commanders no doubt felt pressure to report contact with the enemy, but Ewell went a step further. Daily briefings charted not only the number of contacts, but the number of successful contacts. Units achieved success when they "either killed somebody, or wounded them, or they dropped their supplies and you picked them up."[32] Within this philosophy, body counts, while important, mattered less than elimination or exchange ratios. These measurements of VC versus American dead drove operations like Speedy Express and surely accounted for the high number of "enemy" casualties. Still, one officer attending a briefing by Ewell recalled that the first seven charts highlighted body counts with discussion on the topic lasting for twenty minutes.[33]

Ewell's defense of kill ratios and body counts masked unresolved issues with these well-worn statistics. Certainly, killing the enemy remained important to both Abrams's "one war" approach and counterinsurgency in general. Ewell's infatuation with combat patrol output, though, slighted continuing deficiencies in language training and intelligence gathering. Lieutenant Colonel David Hackworth, a battalion commander in the 9th Infantry, recalled that in 1969 his unit still "had no way to tell the good guys from the bad guys."[34] The division's emphasis on body counts led even officers as aggressive as Hackworth to worry about their productivity. Infantry commanders were required to carry three-by-five cards with their monthly body count totals, even though the main threat came not from enemy contact but from booby traps. The pressure on subordinates reached new heights, as revealed by one company commander's radio operator. "I don't even need a watch out there in the field," he reported "because I know every 15 minutes, the man's going to be on the horn asking me where his body count is." During Speedy Express, the command even threatened infantry units that they would not be extracted from the field until they had achieved an acceptable body count.[35] Under such circumstances, a 40:1 kill ratio appeared increasingly less surprising.

Ewell's stress on exchange ratios made sense, given Abrams's charge to minimize U.S. casualties in 1969. The same month Speedy Express came to a close in the Delta, the 101st Airborne Division experienced the full force of public condemnation for its own costly operations in the A Shau Valley. Deep in the western portion of I CTZ, the valley served as a major infiltration route for communist forces streaming into South Vietnam from Laos. MACV ordered Major General Melvin Zais, the 101st Division Commander, to destroy enemy caches and installations in the A Shau while preventing escape of enemy forces back into their Laotian sanctuaries. Anchoring the valley stood Ap Bia Mountain (*Dong Ap Bia*), though army maps listed it as Hill 937 according to its elevation. Unable to ignore this key piece of terrain, Zais directed an infantry battalion to assault the hill on May 10. U.S. troops soon encountered a well dug-in enemy with no intentions of surrendering his base areas. The stubborn defenders stunned unit commanders who had become accustomed to recent NVA tactics of avoiding heavy combat. Zais nonetheless pressed his men forward. The heavy, close fighting raged for nearly two weeks, marked by five abortive attempts to capture the hill. On May 20, Zais's men finally succeeded, though the battle exacted a heavy price: 56 Americans lay dead, another 420 wounded.[36]

The media storm over such high casualties for an insignificant piece of terrain (U.S. forces immediately abandoned the hill and moved on) replicated public outcry in the wake of Tet. American troops dubbed the battle "Hamburger Hill," a morbid reminder of being chewed up like hamburger meat. Reporters questioned the sense of MACV's "aggressive posture" when the war was supposed to be winding down. Correspondent Jay Scharbutt, observing the battle, quoted one trooper who snarled that his battalion commander "won't stop until he kills every damn one of us."[37] Both soldier and reporter could not understand why Zais had not backed off to let B-52 bombing runs demolish the hill. American lawmakers voiced equal outrage. Senator Edward Kennedy called the attacks "senseless and irresponsible," arguing that "American boys are too valuable to be sacrificed for a false sense of military pride." Texas representative George H. Mason contended that the army was undercutting public confidence with its errors. Even the State Department recoiled from the bloody confrontation, with one official conceding that the "last thing we needed was Hamburger Hill."[38]

Army officials quickly defended the embattled Zais. A Pentagon spokesman stated that "Hamburger Hill was strategically important," while Westmoreland cabled Zais, congratulating him on a "gallant operation." The 101st's commander pointed to more than 600 enemy dead in validation of his men's sacrifices. He argued that bombing runs alone could not have dislodged an enemy deeply dug into Ap Bia Mountain. Besides, Zais reasoned, his mission was to destroy enemy forces. As he told one reporter, "If we find him on any other hill in the A Shau Valley, in Vietnam, I can assure you I'll attack him."[39] Zais's argument underscored the inherent fragility in Abrams's "one war" concept. The call of battle still summoned U.S. Army officers, despite claims that pacification and Vietnamization ranked among the more important missions in South Vietnam. It is doubtful that Zais would have come under such fire in 1966 or 1967. However, the political environment had changed in the aftermath of 1968's Tet offensive. Neither the Nixon administration nor the American public would tolerate further high U.S. casualties. Abrams no doubt realized this shift, accepting his task to minimize losses. Yet officers like Abrams could not shed their profession's cultural predilections for aggressively pursuing the enemy. Even U.S. counterinsurgency doctrine, they could argue, stressed the importance of seizing the initiative from insurgent forces.

Abrams, like Westmoreland before him, was partially to blame. Mixed signals continued to radiate from MACV headquarters. How could combat operations, pacification, and Vietnamization *all* "receive the highest priority?" In the wake of

Hamburger Hill, Abrams told his senior officers to persist in hard fighting but if possible avoid "similar occasions of compressed contact." The army's chain of command emphasized aggressiveness yet suggested MACV avoid the terms "search and destroy" and "reconnaissance in force."[40] Such martial idioms aroused too much excitement in the press. Given this bewildering guidance, few field commanders tied together the threads of Abrams's "one war" concept. Even when units did attempt to synchronize their operations, the cultural pull toward counting bodies upended their efforts. Ewell's 9th Division actually coordinated its area of operations with HES reports in a unique plan to find the enemy and improve pacification. The theory made sense; in its zeal to obtain successful contacts, however, the division alienated much of the population and failed to break the VC's political infrastructure. Ewell defended his approach. "Put maximum military pressure on the enemy. This helps pacification more than anything else."[41] MACV appeared to agree. Ewell received his third star and in April Abrams gave him command of II Field Force, the largest army combat command in Vietnam.

Measuring "Vietnamization"

The media attention accorded to Hamburger Hill and body counts overshadowed larger American efforts to improve and modernize South Vietnam's armed forces. While combat actions and pacification efforts continued unabated, MACV added Vietnamization to its growing list of activities requiring measurement and assessment. Since December 1968, MACV's staff formally had been studying the problem of transferring responsibility to the ARVN under a number of rubrics—military resources, capabilities, missions, and criteria for evaluation.[42] During the early months of 1969, ARVN forces increasingly integrated themselves into U.S. combat operations. Abrams fought hard to break the barriers between allied units. Only by working together could American units help develop ARVN's capacity for providing national security once U.S. forces withdrew. Defense Secretary Laird reviewed for Nixon the numerous actions required to implement the military component of Vietnamization. Abrams would have to develop AVRN leadership and morale while reducing desertion rates. Intelligence and logistic programs needed improvement, as did operational planning. Abrams also had to determine an optimal force structure for ARVN and help develop a strategy and tactical approach best suited to its capabilities. Arguably, MACV had solved few of these issues for its own armed forces.[43]

Fundamental problems faced Abrams in building up South Vietnam's armed forces. After President Thieu announced a national mobilization following Tet in

1968, the size of the regular army and popular and regional forces had increased substantially. In two years, the total armed forces grew by 40 percent. Finding enough competent officers during this rapid expansion proved nearly impossible. Corruption and political favors undermined officer selection and promotion. Additionally, capable leaders in ARVN, of which there were many, too often found themselves and their units relegated to secondary roles prior to Abrams's elevation to MACV command.[44] These officers consequently lacked practical experience in coordinating the multifaceted operations required for effective counterinsurgency. Problems within the enlisted ranks rivaled those among ARVN's leadership. *Newsweek* offered a brutally honest appraisal of the typical South Vietnamese trooper who was "often dragooned into an army where he is poorly trained, badly paid, insufficiently indoctrinated about why he is fighting—and, for the most part, led by incompetent officers."[45] Simply increasing the number of soldiers in the armed forces and supplying them with better weapons would not achieve the larger goals of Vietnamization.

Abrams realized the enormity of his task. Despite years of advisory work, MACV still possessed no accurate measurement system for evaluating South Vietnam's army. As early as mid-1967, Westmoreland's staff had developed a Review and Analysis

FIGURE 7.2 Testing Vietnamization. ARVN soldiers prepare to board American helicopters for an air assault against North Vietnamese Army units operating in the Mekong River Delta.
Source RG123S, Vietnam Photos, Miscellaneous Collection, South Vietnamese Armed Forces, Box 54, Army Folder

System for RVNAF Progress. The review, though, only occurred semi-annually and left unanswered a number of critical questions. How, for example, should MACV measure ARVN confidence or morale? Staff officers, steeped in the process of accumulating vast amounts of quantitative data, turned to metrics affording calculation. In assessing ARVN's progress, MACV counted strength totals, desertion rates, training programs, weapons upgrades, and of course numbers of enemy killed.[46] The data collection effort provided little clarity. In early June 1969, Secretary Laird described for Nixon the perpetual "number of unknowns" affecting ARVN improvement. These included "the quality of leadership, the motivation of the armed forces, the psychological reaction of the South Vietnamese to US redeployments, and the ability of the South Vietnamese to find a stronger organizational structure." American officers remained uncertain over ARVN's ability to handle alone the dual threat of Vietcong and North Vietnamese forces.[47]

This uncertainty stemmed not only from difficulties in measuring intangibles like morale and leadership, but also arose from discouraging reports filtering into MACV headquarters from U.S. advisors in the field. Little had changed here since the early 1960s. Officers remained separated from their Vietnamese counterparts by cultural and linguistic divides. Often making slow headway training ARVN mechanics and technicians, many advisors spent more time teaching English than specialty skills needed to maintain modern American equipment. The CORDS Advisor Orientation Course offered slight assistance in preparing army officers for their duties. One newly assigned advisor reported that classes "were taught by unprepared instructors or by substitutes who were as young and inexperienced as the new Lieutenants in the group."[48]

Poor relations between these advisors and U.S. combat units proved equally trying. In the 25th Infantry's sector, a senior division officer sought to gerrymander the border lines between three contested hamlets to produce one relatively secure hamlet. When the local U.S. district advisor refused, the relationship between the division and the advisory team, already among the worst in Vietnam, deteriorated further. While Abrams considered American advisors the "glue" holding ARVN together, these officers faced a daunting task. Several in fact doubted that they could help build an effective fighting force in time to meet Nixon and Laird's withdrawal plans.[49]

Unfortunately, advisors maintained poor relations with ARVN units as well. Many Americans, advisors and combat troops alike, looked upon South Vietnamese soldiers with unreserved scorn. They referred to their allies as "little people," "squint eyes," "gooks," "Marvin the Arvin," and "Marvelous Marv." U.S. commanders lamented the lack of motivation among ARVN troops when compared to the Vietcong. *Newsweek* captured the sentiment, running a story under the byline "Their Lions—Our Rabbits."

Vietnamese peasants fared no better in Americans' eyes. One soldier wrote home in July, "I still can't believe how these people live. They're just like animals. They live way out in the middle of nowhere."[50] Soldiers made few distinctions in their general disdain for all Vietnamese, especially in an environment where it remained so difficult to tell friend from foe. The army's one-year rotation system likely exacerbated the contempt. It is doubtful the U.S. battalion commander who dubbed his helicopter a "Gookmobile" and recorded his kills on the fuselage with a painted row of conical hats held his South Vietnamese counterparts in high regard. Vietnamization could not undo racism or years of critical attitudes held toward Asians. Advisors certainly treated their allies with greater respect than most combat soldiers, for daily contact often broke down many of the cultural barriers. They understood better than most the suffering that the Vietnamese had endured in living with war for so long. Still, racial prejudices impinged on assessments of ARVN effectiveness.[51]

These prejudices crept into MACV's reporting system for measuring the progress of Vietnamization because MACV had to address those "unknowns" reported by Secretary Laird. U.S. withdrawals depended upon the intangibles of ARVN leadership, morale, and will to fight. In 1966 and 1967, advisors in the field reported their assessments using the Senior Advisor Monthly Evaluation (SAME) reports. They rated ARVN units simplistically as satisfactory, marginal, or unsatisfactory. While the report contained a variety of statistics, it left the overall unit evaluation to the advisor. Thus, an advisor might mark an ARVN regiment as low in combat effectiveness yet award the unit an overall satisfactory rating. In early 1968, Westmoreland called for a new report offering a "quantified objective evaluation" of ARVN development.[52] Named the System for Evaluating the Effectiveness of RVNAF (SEER), the new scheme addressed the three broad areas of military performance, personnel and logistic statuses, and historical trends. Advisors filled out a 157-question survey that covered topics ranging from leadership and unit discipline to training and equipment. One advisor described it as a "multiple guess-type report which requires about three hours." The MACV quarterly report included a chart titled "distribution of effort," placing heavy emphasis on combat operations. In an effort to target weaker units for remedial training, MACV used the SEER reports to rank similar South Vietnamese units against one another. By 1969, the reporting system had become one of Laird's basic tools for measuring RVNAF progress and thus determining U.S. withdrawal schedules.[53]

While the SEER measured regular unit effectiveness, MACV instituted yet another program to evaluate South Vietnam's regional and popular forces. The Territorial Forces Evaluation System (TFES) collated the standard range of tactical statistics—total days of combat operations, friendly and enemy losses, and weapons captured. Like SEER, however, TFES included numerous subjective questions relating to unit performance. Advisors were asked multiple choice questions (good, satisfactory, marginal) on unit aggressiveness, morale, and leadership.[54] Both reports on South Vietnamese military effectiveness filtered into an ever-growing data bank that included statistical information from hundreds of sources. MACV processed information not only from SEER and TFES but from other analytic tools as well: the Hamlet Evaluation System, the Terrorist Incident Reporting System, the Revolutionary Development Cadre Evaluation System, and the National Police Evaluation System. Abrams's staff realized that the sheer weight of data threatened to collapse its reporting structure. In mid-1969, MACV attempted to coordinate its reporting requirements, reduce the flow of information, and make the system more responsive.[55] The system changed little, however, because the "one war" concept demanded measurement in all areas of allied political and military activity. MACV's reporting framework would remain a churning pool of unreliable data.

Though both Laird and Abrams relied on them, SEER and TFES proved to be flawed assessment tools. American advisors too often assessed South Vietnamese effectiveness by American standards. Army officers denigrated their counterparts' lack of aggressiveness and continued measuring results by enemy KIA and weapons captured. According to MACV's command history for 1969, high body counts were "indicative of improved leadership" among ARVN units.[56] Advisors frequently underrated training and rehabilitation in favor of combat and security missions. Additionally, ARVN, like the U.S. Army, conducted diverse missions across South Vietnam's wide-ranging geographical regions. SEER did not distinguish between performance in pacification missions or combat actions or if ARVN units operated in friendly or hostile territory. Defining effectiveness against different types of threat proved equally problematic. Should ARVN prepare for conventional battle against North Vietnamese regulars or for counterinsurgency against Vietcong guerrillas? Effectiveness against main force units did not translate necessarily into effectiveness against insurgents, a point of which many American commanders were well aware. Abrams discussed the inconsistencies with his staff, yet MACV continued building ARVN in the image of the U.S. Army. The SEER reporting framework never considered whether American tactics, equipment, and organizational structures might not be those best suited for South Vietnam's armed forces.[57]

Like nearly all of MACV's metrics, pressure to demonstrate progress biased reporting on ARVN effectiveness. As early as mid-1968, U.S. officials worried about how to dramatize South Vietnamese participation in the war. By 1969, Wheeler was pressing Abrams for SEER reports highlighting progress that could "give us ammunition to use in our contacts with the press." Despite these internal pressures, media accounts admitting forward steps still described ARVN's performance as "mediocre." One senior officer confirmed this appraisal. "Improvement is painfully slow," he lamented. "It takes a tremendous amount of effort. If you want to be discouraged, this is the place to settle down."[58] MACV continued to press for positive reports because the goal of U.S. withdrawals depended on Vietnamization's success. As the *New York Times* noted, mimicking Kissinger, the problem was how to disengage without causing collapse. Anti-war critics claimed the pace of withdrawal too slow, while U.S. advisors worried they were proceeding at a rate faster than ARVN could improve. Consequently, many South Vietnamese military and civilian officials felt increasingly abandoned by their American allies. As one ARVN general recalled, "the withdrawal was accomplished too quickly, to meet the political objectives of the Nixon administration, while forgetting the needs of the fighting front."[59]

This complicated balancing act between political and military realities underscored one of the core problems with measuring the improvement of ARVN forces. As Americans viewed Vietnamization, the effectiveness of the South Vietnamese army became conflated with progress in the war, a mistake that ignored the problems of rooting out the Vietcong, creating lasting security, and developing a sense of national loyalty to the Saigon government. In turning over the conduct of the war to South Vietnamese forces, MACV defined progress in simplistic terms of allied combat effectiveness. As one report noted, "Combat is the final test."[60] But was it? Under certain circumstances, ARVN might fight well in the field, yet corruption, desertions, and a lack of skilled technicians to maintain its equipment wracked the army's organizational foundation. Officers had been unable to keep pace with the influx of new recruits, many of whom were paid less than garbage collectors in Saigon. In the first half of 1969, 66 percent of ARVN maneuver battalions conducted no training. Of greater significance, many ARVN soldiers lacked faith in their government, a fact that often led to young recruits deserting from their units. Thus, while U.S. advisors reported on tactical and operational weaknesses affecting combat effectiveness, the root causes of ARVN's poor performance remained of peripheral concern.[61]

This bias in MACV reporting coincided with a larger omission in assessing the effectiveness of South Vietnam's government. Though counterinsurgency doctrine advocated coordination of political and military efforts, evaluating the GVN's political progress fell largely outside of Abrams's reporting system. ARVN soldiers often felt little ideological bond to a government seemingly out of step with rural peasant life. American officers overlooked this important element of morale and esprit de corps. In the countryside, MACV concentrated almost exclusively on collecting pacification statistics, failing to differentiate between military security and political legitimacy. Correspondent Robert Shaplen appreciated MACV's admirable efforts at the village level. "But we still have no philosophy of government, no fundamental sense of direction in which we are going, and, above all, no system of political organization, which must inevitably begin at the bottom." Shaplen touched upon a central oversight in assessing the progress of Vietnamization. By concentrating on ARVN's ability to combat enemy forces, MACV had minimized the importance of preparing for the imminent political competition with Vietnamese communists once the Americans had departed.[62]

On Other Fields of Battle

Naturally, Vietnamization did not transpire in a vacuum. Abrams preached throughout 1969 the importance of fighting "one war." He called it "working the system." MACV concentrated on the entire enemy system—main force units, insurgents, logistic caches, supply lines, and political infrastructure. In supporting his allies against this structure, Abrams lectured his staff that "we mean all of the army, all of the navy, all the air, all the Vietnamese. We mean the province chief and the district chief, the RF and the PF and the Provincial Reconnaissance Units and the police. *Everybody* in here has got to work together."[63] The task of directing and synchronizing this combined effort ranked as one of MACV's most difficult missions. A "one war" approach demanded tremendous coordination. A host of political and military activities and programs influenced the progress of Vietnamization. Rural pacification, Saigon politics, and continuing infiltration of NVA forces all affected the pace and success of improving South Vietnam's armed forces. Unfortunately, Abrams faced a number of major factors working against him as he sought to improve and modernize his host nation's military forces.[64]

Pacifying the countryside served as a crucial element to both Vietnamization and U.S. withdrawal timetables. In early 1969, the MACV commander styled pacification as "the 'gut' issue for the Vietnamese." Momentum seemed to be on Abrams's side. Reports suggested improving numbers in three important areas—Vietcong defections, civilians living in relatively secure areas, and secured line of communications. A defense systems analysis study found HES scores improved most when regional and popular forces operated close to the hamlet, apparently validating the "one war" concept. By December, HES reports indicated more than 90 percent of South Vietnam's total population living in secure or relatively secure hamlets.[65] Suspicious officers, however, questioned the validity of such optimistic figures. Colonel Donn Starry, one of Abrams's key redeployment planners, found no relationship between allied military activity and population security. In fact, Starry feared that insistence on the wrong aspects of the war "may have lured us into a vast effort to collect the wrong kind of data." The future four-star general confessed that he was "not at all sanguine about the outcome of further efforts to quantify progress using the numbers we have now." The numbers used for pacification, though, had changed little. While MACV would revise the hamlet evaluation system in early 1970, the report's statistical foundation remained intact. Evaluations of CORDS pacification programs, and their connection to Vietnamization and internal security, lingered in a cloud of "widespread skepticism."[66]

Assessing enemy strength and intentions remained equally challenging. American field commanders reported a noticeable decline in enemy activity during July and August. One general declared, "The Communists are simply avoiding contact with us. The reasons are not clear. But there is no doubt that right now there is a very peculiar situation on the battlefield." Intelligence analysts scrambled to explain this "lull" in fighting.[67] Despite its losses, the National Liberation Front had survived the onslaught of U.S. firepower in the eighteen months following the Tet offensive. The enemy now was shifting its tactics, returning focus to rural areas in hopes of disrupting the allies' pacification plans. Rebuilding its strength, the NLF turned to a strategy of "three clingings," staying close to the land, the people, and the enemy. Clinging to the enemy while avoiding major battle proved a delicate balancing act, yet U.S. patrols made few successful contacts throughout the summer months. In the meantime, Hanoi drove thousands of NVA replacements into South Vietnam to shore up battered revolutionary forces. If American withdrawals calmed U.S. public opinion, Hanoi feared, MACV might be able to maintain a presence in Vietnam. Communist forces had to preserve their strength for the fighting ahead.[68]

North Vietnamese leaders approached peace negotiations in Paris with an eye toward conserving and rebuilding their battlefield strength. This fact was lost on neither Kissinger nor U.S. Army officers. Unlike Laird, Nixon's national security advisor resisted Vietnamization, believing the United States had to maintain pressure on all fronts to be successful at the negotiating table. As Kissinger recalled, "Each unilateral withdrawal tended to weaken our bargaining position." Why should Hanoi's leaders compromise, he argued, if they knew U.S. forces were being withdrawn? Once withdrawals began, they would be difficult to stop.[69] Nixon obviously needed to weigh the impact of U.S. redeployments on negotiations in Paris, but he also had to consider public opinion at home and relations with the Saigon government. Some analysts in fact doubted if Vietnamization and negotiations could be pursued simultaneously. American officers tended to agree, recollecting the protracted deliberations at Panmunjom during the Korean War. They worried that any decline in battlefield effectiveness would result in an attendant loss of leverage in negotiations.[70]

For both administration officials and MACV officers, an ostensibly hostile press only worsened these prospects for successful Vietnamization. Nixon groused after the war that "news media coverage continued to concentrate primarily on the failings and frailties of the South Vietnamese and of our own forces." *Time* noted the differences between firepower and spirit, American infusion of the former having little to do with ARVN development of the latter. The *New York Times* declared in June that the day when South Vietnam's armed forces "will be able to stand alone does not seem to be in sight." Near year's end, *Newsweek* ran a story headlined "Baby-Sitting with ARVN."[71] Such condemnatory reporting not only riled Nixon but infuriated Abrams and his officers. Command relations with the press corps degenerated steadily. The level of mistrust escalated to the point where field commanders purposefully blocked media coverage of their operations. In October, Melvin Zais, now in command of XXIV Corps, unleashed his frustrations on Abrams. Already stung over the press coverage on Hamburger Hill, Zais charged the media with "perpetrating a hidden form of censorship on the American people. By slanting, distorting, reporting by exception . . . they are withholding from the American people and from the armed forces the fruits of victory which they so justly deserve and for which so many have laid down life and limb." From the White House to the front lines, U.S. officials denounced the media's unwillingness to criticize Hanoi while displaying few qualms about condemning American efforts to bring the war to a successful conclusion.[72]

If the press threatened Vietnamization through its refusal to emphasize South Vietnam's progress—a contentious argument at best—it further exasperated Nixon's camp by seeming to inflame anti-war public opinion at home. For the president, domestic support played an integral role in maintaining credibility with Hanoi. Yet in the fall of 1969, Nixon faced two major anti-war rallies—the Moratorium and the Mobilization Against the War. The mid-October Moratorium attracted broad national support, threatening to undermine Nixon's designs for an orderly disengagement from Southeast Asia. As correspondent Jonathan Schell remarked, the Vietnam issue was becoming "a problem more of ending dissent against the war than of ending the war itself."[73] Matters worsened on November 17, when the *New York Times* reported on the My Lai massacre. In March 1968, with the Tet offensive still raging, Americal Division soldiers on a search-and-destroy mission had summarily executed more than 300 unarmed civilians. In his after-action report, the task force commander described the operation as "well planned, well-executed, and successful." MACV even awarded the infantry brigade in overall charge of the operation a special commendation for its high body count. Claims of civilian casualties prompted an informal inquiry, but army investigators covered up the story for nearly eighteen months.[74]

By the time the My Lai story broke in late 1969, the wave of public discord appeared to be spilling inexorably into the legislative branch. While most congressional leaders still supported Nixon, many began questioning openly the war's conduct. Edward Kennedy already had denounced the heavy casualties at Hamburger Hill. In early November, Mike Mansfield appeared on NBC's *Today* show, calling Vietnam a "cancer." "It's a tragedy," argued the Montana senator. "It's eating out the heart of America. It's doing us no good." Senator George McGovern joined the growing chorus of dissenters after the My Lai story ran. McGovern implored Nixon to "stop our participation in the horrible destruction of this tiny country and its people." The loss of support incensed the president. Nixon argued forcefully that the pace of Vietnamization, not the level of dissent, should determine U.S. troop withdrawals. He knew, however, that legislative support and funding had its limits. The Joint Chiefs already had battled Secretary Laird earlier in the year over budget reductions that limited the number of B-52 bombing sorties. In mid-1970, McGovern and Senator Mark Hatfield ratcheted up the pressure by proposing a congressional amendment to cut off all funding for the war. The legislation failed to pass, yet domestic events clearly were circumscribing Nixon's strategic options.[75]

Despite the steady decline in both congressional and public support, MACV could not increase the pace of Vietnamization enough to alter the war's course. Abrams rightfully approached counterinsurgency and ARVN effectiveness as an integrated system. However, the problems of directing, coordinating, and evaluating the myriad tasks of combat actions, pacification, and Vietnamization proved insoluble for MACV's staff. Still relying on flawed statistics, officers could not penetrate the fundamental issues on which victory or defeat in Vietnam depended. Statistics on kill ratios, extent of control over rural areas, and incidents of enemy rocketing and terrorism continued to pour forth from combat units and district advisors without much analysis of their meaning in a new strategic environment. Even a greater reliance on systems analysis computers at the division level could not provide clarity. *U.S. News & World Report* maintained convincingly that MACV's benchmarks were "important only when measured by their impact on U.S. public opinion, on the confidence of the South Vietnamese people, and on Hanoi's assessment of whether it will gain most by fighting, talking or stalling the negotiations in Paris." Based on MACV's new mission statement, the nature of the conflict arguably had changed in 1969. The command's familiar metrics for progress and effectiveness, though, had not.[76]

Impending Departures

Against this backdrop of apparent progress in pacification and Vietnamization, U.S. forces began withdrawing from South Vietnam during the final five months of 1969. The first increment of 25,000 American troops began their redeployment in late summer. In July and August, the 3rd Marine Division departed I Corps' northern provinces. The 9th Infantry Division began leaving the southern Mekong Delta those same months. MACV selected these units based on signs of military progress in their areas of operation and on the apparent effectiveness of their South Vietnamese replacements. The 1st ARVN Division, taking over in I CTZ, had scored an impressive 16:1 kill ratio over enemy forces during the summer. Surely, MACV's staff believed, the division's battlefield effectiveness pointed toward progress in Vietnamization. Few officers considered that such progress actually might lead to increased vulnerabilities. By narrowly defining progress in terms of combat effectiveness, MACV had underrated the importance of solving ARVN's more deep-seated problems. Low pay and morale, corruption, and poor leadership continued to undermine ARVN's ability to fight in the political-military environment against communist forces. Thus, as Vietnamization moved forward, MACV was handing the war over to a force increasingly susceptible to defeat by NVA units and VC insurgents.[77]

This continuing dual threat from the NVA and VC underscored yet another problem with using South Vietnamese military effectiveness as a metric of progress. What was the purpose of Vietnamization? Was MACV improving and modernizing ARVN to counter a conventional or insurgent enemy threat? Were improvements aimed at building GVN political stability or simply permitting a U.S. withdrawal? All of these areas surely related to one another (and to Nixon's Vietnam policy), yet the overall strategy remained vague. On the most pressing threat, MACV leaned tentatively toward preparing ARVN for conventional operations. An enervated NLF seemed no longer a danger. All the while, ARVN forces continued to face the one interminable problem of counterinsurgency in South Vietnam. They needed to combat enemy main force units while also performing administrative and territorial security missions across the countryside. In the process, U.S. ground and air support, logistical aid, and advisory assistance decreased at a steady rate. Kissinger recalled Abrams's unhappiness over the initial withdrawal of 25,000 U.S. troops. "He knew then that he was doomed to a rearguard action, that the purpose of his command would increasingly become redeployment and not success in battle."[78] Melvin Zais characterized his new mission as "working yourself out of a job."[79] U.S. Army officers serving in Vietnam, many now on their second tours, speculated if the final test of Vietnamization would adequately reflect their own successes after more than four years of hard fighting.

These ruminations occurred at a time when some MACV and White House officials viewed Vietnamization's progress with deep uncertainties. Despite a flurry of optimistic reports coming from Saigon at the end of 1969, the South Vietnamese armed forces had yet to be tested in a major battle without U.S. assistance. One young field artillery officer revealed his concerns over the uneven degree of progress. "I've seen some South Vietnamese units that can't fight their way out of a paper bag but then again there are some ARVN units that really show up well."[80] Critical reports continued to question ARVN motivation and ability to stand against enemy attacks. Still, MACV staff officers defended their statistics, discussing but not solving the perennial problems of large volumes of data and questionable reliability. At the White House, Henry Kissinger cautioned the president on the supposed progress of Vietnamization. "We have not seen proof that ARVN has really improved," Nixon's advisor warned in January 1970. "There could be too much pressure from the top for optimistic reporting." Kissinger's misgivings warranted attention. As had been the case for years in Vietnam, one could find evidence to support any case with any number of American or Vietnamese officials available to substantiate or refute any thesis. Firm conclusions were hard to come by on the eve of a new decade.[81]

As 1969 drew to a close, the U.S. mission had spent more than a year working on the innumerable problems associated with Vietnamization. While Abrams advocated measuring progress in the war as a "total system," the ARVN's effectiveness and long-term sustainability emerged as the primary concern of MACV planners and White House officials. Achieving peace with honor depended on how much South Vietnamese armed forces could improve. In 1970, however, U.S. Army effectiveness appeared just as crucial to obtaining the goals of Nixon's strategy for an honorable peace. Army Chief of Staff William Westmoreland remarked in early 1969 that "Strength on the battlefield is a direct function of the quality of men that fill the ranks."[82] Throughout the past year, MACV had criticized the quality of ARVN soldiers and their leaders. By early 1970, the first American units had already departed Vietnam and more were scheduled to leave, and U.S. Army officers placed increasing attention on how the prospect of withdrawal was affecting their own soldiers' will to fight. MACV now faced a new challenge of maintaining American combat effectiveness amid morale and discipline problems. Despite all the reported progress in Vietnamization, not just ARVN, but the U.S. Army as well, seemed vulnerable to defeat in the jungles and rice paddies of South Vietnam.[83]

"Vietnam has become a poison in the veins of the U.S. Army."
—Senior American officer in Saigon, quoted in *Newsweek*

8 Soldiers' Interlude: The Symptoms of Withdrawal

"IT LOOKED LIKE a different Army to me," remarked Lieutenant General Arthur S. Collins, Jr., on his inspection tour of South Vietnam in January 1970. Though Vietnamization ranked as MACV's most pressing mission, Collins was speaking not of an improved ARVN, but rather of a decaying American army. "One of the things I noticed as I went around," the I Field Force commander recalled, "was what I considered a deterioration in the appearance of the troops, the discipline, and other things I had seen when I first came to Vietnam in 1966, and when I first left in January 1967." The contrast shocked officers other than Collins. A battalion commander at a firebase southwest of Danang lamented the loss of "intense aggressiveness" among his men.[1] A company commander operating along the Cambodian border with the 1st Cavalry Division found declining motivation among his troops disrupting unit effectiveness. "The colonel wants to make contact with the enemy and so do I," reported the young captain, "but the men flat don't." Combat after action reports in the 101st Airborne Division offered similar accounts. One evaluation drew particular attention to a poorly planned night ambush in which the enemy passed unscathed through the projected killing zone. Thus, while MACV continued to collect piles of statistics on ARVN performance and the progress of Vietnamization, U.S. commanders in the field became increasingly distracted by issues with their own army's effectiveness.[2]

As the U.S. Army continued its withdrawal from Vietnam, the problem only appeared to worsen. In the spring of 1971, President Nixon candidly told the graduating West Point class that "discipline, integrity, patriotism, [and] self-sacrifice... can no longer be taken for granted in the Army in which you serve." In June, *Armed Forces Journal* published a scathing commentary titled "The Collapse of the Armed Forces." Written by recently retired Marine Colonel Robert D. Heinl, Jr., the article portrayed the U.S. Army in Vietnam as a dispirited mob of drug-ridden units with soldiers refusing combat missions and murdering their officers. Because "national armies closely reflect societies from which they have been raised," Heinl maintained that the army's disciplinary troubles stemmed from "the kind of manpower with which the Armed Forces now have to work." Certainly, commanders were responsible for maintaining order within their units, and Heinl blamed them for the army's plight. The article clearly implied, however, that substandard draftees were undercutting the efforts of these professional officers. With the army extricating itself from an unpopular war, Heinl left a marked impression that American soldiers in Vietnam hardly were matching their World War II predecessors in combat effectiveness.[3]

This general criticism of poor quality, uneducated, and politically charged draftees degrading the army's performance in Vietnam demanded growing attention within MACV by late 1969. At a time when senior American officers still were undecided about how best to measure the war in general or Vietnamization in particular, such critiques added yet another aspect to MACV's measurement problems. The army seemed to be mirroring an American society disgusted with war and increasingly fractured along social, racial, and generational lines. Sociologist Charles Moskos, Jr., argued in 1970 that the military had "come to be portrayed as the *bête noire* of American society." A later critique maintained the draft had served as an "instrument of Darwinian social policy" leaving the "fittest" to escape military service through deferments and exemptions. Yet another appraisal noted that draftees from the United States' lower socioeconomic strata often were "stereotyped as persons subject to impulses of immediate gratification, sudden urges toward violence, and a higher incidence of inability to adapt to military life."[4] With the best and brightest of America's youth safeguarded from conscription, the popular argument went, the army fought in Southeast Asia with society's lower-class remains. By the early 1970s, as Paul L. Savage and Richard A. Gabriel contended, "the American Army had begun to disintegrate under relatively minimal stress."[5]

This accepted wisdom on the quality of U.S. Army soldiers in the early 1970s rested, however, on tenuous and at times highly circumstantial evidence. When Moskos visited South Vietnam in the mid-1960s, he reported on the social origins of the field soldiers he interviewed. Two-thirds of his respondents came from working-class backgrounds, with the remainder from the lower middle class. Nearly a third had dropped out of high-school and none had graduated from college. Except for the non-commissioned officers (NCOs), the soldiers' average age was twenty years old. Moskos, though, had visited only infantry rifle squads, an important qualifier, and had interviewed merely thirty-four soldiers. From this small sampling, he made not only broad observations about combat morale and motivation, but also indirectly reinforced emerging social stereotypes of the American soldier in Vietnam—young, lower-class, and uneducated.[6]

For many career officers serving in Vietnam during the early 1970s, it made sense that army effectiveness would decrease with the infusion of lower-quality soldiers. Lieutenant General William J. McCaffrey reported in July 1971 that "discipline within the command as a whole has eroded to a serious but not critical degree." "Mission accomplishment," he noted, "has undergone degradation in some units, primarily in terms of lowered quality of performance." Evidence suggested, however, that while soldier discipline may have eroded, the performance of the U.S. Army in Vietnam, at least according to MACV's measurements of effectiveness, did not suffer greatly as a result. These class-based arguments about the impact of poor quality draftees on military performance were not borne out by studies of organizational and operational effectiveness in the field. Lower intellectual standards for draftees did not correlate with a sharp decline in performance over time. Throughout the course of a long war, the quality of the army's drafted soldiers, in fact, remained remarkably consistent. Dissension in the army's ranks during 1970 and 1971, however, was a critically important issue. As contemporary officers bemoaned their profession being at a "point of virtual disintegration," MACV spent vital time and resources worrying about its internal organizational effectiveness rather than on the progress of Vietnamization and the war effort as a whole.[7]

A Case for Working-Class Warriors

Most young men coming of age in the early 1960s viewed the draft as an accepted part of American life driven by the Cold War. Under the Selective Service System, draftees who supplemented voluntary enlistees to fill out the armed forces' ranks often viewed conscription as an inconvenient yet expected civic obligation. Since the end of World War II, low monthly peacetime draft calls left most men at small risk of being inducted. The draft consequently stirred little public debate. The war in Korea, and the call-up of 220,000 men by the end of 1950, helped change this by setting an important precedent in the nation's draft policies. Some congressional members believed that the Armed Forces Qualification Test (AFQT) prevented too many potential draftees from serving overseas. South Carolina Congressman L. Mendel Rivers backed lowering the exam's intelligence standards because "Korea has taught us one thing if it has taught us anything. You don't need a Ph.D. degree to fight those Chinks."[8] Based on this rather imperfect logic, draft boards began awarding deferments in 1951 to students in the top half of their college classes and to those who performed well on a national aptitude test. Intelligence thus served as a central determinant for who served throughout most of the 1950s and early 1960s.

Support for the structure and selectivity of the peacetime draft remained high, even as the United States began to escalate in Vietnam during the Kennedy administration. With only 10,000 young men drafted monthly between 1955 and 1964 out of an average eligible population of some 25,580,000, the draft's deferment inequities aroused little attention when so few were affected. By 1966, however, the number of draftees called for induction had quadrupled in less than two years. The global war against communism necessitated that the army, bearing the brunt of fighting in Vietnam, also maintain its force levels in Europe and other potential engagement areas around the world. (The troop strength of U.S. armed forces serving in Vietnam reached its peak of 543,482 in April 1969.) Not surprisingly, increased requirements for manpower resulted in increased criticism of the Selective Service process. While Pentagon officials recognized the draft's importance in motivating enlistees to join up—nearly one-third of enlistees stated early in the war that potential drafting induced them to volunteer—the Johnson administration initially did little more than acknowledge the political sensitivity of the draft's deferment system.[9]

As deferments to the educated provoked controversy, so too did the inability of the underprivileged to enjoy the benefits of military service. In 1963 Daniel P. Moynihan, the Assistant Secretary of Labor for Policy Planning, reported that one-third of eighteen-year-olds reporting for draft examinations were deemed unqualified because of deficient aptitude. Nearly half of those who failed the AFQT came from families with annual incomes below $4,000. For Moynihan this amounted to "de facto job discrimination" against the nation's "least mobile, least educated young men."[10] Two years later, Moynihan reiterated his concerns in a disturbing report on the deterioration of black families caused by racial discrimination and a continuing legacy of social and economic subjugation. Military service appeared to Moynihan an attractive vehicle for educating and employing the nation's youth and instilling confidence and pride in African American families. As the Labor Department saw the problem, military veterans would return to their communities as more productive members of society, stronger father figures, and possessed of skills which would lead to economic independence.[11] For a Defense Department in need of manpower given the increasing requirements in Vietnam, Moynihan's recommendations soon would make a sizable impression inside the Pentagon.

On August 23, 1966, Secretary of Defense Robert S. McNamara announced the creation of Project 100,000. Promising to "uplift America's 'subterranean poor' and cure them of the 'idleness, ignorance, and apathy' which marked their lives," McNamara decreed Project 100,000 would offer new opportunities to those citizens who previously had been shunned by their government.[12] The Defense secretary ordered the armed forces to accept 40,000 previously rejected draftees that fiscal year, with an annual 100,000 thereafter. These "New Standards Men" would receive the same training and advantages as regular soldiers. (The Pentagon never identified publicly those recruits who entered under Project 100,000.) In all, the U.S. military accepted roughly 350,000 low-aptitude inductees under the new program, effectively addressing practical military manpower needs while confronting political criticism of the draft's inequities during increasing conscription calls.

At first glance, the induction of these lower-aptitude draftees augured problems for an army already at war. The median New Standards Man read at a sixth-grade level (14 percent read below fourth-grade level) and only 43 percent had graduated from high school. Many came from broken homes and nearly 10 percent had prior criminal convictions. Forty percent were black, an astonishing figure given that African Americans comprised only 11 percent of the U.S. population in the 1960s. (Blacks represented only 8.5 percent of the armed forces in 1964.) Highlighting the correlation between intellectual aptitude and economic standing, New Standards Men, averaging 20.4 years of age, came largely from the working class or below. Over 46 percent earned less than $60 per week when they entered service. Nearly 40 percent were unemployed before induction.[13] Compared to a Department of Defense control group, Project 100,000 draftees underperformed in every significant indicator for potential to succeed in the military. While the Pentagon affirmed that New Standards Men were not "singled out or stigmatized," several uniformed officers objected to the establishment of what they deemed a military "Moron Corps."[14] Many critics in the armed forces and even some congressional leaders argued that social welfare should not be a priority of the military during a time of war.

During its first year, Project 100,000 brought 149,000 men into the armed forces. McNamara stated publicly that the Great Society's social uplift program was "succeeding beyond even our most hopeful expectations."[15] Anecdotal evidence from the front lines seemed to claim otherwise. One battalion level commander serving late in the war remembered the quality of soldiers had declined noticeably. "Thanks to Project 100,000 they were just flooding us with morons and imbeciles. It doesn't mean they couldn't eat and talk and move around, but they couldn't learn well and they'd get frustrated and become aggressive."[16] For an army still trying to cultivate relationships with the Vietnamese population and separate them from VC insurgents, frustrated and angry infantry soldiers posed obvious concerns for unit commanders. The U.S. Army might not need PhDs to fight in Asia, but critics wondered if less capable soldiers might be undermining military effectiveness in South Vietnam.

The National Advisory Commission on Selective Service entered the debate in early 1967. The commission recommended maintaining national conscription yet proposed a number of reforms, the most contentious urging a discontinuation of student and occupational draft deferments. The commission acknowledged that student deferments ostensibly had satisfied a public need, for the nation had been "assured of a steady flow of college-trained manpower in pursuits necessary to the national interest." However, deferments had "become the occasion of serious inequity."[17] The head of Selective Service, General Lewis B. Hershey, understood the injustices created by deferments but believed they served a greater good. Officially labeled a policy of "channeling," manpower deferments based on mental and occupational tests allowed for teachers, engineers, and scientists to continue working in fields vital to national interest. (How the Selective Service defined "national interest" remained unclear.) The system might advance inequalities in the potential military manpower pool, but channeling, the argument went, contributed to the larger goals of economic strength and national progress.[18]

Channeling also occurred within the army, shaping the composition of front-line forces carrying out the fighting in Southeast Asia. Army draftees under the age of twenty with low AFQT scores statistically had the greatest chance of being selected for combat arms assignments (such as infantry) and of being sent to Vietnam. High school dropouts drafted into the army had a 70 percent chance of serving in Vietnam, compared to 42 percent of those enlisted soldiers with a college education. The high correlation between education and social status created the impression that those who died came from working-class, low-income backgrounds. (Compared to AFQT scores, race was not a significant factor in being assigned to a front-line unit or in being sent to Vietnam.) Given the educational background of draftees brought in under Project 100,000, New Standards Men accordingly shared increased chances of receiving a combat arms assignment in Southeast Asia.[19]

Despite Project 100,000's aim of returning them to society with new skills, New Standards Men found their assignments limited to the relatively nontechnical and manual trade jobs of the combat arms. The army detailed the highest percentage of these draftees, nearly 30 percent, into the infantry and artillery. Alfred B. Fitt, the Deputy Undersecretary of the Army for Manpower, explained the assignment process in extremely practical terms. "We can generate more riflemen very rapidly, but you can't generate more pilots very rapidly."[20] From the army's viewpoint, a college graduate and a high school dropout equally were capable of shooting a rifle. It simply made good management sense during wartime to place higher intellects into jobs requiring specialized skills.

The infusion of 350,000 New Standards Men into the armed forces during the Vietnam War appeared to support the claim that unintelligent, working-class men did much of the fighting, while their higher-class contemporaries either served in support positions or avoided conscription through student or occupational deferments.[21] The surprising fact regarding the induction of Project 100,000 draftees is how little they changed the social and intellectual composition of the army. In 1963, more than 27 percent of the army's enlisted men had less than a high school education. In 1966, just prior to New Standards Men entering in large numbers, over 21 percent of the army's enlistees came from the lowest AFQT mental group (Category IV). Thanks to the ending of student deferments, from 1967 to 1970 the number of soldiers with one to three years of college actually rose every year. While high school dropouts were three times more likely to engage in combat than those with college experience—due to occupational channeling within the army—the intellectual aptitude and educational makeup of the army remained fairly consistent before and after the induction of New Standards Men into the army.[22] Battalion commanders late in the war bemoaned the poor quality of draftees and their inability to learn military-related skills as quickly as their predecessors. Evidence suggests, however, little disparity in the capacity for New Standards Men to function as capable soldiers, compared to those serving in the army before the inception of Project 100,000.

The Enemy Within

Despite these consistencies, the fact remained that by 1970 the U.S. Army in Vietnam seemed to be unraveling. If New Standards Men did not significantly alter the social or intellectual composition of the army, why did commentators such as Colonel Heinl imply that the army was nearing a state of collapse due to the declining quality of its conscripted manpower? In virtually all areas the army appeared to be at war with itself. Even MACV acknowledged the wide-ranging nature of its problems. "Unusual psychological pressures were placed upon US military personnel in the Republic of Vietnam (RVN) during 1970," the command history noted. "US troops were being withdrawn, with some loss of a sense of mission by those remaining. Criticism from home of US policies and actions in Vietnam helped create dissidence. Activities of undisciplined soldiers attracted public attention. Many troops were bored or restless."²³ The quality of draftees did not solely account for the army's assumed ineffectiveness. Yet the apparent disintegration within the army's ranks burdened MACV headquarters with additional troubles that took focus away from measuring progress in the larger war effort.

The process of Vietnamization certainly added to MACV's frustrations. Field commanders struggled to maintain an offensive spirit deemed so necessary by Abrams for limiting U.S. casualties as Americans transferred responsibilities to their South Vietnamese counterparts. Herbert Y. Schandler, a battalion commander in 1970, recalled that his soldiers were "not too eager" to attack the enemy with the "war obviously drawing down." Such reasoning did not sit well with seasoned veterans who had spent previous tours in Vietnam aggressively searching down VC and NVA units. "These young GI's make me sick," complained one first sergeant. "They're soft. They have no guts. They're afraid of being shot at. They've been spoiled because their parents made it too easy for them."²⁴ Career soldiers—scornfully dubbed "lifers" by young draftees—often discounted the army's changing mission as a reason for their unit's troubles. Conscripts felt otherwise. Few wanted to be fighting in Vietnam in the first place and even fewer wanted to risk being killed in an army that clearly was withdrawing from the conflict.

The first sergeant's claims that young recruits had no "guts" underlined a generational divide that influenced opinions on army effectiveness in the early 1970s. Career officers bewailed the growing "permissiveness" among the youth of American society. They argued that political dissent, materialism, a lack of respect for authority, and a growing drug culture all were spilling into the armed forces. Army Chief of Staff William Westmoreland blamed the military's disciplinary breakdown on this new culture of social permissiveness, "for inevitably, the problems of society are mirrored in the Army."²⁵ A 1971 Pacific Command report surveying military discipline supported Westmoreland's stance. The report noted an increased "presence within the ranks of a sizeable number of individuals of 'anti' persuasion—antiwar, antimilitary, antiestablishment, antidiscipline." The study did acknowledge, however, that the army's withdrawal from Vietnam was contributing to the general malaise and maintained that a weak chain of command, especially at lower levels, had played a significant role. Officers accustomed to willing obedience from their soldiers were at a loss. Instead of looking inward, their first reaction was to attack society for their disciplinary woes. One general officer railed against the "New Left Movement" which, encouraged by its success on college campuses, was now mounting "an all-out attack on the armed services." In the process, communication between "lifers" and draftees broke down in 1970, further adding to the divide between the two groups.²⁶

While the army in Vietnam struggled with indiscipline, its leaders faced yet another new challenge in the form of public dissent. Soldiers in the ranks increasingly organized political opposition and resistance groups to the war. Career officers warned that such dissidents required command attention, for they had "a way of creating and spreading infection."[27] Officers themselves apparently were not immune from the dissent contagion. In early 1971, three West Point graduates publicly condemned the army's emphasis on body counts. At a news conference in April, the three recently resigned captains contended that "war crimes are a way of life in Vietnam." That same year, Lieutenant Colonel David Hackworth cited numerous army failures in a nationally broadcast interview. Hackworth, a much-decorated veteran of both Korea and Vietnam, followed his televised indictment with a scathing denunciation of army leadership in the *Washington Post*. Another highly decorated veteran, Lieutenant Colonel Anthony Herbert, was forced to resign after publicly accusing his superior officers in Vietnam of covering up war crimes.[28] If young, undisciplined recruits were the source of the army's troubles, how could the command account for such public dissension from its professionally educated and trained leadership? Clearly, the problem of a dissenting army did not rest solely on the shoulders of inexperienced, working-class draftees or Project 100,000 New Standards Men.

While Abrams in Vietnam and Westmoreland in Washington attended to damage control over Hackworth's comments, MACV clamped down on anti-war mail and organizations. The Department of the Army's 1969 "Guidance on Dissent" authorized soldiers to work on underground newspapers so long as they did not advocate refusal of duty or disloyalty to the United States. However, by 1971, MACV ordered the confiscation of any mail containing anti-war or dissident publications. GI newspapers like *FTA*, *Fatigue Press*, and *Your Military Left* voiced soldiers' misgivings with the war and became prime targets for official military mail handlers. The U.S. Postal Service argued that the government could not confiscate first-class mail without a court order. MACV defended its authority to seize any correspondence that was "inflammatory" or "critical of the military effort in Vietnam."[29] Despite MACV's efforts, underground newspapers made their way into Vietnam. Soldiers reading these periodicals readily joined grassroots organizations that opposed the war. By the early 1970s, anti-war groups like the American Serviceman's Union (ASU) and the Movement for a Democratic Military (MDM) counted thousands of members in Vietnam. Eager for peace and unconvinced of Vietnamization's worth, young draftees eagerly embraced these anti-war convictions. As one 1st Infantry Division GI sneered, "I don't want to get killed buying time for the gooks."[30]

Buying time would become a catch-phrase for the Nixon administration in explaining military incursions into Cambodia and Laos in 1970 and 1971. Such idioms, though, met with growing resistance in MACV's field units. The link between dissent and military effectiveness found no greater expression than in combat refusals. In September 1969, *Newsweek* reported how a company in the 196th Infantry Brigade rejected their commander's orders to recover a downed helicopter. "I'm sorry, sir," the twenty-six-year-old captain radioed his battalion commander, "but my men have refused to move out."[31] Other incidents of battle avoidance followed. In March 1971, fifty-three soldiers in the 1st Cavalry Division refused a similar vehicle extraction mission. The commanding general pressed no charges and blamed the troop commander for an "error in tactics." In October, men occupying Firebase Pace near the Cambodian border refused to go out on night patrols. These soldiers from the 12th Cavalry Regiment then wrote Senator Edward Kennedy imploring him to "enlighten public opinion." As they argued, "We are ground troops who are supposedly in a defensive role (according to the Nixon administration) but who constantly find ourselves faced with the same combat role we were in ten months ago." Unit commanders increasingly were obliged to negotiate and debate with their troops, dubbed "working it out" by young draftees. In the process, "search-and-avoid" missions at times replaced search-and-destroy operations. As one captain recalled, "We did a very good job of avoiding the bad guys. As a matter of fact, we religiously avoided the bad guys."[32]

If combat refusals and "search-and-avoid" missions impinged upon military effectiveness, ground combat officers often faced little choice. Aggressive officers intent on scoring high body counts risked threats from their own subordinates. "Fragging" entered the military lexicon during these final years in Vietnam, a label for assassination attempts by one's soldiers using fragmentation grenades. Incompetent leaders stood similar chances of being murdered by their own men, as did overly assertive officers and NCOs. Senator Charles Mathias of Maryland told his colleagues that fraggings implied a "total failure of discipline and depression of morale, the complete sense of frustration and confusion and the loss of goals and hope itself."[33] By 1972, MACV reported more than 800 incidents which left 86 soldiers dead and more than 700 injured. The army literally was at war with itself. Of course, fraggings held serious implications for military effectiveness. While most incidents occurred in support units rather than on the front lines, some officers went so far as to curtail their unit's access to firearms and explosives. A colonel in the 440th Signal Battalion, as an example, refused to hand out weapons to his troops for fear of potential fraggings.[34]

Soldier-on-soldier violence had the potential to squash military effectiveness because of its devastating impact on unit cohesion. The 1971 Pacific Command disciplinary study found that "a distinct dichotomy of dedicated life styles exists between a significant portion of the young, first term military members, and the older, career-oriented noncommissioned and commissioned officers."[35] The army's one-year rotation policy surely accounted for some of the alienation experienced by draftees. New Standards Men often found little common ground with career NCOs and officers who scorned recent cultural shifts in American society. For draftees, there seemed little reason to conform to institutional values in an army that appeared only to be marking time before its final withdrawal from Southeast Asia. In early 1971, *Newsweek* exposed the growing cracks in unit cohesion by reporting on soldiers who cheered when they heard their own officers had been killed in a VC ambush. Lieutenant Colonel Benjamin E. Smith, a chaplain serving in Vietnam, further stressed the obstacles MACV faced in building *esprit de corps* as it withdrew from Vietnam. Smith believed "fragmented groups within the contemporary army" were weakening the lines of communication between leaders and their men. As a result, unit cohesion and morale suffered while incidents of inter-army violence rose.[36]

If gaps existed along generational and class lines, they were arguably most serious along racial lines. Like fragging incidents, racial polarization increased the farther one moved from the front lines. Politically conscious African Americans not only mistrusted their often unresponsive, discriminatory chains of command but questioned the war's very foundation. Many blacks watched in frustration as whites garnered the most desirable, least dangerous jobs. Promotions, awards, and rear-area assignments all seemed weighted toward white soldiers.[37] Concluding that the army reflected a racist society back home, many African Americans denounced the ideal of bringing democracy to South Vietnam when they were denied so many freedoms in the United States. As Private James Barnes recalled, "They say we're fighting to free the people of South Vietnam. But Newark wasn't free. Was Watts? Was Detroit? I mean, which is more important, home or here?" Faced with so many inequities, blacks increasingly bonded together in solidarity groups to form their own brand of political resistance. Black Power salutes replaced formal military greetings. Demonstrations supporting black activism grew in size and number. One group, the Black Liberation Front of the Armed Forces, staged a rally in the spring of 1971 that included more than forty participants. As one officer remarked, "black and white friction is growing and portends new proportions of a serious nature and challenge to military leaders."[38]

Too many army officers blamed racial tension within their ranks on a preferred target—American society. Such charges masked the inequities of internal army channeling during conscription and did little to address African Americans' concerns that their officers cared little for their personal and professional well-being. Senior army leaders equally blamed a permissive society for the drug problem in Vietnam. A medical officer at MACV headquarters argued that almost "all the 'pot heads' we get were on the stuff before they came in the Army, so we really do not consider them the Army's problem alone."[39] Soldiers using drugs in Vietnam certainly were the army's problem. A 1970 Department of Defense sponsored study found more than 50 percent of MACV soldiers had smoked marijuana, nearly 30 percent had used narcotics such as heroin, and more than 30 percent had used other psychedelic drugs. While these high percentages did not represent daily usage, Abrams belatedly directed his field commanders to develop counter-drug programs in early 1971. That same year, while only 5,000 troops went to hospitals for combat related injuries, roughly 20,500 sought treatment for drug abuse. One general officer noted that heroin use was "the worst problem a commander faces" while a cavalry troop commander in the Americal Division estimated that 20 to 30 of his assigned 210 men were addicted to or heavily using heroin. Drugs may not have incapacitated the army, as many media reports suggested, but widespread usage forced MACV to contend with yet another internal issue that diverted focus away from the problems of Vietnamization.[40]

The range of internal personnel crises raised an important question in army leaders' minds on what appeared to be the declining morality among young draftees. Was society or the war in Vietnam to blame? Hearings in the U.S. Senate on the moral aspects of the war pointed toward Vietnam in increasing violence at home. One testimonial maintained the "collection of ears of Vietcong by Americans is a symbol of the effect of the war upon people who would often be otherwise normal."[41] Even some military officers contested MACV's standard charges that the army's problems lay within American society. In early 1969, three soldiers were tried by general court-martial for raping a sixteen-year-old Vietnamese girl. When one soldier was asked why he raped the girl, he replied, "Because of hate for the Vietnamese people." The defense counsel for another offender, a corporal, explained his client's actions to the court members in terms of a frightening transformation caused by a corrupted environment. "Gentlemen, these young men get out in the field and do these things because they are no longer what they were in civilian life." Unmoved, the presiding judge sentenced the corporal to a dishonorable discharge and two years of hard labor. Recalling these events, the judge (a colonel) argued that the burden of the draft "should not fall upon the disadvantaged and those who are not sophisticated enough to know how to escape being made part of the military."[42]

Arguments of a corrupting environment overlooked the vital importance of small-unit leadership. The prime responsibility for instilling values of moral behavior in Vietnam rested with MACV's officers and NCOs. So too did the responsibility for waging an effective counterinsurgency campaign. Senior officers may have condemned the ills of society for overlapping into the army's ranks, but such claims equally excused leaders who were unable to enforce discipline and operate effectively in an ever-shifting environment. Just as the war changed in Vietnam from province to province and year to year, so too did the values and ideals that American soldiers brought with them into the army's ranks. While Hackworth overstepped the boundaries for serving officers by publicly criticizing official policies, his message nonetheless rang true. "The draftee soldier today cannot be blamed for the Army's failures to recognize the nature of the Vietnam war and adjust its tactics accordingly," Hackworth argued. Internal officer debriefing reports, supporting such views, spoke of NCOs who had "abdicated [their] leadership" and left young draftees "basically cast adrift." Others mentioned officers applying situational ethics in pursuit of laudatory efficiency reports and awards for heroism. Rather than blaming society, Hackworth directed his wrath at fellow officers who were not skilled enough to adapt either to their soldiers' changing social values or their enemies' flexible insurgency tactics.[43]

Assessing the Effectiveness of a Troubled Army

In arguing that the American army already had "lost the guerrilla war in Vietnam," Hackworth exposed a fundamental debate over military effectiveness in 1970 and 1971. The conflicting claims of progress and effectiveness in Vietnam had been a centerpiece of military reporting since at least the Harkins era. By the early 1970s, though, much of the blame for the army's problems shifted ever so slightly from external to internal factors. Throughout the mid-1960s, senior officers in the Pentagon and MACV headquarters blamed any inertia in the army's counterinsurgency campaign on waffling administration policies that refused to either escalate or abandon the conflict. MACV's statistics on the war's progress all the while attested to soldier effectiveness through high body counts, increases in population security, and improvements in ARVN training. If units, leaders, and soldiers failed, it was only because of civilian constraints imposed on professional military men. The tone of these recriminations shifted in late 1969 and early 1970 as officers increasingly blamed the quality of their soldiers for reduced military effectiveness. Denouncing "social permissiveness," army leaders argued sophistically that the raw material with which they had to work no longer met the high standards of the men who fought at Ia Drang or in operations like Cedar Falls and Junction City.

Such arguments rested on questionable evidence, at least by the Pentagon's own metrics for soldier effectiveness. Empirical data suggested that in both combat arms training and field operations, draftees performed just as well as volunteers. In Project

100,000's first year, over 96 percent of New Standards Men successfully completed basic training. Between 1969 and 1970, less than 6 percent were discharged from basic training. Held to the same performance standards for all recruits, lower-aptitude draftees did require additional remedial training (8.75 percent of total trainees) and their rates for non-judicial punishments and court-martial convictions were higher than average.[44] Still, the high percentages of New Standards Men passing infantry basic training demonstrated an acceptable level of success for Project 100,000. With additional training for those requiring remediation, the army could produce qualified infantrymen able to serve in combat positions from a pool of lower-aptitude draftees.[45]

Assessing the effectiveness of these soldiers in battle proved more complicated. By the time Project 100,000 draftees began entering the ranks, MACV already had amassed over a full year of ground combat experience against both Vietcong insurgents and NVA regular units. Tactical performance by U.S. ground troops in 1965 and 1966, though, suggested an unimpressive start in combating the spread of Vietcong influence within the countryside. One Department of Defense study analyzed the types of engagements in which American soldiers participated during 1966. The report found that Vietcong and NVA units initiated nearly 80 percent of all combat engagements, while U.S. forces had prompted only 14 percent. Nearly 50 percent of combat was described as ambushes where the enemy had surprised American units from concealed positions. In only 5.4 percent of all engagements was the U.S. tactical commander reasonably certain of enemy positions and strength before committing his unit. Thus, well before the introduction of Project 100,000 draftees into theater, the enemy clearly possessed the initiative over U.S. soldiers at the lowest levels of fighting. While not a comprehensive gauge of counterinsurgency effectiveness, the fact that Americans had initiated fighting less than 15 percent of the time indicated their inability to control the tempo and shape of military operations. VC insurgents had been frustrating MACV long before Project 100,000 draftees arrived.[46]

By the war's final years, little had changed in regard to this one measure of combat effectiveness. In 1972, the Joint Chiefs of Staff reported that "three-fourths of the battles [in Vietnam] are at the enemy's choice of time, place, type, and duration."[47] Reverting back to guerrilla tactics in the aftermath of their conventional defeat during Tet 1968, the Vietcong had achieved results similar to those attained before the arrival of Project 100,000 soldiers. Certainly, enemy units in 1966 frequently targeted moving U.S. patrols, whereas in 1971 and 1972 they more often attacked isolated firebases and outposts. These statistics, however, conveyed the continuing fruitless nature of combat missions late in the war. One rifleman described his unit's pursuit of the enemy in familiar terms. "Just walkin' around don't accomplish nothin'," remarked a soldier in the 101st Airborne Division. A military intelligence interrogation officer also noted the undiminished resourcefulness of the Vietcong. "They'd do their operation and evaporate to nowhere again, out to the hamlets."[48] While the Pentagon did not maintain performance records or casualty rates of New Standards Men serving in infantry units during the war, Project 100,000 soldiers appeared to perform their combat assignments no less satisfactorily than did earlier draftees.

In fact, the decisive battles of Tet in 1968 should have exposed the weaknesses of Project 100,000, given the high percentage of these draftees serving in combat arms units inside Vietnam. By early 1968, the program had been in effect for well over a year with more than 200,000 draftees entering the armed forces. While Tet and the subsequent draft call for 48,000 new conscripts shocked the American public, the U.S. Army successfully blunted the enemy's greatest offensive to that point in the war. By all accounts, American soldiers performed every tactical task assigned to them and performed well. It seemed misleading to argue that the army which functioned so capably during the summer and fall of 1968 within a year was nearing collapse due to unskilled manpower. Claims that the "draft caused havoc in the army" simply did not measure up.[49] Many drafted in the aftermath of Tet possessed intellectual attributes that were equal to, if not higher than, their predecessors, even if their social values somehow had changed. Some officers even embraced the entry of lower-aptitude recruits. As one noted, "These men make the best infantrymen, mortarmen, and mechanics. Practically all will do their best to do a good job. I'd prefer a company of riflemen with fifth-grade educations over a company of college men anytime."[50]

Despite contemporary allegations of increasing dissent and decreasing morale among its lower-quality ranks, MACV made scant changes to its measurement systems during 1970 and 1971. Some ex-officers suggested that in accepting inferior junior officers, MACV should have changed its approach to "account for this reality" and by not doing so, it insured "a diminished combat effectiveness." As in nearly all its assessments for both progress and effectiveness, though, Pollyannaism reigned supreme in MACV headquarters. "All indications are that morale is good," declared one personnel officer. To stress this theme, MACV began emphasizing in its press reports the low number of American casualties. At one briefing in August 1971, the MACV spokesman declared proudly that the weekly average of 19 Americans killed in action had dropped significantly when compared to the weekly average of 81 killed the year prior.[51] This reliance on hard statistics raised several questions. Were American casualties lower because the enemy was no longer capable militarily, or were U.S. troops in the field conducting "search-and-avoid" operations? Did lower casualties truly mean progress if the enemy had decided to divert its resources to the political arena while Vietnamization ran its course? Such

FIGURE 8.1 Anabasis. Soldiers from the 9th Infantry Division wade across a stream in the Mekong Delta in search of an elusive enemy.
Source RG124S, SLA Marshall Collection, Box 4, Folder 336

unanswered questions arose from Abrams's conflicting guidance to remain on the offensive while simultaneously directing field commanders to minimize their losses. At its core, the morale of the U.S. Army in Vietnam was being undermined not from external social factors, disruptive as they were, but rather from an inability of its soldiers in the field to reconcile the contradictions in American strategy during a time of withdrawal.

MACV largely overlooked soldiers' discomfort with a strategy of fighting while withdrawing. Blaming society proved easier than dissecting an incongruent strategy. MACV's staff officers and commanders concentrated their inquiries about soldiers' moral and effectiveness on quantifiable metrics to confirm their assumptions that "social permissiveness" was ruining their army. They used numerous statistical measures to gauge the declining health of their units—desertions, disciplinary actions for drug use or racial unrest, and courts martial for fragging incidents. Field indicators continued to rely on metrics such as numbers of missions completed and numbers of successful engagements against the enemy. One division commander criticized his subordinate leaders in early March 1970 for an 18:1 kill ratio in February that had dropped from previous monthly averages of 45:1.[52] More circumspect officers realized, however, that disciplinary unrest and morale problems required more insightful examination than a reliance on cold statistics. Chaplain Benjamin Smith argued that his fellow officers were not going to recognize the root causes of unit difficulties by using "some of the normal criteria of military effectiveness and discipline." Soldiers might continue being effective in their duties while being polarized by racism or impaired by drug use. Abrams held a special commander's conference in May 1971 to deal with the problems of military discipline. Constrained, however, by traditional metrics, few commanders were apt to assess their problems with fresh insights that might help soldiers reconcile themselves to a war that increasingly made little sense to them.[53]

Withdrawal Pains

In April 1970, Westmoreland asked the U.S. Army War College for an assessment of the army's moral and professional climate. The resulting two-hundred-page report, titled the "Study on Military Professionalism," was completed in June. Surveying a sample of 450 officers of all grades, the study found a troubling "disharmony between traditional, accepted ideals and the prevailing institutional pressures. These pressures," the report contended, "seem to stem from a combination of self-oriented, success-motivated actions, and a lack of professional skills on the part of middle and senior grade officers." Much of the blame rested on an "environment that rewards relatively insignificant, short-term indicators of success" that undermined effective communication between junior and senior officers. In the process, the army's moral and organizational strength had weakened considerably. Representative remarks within the survey included testimony from a captain who spoke of reluctance among middle-grade officers to render reports reflecting the true status of their units. One major confessed he was "concerned with honesty—trust—and administrative competence within the Officer Corps. . . . Command influence impairs calling a 'spade a spade.'" The study maintained that inaccurate reporting was "rampant throughout the Army," spurred by an incessant need to "quantify progress and compare efficiency." Army officers had failed to recognize "the importance of the non-quantifiable variables in a valid equation of personal or organizational success."[54]

The War College's findings underscored many of the unseen consequences of relying so heavily on statistics without considering context. Lacking tangible signs of progress, senior officers in a counterinsurgency environment pressured their subordinates to emphasize measureable, rather than useful, short-term objectives. The fact that Vietnamization had become the driving element of U.S. strategy in Southeast Asia helped little. MACV's main task no longer consisted of destroying the enemy but rather of training ARVN to a level of proficiency at which Americans could disengage promptly from a long war. Quantifying progress in such an intangible assignment proved as frustrating as measuring progress in the war. Some officers even doubted whether Vietnamization constituted a mission at all. "There was no doubt that people didn't see a mission over there," recalled one company commander. Thus, with the conflict winding down, career officers continued to look for ways to demonstrate their proficiency and their own potential for promotion even if the possibility of achieving high body counts no longer existed. They twisted conventional statistics to meet their own professional needs, highlighting low American casualties instead of high enemy body counts, accentuating the high number of battalion days in the field instead of instances involving "search-and-avoid" missions. In the process, the moral climate of the army deteriorated while the ability to measure progress in the war, so flawed in other ways, was further undermined.[55]

Some observers equally doubted whether MACV could draw down while maintaining both combat effectiveness and its moral bearings. By early 1971, many commanders and their soldiers were experiencing a new enemy in Vietnam—boredom. With greater responsibilities shifting to ARVN, the U.S. Army found itself simply waiting to depart the war-torn country. Surviving replaced fighting. One popular motto avowed, "You owe it to your body to get out of this alive." It is important to note, however, that the strategic shift toward Vietnamization and disengagement resulted not from a deterioration in soldier performance but from social and political factors well outside the purview of tactical units. Racial and drug problems certainly affected the army by the early 1970s, and discipline did break down in some units. An increasingly unsupportive home front surely conditioned draftees long before they came to Vietnam. Soldiers were reluctant to risk their lives during a time of withdrawal. As one noted, "We're getting out anyway. So why should I be the last man killed in this no-good war?"[56]

Despite a deterioration of performance in some areas, suggestions of a complete disintegration within the army seem overstated. As General Bruce Palmer recalled, leaders still held their units together and carried out their missions "right up to the end." In general, the quality of the army's soldiers remained remarkably consistent throughout the war. In 1971, the Department of the Army dispatched interviewers to South Vietnam and found "the American soldier serving in combat arms units . . . is still a responsible, disciplined individual."[57] Of course, a number of variables influenced MACV's overall performance. The personnel rotation system of one-year combat tours often inhibited development of a lasting institutional knowledge in counterinsurgency warfare. Manpower requirements throughout the conflict curtailed training periods for new draftees who entered Vietnam not in cohesive units but as disoriented individuals. The professionalism of the officer corps, at least according to the War College study, seemed to be in decline. So too did the experience level of the NCOs corps. The army's tendencies of weighting too much effort toward combat and not enough toward the social, cultural, and political aspects of Vietnam often proved counterproductive. Still, the army fared no worse in the early 1970s than it had during the initial years of fighting against the complex insurgency within South Vietnam.[58]

In the end, no correlation appeared to exist between army effectiveness in the counterinsurgency environment of Vietnam and lower draft standards as seen in Project 100,000. Critiques that the social experiment program "created severe disciplinary problems" and thus degraded army performance seem overblown.[59] Project 100,000 unquestionably helped to encourage negative perceptions of draftees. The introduction of New Standards Men into combat, however, did not affect, one way or the other, the army's inability to wrest the initiative away from an elusive enemy. Yet the debate over organizational effectiveness had a profound impact on how MACV approached the overall war effort in the early 1970s. The command shifted its focus away from measuring effectiveness and progress in combating the insurgency and winning the war to measuring the internal effectiveness of the U.S. Army still in Vietnam. A distracted MACV redirected precious energy and command attention away from the problems associated with Vietnamization—and beyond that, whether the overall American effort was defeating the communist insurgency—while the army sought to manage its own troubles.

By 1970, MACV increasingly left the mission of wresting initiative away from the enemy to the Army of the Republic of Vietnam. Unlike World War II, the U.S. Army's leaders were disengaging their units from combat before the fighting had ended. Ironically, MACV, which had disparaged its allies for years, now depended on them to demonstrate sufficient progress and effectiveness so that Americans finally could depart South Vietnam. U.S. soldiers doubted that ARVN would fare well against an enemy that continued to show a level of resilience worthy of grudging admiration. "The dinks are just playin' with us, waitin' for us to go home, then they'll beat the—out of the ARVN," growled one rifleman. In early 1970, Nixon and Abrams decided to buy additional time for the South Vietnamese Army. The concluding act of a diminishing war would see incursions into Cambodia and Laos. For Americans, the Vietnam War officially would become a Southeast Asia war. How ARVN fared in these operations, and how MACV evaluated their allies' progress and effectiveness, would demonstrate one last time the unresolved problems of measuring performance in a long and unconventional war.[60]

> "In the process, we lost sight of one of the cardinal maxims of guerrilla war: the guerrilla wins if he does not lose. The conventional army loses if it does not win."
> —HENRY KISSINGER, *Foreign Affairs*

9 Staggering to the Finish

WITH THE WITHDRAWAL of U.S. troops foremost on his mind, Secretary of Defense Melvin Laird visited South Vietnam in early 1970. After a series of briefings and conferences, Laird reported upon his departure that "Vietnamization is working." To the president he characterized the atmosphere in Saigon as one of "cautious optimism." General Creighton Abrams ranked among those more cautious American and South Vietnamese officials with whom Laird spoke. The general's assessment of the situation in January noted several bright spots—declining intensity of enemy activity, increased frustrations in enemy recruiting drives, and gains in population security. Still, Abrams fretted over a sharp rise in enemy logistical activities that suggested preparations for large-scale offensive operations. MACV's commander also faced seemingly intractable problems within ARVN. The South Vietnamese army continued to show a lack of leadership, confidence, and aggressiveness. U.S. advisors had yet to resolve structural weaknesses within ARVN's combat support units and among the country's territorial forces. Abrams argued that if military difficulties ensued in the wake of U.S. troop redeployments, they would have a severe psychological impact on ARVN. Whether the South could withstand a determined North Vietnamese attack once American combat troops departed remained a key unanswered question.[1]

These uncertainties in gauging ARVN effectiveness typified other problems in measuring the progress of Abrams's "one war" strategy in early 1970. Facing mounting pressure to reduce U.S. casualties, Abrams insisted nonetheless on offensive operations to keep the enemy off balance. In many ways, little had changed since the Westmoreland era. During Operation Randolph Glen, MACV assigned the 101st Airborne Division the mission of maintaining a "shield of security for the protection of the people" while also providing "maximum support" for pacification and rural development. The allies, though, failed to gain the upper hand. NVA forces avoided the Americans' security sweeps, while VC insurgents hid among the population. Enemy casualties resulted mostly from enemy-initiated actions.[2] Late that spring, the 101st exposed the hazards of pursuing Abrams's offensive strategy at Firebase Ripcord. Overlooking the A Shau Valley, still a major storage and transition area for the North Vietnamese, Ripcord became surrounded by the bulk of an entire NVA division. During the resulting twenty-three day siege, the 101st suffered over 400 killed and wounded. The enemy might have adopted a protracted war strategy relying on small unit actions, but he still could deliver serious blows under the right conditions.[3]

This unremitting dual threat from both regular NVA units and Vietcong insurgents left MACV assessments on population security in chronic doubt. While the Phoenix Program had weakened the VC infrastructure, the Vietcong remained a viable threat. Terrorist incidents rose in early 1970. The Vietcong still found ways to tax, recruit, and propagandize in rural areas, albeit at levels far less than pre-Tet offensive days. Many subversives remained unrecognizable, evading allied efforts to identify those not supporting the GVN. Among the most disquieting indicators, Ambassador Ellsworth Bunker reported a "lack of resistance to night incursions of VC into rural hamlets." Though MACV reported gains in pacification, the CIA argued that "internal security in the rural areas of [South Vietnam] is inadequate."[4] While Abrams noted correctly that the enemy operated "at about five or six levels," the population security picture remained as murky as ever. Hamlet evaluation statistics showed more than 90 percent of the population living in secured areas, yet soldiers returning on their second or third tours in 1970 and 1971 found areas once deemed secure now to be contested. Correspondents focusing on official statistics likewise believed MACV's evidence to be "ambiguous, confusing and contradictory." Robert Komer, visiting in mid-1970, reported that "Vietnam analyses are still a dime a dozen, and still run the whole gamut from overconfidence to despair."[5]

Laird's visit, however, confirmed that America's Vietnam policy was entering its final stages regardless of the political-military situation. Committed to withdrawing U.S. troops, Nixon and Kissinger compared MACV's population control assessments to ARVN's potential for providing security against external aggression with bleak results. Neighboring Cambodia was reeling in the throes of its own rebellion. Increasing communist presence within the Cambodian borders was fueling not only internal anarchy but threatening to destabilize the entire region. Senior U.S. officers warned that Cambodia's fall to the communists "would send severe repercussions rolling across Southeast Asia."[6] Nixon, taking cues from Abrams, doubted ARVN's readiness to defend itself if Hanoi exploited this chaos and attacked into South Vietnam. Vietnamization simply needed more time. Thus, in early 1970, the president ordered an incursion into Cambodia to buy that time for both Abrams and the GVN. As Nixon recalled, our "principal purpose was to undercut the North Vietnamese invasion of that country so that Vietnamization and plans for the withdrawal of American troops could continue in South Vietnam." Less than a year later, the president followed suit with a military strike into Laos. Nixon was widening the war to shorten it.[7]

These final tests of Vietnamization—along with Hanoi's 1972 offensive against South Vietnam—demonstrated how little MACV's system for measuring progress and effectiveness had evolved after five years of fighting. Two months before the Cambodian incursion, Abrams acknowledged that there were so many factors affecting the progress of the war that "there's no way we know of yet to deal with it."[8] Exasperated with the uncertainty, MACV reverted to traditional World War II metrics to measure ARVN effectiveness in Cambodia and Laos and during the 1972 Easter Offensive. Abrams's staff measured enemy troops killed, prisoners taken, and supplies captured. Geography returned as a scorecard. The metrics offered little clarity, though, for ascertaining how well ARVN eventually would stand on its own. Debates during the Cambodian and Laotian incursions revealed uncertainty over Vietnamization's progress. Optimists cited high enemy body counts and Hanoi's inability to launch a cross-border invasion until 1972. Pessimists pointed to mammoth inflation problems and widespread corruption inside South Vietnam. The ambiguity persisted to the war's closing stages. MACV never resolved the problems of assessing a "one war" strategy that simply contained too many variables.[9] In the end, a disenchanted U.S. Army left Southeast Asia still unable to measure objectively whether it had succeeded.

Unrefined Theory, Unchanged Metrics

By 1970, U.S. Army officers could refer to a decade's worth of counterinsurgency theory as they planned for the final phase of their involvement in Southeast Asia. The earlier theoretical precepts spoke of now familiar themes for most army officers. By merely surviving, Robert Taber had argued back in 1965, insurgents could win a political victory. While social and economic ills ranked as the government's chief weaknesses, the "relationship to a disconnected people" ranked as the insurgent's greatest strength.[10] Frenchman Roger Trinquier had maintained that counterinsurgents could not rely solely on military operations. "Counterguerrilla operations have two objectives—the destruction of guerrilla forces, and the eradication of their influence on the population."[11] With the civilian population at stake, the struggle necessarily assumed both military and political aspects. David Galula had expanded upon these political-military facets of counterinsurgency warfare in defining success. A victory, Galula contended, came not simply by destroying the insurgent's forces and his political organization. Rather, it rested on the "extent of support from the population." In short, defeating an insurgency required more than just military might.[12]

These theoretical principles changed little in the late 1960s and early 1970s. Adjuncts to counterinsurgency literature reiterated the importance of intelligence and retaining the initiative. New treatises reaffirmed the need to coordinate military, political, social, and economic actions. Mao's three stages of strategic defense, equilibrium, and strategic offense remained a crucial element in understanding revolutionary warfare. So, too, did the belief that counterinsurgents fought primarily among and for the population. The key dilemma remained one of isolating the insurgent without alienating the civilian population.[13] Unsurprisingly, army doctrine mirrored this continuity in counterinsurgency literature. Army field manuals, revised in 1967 and 1968, reinforced earlier convictions of applying constant pressure on insurgents through offensive operations. As in the past, doctrine advised commanders to "devote resources not only to the primary tactical mission, but also to others not traditionally military." Local sociopolitical considerations required as much attention as security operations. Officers in Vietnam thus found a great deal of theoretical and doctrinal consistency when considering the competing demands of internal development and internal defense in counterinsurgency warfare.[14]

Continuity in MACV's metrics system paralleled these slight refinements in counterinsurgency theory. Few of the new academic works added fresh insights into the problem of measuring progress or effectiveness in an unconventional environment. Those that did address the issue offered only hazy references to evaluating the population's loyalty or enthusiasm for the struggle. One review asserted vaguely that soldiers killed or ground-occupied meant less than "intangibles such as shifts in popular support, altered perceptions, and altered behavior on the part of segments of the populace."[15] Among these new works, only Nathan Leites and Charles Wolf, Jr., viewed insurgencies as systems against which counter operations could be measured. In *Rebellion and Authority* (1970), the two RAND analysts posited that insurgencies required inputs (such as recruits, information, or shelter) from their internal environment before converting them into outputs of sabotage, political demonstrations, or military attacks. Leites and Wolf argued that the best indicators of success should concentrate on disrupting both the insurgent's access to inputs and his mechanisms for converting inputs into outputs. The rate at which counterinsurgents "acquired" the insurgency's mid- and higher-level officers and cadre, either by defection or capture, served as a key indicator for success.[16]

Analyzing an insurgency as a system seemed to match well with Abrams's "one war" concept. Yet, for an army already withdrawing from Vietnam, the highly theoretical work of Leites and Wolf proved indecipherable for a MACV staff habituated to reporting only statistical figures. Officers in 1970 certainly appreciated the potential of operational analysis techniques, and MACV acknowledged the need for indicators to supplant body counts as a measure of progress. In late January, MACV's chief of staff directed that more attention be placed on metrics such as ARVN operational effectiveness and population security. A closer examination, however, revealed that the more than 180 statistical elements used by MACV headquarters rehashed the same old indices: kill ratios, weapons captured, combat strength totals, and caches discovered.[17] Even the 1970 revision of the Hamlet Evaluation System disclosed scant new thinking in how population security should be measured. In an attempt to overcome biases, HES/70 relied on a centralized mathematical scoring system, rather than on grading by advisors, to measure governmental control. The report's basic framework, though, remained unchanged, leaving at least some advisors in the field doubting MACV's interpretations of the statistics. By the end of the year, HES reported over 95 percent of the population living in secure areas.[18]

Beneath the surface, the positive HES trends masked the realities of a resurgent communist terror campaign, creating what one correspondent deemed "an atmosphere of fear among the people and a loss of confidence among many pacification officials." Other reports similarly hid deep fractures within the Vietnamization process. MACV's Ground Operations Reporting Guide continued to stress the number of enemy killed in action, despite the chief of staff's apparent dissatisfaction with body counts.[19] In the field, the drawdown left fewer American advisors working with ARVN units. The number of reports submitted to MACV headquarters, however, had not subsided. One U.S. officer grumbled that "as the amount of voluminous paper shuffling created by the inordinate number of reports increases, the amount of advisory time appreciably decreases." Nor had MACV solved the problem of providing timely feedback to commanders and advisors in the field. Information continued to flow only one way. Intelligence reports that might have been advantageously shared between province advisors remained stacked in MACV headquarters.[20]

While most of these reports simply replicated data requirements from the earliest days of MACV's existence, the Pacification Attitude Analysis System (PAAS) attempted to establish trends in rural attitudes toward pacification and development. This long overdue report, established in late 1969, sought to evaluate shifts in opinion and public reactions to specific events. Questions probed villagers to reveal if they felt more secure as the year passed, how often they turned to local officials for information, and their opinion on ARVN forces. Of course, any system attempting to portray attitudes and opinions was subject to error. PAAS, however, served as the only survey providing insights into Vietnamese public opinion. Loyalty to the government might be difficult to measure, but ascertaining political awareness among the civilian population surely aided MACV in gauging progress against the Vietcong infrastructure. Likewise, determining a sense of security among the populace reflected important trends in the relationship between enemy activity and ARVN security forces. Unfortunately, PAAS was a case of too little, too late. Within MACV's bloated reporting system, a new report analyzing rural attitudes simply joined the host of other established data collection tools requiring staff review and processing.[21]

PAAS would remain an anomaly in these final years of U.S. involvement in Vietnam. Its innovative approach to measuring progress and effectiveness was not matched elsewhere in the American command, despite continuing concerns over the validity of its statistical reports. MACV headquarters had no motivation to revise metrics for an army already withdrawing from the conflict. In both Washington and Saigon, the most important indicators were those that tangibly demonstrated that ARVN was capable of assuming full responsibility for the war. Military information officers suggested unit publications replace "hard combat news" with "reports of the progress of our efforts in the fields of Vietnamization, pacification and civil action." In the process, civilian officials complained to Kissinger that the allied leadership was giving "lip service" to the fundamental problems of attacking the Vietcong's political infrastructure and improving ARVN leadership. The MACV staff and the U.S. embassy, according to one former CORDS administrator, "seem to have settled down into a rather bland bureaucratic routine."[22]

This bureaucratic stagnation reflected the intellectual inertia characteristic of the U.S. Army's final years in Vietnam. The basic premises underlying both counterinsurgency theory and MACV's metrics for progress remained remarkably consistent throughout the 1960s and early 1970s. Because of this continuity, imprecise assessment mechanisms persisted, leaving officers still unclear of the war's true state. The Chairman of the Joint Chiefs of Staff admitted in late 1971 that the "accuracy of enemy body count statistics is difficult to assess." MACV conceded that advisors' evaluations of ARVN units were "subjective evaluations" and "not necessarily indicative of the operational results achieved by those units." Officers in the field complained they had "now reached a point that data collection is becoming an end unto itself."[23] Amazingly, MACV's reporting problems in the early 1970s mimicked those of the early 1960s. MACV had found no dominant indicators to reliably gauge its progress. The effectiveness of its programs languished in doubt and uncertainty, overwhelmed in a sea of statistical gabble. Evaluating counterinsurgency operations remained an enigma.

Of Peace and Victory

William Westmoreland often reminded his aides that it was the political leadership, not the military leadership, which had the duty of defining "victory." Whether, for example, to accept a political settlement on terms less favorable than those anticipated in 1965 was a decision for the president. By 1970, the Nixon administration's definition of victory had changed in subtle yet important ways from the Johnson years. MACV's mission now focused on allowing "the people of the RVN to determine their future without outside interference." Strategic guidance furtively left unspoken whether U.S. officials considered the Vietcong insurgency an "outside interference." Defense Secretary Laird emphasized that MACV's military strategy should be directed toward four goals: successful Vietnamization, reduction of U.S. casualties and costs, continued troop withdrawals, and stimulation of meaningful negotiations. After years of searching for a coherent strategy, the United States, in Kissinger's words, now simply was hoping for an agreement that left the GVN with a "reasonable chance to survive."[24]

Expanding the war into Cambodia offered an opportunity to fulfill MACV's strategic goals and increase South Vietnam's chances for survival, even if violating the Nixon Doctrine that Asian nations were responsible for their own defense. From his first day in office, the president sought ways to "quarantine" Cambodia. Hanoi had taken advantage of the neutral country by building supply caches and base areas from which NVA units could infiltrate into South Vietnam. As Kissinger recalled, "Without challenging the North Vietnamese logistic bases, no conceivable American withdrawal strategy could have worked."[25] Cambodia's growing instability worried the administration even further. If Cambodia fell to the communists, Hanoi might be able to launch large, cross-border offensives that would increase American casualties and slow withdrawals. South Vietnam's survival, and American credibility, seemed very much at stake. So, with minimal input from the Joint Chiefs of Staff, the White House began taking its initial steps toward an expansion of the war outside of South Vietnam's borders.[26]

By striking NVA sanctuaries in Cambodia, and eventually in Laos, Nixon and Kissinger were forced to reconceptualize the war in Southeast Asia. If the United States could not achieve its goals within the confines of South Vietnam, the war would have to be expanded. In one sense, the United States at long last was viewing the war from the enemy's perspective. For years, Vietnamese communists had regarded Indochina as a "strategic unity, a single battlefield"—a fact underlying MACV's perennial argument to widen the war into Cambodia, Laos, and North Vietnam. Such appeals, however, often discounted presidential wishes to keep the Vietnam conflict limited within the larger framework of the Cold War. No administration, not even Nixon's, wanted a direct confrontation with China or the Soviet Union over Vietnam. Nixon faced the same dilemma as every president since Eisenhower: How could the United States contain communist expansion without risking general war? The vitriolic debate over the Cambodian incursion illustrated the strategic predicament concerning America's involvement in Southeast Asia. In a limited war, Nixon and his predecessors needed to define victory in such a way that achieved the United States' strategic goals and maintained the credibility of containment and deterrence while avoiding escalation.[27]

Defining victory and having the means to achieve that victory were, of course, two separate matters. The continuing withdrawal of U.S. troops left MACV with a decreasing capacity to influence the war's direction. American military and civilian officials not only lost leverage in bargaining with Hanoi but, according to one journalist, exercised "little control over internal South Vietnamese politics." Officers in the field echoed this opinion. One colonel remarked that his fellow advisors "have time and again been disgusted and disheartened by their inability to prevent the enormous squandering of precious American assets and dollars that they observe constantly."[28] Such critiques raised the question of whether expanding the war into Cambodia would help produce victory. Attacking NVA sanctuaries would not force Saigon to address persistent, fundamental problems within Vietnamese society. Lieutenant General Melvin Zais told Abrams in mid-1970 that neither the GVN nor the U.S. advisory effort had been able "to devise and execute meaningful programs to raise the economic and social level of the vast number of people in I Corps." Political power had yet to be distributed among the Vietnamese people, and Saigon remained totally dependent on U.S. aid and support.[29]

Nixon countered that disrupting NVA sanctuaries in Cambodia and Laos allowed Vietnamization to proceed in relative safety. Social and economic programs needed time to develop. ARVN needed time to train. Though Laird reported publicly that Vietnamization was working, troubles were brewing below the surface. MACV reports on ARVN effectiveness indicated ongoing problems with weak leadership, desertions, and unavailability of equipment repair parts. One survey revealed that 35 percent of

ARVN infantry battalions were commanded by captains, positions normally held by lieutenant colonels. Thirty percent of units were undermanned.[30] Lieutenant General Arthur S. Collins, Jr., the I Field Force commander, worried more about the "pervasive lack of will or determination to get on with the job." In a spring 1970 report, Collins listed familiar obstacles to ARVN's progress: lack of aggressive leadership, failure to plan ahead, a tendency to substitute firepower for maneuver, and an inability to coordinate actions against the enemy. If ARVN had "matured considerably," as some officers believed, Collins surmised that "somewhere along the line they had again slipped back a long way."[31]

The dubious state of Vietnamization in early 1970 illustrated the precarious foundation upon which Nixon was building his version of victory. Incredibly, the American mission in Vietnam still had not agreed upon the principal threat to GVN stability. Reports indicated that, while programs like Phoenix were making inroads, the communist political infrastructure remained intact. In late 1969, Hanoi even established the Provisional Revolutionary Government (PRG) to supersede the National Liberation Front and represent the southern communists in peace talks. To some Americans, however, fragile gains in pacification mattered only if South Vietnam's borders were secure. Alexander Haig, Kissinger's military aide, believed "statistics on the internal security situation in South Vietnam meant little even if they were accurate" because the main threat came from NVA sanctuaries inside Cambodia. To White House officials, Hanoi clearly was moving to the final, more conventional, phase of revolutionary warfare.[32]

Nixon and Kissinger realized that, despite the secret bombing of Cambodia a year earlier, the North Vietnamese were expanding their sanctuaries and merging them into a "liberated zone." Supplies continued to flow uninterrupted down the Ho Chi Minh Trail. This strategic supply route, in use since the French-Indochina War, ran along the Laotian-Vietnamese border and terminated in the eastern part of Cambodia flanking South Vietnam. The trail's complex system of jungle paths and mountain trails had been sustaining Hanoi's war effort in the south for years, a point not lost on MACV planners. In 1969 alone, U.S. bombers dropped more than 433,000 tons of munitions on the trail. Still, the supplies continued to move southward, on bicycles and ox carts if necessary. By 1970, the trail once again was supporting truck convoys of forty to sixty vehicles. Even when infiltration rates diminished under the onslaught of American air power, Hanoi pushed supplies and manpower through the Cambodian port of Sihanoukville. Kissinger believed that, if left unopposed on the ground, these communist sanctuaries "would be organized into a single large base area of a depth and with a logistics system which would enable rapid transfer of units and supplies."[33] South Vietnam thus would remain vulnerable to external attack, and the United States never would meet its goal of withdrawing successfully from the war. There seemed little choice. The war had to be widened to declare victory and peace.

Testing Vietnamization: From Cambodia to Laos

By early 1970 Cambodia was teetering under the strains of political and economic chaos. Prince Norodom Sihanouk, acquiescing to NVA and VC base camps within his borders, found it increasingly difficult to steer a neutral course for his beleaguered country. The American bombing campaign and internal tensions with Cambodian communists (the Khmer Rouge) had left the economy in shambles and Sihanouk vulnerable to overthrow. In March, Prime Minister Lon Nol deposed the prince. The country sank immediately into civil war. Lon Nol, believing he had the support of Nixon, issued an ultimatum to Hanoi to remove its troops from Cambodian soil. Throughout late March and early April, war raged across the country, leaving Lon Nol little choice but to appeal for American assistance.[34] Nixon did not disappoint. On April 30, 1970, the president announced to the nation that American combat troops were fighting in Cambodia. The purpose, Nixon stated, was to "protect our men who are in Vietnam and to guarantee the continued success of our withdrawal and Vietnamization programs." Nixon clearly affirmed that this was not an invasion, but a limited "incursion" to drive out the enemy and destroy his military supplies. U.S. officers, in an impressive manipulation of the military lexicon, described the operation as a "preemptive defensive raid."[35]

Nixon's decision threw MACV headquarters into a spasm of planning. While officers for years had pined to attack communist sanctuaries, they had not developed contingency plans for such an event. The 1st Cavalry Division, one of the lead American units for the operation, had no maps of Cambodia and received only four days' notice before moving out. Excluding Vietnamese staff officers from the planning process, MACV issued the attack orders and on April 29, ARVN reconnaissance units crossed into Cambodia.[36] Two days later, roughly 10,000 American and South Vietnamese troops followed in behind waves of B-52 attacks. It was the first time that ARVN operated in such large numbers for a single operation. As allied troops fanned into the "fishhook" border region, they pushed Vietnamese communists deeper into the Cambodian countryside. NVA and VC combat units purposefully avoided heavy contact, knowing the incursion to be limited in space and time. Nixon had announced publicly that U.S. troops would venture no deeper than 30 kilometers into Cambodia and would be out of the country by the end of June. To further mollify a wary public, Laird stressed that Abrams should keep his casualties to a minimum.[37]

As American troops returned to South Vietnam, officials in Saigon and Washington heralded the operation's accomplishments. Nixon stated that the "performance of the ARVN had demonstrated that Vietnamization was working." Afterward he recalled that the "Cambodian incursion was the most successful military operation of the entire Vietnam War." Alexander Haig deemed it "a military and strategic success by any rational standard of judgment."[38] Officers at MACV were no less sanguine, providing impressive numbers to bolster their claims of progress and effectiveness. The allies had captured 22,892 individual weapons, secured 14 million pounds of rice, cleared 1,600 acres of jungle, and achieved a kill ratio of 11 to 1. The U.S. II Field Force commander boasted that the operation "demonstrated that ARVN commanders possess the professional skills and leadership qualities required to conduct aggressive combat independently." According to one ARVN general, driving enemy main force units away from the South Vietnamese border ranked as the most important result of the incursion. Nixon indeed had bought the time needed for Vietnamization to continue. ARVN's fine performance, the administration argued, warranted further U.S. troop withdrawals.[39]

Such heady optimism obscured the Cambodian incursion's substantial limitations. As the II Field Force commander conceded, "since most main force enemy units avoided contact, a large portion of the losses were suffered by rear service elements." More importantly, NVA and VC units, though beaten, returned to their original base camp areas when American ground troops departed Cambodia. By early June, the allies had searched only 5 percent of the 7,000 square miles of borderland, despite intense pressures to show progress in disrupting the enemy's logistical bases. As one brigade commander commented, "We're not body counters on this operation. We're cache counters."[40] Statistics trumpeting captured stores hid more deep-seated problems within ARVN. Their reliance on American firepower throughout the operation did not augur well for a future without U.S. air and artillery backing. ARVN leaders might be aggressive in the field, but they were sustained by U.S. advisors and massive amounts of fire support. Additionally, the ancillary mission of finding and destroying COSVN, the communists' Central Office for South Vietnam, failed to eliminate the enemy's command and control network. Perhaps the incursion was not in fact a success by any rational standard of judgment.[41]

If the military results fell short of Nixon and Haig's fulsome praise, the Cambodian incursion's political results offered even more cause for concern. At home, protests erupted in the wake of Nixon's Cambodian address. Ohio National Guardsmen fired into a demonstration at Kent State University on May 4, leaving four students dead. A wave of campus anti-war rallies swept the nation, closing nearly 450 colleges and universities. In Paris, Hanoi suspended negotiations. In South Vietnam, MACV noted that pacification was making gains but "most 1970 programs fell short of their goals."⁴² Perhaps worst of all, allied operations in Cambodia left behind a path of homeless refugees, further destabilizing the countryside. In retaliation for the murder of Vietnamese living inside the Cambodian borders, several ARVN units had raped, looted, and burned their way into the country. Cambodia descended into a full-scale civil war that ultimately led to genocide under the direction of the Khmer Rouge. Nixon might declare that the incursion eliminated the immediate danger to U.S. forces still in Vietnam, but such security came at a steep price. As one correspondent quipped, claiming Cambodia as "the greatest victory yet achieved" was "a little like praising the fairest damsel in the leper colony."⁴³

The aftermath of the Cambodian incursion left many Americans wondering if the United States and its allies had scored a victory. As with so many other Saigon-based progress reports, accounts contradicted one another, depending on which indicators were used. Some reports highlighted ARVN's growing confidence, while others warned of widespread economic inflation and incessant corruption in Saigon. Journalists continued to question MACV's optimistic reporting. *The New Yorker's* Jonathan Schell wrote in December that government-sponsored measurements of success

FIGURE 9.1 Counting caches. Soldiers from the 33ʳᵈ Ranger Battalion, 5th ARVN Ranger Group tally grenades, mines, and weapons unearthed southwest of Saigon, November 1968.
Source RG282S, Kerwin Collection, Box 1

reminded one of "a doctor who tries to judge the health of his patient by taking his own temperature."[44] Nevertheless, American troop withdrawals progressed at a steady pace. By the end of 1970, U.S. Army strength dropped to some 254,800 soldiers remaining in country. Kissinger warned the president that such unilateral withdrawals were weakening the United States' bargaining position in Paris, but Nixon continued with the redeployments to prove that Vietnamization was on track.[45]

As 1971 opened, ARVN forces assumed most responsibilities from U.S. ground combat troops. With the new year, however, came the realization that the Cambodian incursion had not shattered Hanoi's logistical bases. While the operation had denied Hanoi the use of the Sihanoukville (now Kâmpóng Sâom) port, the Ho Chi Minh Trail continued to serve as a major infiltration route into South Vietnam. "An invasion of the Laos Panhandle," one ARVN officer recalled, thus "became an attractive idea." Such an operation would "retain the initiative for the RVNAF, disrupt the flow of enemy personnel and supplies to South Vietnam, and greatly reduce the enemy's capability to launch an offensive in 1971."[46] There would, though, be significant differences between the incursions into Laos and Cambodia. In late December 1970, Congress passed the Cooper-Church Amendment, which prohibited U.S. forces from further operating outside the borders of South Vietnam. For the Laotian operation, code-named Lam Son 719, American combat units would secure lines of communication along Route 9 inside Vietnam while advisors coordinated air support. For the first time, ARVN would be operating on its own. If successful, Lam Son 719 not only would confirm Vietnamization's progress to date but also provide another year's grace by further disrupting the enemy's logistical buildup.[47]

On February 8, the ARVN 1st Airborne Division and 1st Armored Brigade pushed into Laos under an umbrella of U.S. airpower. (American units flew 90,000 helicopter sorties in support of the incursion.) Nearly from the beginning, Lam Son 719 bogged down. As Kissinger recalled, the "operation, conceived in doubt and assailed by skepticism, proceeded in confusion."[48] ARVN officers set Tchepone as their objective and the North Vietnamese quickly, and correctly, identified the threat. As a result, 60,000 communist troops were defending the area when Lam Son 719 launched. On the second day, bad weather cancelled U.S. air support. ARVN units, unfamiliar with the terrain, advanced cautiously, allowing the communist defenders to push reinforcements into the battle zone. As fighting intensified, MACV forwarded optimistic reports to Washington, despite a growing stalemate on the ground. South Vietnamese losses mounted under withering NVA artillery fire, further slowing ARVN's advance. Finally securing Tchepone, President Thieu ordered a withdrawal on March 16, well before the scheduled end date of the operation. Nixon raged, fearing negative press reports of a rout, and spoke angrily of relieving Abrams. Later the president contended that ARVN commanders "decided to withdraw early" because "most of the military purposes of Lam Son were achieved within the first few weeks." A young American soldier offered a slightly less upbeat perspective. "ARVN is making an orderly withdrawal they say. In other words, they got their ass kicked and they are hightailing it back."[49]

Allied officials did their best to accentuate the positive when assessing Lam Son 719. MACV dutifully reported more than 14,000 enemy killed in action, 6,600 weapons captured or destroyed, and 176,000 tons of ammunition no longer in enemy hands. To his staff, Abrams claimed that the enemy had "been badly hurt." President Thieu proclaimed Lam Son "the biggest victory ever," while Ambassador Bunker believed that by seizing the initiative, ARVN had "preempted enemy plans for a winter/spring campaign." Nixon declared the campaign had "assured" the next round of troop withdrawals.[50] Privately, however, ARVN's shaky combat performance troubled the Americans. Kissinger worried that the Laotian operation had exposed many "lingering deficiencies" that raised questions over South Vietnam's ability to bear the full burden of the ground war. Even Abrams wondered if they were pushing ARVN too hard. Without American oversight, South Vietnamese officers struggled with planning and the coordination of fire support and resupply. ARVN undeniably fought well in many instances and, thanks to heavy U.S. firepower, inflicted a serious toll on the communists. Yet despite their continuing losses, the enemy, though seriously weakened, had not been incapacitated. The loss of nearly 100 U.S. helicopters during Lam Son 719 suggested that Hanoi still had the means and the will to achieve victory once the Americans finally departed.[51]

The ambiguous military results of Lam Son 719 reflected the political uncertainties of the Vietnam War in 1971. Both Nixon and Thieu would be running for reelection later in the year, and neither could afford a defeat in the Laotian jungles. The press, however, were at best skeptical, at worst incredulous. U.S. government officials lashed back, railing against the media for turning what Nixon believed a "military success" into a "psychological defeat."[52] The president exhorted his chief advisors to speak only of victory with the press, and in May, Secretary of the Army Stanley R. Resor proclaimed obediently that Vietnamization was making encouraging progress. More pessimistic assessments nonetheless crept their way into the media. In early August, *Newsweek* quoted an American official in Saigon who cast doubt on the progress being offered up by his superiors. "As usual, we've been guilty of self-delusion," the official stated. "Vietnamization was supposed to be the theme upon which we were going to slide out of this mess. And nobody wants to recognize the fact that Vietnamization does not reflect the reality on the ground."[53]

In terms of measuring the progress of Vietnamization, the reality of the Cambodian and Laotian campaigns in 1970 and 1971 actually meant little. Certainly, ARVN temporarily had disrupted the North Vietnamese buildup outside of South

Vietnam's borders. These military tests of Vietnamization, however, failed to reveal the effectiveness of other, more important aspects of Abrams's "one war" strategy. MACV contented itself with demonstrating progress through supplies captured and enemy killed, without calculating if these results mattered in the broader political context of the war. In mid-June 1971, Lieutenant General James W. Sutherland, Jr., reported favorably on Lam Son 719 yet recognized that the enemy in the lowlands still had not been "effectively separated from his source of survival, the people."[54] Ambassador Bunker worried over increasing manifestations of anti-American sentiment and a bleak economic outlook. MACV's optimistic reports on Cambodia and Laos largely ignored these underlying problems. While Abrams talked of systems, his staff continued measuring only traditional indices of military progress. Tucked away in the command history for 1971, MACV admitted that it was increasingly losing its ability to gauge the course of the war. The "capability to provide independent evaluation of programs" had been "significantly curtailed at all levels" by the ongoing troop reductions. As 1971 came to a close, the U.S. Army in Vietnam could not calculate the results of its Vietnamization programs with any level of confidence.[55]

The Final Evaluation

At the beginning of January 1972, only sixteen U.S. maneuver battalions remained in South Vietnam. On all fronts the war seemed to be deadlocked. Negotiations in Paris had stalled, despite Kissinger conceding to a cease-fire-in-place and assuring Hanoi that all U.S. forces would depart Vietnam within six months of an agreement. On the ground, an uneasy stalemate settled over the combatants. The enemy avoided large-scale engagements while increasing its terrorist attacks against isolated Territorial Force outposts and government offices. Infiltration of NVA forces into South Vietnam continued unabated. So too did U.S. troop withdrawals. The American mission reported Saigon making substantial economic progress in spite of a rising budget deficit. MACV emphasized ongoing progress in Vietnamization, yet the confidence of ARVN forces remained badly shaken in the wake of Lam Son 719. As American forces turned over their ammunition depots and storage facilities to the South Vietnamese, few doubted that ARVN soon would be fighting on its own, regardless of the state of Vietnamization.[56]

By early March, Abrams reported signs of increased enemy activity. In fact, far from acknowledging a stalemate, Hanoi had been planning for an offensive in South Vietnam since the spring of 1971. The Politburo hoped such an invasion would "defeat the American 'Vietnamization' policy, gain a decisive victory in 1972, and force the U.S. imperialists to negotiate an end to the war from a position of defeat."[57] MACV spotted warning signs but remained unclear of enemy intentions. Was this an act of desperation, as Nixon believed, or a way to gain leverage in negotiations by controlling South Vietnamese territory? North Vietnamese strategists certainly were taking risks, but not out of desperation. The 1972 Nguyen-Hue Campaign plan aimed for a collapse of South Vietnam's armed forces, Thieu's ouster, and the formation of a coalition government. Failing these ambitious goals, the Politburo envisioned the struggle continuing against a weakened ARVN. Hanoi, while not underestimating Nixon, calculated that the United States would provide minimal assistance to Saigon once negotiations concluded. In either case, the Politburo believed that its "actions would totally change the character of the war in South Vietnam."[58]

In the early morning of March 30, under the cover of a heavy artillery barrage, NVA units crashed across the demilitarized zone in Quang Tri province. One of three separate thrusts into South Vietnam, North Vietnamese tanks and infantrymen sliced their way through ARVN firebases and defensive positions. In the following days, a second front opened in Binh Long province as communist units streamed across the Cambodian border toward Saigon. A third attacking force cut into Kontum province in the Central Highlands. In the north, ARVN's Third Division reeled under the combined weight of enemy artillery and tank fire. U.S. advisors strained to get accurate assessments on the fighting but found their counterparts had learned an unfortunate lesson from the Americans. ARVN commanders were hesitant to report bad news. As one advisor noted, "There were a lot of false reports to save face which resulted in extremely drastic losses of territory and personnel."[59] Unskilled in anti-tank warfare or conventional defensive operations, the South Vietnamese had little choice but to give ground. In some areas, ARVN fought bravely; in others, soldiers broke and ran. Abrams responded by throwing B-52 bombers into the battle as Nixon ordered resumption of bombing in the north and the mining of Haiphong harbor. Gradually, yet perceptibly, the offensive's momentum began to slow.[60]

As B-52s pounded enemy units, throughout April and May the NVA launched three separate assaults on Binh Long province with hopes of seizing a base from which to attack Saigon. Thieu ordered the provincial capital of An Loc held at all cost. For the next three months, the besieged An Loc stood as a symbol, far outweighing its strategic value as NVA and ARVN forces battled over the small town. U.S. airstrikes pummeled the attackers, barely keeping the North Vietnamese at bay. As one advisor recalled, the "situation was very confused because the NVA and ARVN were so closely intertwined; from the air, the pilots had a difficult time separating friend from foe."[61] Walter F. Ulmer, Jr., an American officer with

ARVN's Fifth Division, was surrounded for sixty-two days. For him, the measurement of success returned to the classic metrics used in World War II—"a unit was either holding its ground or it was not holding." By the end of June, with An Loc in ruins, the fighting subsided as NVA units pulled back toward their Cambodian sanctuaries. The ARVN defenders had held, sustaining 5,400 casualties, including 2,300 killed and missing. Although North Vietnam's spring offensive had ended with no dramatic battlefield victory, it had met its goal of changing the character of the war.[62]

With ARVN effectively blunting Hanoi's Nguyen-Hue campaign, U.S. officials proclaimed Vietnamization a final success. American units and advisors, they argued, were no longer needed in South Vietnam. Such optimistic military assessments unsurprisingly overlooked several caveats to ARVN's performance. Many ARVN units did fight well in the spring of 1972. However, overwhelming U.S. air support quite literally saved many from being overrun and, more intangibly, helped sustain morale during hard months of fighting. John Paul Vann noted graphically that B-52 strikes were "turning the terrain into a moonscape" where one could "tell from the battlefield stench that the strikes are effective."[63] Equally important, North Vietnamese leaders made several errors during the campaign. The three separate thrusts into South Vietnam dissipated combat strength while placing overwhelming strain on logistical support capabilities. Tactical commanders lacked experience in employing armor in battle and squandered infantry units in suicidal assaults. As one U.S. advisor saw it, "Maybe the South Vietnamese Army is not very good. But neither is the enemy any more."[64]

Suffering more than 100,000 casualties and losing more than half its tanks and heavy artillery, the North Vietnamese Army certainly paid a heavy price for the spring offensive. As in past battles, however, battlefield statistics told only half the story. The political appraisal of the Nguyen-Hue campaign offered more sober insights into the GVN's position in mid 1972. According to MACV, "the unprecedented scale of the enemy invasion during April and May left the people and Government of South Vietnam shaken."[65] Saigon officials suspended local elections, the economy faltered, and pacification had been set back in numerous areas. More than 25,000 South Vietnamese civilians had died during the campaign, another million uprooted from their homes. While media reports exaggerated that pacification programs had been "brought to a halt," the rural population realized that Saigon had escaped defeat only through American assistance. With the final U.S. withdrawals taking place in the wake of the offensive, villagers in the countryside cautiously decided to wait before committing to the GVN. The fact that nearly 125,000 NVA troops remained on South Vietnamese soil did little to convince local villagers of Saigon's ability to survive on its own.[66]

The final assessments of the 1972 campaign matched the uncertainty surrounding ARVN performance during the incursions into Cambodia and Laos. Perhaps it was unrealistic to expect honest appraisals of Vietnamization, given the political climate in the United States. "Peace with honor" required leaving South Vietnam with a military machine capable of providing for national security. Yet by mid-1972, withdrawing U.S. troops ranked as the top American priority, regardless of Vietnamization's progress. At the White House, Nixon declared that the United States had achieved its mission of allowing South Vietnam to determine its future without outside interference. On the ground, remaining U.S. advisors were not so sure. Many believed that ARVN still possessed major weaknesses. "Poor or listless leadership, not only at junior levels, is widespread," reported one advisor, "and aggressiveness is found among only a few ARVN units."[67] Pacification evaluations indicated that the government controlled high percentages of the Mekong Delta, yet local officials admitted they were afraid to venture outside of town. VC tax collection, propaganda, and terrorist acts continued throughout the countryside. As Maxwell D. Taylor editorialized in the *Washington Post* that fall, no victory was in sight for either side in Vietnam.[68]

By the end of June, only 49,000 U.S. troops remained in South Vietnam. Creighton Abrams was not among them. On June 30, Abrams entrusted MACV to his deputy, Frederick C. Weyand, and headed to Washington to once again replace Westmoreland, this time as the Army Chief of Staff. The *New York Times* reported that Abrams was "leaving to the South Vietnamese and to his successor ... an unfinished job."[69] No one knew that better than Abrams. Throughout the summer and fall, stalemated discussions in Paris rivaled the military standoff in South Vietnam. In October, Kissinger reported to Nixon a breakthrough with the North Vietnamese delegation and announced an impending cease-fire. President Thieu fumed that Kissinger had conceded too much, allowing NVA units to remain in South Vietnam and granting legal status to the Provisional Revolutionary Government. On October 24, Thieu pronounced his objections to the South Vietnamese National Assembly and refused to sign any agreement. "They want to offer this remaining South Vietnamese land to the Communists on a golden platter," cried Thieu.[70]

The resulting diplomatic impasse, fueled by Thieu's defiance and Hanoi's intransigence, infuriated Nixon. By December, the president had reached his limits and ordered a massive air campaign against North Vietnam to break the deadlock. Nixon intended the bombing assault, codenamed Linebacker II, to induce both Hanoi and Saigon to return to the negotiating table. The president hoped to illustrate to both sides that he would intervene in any civil war potentially looming on the horizon. The press reacted strongly, referring to the bombing as "war by tantrum" and an act of "senseless terror."[71] On December 26, however, the Politburo agreed to resume talks while Nixon pressed Thieu to support the armistice agreement's key points. The final settlement changed little from the principles outlined in October. North Vietnamese units were allowed to remain in the south and the PRG was recognized in the signing procedures. One month later, on January 27, 1973, the United States, North and South Vietnam, and the PRG signed the Paris Agreement on Ending the War and Restoring Peace in Vietnam.[72]

"We had won the war militarily and politically in Vietnam," recalled Richard Nixon. "But defeat was snatched from the jaws of victory because we lost the war politically in the United States." The U.S. Army echoed this argument as the war drew to a close. Based on their metrics, many officers and soldiers believed they successfully had completed their task. On March 29, 1973, the last U.S. combat troops departed South Vietnam. "Our mission has been accomplished," announced General Weyand at a final ceremony.[73] Such assessments rested on criteria that incompletely defined success in a counterinsurgency environment. Despite years of doctrinal and theoretical advice on viewing counterinsurgency as a political-military whole, MACV ended the war focusing on the military ability and effectiveness of ARVN, stressing its progress using conventional, military metrics. Certainly, the final battles unfolded along conventional lines, but they comprised, as often had been the case in Vietnam, only one aspect of the overall war. The political-military struggle always had included more than just battlefield engagements. Such remained the case at the end of 1972, where, according to one estimate, VC insurgents still had access to nearly two-thirds of the population. MACV's confident appraisals aside, the U.S. Army in Vietnam ultimately had not broken the will of its enemy.[74]

The Avalanche Falls

The end of American intervention did not mean an end to the war. Viewing the Paris agreement as little more than a temporary truce, Hanoi pushed new equipment and units into South Vietnam. Local revolutionary organizations in the south meanwhile consolidated their political bases of support. The Easter Offensive's outcome had disrupted only briefly the protracted struggle for control of the population. As the communists attempted to shift the military balance to their side, Thieu sought to expand the GVN's territorial control in the countryside. Lacking competent administrators and unable to provide effective security, the program foundered.[75] The United States equally prepared for what it believed was an imminent return to open conflict. Still focusing on the military aspects of Vietnamization, the Defense Department funneled ground and air equipment into the beleaguered country. Under Operation Enhance, Pentagon officials aimed to fill

ARVN shortfalls to pre-Easter Offensive levels. The few U.S. advisors remaining in Vietnam doubted that the infusion of tactical equipment would influence greatly the war's final outcome. One frustrated American colonel railed in mid-1973 that unsolvable problems continued to weigh down ARVN's progress. "Their conduct of the war is hampered by certain national characteristics such as laziness, corruption, unwillingness to close with the enemy, lack of motivation, dullness and stupidity which no amount of advice or assistance can overcome."[76]

The colonel's rant suggested not only that Americans had been unable to bridge the cultural gap between their Vietnamese allies, but, more importantly, that U.S. advisors had not realized fully the goals of Vietnamization. ARVN appeared tactically proficient in many areas and soldiers fought well when properly led. However, the final 1975 communist offensive and collapse of South Vietnam exposed how MACV's extensive Vietnamization program had failed to measure up to its own reports of progress and effectiveness. Once MACV departed, South Vietnamese forces faced alone a host of diverse threats from both VC insurgents and conventional NVA units.[77] Despite confident evaluations in the wake of Lam Son 719 and the Nguyen-Hue Offensive, ARVN simply could not meet the challenges it faced in early 1975. When Hanoi invaded in March 1975, South Vietnamese forces revealed countless unresolved issues, despite years of American advisory efforts—uneven leadership, reliance on U.S. air and artillery support, faulty command and planning structures, lack of mobile reserves, and a static defensive posture. NVA attackers bypassed ARVN strong points in what one ARVN general described as a "succession of successful envelopments." Province capital after province capital fell with alarming rapidity. "It is like an avalanche," despaired one government official.[78]

When the North Vietnamese launched their last attacks against ragged ARVN units defending the Saigon perimeter, the conquest of South Vietnam seemed all but inevitable. On April 30, 1975, the war of unification finally ended. MACV's mission of allowing "the people of the RVN to determine their future without outside interference" had crashed under the combined weight of NVA tanks and infantry units and local and regional insurgent forces. In the end, Vietnamization had failed. The dubious successes of ARVN between 1970 and 1972 had done little to revitalize the American advisory effort or to force U.S. officials to come to grips with a decade's worth of overly optimistic reporting. To the closing stages, MACV officers preferred relying on statistics that displayed ARVN tactical effectiveness while minimizing problems in South Vietnamese political leadership and popular morale.[79]

For years, "Vietnamization is working" served as the mantra for Washington and Saigon officials. Yet Vietnamization had not solved the Americans' own problems of organizational and intellectual rigidity. The U.S. Army in Vietnam never squared its obsession with ARVN military effectiveness with the knowledge that a politically inspired insurgency could be defeated only when the indigenous regime became a viable government. Only then could the South Vietnamese separate the Vietcong from the people and connect the rural population to Saigon. MACV's data collection efforts certainly continued unabated. However, by 1970, the U.S. mission worried most about demonstrating ARVN effectiveness to prove that American forces could complete their withdrawal safely from Southeast Asia. MACV metrics accordingly ignored Robert Thompson's claim that "an insurgency is only defeated by good government which attracts voluntary popular support." In short, the U.S. mission measured only what facilitated disengagement.[80]

The final years of U.S. involvement in Southeast Asia highlighted MACV's intellectual rigidity toward gauging progress in a largely unconventional war. To the very end, staff officers measured and briefed innumerable statistics in an attempt to quantify how well their South Vietnamese allies were faring against the enemy. In no instance had the staff established useful indicators revealing the war's true trends. A MACV briefing in June 1972, just prior to Abrams's departure, revealed how little the staff had progressed in thinking about measuring progress and effectiveness in army operations. The presentation offered faintly more than a laundry list of well-worn statistics—enemy infiltration numbers, manpower and equipment losses, counter-pacification efforts—without any penetrating staff analysis. Few officers asked if any of these yardsticks were meaningful to the ultimate political success of Vietnamization and beyond that to victory in the war. The staff simply continued amassing vast amounts of statistical data without considering their usefulness in helping better prosecute a long war and difficult war. As in so many previous years, MACV had attempted measuring everything and ended up measuring nothing.[81]

> Guerrilla war is far more intellectual than a bayonet charge.
> —T.E. LAWRENCE, *The Science of Guerrilla Warfare*

Conclusion

THE UNITED STATES Army failed in Vietnam in part because its metrics for success masked important operational and organizational deficiencies. Flawed measurements validated imperfect counterinsurgency methods and provided MACV with a false sense of progress and effectiveness. These measurements were symptomatic of a larger failure in thinking about the war's deepest issues. With respect to metrics, it was both how the army fought the war and how the army thought about the war that helped lead to its eventual outcome. While MACV's officers claimed that they were making consistent progress in Vietnam, in truth they never reached a consensus over how they were doing in an extremely complex war.

Contemporary critics identified a number of reasons for the army's failure in Vietnam: a politically unstable and vulnerable GVN, an improperly trained and organized American military force, an incremental expansion of the war, and a lack of coordination between U.S. and South Vietnamese efforts. Many of these critiques rightfully condemned senior military and civilian officials for not establishing clear strategic goals and priorities. Few of these assessments, though, examined MACV's failure to develop a practical measurement and reporting system on which to gauge progress and connect operations to the larger political and military strategy. Most officers, in fact, overlooked the connection between metrics, operations, and strategy. Thus, as the war proceeded, MACV increasingly lost the ability to draw accurate conclusions from the massive amount of data it was collecting.[1]

The army needed some means of determining how well it was doing in Vietnam. For much of the war, it defined "victory" as an independent, non-communist South Vietnam that could survive indefinitely without the American army fighting in its defense. Yet, as one veteran journalist asked in 1967, "In a war where territory won is not held, how is progress measured?"[2] MACV answered by attempting to measure nearly all aspects of the war. While their metrics were grounded in contemporary counterinsurgency theory, army staff officers in truth had few examples on which to build their framework for evaluation. Early MACV directives for gauging progress indicated that officers realized the inadequacies of conventional yardsticks. Constant pressure from the Department of Defense and the White House to demonstrate progress, however, demanded that the army's officers cast a wide net in their search for indicators that might provide clarity in a complex, often incoherent war.

Metrics for mission success thus gathered statistics on pacification security, ARVN training programs, the damage being inflicted on the enemy, and, later in the war, even popular attitudes. Other indicators reported on the effectiveness of South Vietnamese regional and territorial forces and on progress being made in economic and social development projects. Metrics of the army's organizational effectiveness, often conflated with progress in the war, covered a similarly wide spectrum of evaluations. MACV assessed not only the efficacy of airmobility but, in the early 1970s, the supposed deterioration of U.S. troop performance due to drug use, racial tension, and a breakdown in discipline. Only in its metrics of mission failure did MACV seemingly retreat from its otherwise enthusiastic pursuit of calculable data. The pursuit, however, had satisfied few. As William Westmoreland reported, "All of these measurements have been imperfect and without exception there have been skeptics and critics."[3]

These imperfections stemmed from MACV erring on both sides of the measurement problem. The military assistance command wrongly applied too many indicators of insignificant value. Simultaneously, MACV failed to isolate those metrics that identified trends essential to a stable, successful GVN state which could connect to its population and gain, if not its trust, at least its acquiescence. In short, there were too many metrics but not enough meaningful metrics. Too much of MACV's statistical data simply counted and organized events or activities. The military staff—whether under Harkins, Westmoreland, or Abrams—valued data collection over trend analysis. And yet, so often, the quality of the data was suspect. In an unconventional environment like South Vietnam, such an approach held "severe limitations," according to one analyst. "It is difficult to meaningfully lump together events in a counterinsurgency, where there are political, economic and military factors."[4] MACV's efficiencies in information gathering did not equate to an understanding in either counterinsurgency effectiveness or the true nature of a complex war.

At times, it seemed MACV made a sincere, good-faith effort at gauging its efforts. That officers developed indicators for evaluating counterinsurgency progress in Vietnam as early as 1963 spoke to their realization that traditional measures of enemy forces destroyed or ground taken no longer sufficed. At other times, however, it appeared that MACV did not push the issue too hard. Few officers, either on the staff or in command positions, prioritized which indicators were essential for gauging progress in the war. Worse, there appeared to be little intellectual effort placed on the subject of accurately defining measurements of effectiveness and progress. Once MACV established its measurement framework, it adjusted the system only on the margins over the course of a long war. Thus, the problem was not just one of flawed metrics but of how MACV thought about and defined its system for measuring progress and effectiveness. A lack of institutional flexibility, combined with bureaucratic and intellectual stagnation, had created an organization with a deeply flawed mentality for imposing simple measurements on a multifaceted conflict.

The Problem of Metrics

The U.S. Army in Vietnam encountered considerable obstacles in assessing its progress and effectiveness largely because its officers could not develop a practical framework for a counterinsurgency environment. The area war of Vietnam certainly did not lend itself to meaningful calculation. Lieutenant General Julian Ewell recalled the war being so involved that "it was sort of like making a watch." MACV's structure for evaluating progress mirrored this complexity. The indicators developed in late 1963 were so numerous and varied that merely supervising the collection of information was a major staff undertaking. Coordination and management of all this statistical data added further requirements to an organization already overburdened with the day-to-day activities of running an unconventional war. One senior officer bemoaned the MACV staff's lack of "central focus to the analytical effort. So not only is the analytical talent dissipated, but the analysis effort is fragmented."[5]

Early systems analysis advocates largely had overlooked these potential drawbacks of relying on computers. McNamara's efficiency-minded whiz kids had assumed that they could quantify, and thus explain, nearly all facets of large-scale human activity. Further, McNamara's requests for both progress and statistical confirmation drove a military institution already accustomed to approaching problems with an engineering mentality toward the mechanical system MACV instituted. While some warned of the differences between measuring and understanding, few realized that computers might also become a crutch for MACV. In fact, as one Defense

Department report surmised, the U.S. mission in Vietnam "became mesmerized by statistics of known doubtful validity, choosing to place [its] faith only in the ones that showed progress."[6] Still, most officials honestly viewed systems analysis as a way for commanders in Vietnam to make rational decisions and choices while prosecuting the war. Few considered that in counterinsurgency operations, commanders might be overwhelmed with statistics, limiting the data's utility. No one had contemplated that statistics might come to dominate MACV's hierarchical organization as it sought to demonstrate that it was winning.[7]

McNamara's systems analysts also assumed they could measure the sociological and cultural aspects of counterinsurgency. It was, of course, difficult to measure the pulse of revolutionary warfare in the context of village life in South Vietnam. Understanding the social and political aspects of the Vietcong insurgency was challenging for even the most perceptive of officers. Americans literally were strangers in a strange land. How could they gauge political and moral legitimacy, what the Vietnamese knew as the Mandate of Heaven? One advisor late in the war maintained that the "really meaningful success indicators are the smiles I see on the people's faces as I walk though the hamlets."[8] Smiles, however, were a fickle indicator.

Measuring will, social development, and political growth ultimately proved impractical. Early lessons learned reports acknowledged that there were "many intangible elements that cannot be portrayed by statistics," yet MACV persisted in trying.[9] It appeared, as Edward Lansdale confessed, that Americans felt more comfortable providing money, equipment, and technical advice rather than "finding the motivation for conducting a successful counter-insurgency effort." Ignorant of Vietnamese language and culture, Americans focused instead on numbers—fortified hamlets, friendly kill ratios, or the number of days ARVN committed to offensive operations.[10] Most likely, MACV staff officers realized that something as intangible as will defied measurement.

The mosaic nature of the Vietcong insurgency added further complications for MACV's staff. Metrics for progress and effectiveness often overlooked the considerable variations between South Vietnam's provinces. As one officer recalled, the war "changed from year to year, from unit to unit, from place to place. There were no typical experiences."[11] In such an environment, using all-inclusive statistics did have severe limitations. Tracking body counts might be informative in the Central Highlands' unpopulated areas yet be irrelevant, perhaps even counterproductive, in the provinces surrounding Saigon. MACV's metrics system rarely accounted for such deviations. Fixations on body counts in Bien Hoa or Hau Nghia offered few insights into the Vietcong's political infrastructure. Hamlet evaluation statistics told little of VC influence within the villages. The number of days ARVN spent on field operations hardly addressed the glaring weaknesses in reporting on Vietcong operations and movements. Officers seemed to have realized early on the inchoate character of the VC insurgency. Their measurement and reporting system, however, never came to grips with this central feature of the war. Broad statistical indicators failed to capture the nuances of the insurgency's revolutionary approach.[12]

As MACV struggled to find metrics most representative of the overall war effort, the massive data collection effort soon overwhelmed its officers. MACV's chief intelligence officer remembered that "information poured in and was processed and whatnot, but not very much use was made of it." This lack of data analysis undermined senior commanders' ability to understand and explain the war's trajectory. Creighton Abrams might lament getting "wrapped around the axle" watching "fucking *charts*" but neither he nor his predecessors directed the staff to spend less time collecting data and more time analyzing it.[13] In the process, contradictory assessments resulted from different agencies drawing different conclusions from the mountains of statistics. A special studies group under Henry Kissinger identified one of the underlying deficiencies in MACV's measurement framework. "For an indicator to be useful for policy, other than serving as a scorecard, we need to look at the reasons for the change it records."[14] Unfortunately, by the time of the group's report in late 1969, U.S. troop withdrawals already had begun, leaving MACV little incentive to spend much intellectual energy on complicated data analysis.

Insufficient analysis often led to faulty evaluations, whether of ARVN effectiveness or VC political strength, in large part because MACV had created no verification procedures or feedback mechanisms for its metrics system. Staff officers rarely questioned the validity of sources feeding their reports. Did someone really weigh the millions of pounds of rice seized during the Cambodian incursion? Few senior American officers bothered to investigate if the system they created was accomplishing that for which it was designed. Did the captured rice really provide insights into ARVN effectiveness upon which U.S. withdrawals so heavily relied? Rarely did the staff subject its reporting system to such scrutiny.[15] Given the short time that most officers spent on the MACV staff, perhaps this was to be expected. Frequent rotation of staff officers left MACV with a short institutional memory. Career officers had no interest in rocking the boat while they waited for a coveted command assignment. Thinking about higher level, long-term problems likely was not rewarded in a staff facing so many day-to-day operational problems. Thus, as the army's organizational memory was "erased every twelve months" like a recording tape, the framework for its metrics system saw very little change over time. If progress reports were not encouraging, it was not a problem of imperfect metrics in the psychology of senior commanders but rather one of flawed implementation in the field.[16]

While MACV's staff succumbed to a sort of bureaucratic and intellectual inertia in relation to its indictors for success, it often turned a blind eye to metrics that might suggest failure. Without question, it was hard to get reliable data and even harder to confirm the accuracy of that data. Yet in numerous cases MACV played down or ignored acts involving unwarranted collateral damage or civilian deaths. Operation Masher/White Wing in early 1966 set an unfortunate precedent in MACV's reporting system: discounting the numbers of hamlets destroyed, civilians killed, and refugees created in the course of combat operations. By the time of Operation Cedar Falls a year later, the destruction of villages like Ben Suc warranted only passing attention as eradication of VC strongholds. Perhaps MACV was afraid to use such metrics because they might reveal trends at cross-purposes with its overly optimistic reporting. Destroyed hamlets did not substantiate claims of security gains. Depopulation of the countryside did not corroborate declarations of progress in pacification. Disappointments in Cambodia and Laos did not help publicize ARVN improvements under Vietnamization. In some instances, it appeared MACV did not push too hard in assessing its progress because officers knew what the answer might be.

There seemed, of course, an inherent need to demonstrate that MACV was winning. Pressures for accentuating and even inflating positive numbers grew as the war proceeded. Harkins's upbeat appraisal of the 1963 Ap Bac battle illustrated early on MACV's proclivity for optimism. In due course, the military command's metrics became politicized. Senior officials in both the Johnson and Nixon administrations pursued favorable reports to prove to skeptical news correspondents, an increasingly war-weary public, and even to themselves that the U.S. mission was making progress in Vietnam. Careerist army officers purposefully sought ways to highlight their own progress, as well as the efficacy of their units and the army's operational concepts. As senior leaders devalued or discounted negative reports, the realities of Vietnam's political and military situation soon came into doubt. Visiting a Mekong Delta outpost in 1963, one U.S. embassy official illustrated the early impacts of selective reporting. "The senior officer told me that things were going exceptionally well. After he left, his deputy told me that the situation was rapidly deteriorating. The deputy, frankly, was more persuasive."[17] The senior officer likely felt pressure to report short-term progress during his one-year tour. Ironically, all this pressure to demonstrate progress left unanswered a key question. What, in fact, constituted progress?

The Problem of Language

While MACV suffered from a poor conception of counterinsurgency metrics, at the same time it wrestled with defining success in an unconventional environment. Lack of coherent strategic objectives bedeviled MACV throughout the war.

Contemporary officers and analysts spoke often of the need for clarity and consistency in both political and military aims. Yet there was no agency below the White House responsible for formulating grand strategy. The Joint Chiefs of Staff played almost no role in shaping strategy within the theater of operations, leaving the MACV commander to develop his own concept of counter-revolutionary warfare. As one senior officer recalled, "the strategy of the Vietnamese War was so screwed up that trying to win the war tactically was like swimming up Niagara Falls with an anvil around your neck."[18] Poor coordination between U.S. agencies only intensified the strategic muddle. American assistance to South Vietnam comprised not just military advisors but a host of bureaus and departments offering civic, political, and economic advice and support. Lacking a common approach and direction, American civil and military organizations at times feuded with each other as much as they battled the VC. As one RAND analyst remarked late in the war, it was "not possible to measure progress toward ultimate victory because that goal has never been clearly defined."[19]

If MACV had trouble defining victory, it faced similar problems agreeing on the nature of the enemy's strategy in a largely political environment. Army officers surely realized that the war could not be won solely on the basis of military might and faithfully attempted to achieve some political-military balance in their operations. They failed to reach consensus, however, on where the main threat lay, on whether it was a conventional invasion from the north, an insurgency-based revolution in the south, or a mixture of both. General Bruce Palmer rightfully asserted that "few Americans understood the true nature of the war—a devilishly clever mixture of conventional warfare fought somewhat unconventionally and guerrilla warfare fought in the classical manner."[20] Consequently, MACV's metrics never revealed if U.S. troops and their ARVN allies were making progress against the enemy. Vietnamization indicators trumpeted ARVN effectiveness yet evaded questions of whether the South Vietnamese truly were prepared to defend against NVA main force units, Vietcong insurgents or, more important, both. Worse, MACV statistics rarely captured how the enemy's political and military operations worked together to prevent the South Vietnamese government from gaining the confidence and loyalty of the population. By the war's final years, Vietnamization metrics concentrated almost exclusively on the RVNAF, ignoring assessments of Saigon's long-term political viability or the insurgents' control of the population.

This inability to articulate strategic objectives or accurately define the threat helped create dissent over measurements of progress and effectiveness. In short, the wide range of metrics revealed much about American strategy in Vietnam. MACV could not measure only one aspect of a complex counterinsurgency, especially if the U.S. mission had not settled upon its strategic aims. Though some metrics might have had more explanatory power, such as voluntary information given by the population, there simply were too few moments in the war when most of the actors agreed on either strategy or metrics. Throughout, administration officials and the media remained skeptical of MACV statistics. *Time* reported accurately in early 1970: "For each good sign, there can still be found another, less hopeful sign. . . . As a result, every assessment of the war is self-contradictory."[21] Both optimists and pessimists easily justified their positions from the mounds of conflicting data. Without linkages to coherent strategic aims and sound threat assessments, it seemed any balance sheet or prognosis was as good as the next. As one reporter quipped, the question of what to make of all these conflicting evaluations was "a little like the old vaudeville query: 'How's your wife?' with the wag replying, 'Compared to what?'"[22]

The army's unpreparedness for counterinsurgency in the early 1960s surely encouraged this confusion. Conventional officers had little experience in developing a counterinsurgency reporting system and applying it within a larger strategic context. It would be simplistic, however, to argue that these officers were interested solely in body counts. Rather than relying on this one military metric, MACV's staff instead cast a wide net in search of indicators for measuring a war without fronts. In some instances, they collected important data like the amount of useful information voluntarily provided by the local population. Unfortunately, the officer corps' experience and educational system offered slight assistance in helping conceptualize the overall strategic problem. The lack of theoretical and doctrinal discussion on counterinsurgency metrics left the army ill-equipped to gauge how it was doing across Vietnam. Here, systems analysis statistics filled a gaping hole in the army's understanding of revolutionary warfare. By counting activities, quantifying effort, and calculating performance MACV hoped to illuminate where it was making progress.[23]

In fact, under all of its commanders, MACV presupposed that effort equated to progress. Most Americans assumed that progress in Vietnam would be linear. The more effort expended, the more progress achieved. Instead, the Vietcong insurgency naturally ebbed and flowed depending on a host of political and military variables. The enemy's flexible implementation of revolutionary warfare thus disrupted MACV's reliance on statistics, making any trend analysis a demanding task. As one advisor noted, the "situation in the Vietnam countryside was uncertain and changing. A man might walk unmolested from hamlet to hamlet for months at a time, only to be taken prisoner or killed in an ambush without warning. In that environment it was very difficult to know just what the condition of security was."[24] For a task-oriented army expecting immediate results from its efforts, these fluctuations proved infuriating. As a result, MACV placed undue emphasis on any indicators it believed were measuring progress. In short, as one former brigade commander recalled, "the word measure got in the way." Instead of asking if they understood the reasons behind failure or success, MACV's officers instead fretted over ensuring progress was a constant, linear process.[25]

Part of this problem, correctly identified by Abrams, stemmed from the NLF insurgency operating as a coordinated system. To succeed, U.S. forces had to triumph simultaneously in a number of diverse areas: in pacification, in Vietnamization (both its political and military aspects), in combating the NVA and VC threat, and in stabilizing the Saigon government and improving its effectiveness. Unfortunately, while Abrams viewed the war as a system, neither he nor his staff determined how best to measure progress in a systematic way.[26] None of the MACV commanders developed an integrated system of assessment. Rather, they relied on disparate measurements of varied military and political programs. No one asked how the hundreds of indicators and thousands of statistics related to one another and to the larger struggle. In truth, Westmoreland's sequential view of counterinsurgency—where security preceded improvements in pacification and governmental stability—never disappeared fully from the army's conception about how to win in South Vietnam. One correspondent spoke for many officers who believed security a prerequisite for larger aims. "We are not going to get much cooperation from the civilian population until we can offer them some measure of protection and security."[27]

Defining security, however, remained one of the more complicated aspects of MACV's measurement system. Indeed, imprecise definitions plagued nearly all facets of U.S. reporting. How should "security" be defined? Quantitative reports like the HES never really said. Was control different from security? MACV's criteria, much like that of the French, often made little distinction between the two. Marine General Lewis Walt maintained that "control over the people must be absolute to be effective."[28] In Vietnam, that seemed a difficult benchmark to achieve. When was a "clear and hold" operation deemed successful? MACV simply assumed most were, reporting metrics on the clearing rather than on the holding. How should progress in achieving popular support for the GVN be measured? According to most evaluations, it was difficult to say. Even defining victory itself was problematic. Was the battle of Ia Drang truly a victory? Hal Moore, Harry Kinnard, and William Westmoreland all believed so at the time. All of these unanswered questions created a tremendous void in MACV's measurement and reporting systems. Without agreeing on what success actually meant, officers attempting to assess progress and effectiveness spent much of their time stuck in a definitional morass.[29]

Ultimately, MACV never designated any dominant indicators that might help officials better evaluate the state of the war. Its staff and commanders never articulated what needed to be the central focus in their narrative on counterinsurgency. Critical information instead remained hidden, lost in a sea of statistics. Ambiguous yardsticks left civilian and military officials alike doubtful of the reporting system's worth. As one staff officer recalled, MACV had failed to define and identify those elements of information "essential to prosecuting and winning the war."[30] In the end, the U.S. Army found that measuring progress in conventional operations was far less complicated than dealing with the intricacies of counterinsurgency. It seemed no wonder that they craved for a return to the European battlefields of World War II.

New Perspectives on Old Metrics

The army did return to Europe after the Vietnam War, at least in its focus, organization, planning, and doctrine. The institution of an all-volunteer force in 1973, together with military implications of the Yom Kippur War, refocused officers on conventional warfare and facilitated a turning away from their unpleasant experiences in Vietnam. The Mideast war suggested that the army should train for high-intensity conflict if it were to deter the Soviet threat in Europe. Post-Vietnam revisions to army doctrine thus emphasized conventional operations. Over the next few decades, only rarely did the army evaluate its performance in Vietnam or discuss the issues of revolutionary warfare. Measurements of productivity, efficiency, and effectiveness settled on traditional training indicators—tank gunnery scores, performance during field training exercises, maintenance readiness rates, and soldiers' physical fitness scores. In the process, through a spate of small conventional wars and peacekeeping operations in the 1980s and 1990s, the army resurrected itself from defeat in Vietnam.[31]

By the time of the 2003 Iraq War, the U.S. Army had achieved an unprecedented level of excellence in conventional operations. However, the subsequent insurgency inside Iraq's borders, along with the concurrent struggle in Afghanistan, involved the army once more in unconventional war. As in Vietnam, years of fighting in a war without fronts called into question reports of progress and effectiveness, even though for some years prior army schools and some military thinkers had been addressing what was termed "operations other than war." Even the army's new field manual on counterinsurgency, published in late 2006, discussed formally the problems associated with assessments. For the first time, army doctrine offered insights into developing measurement criteria for a counterinsurgency environment. The manual distinguished between measures of effectiveness and performance. All metrics, the doctrine writers counseled, should have the four characteristics of being measurable, discrete, relevant, and responsive. Of note, FM 3–24 acknowledged the difficulties in assessing complex counterinsurgency operations. "Numerical and statistical indicators have limits when measuring social environments." Interestingly, though, the manual's examples of progress indicators covered a wide range of quantifiable metrics—acts of violence, numbers of dislocated civilians, level of agricultural activity, government services available, and the activity of small businesses—similar to those indicators used four decades earlier in Southeast Asia.[32]

An increasing amount of debate in professional journals accompanied this doctrinal discussion on counterinsurgency assessment. Articles deliberated the use of statistics and their appropriate sources of information. Performance analysts compared the definitions of success in traditional versus irregular warfare. The French experience in Algeria resurfaced, Americans seemingly more receptive now to learning from their European allies. Articles on "systems thinking" in counterinsurgencies advocated the use of feedback loops. One serving officer recommended organizing measurements of progress into "leading" indicators and "lagging" indicators. "Leading indicators forecast progress. Lagging indicators confirm whether existing strategies are working."[33] Yet another commentary considered the Hamlet Evaluation System as a potential starting point for measuring progress and effectiveness against the insurgency in Afghanistan. Sample assessment tools for "strategic counterinsurgency modeling" included indicators on human-relations training, medical care, law enforcement, and reimbursement of collateral damage.[34] As in Vietnam, the potential existed for data threatening to overwhelm the war's managers.

In fact, the conflicts in Iraq and Afghanistan illustrated the continuing challenges of defining progress and success in a counterinsurgency environment and of developing a coherent war strategy. Commanders in Iraq struggled to determine whom to trust among the local population, where the insurgents' main bases were located, and what organized groups posed the greatest threat to government stability. Perhaps unsurprisingly, the pressure to measure and report progress had not dissipated from the Vietnam era. According to one correspondent, scores of analysts were "assigned to crunch numbers—sectarian killings, roadside bombs, Iraqi forces trained, weapons caches discovered and others—in a constant effort to gauge how the war is going."[35] In Afghanistan, other analysts wrestled with defining success, both "from the perspective of the international community and from that of ordinary Afghans."[36] The surplus of indicators, metrics, and differing opinions on the state of progress in both Iraq and Afghanistan seemed to indicate the unresolved difficulties of measuring what matters most in a counterinsurgency environment. As the *New York Times* reported, "even the best-constructed measures can miss the larger truth."[37]

The Sorcerer's Apprentice

In Goethe's famous poem, an old sorcerer's apprentice, weary of his chores, enchants a broomstick to carry water by pail for him. The young novice, though, is practicing magic in the sorcerer's absence and well before he has learned to control his master's spells. Unable to stop the broom from carrying water into a room now submerged in water, the apprentice takes an axe, cutting the broomstick in two. The pieces, however, transform into new brooms and resume filling pails at an even faster pace. Returning to a flooded workshop, the sorcerer breaks the spell, chiding his apprentice for starting something he could not finish.[38]

So it was for the U.S. Army in Vietnam. Insufficiently versed in the mysteries of counterinsurgency, officers turned to statistics to assist them in measuring and reporting progress and effectiveness. Statistics, though, bred more statistics, and the MACV headquarters soon became awash in a flood of numbers, facts, and figures. The commanders and their staffs had started a process they could not stop. Officers' understanding of their craft proved inadequate to prevent the systems analysis computers from pouring forth greater and greater amounts of reports and data.

Arguably, the army needed to measure its progress in Vietnam. Americans in general and army officers in particular were (and perhaps continue to be) uncomfortable with ambiguity, especially in a time of war. Useful indicators for progress and success certainly existed during the Vietnam War. Numerous commentators spoke of the importance of information voluntarily provided by the population. Some officers believed that the most reliable metrics measured freedom of movement or tracked how many village leaders were sleeping in their villages. Still others counseled that more weight should be placed on the number of insurgents surrendering rather than on the number killed and wounded in battle. The problem for MACV, one unresolved throughout a long war, was linking the most dominant indicators of success to a well-articulated strategy and vision for victory. As a substitute for understanding the war, statistics had become an end unto themselves.[39]

In the end, it seems that much perspective can be gained from a long war in which too many American officers and soldiers never truly knew if they were winning or losing. Of course, one must be careful of attempting to draw "lessons" from the Vietnam experience. As Henry Kissinger accurately maintained, "Vietnam represented a unique situation, geographically, ethnically, politically, militarily and diplomatically."[40] Still, the American experience in Southeast Asia can offer exceptional insights into developing measurements of progress and effectiveness for complex political-military problems. That experience, however, also offers a word of caution to armies searching for numerical formulae as a substitute for a deeper understanding of their operational and strategic environments. In the process of collecting data during the Vietnam War, MACV had lost sight of what winning truly meant. Armies employed in counterinsurgencies cannot be so focused on counting that they forget the reason why they were counting in the first place. In short, there is more to winning than counting.

Notes

INTRODUCTION

1. John Zmudzinksi quoted in Ronald J. Drez, ed., *Voices of D-Day: The Story of the Allied Invasion Told by Those Who Were There* (Baton Rouge: Louisiana State University Press, 1994), 239.

2. Omar Bradley, *A Soldier's Story* (New York: Henry Holt, 1951), 271.

3. Lt. Jack Shea quoted in Joseph Balkoski, *Beyond the Beachhead: The 29th Infantry Division in Normandy* (Harrisburg, Pa.: Stackpole Books, 1989), 138.

4. Bradley, *A Soldier's Story*, 272. Emphasis in original.

5. D-Day operational objectives in Russell F. Weigley, *Eisenhower's Lieutenants: The Campaign of France and Germany, 1944–1945* (Bloomington: Indiana University Press, 1990), 94. Casualty figures in Max Hastings, *Overlord: D-Day and the Battle for Normandy* (New York: Simon and Schuster, 1984), 102.

6. Bradley, *A Soldier's Story*, 317.

7. J. Lawton Collins, *Lightning Joe: An Autobiography* (Baton Rouge: Louisiana State University, 1979), 229.

8. Dwight D. Eisenhower, *Crusade in Europe* (Garden City, N.Y.: Doubleday & Company, Inc., 1948), 265.

9. While the term "Vietcong" was used contemptuously by the South Vietnamese government to describe the National Liberation Front's political organization and armed forces, I have decided to apply that idiom in this work in hopes of avoiding some confusion for general readers, since many of the contemporary references and quotations made by U.S. Army officers and soldiers relied so heavily on the word "Vietcong."

10. William C. Westmoreland, "American Goals in Vietnam," in *The Lessons of Vietnam*, eds. W. Scott Thompson and Donaldson D. Frizzell (New York: Crane, Russak & Company, 1977), 10–11. On Johnson, see Langguth, *Our Vietnam*, 421.

11. George L. MacGarrigle, *Taking the Offensive: October 1966 to October 1967* (Washington, D.C.: Center of Military History, 1998), 32.

12. William C. Westmoreland, *A Soldier Reports* (Garden City, N.Y.: Doubleday, 1976), 218.

13. Shelby L. Stanton, *The Rise and Fall of an American Army: U.S. Ground Forces in Vietnam, 1965–1973* (Novato, Calif.: Presidio Press, 1985), 107–108. On Attleboro's gains being temporary and limited, see George Donelson Moss, *Vietnam: An American Ordeal*, 5th ed. (Upper Saddle River, N.J.: Pearson Prentice Hill, 1990, 2006), 216–217.

14. MacGarrigle, *Taking the Offensive*, 47.

15. Ibid., 55–56. For a company level view of the Attleboro fighting, see S. L. A. Marshall, *Ambush: The Battle of Dau Tieng* (Nashville, Tenn.: The Battery Press, 1969).

16. Phillip B. Davidson, *Vietnam at War, The History: 1946–1975* (Novato, Calif.: Presidio Press, 1988), 359. William E. DePuy, *Changing an Army: An Oral History of General William E. DePuy, USA Retired* (Washington, D.C.: U.S. Army Center of Military History, 1988), 144–145. On problems associated with body counts, see MacGarrigle, *Taking the Offensive*, 57.

17. Only later did DePuy acknowledge problems in fighting the Vietcong. "I was surprised . . . [at] the difficulty we had in trying to find the VC. We hit more dry holes than I thought we were going to hit. They were more elusive. They controlled the battle better." Quoted in Andrew F. Krepinevich, Jr., *The Army and Vietnam* (Baltimore and London: The Johns Hopkins University Press, 1986), 190. On differences between military and political successes, see Guenter Lewy, *America in Vietnam* (New York: Oxford University Press, 1978), 58.

18. Quoted in Stanton, *The Rise and Fall of an American Army*, 109.

19. Counting enemy dead as a measurement tool was not a phenomenon new to the Vietnam War. Military forces engaged in the attrition of enemy forces, such as at the World War I battle of Verdun, often have used casualties as the primary yardstick for progress.

20. Survey data taken from Douglas Kinnard, *The War Managers: American Generals Reflect on Vietnam* (Hanover, N.H.: University Press of New England, 1977; DaCapo Press, 1991), 73–74. For an example of MACV's progress briefings, see Robert E. Lester, ed., *The War in Vietnam: The Papers of William C. Westmoreland* (Bethesda, Md.: University Publications of America, 1993), text-fiche, Reel 8, Folder 12, History File, December 13, 1966–January 22, 1967, January 22, 1967 MACV Commander's Conference, Measurement of Progress Briefing.

21. Scott Sigmund Gartner, *Strategic Assessment in War* (New Haven and London: Yale University Press, 1997), 26, 44–45.

22. Among the several histories of the Vietnam War which note the body count as the primary indicator of success are: Dave Richard Palmer, *Summons of the Trumpet: U.S.-Vietnam in Perspective* (San Rafael, Calif.: Presidio Press, 1978), 119; Loren Baritz, *Backfire: A History of How American Culture Led Us into Vietnam and Made Us Fight the Way We Did* (Baltimore and London: The Johns Hopkins University Press, 1985), 311; George C. Herring, *America's Longest War: The United States and Vietnam, 1950–1975*, 2d ed. (New York: Alfred A. Knopf, 1979, 1986), 153; Robert D. Schulzinger, *A Time for War: The United States and Vietnam, 1941–1975* (New York and Oxford: Oxford University Press, 1997), 182.

23. On different missions performed by U.S. ground troops, see Shelby L. Stanton, *Vietnam Order of Battle: A Complete Illustrated Reference to U.S. Army Combat and Support Forces in Vietnam, 1961–1973* (Mechanicsburg, Pa.: Stackpole Books, 2003), 8.

24. Lack of consensus over metrics mirrored the lack of consensus over strategy. Lieutenant General Julian J. Ewell, commander of the 9th Infantry Division and later II Field Force, defended

the use of body counts while General Creighton Abrams, Westmoreland's successor at MACV, thought the appropriate measure of merit was not body count but population security. Abrams, however, never revised MACV's metrics. Julian J. Ewell and Ira A. Hunt, *Sharpening the Combat Edge: The Use of Analysis to Reinforce Military Judgment* (Washington, D.C.: Department of the Army, 1974), 227–228. On Abrams, see Lewis Sorley, *A Better War: The Unexamined Victories and Final Tragedy of America's Last Years in Vietnam* (New York, San Diego, and London: Harcourt Brace & Company, 1999), 22.

25. Allan R. Millet, Williamson Murray, and Kenneth H. Watman, "The Effectiveness of Military Organizations," in *Military Effectiveness, Volume I: The First World War*, ed. Allan R. Millett and Williamson Murray (Boston: Unwin Hyman, 1988), 1–30. On definition of military effectiveness, see p. 2.

26. Definition and discussion of combat power in ibid., 2–12.

27. Colonel T. N. Dupuy, *Numbers, Predictions and War: Using History to Evaluate and Predict the Outcome of Armed Conflict*, rev. ed. (Fairfax, Va.: Hero Books, 1985). Dupuy's focus is on quantitative methodology where even intangible variables such as morale have their own mathematical tables.

28. John Lewis Gaddis, *Strategies of Containment: A Critical Appraisal of Postwar American National Security Policy* (New York and Oxford: Oxford University Press, 1982), 208. Walter LaFeber, *America, Russia, and the Cold War, 1945–1984*, 5th ed. (New York: Alfred A. Knopf, 1985), 216–218.

29. Fall quoted in Palmer, *Summons of the Trumpet*, 24. Examples of widely discussed insurgency literature include Che Guevara, *Guerrilla Warfare* (New York: Monthly Review Press, 1961; Lincoln: University of Nebraska Press, 1998) and Sir Robert Thompson, *Defeating Communist Insurgency: The Lessons of Malaya and Vietnam* (New York and Washington: Frederick A. Praeger, Publishers, 1966).

30. Bernard Fall, *Street Without Joy* (Mechanicsburg, Pa.: Stackpole Books, 1994), 375.

31. See, as one example, Franklin A. Lindsay, "Unconventional Warfare," *Foreign Affairs*, Vol. 40, No. 2 (January 1962): 264–274.

32. For this study, I rely on the definition of revolutionary war as an "armed conflict between a government and opposing forces, wherein the latter rely mainly on guerrilla warfare and subversion rather than on formal warfare. The revolutionary side operates by establishing a rival state structure which embodies a political ideology, and which is intended to replace the existing order. This competing administration is itself the chief instrument of warfare." Edward Luttwak and Stuart Koehl, *The Dictionary of Modern War* (New York: HarperCollins Publishers, 1991), 487. On Malaya, see Rowland S. N. Mans, "Victory in Malaya," in *The Guerrilla—and How to Fight Him*, ed. T. N. Greene (New York: Frederick A. Praeger, 1962), 121.

33. Edward G. Lansdale "Viet Nam: Do We Understand Revolution?" *Foreign Affairs*, Vol. 43, No. 1 (October 1964): 76.

34. Westmoreland, *A Soldier Reports*, 82. Westmoreland argued, rightfully so, that "the insurgency in Malaya had been mounted by ethnic Chinese who, unlike the Viet Cong, were distinguishable from the bulk of the populace."

35. On quality of information, see Sir Robert Thompson, *No Exit from Vietnam* (New York: David McKay, 1969), 142. On attracting popular support, see p. 176.

36. T. N. Dupuy, *Understanding War: History and Theory of Combat* (New York: Paragon, 1987), 106.

37. On the "mosaic" aspect of revolutionary warfare, see Phillip B. Davidson, *Secrets of the Vietnam War* (Novato, Calif.: Presidio Press, 1990), 20–21.

38. Thompson, *No Exit from Vietnam*, 136.

39. On validity of statistics, see Lewy, *America in Vietnam*, 81.

40. Department of the Army, Field Manual 31–16, *Counterguerrilla Operations*, March 1967, 40.

41. Weyand quoted in Stanley Karnow, *Vietnam: A History* (New York: The Viking Press, 1983), 512.

42. Russell F. Weigley, "The Political and Strategic Dimensions of Military Effectiveness," in *Military Effectiveness*, Volume III: *The Second World War*, eds. Allan R. Millett and Williamson Murray (Boston: Allen & Unwin, 1988), 342.

43. See Herring, *America's Longest War*, 153.

44. Palmer, *Summons of the Trumpet*, 114.

45. For a discussion on the effectiveness of airpower in Vietnam, see Mark Clodfelter, *The Limits of Airpower: The American Bombing of North Vietnam* (New York and London: The Free Press, 1989). On objectives of the air campaign, see William W. Momyer, *Airpower in Three Wars* (Maxwell Air Force Base, Ala.: Air University Press, 1978, 2003), 194.

Chapter 1

1. Robert E. Osgood, *Limited War: The Challenge to American Security* (Chicago: The University of Chicago Press, 1957), 4, 13, 15.

2. See T. R. Fehrenbach, *This Kind of War: The Classic Korean War History* (Washington and London: Brassey's, 1963, 1994), 419, 452. On the effectiveness of military power depending on the nature of the threat and the relation of war to politics, see Osgood, *Limited War*, 20.

3. On Mao's shift to a harder line, see Roger Hilsman, *To Move a Nation: The Politics of Foreign Policy in the Administration of John F. Kennedy* (Garden City, N.Y.: Doubleday, 1964, 1967), 418.

4. Osgood's *Limited War*, along with Henry Kissinger's *Nuclear Weapons and Foreign Policy*, was reviewed at length in the January 1958 edition of *Military Review*. G. A. Lincoln and Amos A. Jordan, Jr., "Limited War and the Scholars," *Military Review*, Vol. XXXVII, No. 10 (January 1958): 50–60.

5. On the development of a pervasive conventional, Eurocentric "Army concept," which inhibited the officer corps from effectively executing counterinsurgency warfare in Vietnam, see Krepinevich, *The Army and Vietnam*. John Nagl furthers this thesis in *Learning to Eat Soup with a Knife: Counterinsurgency Lessons from Malaya and Vietnam* (Chicago and London: The University of Chicago Press, 2002) though his general argument that the U.S. Army was not a learning organization in Vietnam is overly simplistic.

6. As an example, see Robert K. Cunningham, "The Nature of War," *Military Review*, Vol. XXXIX, No. 8 (November 1959): 50.

7. Carl von Clausewitz, *On War*, ed. and trans. Michael Howard and Peter Paret (New York and Toronto: Alfred A. Knopf Everyman's Library, 1976, 1993), 580.

8. C. E. Callwell, *Small Wars: Their Principles and Practice* (London: H.M.S.O, 1906; Lincoln: University of Nebraska Press, 1996), 21, 78.

9. T. E. Lawrence, "The Evolution of a Revolt," *Army Quarterly and Defence Journal*, Vol. 1 (October 1920): 22.

10. U.S. Army Infantry School, *Selected Readings on Guerrilla Warfare* (Fort Benning, Ga.: U.S. Army Infantry School, 1962), i, 7.

11. Larry E. Cable, *Conflict of Myths: The Development of American Counterinsurgency Doctrine and the Vietnam War* (New York and London: New York University Press, 1986), 5. For the purposes of this work, Bard E. O'Neill's definitions serve best. O'Neill classifies terrorism as "the threat or use of physical coercion, primarily against noncombatants, especially civilians, to create fear in order to achieve various political objectives." Insurgency is "a struggle between a nonruling group and ruling authorities in which the nonruling group uses *political resources* . . . and *violence* to destroy, reformulate, or sustain the basis of legitimacy of one of more aspects of politics." Finally, guerrilla warfare is defined as "highly mobile hit-and-run tactics by lightly to moderately armed groups that seek to harass the enemy and gradually erode his will and capability." *Insurgency and Terrorism: From Revolution to Apocalypse*, 2nd ed. (Washington, D.C.: Potomac Books, 2005), 15, 33, 35.

12. Department of the Army, Field Manual 31–15, *Operations Against Airborne Attack, Guerrilla Action, and Infiltration*, January 1953, 6. Department of the Army, Field Manual 31–16, *Counterguerrilla Operations*, February 1963, 3, 20.

13. Samuel B. Griffith, *Mao Tse-Tung on Guerrilla Warfare* (New York and Washington: Praeger Publishers, 1961), 4. Political appeal of Vietnamese independence in John Shy and Thomas W. Collier, "Revolutionary War," in *Makers of Modern Strategy: From Machiavelli to the Nuclear Age*, ed. Peter Paret (Princeton, N.J.: Princeton University Press, 1986), 848.

14. C. H. A. East, "Guerrilla Warfare," *Military Review*, Vol. XXXVII, No. 6 (September 1957): 97–98.

15. Carl M. Guezlo, "The Communist Long War," *Military Review*, Vol. XL, No. 9 (December 1960): 16.

16. Quoted in Thomas C. Thayer, *War Without Fronts: The American Experience in Vietnam* (Boulder and London: Westview Press, 1985), 18. See also Mark M. Boatner III, "The Unheeded History of Counterinsurgency," *Army*, Vol. 16, No. 9 (September 1966): 31–36.

17. Henri Navarre, *Agonie de L'Indochine (1953–1954)* (Paris: Librarie Plon, 1956), 89. On the difficulties that French officials encountered because of Vietnamese nationalism, see Ellen J. Hammer, *The Struggle for Indochina, 1940–1955* (Stanford, Calif.: Stanford University Press, 1954, 1966), 68–69.

18. Marshal Jean de Lattre de Tassigny to M. Jean Letourneau, Minister of the Associated States, Saigon, January 23, 1951, Marshal Jean de Lattre, *Ne Pas Subir, Écrits, 1914–1952*, ed. Élisabeth du Réau, et al. (Plon: Paris, 1984), 468–474.

19. Quoted in the Committee of Concerned Asian Scholars, *The Indochina Story: A Fully Documented Account* (New York: Pantheon Books, 1970), 17–18.

20. On French objectives, see Davidson, *Vietnam at War*, 102, 108, 150.

21. Edgar O'Ballance, *The Indo-China War, 1945–1954: A Study in Guerrilla Warfare* (London: Faber and Faber, 1964), 255.

22. Quoted in George C. Herring, "The Legacy of the First Indochina War," in *The Second Indochina War: Proceedings of a Symposium Held at Airlie, Virginia, 7–9 November 1984*, ed. John Schlight (Washington, D.C.: Center of Military History, 1986), 24.

23. Davidson, *Vietnam at War*, 63. On political campaign of the Vietminh, see George K. Tanham, *Communist Revolutionary Warfare: The Vietminh in Indochina* (New York: Frederick A. Praeger, 1961), 63–64.

24. Andrew J. Birtle, *U.S. Army Counterinsurgency and Contingency Operations Doctrine, 1942–1976* (Washington, D.C.: Center of Military History, 2006), 163.

25. For an excellent overview of *guerre révolutionnaire*, see Peter Paret, *French Revolutionary Warfare from Indochina to Algeria: The Analysis of a Political and Military Doctrine* (New York, Washington, and London: Frederick A. Praeger, 1964), 9–11, 55.

26. Quoted in Paret, *French Revolutionary Warfare*, 93. Paret admitted the "success of Opération Pilote is difficult to evaluate." Card catalogues in Alf Andrew Heggoy, *Insurgency and Counterinsurgency in Algeria* (Bloomington, London: Indiana University Press, 1972), 183.

27. Constantin Melnik, "Insurgency and Counterinsurgency in Algeria," (Santa Monica, Calif.: RAND, April 23, 1964), 145. The report was classified "For RAND Use Only."

28. Ibid., 144. Martha Crenshaw Hutchinson, *Revolutionary Terrorism: The FLN in Algeria, 1954–1962* (Stanford, Calif.: Hoover Institution Press, 1978), 112–113.

29. Jean-Jacques Servan-Schreiber, *Lieutenant in Algeria* (New York: Alfred A. Knopf, 1957),

30. On the relation between casualty estimates in Algeria and Vietnam, see David L. Schalk, *War and the Ivory Tower: Algeria and Vietnam* (New York, Oxford: Oxford University Press, 1991), 30.

30. David Galula, *Counterinsurgency Warfare: Theory and Practice* (New York, Washington, London: Frederick A. Praeger, 1964, 2005), 77, 85.

31. Roger Trinquier, *Modern Warfare: A French View of Counterinsurgency* (Westport, Conn., and London: Praeger Security International, 1964, 2006), 54. Italics in the original. Condemning French tactics in Peter Braestrup, "Partisan Tactics—Algerian Style," *Army*, Vol. 11, No. 1 (August 1960): 33–44.

32. On political organization at the grass roots, see Galula, *Counterinsurgency Warfare*, 79. On measuring progress in Algeria, see David Galula, *Pacification in Algeria: 1956–1958* (Santa Monica, Calif.: RAND, 1963, 2006), 187.

33. Fall, *Street Without Joy*, 375. Donn A. Starry, *Armored Combat in Vietnam* (New York: Arno Press, 1980). Starry notes that Fall's works had more of an influence than did the French army's candid and comprehensive "after action" reports, p. 4.

34. Bernard B. Fall, "Insurgency Indicators," *Military Review* Vol. XLVI, No. 4 (April 1966): 3. Unfortunately, this article was published at a time when MACV had already firmly established their reporting systems for measuring progress in Vietnam. However, Fall's "South Viet-Nam's Internal Problems," *Pacific Affairs*, Vol. 31, No. 3 (September 1958): 255 offers a similar argument.

35. Fall, "South Viet-Nam's Internal Problems," 255. See "Insurgency Indicators," p. 8, for what Fall coined the "Fall Insurgency Nonmilitary Indicators" or "FINI."

36. On the Malayan Emergency, see Daniel Moran, *Wars of National Liberation* (London: Cassell, 2001), 85–91.

37. Richard L. Clutterback, "Communist Defeat in Malaya: A Case Study," *Military Review*, Vol. XLIII, No. 9 (September 1963): 63. The American University Special Operations Research Office highlighted British countermeasures and pacification in Malaya in *Undergrounds in Insurgent, Revolutionary, and Resistance Warfare* (Washington, D.C.: The American University, 1963), 170–173 and 259–262.

38. Moran, *Wars of National Liberation*, 91. On lack of corruption in Malayan politics, see Douglas S. Blaufarb, *The Counterinsurgency Era: U.S. Doctrine and Performance, 1950 to Present* (New York: The Free Press, 1977), 48.

39. Bernard B. Fall, *The Two Viet-Nams: A Political and Military Analysis* (New York, London: Frederick A. Praeger, 1963), 339.

40. William C. Westmoreland, interview by Martin L. Ganderson, 1982, Senior Officer Oral History Program, William C. Westmoreland Papers, Box 1, MHI, 142. See William F. Long, "Counterinsurgency: Some Antecedents for Success," *Military Review*, Vol. XLIII, No. 10 (October 1963): 93 on ethnic factors in Malaya.

41. Birtle notes that the U.S. Army "distributed copies of the British manual *Conduct of Antiterrorist Operations in Malaya* to all its service schools for use in formulating doctrine" but does not indicate how well received they were by American officers. *U.S. Army Counterinsurgency and Contingency Operations Doctrine*, 162.

42. On Philippines, see Brian McAllister Linn, *The U.S. Army and Counterinsurgency in the Philippine War, 1899–1902* (Chapel Hill and London: The University of North Carolina Press, 1989). On Greece, see Robert B. Asprey, *War in the Shadows: The Guerrilla in History* (Garden City, N.Y.: Doubleday & Company, Inc., 1975), 740–742 and Birtle, *U.S. Army Counterinsurgency and Contingency Operations Doctrine*, 47–55.

43. Quoted in John K. Walmsley, "US Military Advisers in Greece: The Development of United States Military Assistance and Counterinsurgency Operations during the Greek Civil War" (Master's thesis, The Ohio State University, 2003), 82. Citing Van Fleet correspondence to Ed Clark, July 11, 1950, Folder 66, Box 32, Van Fleet Papers, Marshall Library.

44. Edward R. Wainhouse, "Guerrilla War in Greece, 1946–49: A Case Study," *Military Review*, Vol. XXXVII, No. 3 (June 1957): 25.

45. George Grivas, *General Grivas on Guerrilla Warfare*, trans. A. A. Pallis (New York and Washington: Frederick A. Praeger, 1965), 12. Cable, *Conflict of Myths*, 29.

46. Quotation from CMH Historian Robert Ross Smith, "The Hukbalahap Insurgency," *Military Review*, Vol. XLV, No. 6 (June 1965): 35. Blaufarb correctly asserts that "the U.S. role was important but secondary to that of Magsaysay and the Philippine leadership." *The Counterinsurgency Era*, 38.

47. Uldarico S. Baclagon, *Lessons from the Huk Campaign in the Philippines* (Manila: M. Colcol, 1960). For a summary of the author's lessons, see 230–240.

48. Napoleon D. Valeriano and Charles T. R. Bohannan, *Counter-Guerrilla Operations: The Philippine Experience* (Westport, Conn., and London: Praeger Security International, 1962, 2006), 59, 62.

49. Ibid, 62–64.

50. Of all Americans involved in these early counterinsurgency efforts, the ubiquitous Edward Lansdale functioned as the leading unconventional warfare expert. An Air Force officer who served as Magsaysay's personal advisor during the Huk rebellion, Lansdale recommended in his post-Vietnam autobiography a rather unorthodox way to measure security of a given area—"in guerrilla territory, the children are a barometer." Edward Geary Lansdale, *In the Midst of Wars: An American's Mission to Southeast Asia* (New York: Harper & Row, 1972), 376.

51. Jonathan F. Ladd, "Some Reflections on Counterinsurgency," *Military Review*, Vol. XLIV, No. 10 (October 1964): 78.

52. Gaddis, *Strategies of Containment*, 239.

53. Department of the Army, Field Manual 31–20, *Operations Against Guerrilla Forces*, February 1951, 75.

54. Quoted in Birtle, *U.S. Army Counterinsurgency and Contingency Operations Doctrine*, 225 citing Memo, Decker for the President, February 15, 1961, sub: U.S. Army Role in Guerrilla and Anti-Guerrilla Operations.

55. On the three missions anti-guerrilla forces must fulfill, see Otto Heilbrum, *Partisan Warfare* (New York: Frederick A. Praeger, 1962), 101. Soviet partisan influence on American doctrine in Birtle, *U.S. Army Counterinsurgency and Contingency Operations Doctrine*, 133.

56. Matthew Ridgway as quoted in Clay Blair, *The Forgotten War: America in Korea, 1950–1953* (New York: Times Books, 1987), 761, citing Command Report, March 1951, telex to MacArthur, March 22, 1951.

57. A.J. Bacevich, *The Pentomic Era: The U.S. Army Between Korea and Vietnam* (Washington, D.C.: National Defense University Press, 1986), 119–120. On the army's fixation with body counts during the Korean conflict, see Scott S. Gartner and Marissa E. Myers, "Body Counts and 'Success' in the Vietnam and Korean Wars," *Journal of Interdisciplinary History*, Vol. 25, No. 3 (Winter, 1995): 377–395.

58. For the most influential argument of the day against relying solely on nuclear capabilities, see Maxwell D. Taylor, *The Uncertain Trumpet* (New York: Harper & Brothers, 1960).

59. Letter from LTC Richard W. Ulrich, *Army*, Vol. 11, No. 11 (June 1961): 6. "Origins" in Che Guevera, *Guerrilla Warfare* (Monthly Review Press, 1961; Lincoln: University of Nebraska Press, 1998), 13. *Army* published the condensation and translation of Che Guevara's book in three installments in March, April, and May of 1961 under the title "La Guerra de Guerrillas."

60. Trinquier, *Modern Warfare*, 54, 65. Galula, *Pacification in Algeria*, 176–177. On American viewpoints, see John E. Beebe, "Beating the Guerrilla," *Military Review*, Vol. XXXV, No. 9 (December 1955): 13, 18.

61. Donald Vought, "American Culture and American Arms: The Case of Vietnam," in Richard A. Hunt and Richard H. Shultz, Jr., eds., *Lessons from an Unconventional War: Reassessing U.S. Strategies for Future Conflicts* (New York and Oxford: Pergamon Press, 1982), 165.

62. FM 31–20, February 1951, 71. On Volckmann's background, see Birtle, *U.S. Army Counterinsurgency and Contingency Operations Doctrine*, 131–132.

63. FM 31–15, January 1953, 44.

64. Department of the Army, Field Manual 31–21, *Guerrilla Warfare*, May 1955, 53. The manual also stressed the importance of synchronizing efforts among various governmental agencies.

65. Department of the Army, Field Manual 31–15, *Operations Against Irregular Forces*, May 1961, 4, 18, 25.

66. FM 31–16, February 1963, 20. See also John S. Pustay, *Counterinsurgency Warfare* (New York: The Free Press, 1965), 136.

67. On officers' understanding the basic principles of counterinsurgency, see Peter M. Dunn, "The American Army: The Vietnam War, 1965–1973," in *Armed Forces and Modern Counter-Insurgency*, eds. Ian F. W. Beckett and John Pimlott (New York: St. Martin's Press, 1985), 80. On revolutionary wars being unique "episodes" see Shy and Collier, "Revolutionary War," 818.

68. Lionel C. McGarr, interview by Mr. McDonald and Mr. von Luttichau, n.d., VNIT Folder 1106, CMH, p. 31. On CGSC course subjects in the 1959–1960 school year, see "Summary of the 1959–1960 Regular Command and General Staff Officer Course," Special Collections, CARL. On 1969 course hours, see Boyd L. Dastrup, *The US Army Command and General Staff College: A Centennial History* (Manhattan, Kans.: Sunflower University Press, 1982), 111.

69. Birtle, *U.S. Army Counterinsurgency and Contingency Operations Doctrine*, 265.

70. "Increased Emphasis—Counterinsurgency and Unconventional Warfare Instruction," *Armor*, Vol. 73, No. 1 (January–February 1964): 58. Program of Instruction (POI) for Associate Armor Officer Career Course, August 1964, and POI for Branch Immaterial, Officer Candidate

Course, September 29, 1965, in Special Collections, USAASL. To see how far the Armor School had progressed, see POI for Armor Officer Orientation Course, July 25, 1961, where two hours of instruction were devoted to a "general knowledge of the history, nature, causes, and background of insurgency movements"—all using a single army pamphlet (p. 24).

71. David A. Duffy, "A Reflection of the Army: West Point and Counterinsurgency, 1962–1968," (LD720 Research Paper, United States Military Academy Tactical Officer Education Program, 1995), 5. Citing Richard G. Stilwell to Office of Deputy Chief of Staff for Military Operations, March 7, 1962, Subject: Counter-Insurgency Instruction at USMA, WPSC. That same year the Department of Social Sciences published a 148-page document titled "Readings in Counterinsurgency" for the Corps of Cadets, covering a wide range of unconventional warfare topics. Allen B. Jennings, ed., "Readings in Counterinsurgency" (West Point, N.Y.: USMA Department of Social Sciences, 1962).

72. Quoted in Hilsman, *To Move a Nation*, 427.

73. Guy J. Pauker, "Notes on Non-Military Measures in Control of Insurgency" (Santa Monica, Calif.: RAND, October 1962), 11.

74. Wesley W. Yale, "The Evaluation of Combat Effectiveness," *Army*, Vol. 12, No. 10 (May 1962): 69. Robert Taber, *The War of the Flea: The Classic Study of Guerrilla Warfare* (New York: Lyle Stuart, 1965; Washington, D.C.: Potomac Books, Inc., 2002), 151.

75. Kenneth E. Boulding explores this issue as a conflict of ideologies in *Conflict and Defense: A General Theory* (New York, Evanston, and London: Harper Torchbooks, 1963), 282, 305.

76. Robert S. McNamara, *The Essence of Security: Reflections in Office* (New York, London: Harper & Row, 1968), 88. On the "management revolution," see Paul Y. Hammond, "A Functional Analysis of Defense Department Decision-Making in the McNamara Administration," *The American Political Science Review*, Vol. 62, No. 1 (March 1968): 57.

77. On McNamara's early influences, see Michael T. Klare, *War Without End: American Planning for the Next Vietnams* (New York: Alfred A. Knopf, 1972), 63. For program budgeting, see Alain Enthoven and K. Wayne Smith, *How Much Is Enough? Shaping the Defense Program, 1961–1969* (New York, London: Harper & Row, 1971), 33. On the "whiz kids" see Fred Kaplan, *The Wizards of Armageddon* (New York: Simon and Schuster, 1983), 251–257.

78. Ralph Sanders, *The Politics of Defense Analysis* (New York, London: Dunellen, 1973), 46. Among the more influential early works on systems analysis was Roland N. McKean's *Efficiency in Government Through Systems Analysis: With Emphasis on Water Resources Development* (New York: John Wiley & Sons, 1958). For specific discussion on the application of analytical aids in government, see 8–9, 15. On uncertainty and the suggestion of looking for "dominance" in tests, see 98.

79. Enthoven and Smith, *How Much is Enough?*, 62. Charles J. Hitch, *Decision-Making for Defense* (Berkeley, Los Angeles: University of California Press, 1965), 53. On the rationalist approach, see Gregory Palmer, *The McNamara Strategy and the Vietnam War: Program budgeting in the Pentagon, 1960–1968* (Westport, Conn., and London: Greenwood Press, 1978), 4–5.

80. On choosing criteria to measure effectiveness, see Sanders, *The Politics of Defense Analysis*, 14. On goals and objectives, see Hitch, ibid., 54. On human judgment, see R. D. Specht, "The Why and How of Model Building," in *Analysis for Military Decisions*, ed. E. S. Quade (Chicago: Rand McNally, 1966), 77. On criterion errors and looking for "dominance" see R. N. McKean, "Criteria," in Quade, 89–90.

81. LeMay as quoted in Enthoven and Smith, *How Much Is Enough?*, 78. On Enthoven exchange, see Kaplan, *The Wizards of Armageddon*, 254. "Computers versus Military Judgment," in

Carl W. Borklund, *Men of the Pentagon: From Forrestal to McNamara* (New York, Washington, and London: Frederick A. Praeger, 1966), 219. On widespread criticism among military officials, see Sanders, *The Politics of Defense Analysis*, 155.

82. Hitch, *Decision-Making for Defense*, 57.

83. James H. Hayes, "Basic Concepts of Systems Analysis," *Military Review*, Vol. XLV, No. 4 (April 1965): 12–13. *Military Review*, Vol. XLIII, No. 1 (January 1963): 7–17. Robert R. Hare, Jr., "Models and Systems Effectiveness," *Military Review*, Vol. XLV, No. 11 (November 1965): 26–30.

84. Delbert M. Fowler, "Strategy and Systems Analysis," *Military Review*, Vol. XLV, No. 6 (June 1965): 6.

85. Bernard B. Fall, *Viet-Nam Witness: 1953–66* (New York, Washington: Frederick A. Praeger, 1966), 294. Westmoreland, *A Soldier Reports*, 332. On intangibles, see George A. Kelly, "Footnotes on Revolutionary War," *Military Review*, Vol. XLII, No. 9 (September 1962): 31–39.

86. Ellen J. Hammer, "Progress Report on Southern Viet Nam," *Pacific Affairs*, Vol. 30, No. 3 (September 1957): 221, 224, 230, 235.

Chapter 2

1. Stephen T. Hosmer and Sibylle O. Crane, *Counterinsurgency: A Symposium, April 16–20, 1962* (Santa Monica, Calif.: RAND Corporation, 1963; reprint 2006), 141.

2. ibid., 142.

3. Force structure numbers in South Vietnam for 1962 from David F. Gordon, ed., *Estimative Products on Vietnam, 1948–1975* (Pittsburgh, Pa.: National Intelligence Council, 2005), xxxiv. On the diverse threat and how, when coupled with an absence of close civil-military coordination, this undermined an effective counterinsurgency strategy in Vietnam, see Peter M. Dunn, "The American Army: The Vietnam War, 1965–1975," in Beckett and Pimlott, *Armed Forces and Modern Counter-Insurgency*, 79.

4. Department of the Army, Field Manual 100–5, *Field Service Regulations Operations*, February 1962, 4, 8.

5. David Kaiser, *American Tragedy: Kennedy, Johnson, and the Origins of the Vietnam War* (London and Cambridge, Mass.: The Belknap Press of Harvard University Press, 2000), 192.

6. Ho Chi Minh experienced his own difficulties in the north. See Karnow, *Vietnam*, 224–225. On the south's diversity, see Hunt and Shultz, *Lessons from an Unconventional War*, xiii. Religious sects' challenge to Diem in Frances FitzGerald, *Fire in the Lake: The Vietnamese and the Americans in Vietnam* (Boston and Toronto: Little, Brown, 1972), 79–80.

7. On the parallel VC government, see Birtle, *U.S. Army Counterinsurgency and Contingency Operations Doctrine*, 305. Diem's repression in Karnow, *Vietnam*, 235.

8. Political consolidation to armed struggle in Eric M. Bergerud, *The Dynamics of Defeat: The Vietnam War in Hau Nghia Province* (Boulder, Colo.: Westview Press, 1991), 22, and FitzGerald, *Fire in the Lake*, 147–148. U.S. commitment to Diem in Timothy J. Lomperis, *The War Everyone Lost—and Won: America's Intervention in Viet Nam's Twin Struggles* (Washington, D.C.: CQ Press, 1993), 56, and David L. Anderson, *The Vietnam War* (New York: Palgrave Macmillan, 2005), 21. U.S. credibility in relation to Vietnam within the Cold War in Michael Lind, *Vietnam:*

The Necessary War (New York: The Free Press, 1999), and Mark Atwood Lawrence, *Assuming the Burden: Europe and the American Commitment to War in Vietnam* (Berkeley, Los Angeles, and London: University of California Press, 2005). MAAG's fears of an NVA invasion in Birtle, *U.S. Army Counterinsurgency and Contingency Operations Doctrine*, 309.

9. Gilpatric to the President, memorandum attachment, May 1, 1961, FRUS, 1961–1963, I: 93. "Telegram from Ambassador Eldridge Durbrow in Saigon to Secretary of State, March, 7, 1960" in *Vietnam: A History in Documents*, ed. Gareth Porter (New York and Scarborough, Ontario: New American Library, 1981), 199. Fall, *Viet-Nam Witness*, 238.

10. MAAG-Vietnam, "Tactics and Techniques of Counter-Insurgent Operations," rev. February 10, 1962, General Historians Files, CMH, 2–3. McGarr's emphasis on counterinsurgency in *The Pentagon Papers: The Defense Department History of United States Decisionmaking in Vietnam* [Senator Gravel ed.] (5 vols.; Boston: Beacon Press, 1971–1972), II: 435–436.

11. Diem quoted in John Michael Dunn, interview, July 25, 1984, LBJL, 3. On competing perceptions of the threat, see Douglas Pike, "Conduct of the War: Strategic Factors, 1965–1968," in *The Second Indochina War*, ed. Schlight, 101, and Robert A. Doughty, *The Evolution of US Army Tactical Doctrine, 1946–1976* (Fort Leavenworth, Kans.: Combat Studies Institute, 1979), 30.

12. Marilyn B. Young, *The Vietnam Wars, 1945–1990* (New York: HarperCollins, 1991), 70–72.

13. Quoted in Bergerud, *The Dynamics of Defeat*, 18.

14. Cablegram in Porter, *Vietnam*, 221–222. CIP in Donald W. Hamilton, *The Art of Insurgency: American Military Policy and the Failure of Strategy in Southeast Asia* (Westport, Conn., and London: Praeger, 1998), 134.

15. On Kennedy and the creation of a Special Group, Counterinsurgency under the auspices of the National Security Council, see William P. Yarborough, "Counterinsurgency: The U.S. Role—Past, Present, and Future," in *Guerrilla Warfare and Counterinsurgency*, eds. Richard H. Shultz, Jr., Robert L. Pfaltzgraff, Jr., Uri Ra'anan, William J. Olson, and Igor Lukes (Lexington, Mass., and Toronto: Lexington Books, 1989), 103. Number of American military advisors in Vietnam in Birtle, *U.S. Army Counterinsurgency and Contingency Operations Doctrine*, 315.

16. As quoted in Asprey, *War in the Shadows*, 986.

17. On "Concepts of Pacification Operations" see FRUS, 1961–1963, I: 276–277. Creation of a Western-style army in Bergerud, *The Dynamics of Defeat*, 24. Advisor quotation in Palmer, *Summons of the Trumpet*, 20. Emphasis in original.

18. McGarr to McNamara, October 30, 1961, FRUS, 1961–1963, I: 449–450. On soldiers pervading Diem's administration at the district level, see Karnow, *Vietnam*, 238.

19. David Halberstam, *The Making of a Quagmire: America and Vietnam during the Kennedy Era* (New York: Alfred A. Knopf, 1964, 1988), 56. Karnow, *Vietnam*, 238. CIA memorandum, January 11, 1963, FRUS, 1961–1963, III: 21.

20. On fleeting gains in 1962, see Fredrik Logevall, *The Origins of the Vietnam War* (Harlow, England: Longman, 2001), 47–48. On the U.S. program not reversing the level or intensity of VC operations, see Burris to Johnson, March 16, 1962, FRUS, 1961–1963, II: 237. Harkins assessment of February 23, 1963, in FRUS, 1961–1963, III: 118.

21. Felt to McGarr, February 8, 1962, FRUS, 1961–1963, II: 111–112.

22. Paul D. Harkins, VNIT Folder 1105, CMH, 8. The war literally was in Harkins's backyard. As he remembered, "they finally found that two of the gardeners who worked in my yard in Saigon were Viet Cong," p. 9.

23. Paul D. Harkins, interview, November 10, 1981, LBJL, 7. On legitimacy in the countryside, see Noam Chomsky, *Rethinking Camelot: JFK, the Vietnam War, and U.S. Political Culture* (Boston, Mass.: South End Press, 1993), 57.

24. Mansfield in Porter, *Vietnam*, 235. Nes in *FRUS*, 1964–1968, I: 91. Robert Komer, *Bureaucracy at War: U.S. Performance in the Vietnam Conflict* (Boulder and London: Westview Press, 1986), 21.

25. National Campaign Plan, Phase II, June 22, 1963, Part I, Historians Background Material Files, Box 1, RG 472, NARA, 206–02. On military and political *dau tranh* see Davidson, *Secrets of the Vietnam War*, 18–19 and Asprey, *War in the Shadows*, 997–998.

26. Douglas Pike, interview (I) by Ted Gittinger, June 4, 1981, LBJL, 13.

27. Senior Officer Oral History Program Interview, Box 1, J.L Throckmorton Papers, MHI, 3. On criticisms of ARVN, see Cable, *Conflict of Myths*, 249.

28. Charles J. Timmes quoted in Fall, *Street Without Joy*, citing *The Pacific Stars and Stripes*, November 1, 1963.

29. CIA report in *FRUS*, 1961–1963, IV: 602. On conflict within the American mission in Saigon, see Michael H. Hunt, *Lyndon Johnson's War: America's Cold War Crusade in Vietnam, 1945–1968* (New York: Hill and Wang, 1996), 63–64.

30. Halberstam, *The Making of a Quagmire*, 7. On Johnson's policy upon taking office, see Hunt, ibid., 78–79.

31. On Johnson and "coercive diplomacy" see Young, *The Vietnam Wars*, 122. On the Vietcong's increasing boldness in attacking U.S. troops and facilities, see Davidson, *Vietnam at War*, 284, 290.

32. Quoted in Schulzinger, *A Time for War*, 125. No further citation noted.

33. Presidential Task Force on Vietnam, April 22, 1961, *FRUS*, 1961–1963, I: 74. The Program for the Presidential Task Force on Vietnam stated the goal was "to counter the Communist influence and pressure upon the development and maintenance of a strong, free South Vietnam." By 1964, the U.S. objective was one of maintaining "the independence and territorial integrity of South Vietnam." Porter, *Vietnam*, 273. For Secretary McNamara's March 16, 1964 recommendations on U.S. objectives in South Vietnam, see Thompson and Frizzell, *The Lessons of Vietnam*, 9.

34. Davidson in *An American Dilemma: Vietnam, 1964–1973*, eds. Dennis E. Showalter and John G. Albert (Chicago: Imprint Publications, 1993), 53. Generals LeMay and Greene quoted in Kaiser, *American Tragedy*, 323. William C. Trueheart, Department of State, interview by Ted Gittinger, March 2, 1982, LBJL, 59.

35. On understanding of the political-military problem, see Hilsman, *FRUS*, 1961–1963, II: 77–78, and Lionel C. McGarr, interview, n.d., CMH VNIT Folder 1106, 39. On mobilizing the civilian population, see Lindsay, "Unconventional Warfare," 269.

36. Thomas C. Thayer, "How to Analyze a War Without Fronts: Vietnam, 1965–72," *Journal of Defense Research, Series B: Tactical Warfare*, Vol. 7B, No. 3 (Fall 1975): 771. Emphasis in the original. On "chronic ambiguity in Johnson's approach to the war" see Peter Braestrup, March 1, 1982, LBJL, 15. Broad policy objectives in "Text of Secretary McNamara's Address on United States Policy in South Vietnam," *New York Times*, March 27, 1964.

37. Lansdale in *FRUS*, 1961–1963, I: 418. Taylor in Porter, *Vietnam*, 223.

38. On indicators, see Gartner and Myers, "Body Counts and 'Success' in the Vietnam and Korean Wars," 390. On analysis of resources for offensive operations or securing the population, see Palmer, *The McNamara Strategy and the Vietnam War*, 117.

39. McGarr, VNIT, CMH, 57.

40. Joseph P. D'Arezzo, "Systems Analysis in the Army," *Military Review*, Vol. XLVII, No. 7 (July 1967): 90. On MAAG reporting being unsystematic, see Laurence J. Legere to Thomas Thayer, November 10, 1971, Folder 90, MACV Info & Reports Working Group, Thayer Papers, CMH, p. 3. Army advocating systems analysis in Carl H. Builder, *The Masks of War: American Military Styles in Strategy and Analysis* (Baltimore and London: The Johns Hopkins University Press, 1989), 99. On analysis not being able to replace judgment, see Alain C. Enthoven, interview, March 12, 1975, LBJL, 22.

41. March 1962 memorandum in *FRUS*, 1961–1963, II: 256. Lansdale's July "X-Factor" memorandum in ibid., 506–510. On indicators used in the Philippines and Malaya, see Pauker, *Notes on Non-Military Measures in Control of Insurgency*.

42. Department of Defense paper, n.d., *FRUS*, 1961–1963, II: 379, 386.

43. Report, Visit to SE Asia by the Sec Def, May 8–11, 1962, Appendix 9, Historians Files, CMH.

44. *FRUS*, 1961–1963, II: 645 and 662.

45. Appendix P to MACV Intelligence Guide and Operating Procedures Manual, January 4, 1963, Historians Files, CMH. On RAND warnings, see "MACV Objectives and Indicators," CMH.

46. CINPAC Conference, November 20, 1963, Historians Background Material Files, Box 16, RG 472, NARA.

47. On control being difficult to measure, see Legere, CMH, 10. On operators' reporting see George A. Martinez, Research Analysis Corporation, "Some Aspects of Indicator Analysis," RAC Project No. 261.8, War Indicators SVN, Folder 86, Thayer Papers, CMH, 9. On analytic models, see Thayer, "How to Analyze a War Without Fronts," 769.

48. Halberstam, *The Making of a Quagmire*, 86. On Harkins's conventional mindedness see: William Colby with James McCargar, *Lost Victory: A Firsthand Account of America's Sixteen-Year Involvement in Vietnam* (Chicago and New York: Contemporary Books, 1989), 115 and Hamilton, *The Art of Insurgency*, 145.

49. Memorandum for record, July 31, 1962, *FRUS*, 1961–1963, II: 528.

50. So unwieldy were these reports that the Advanced Research Projects Agency (ARPA) proposed sending a team to Vietnam to study how the command was employing operations analysis resources and techniques. "Proposal for Operations Analysis Study to Develop Statistical Indicators for Measuring Pacification Progress in Vietnam," ARPA, October 31, 1964, War Indicators, SVN, Folder 86, Thayer Papers, CMH.

51. MACV Directive Number 88, MACV Adjutant General Administrative Division, MACV Directives, Box 5, RG 472, NARA. On over 100 indicators, see Report of General Earle G. Wheeler on visit to The Republic of South Vietnam, April 15–20, 1964, ACSI Intelligence Document FICE, TSC Documents, RG 319, NARA. On operational reports, see Command History, United States Military Assistance Command, 1964, Entry MACJ03, Box 1, RG 472, NARA, p. 54.

52. On reports working group, see MACV memorandum "Reports Evaluations by MACV Information and Reports Working Group," March 27, 1964, MACV Info & Reports Working Group, Folder 90, Thayer Papers, CMH.

53. Thayer, *War Without Fronts*, 137. On Pacification Reports, see Command History, US-MACV, 1964, NARA, 55. On data being based on Vietnamese sources, see Legere, CMH, 14.

54. John H. Cushman in *Strange Ground: Americans in Vietnam, 1945–1975, An Oral History*, ed. Harry Maurer (New York: Henry Holt, 1989), 111.

55. Colby, *Lost Victory*, 122. On McNamara's background, see David Halberstam, *The Best and the Brightest* (New York: Random House, 1969), 226–239.

56. Colby, ibid.

57. Quoted in Lewis Sorley, *Honorable Warrior: General Harold K. Johnson and the Ethics of Command* (Lawrence: University Press of Kansas, 1998), 161. On the State Department and Joint Chiefs' requests for regular reporting from Saigon, see *FRUS*, 1961–1963, II: 727–729.

58. Fact Sheet, "Steps to be Taken and Timetable for Future Implementation of 'Oil Spot' Concept Through End 1964," Historians Background Materials Files, Box 3, Sec. Def. Conf. May 12–13, 1964, RG 472, NARA. On counterinsurgencies proceeding along different directions and on different levels, see William W. Kaufman, *The McNamara Strategy* (New York, Evanston, and London: Harper & Row, 1964), 265.

59. William E. Odom, "Output Measurement," *Military Review* Vol. XLVI, No. 1 (January 1966): 46. See also Harry G. Summers, Jr., *On Strategy: A Critical Appraisal of the Vietnam War* (Novato, Calif.: Presidio, 1982), 44.

60. Chester L. Cooper, *The Lost Crusade: America in Vietnam* (New York: Dodd, Mead, 1970), 422.

61. Thayer in Thompson and Frizzell, *The Lessons of Vietnam*, 192. Example indicators from MACV Directive Number 88, NARA. On RAND report, see Martinez, "Some Aspects of Indicator Analysis," 23. On activities versus impact see Tanham in Harvey Neese and John O'Donnell, eds., *Prelude to Tragedy: Vietnam, 1960–1965* (Annapolis, Md.: Naval Institute Press, 2001), 177.

62. Halberstam, *The Making of a Quagmire*, 86.

63. On control changing "overnight" see Taber, *The War of the Flea*, 84. On the "great disparities in impressions of observers" see Johnson to Cottrell, September 11, 1962, *FRUS*, 1961–1963, II: 644.

64. Stanley Karnow, interview by Ted Gittinger, April 30, 1984, LBJL, 5. On lacking quantitative descriptions on the NLF, see Martinez, "Some Aspects of Indicator Analysis," 16.

65. "Report on Viet-Nam," delivered October 23, 1963. As quoted in Fall, *Street Without Joy*, 387–390.

66. On dual mission of RVNAF, see *FRUS*, 1961–1963, I: 278. On Americans eager for battle and contesting the delta, see Halberstam, *The Making of a Quagmire*, 68, 72. Quotation in David M. Toczek, *The Battle of Ap Bac, Vietnam: They Did Everything but Learn from It* (Westport, Conn., and London: Greenwood Press, 2001), 26. Citing MAAG U.S. Army Section (USASEC) "Lessons Learned Number 9."

67. On Ap Bac, see Toczek, *The Battle of Ap Bac* and Neil Sheehan's treatment in *A Bright Shining Lie: John Paul Vann and America in Vietnam* (New York: Random House, 1988). Vann quoted in Sheehan, 277. Halberstam provides his assessment in *The Making of a Quagmire*, 67–81.

68. July numbers from "Agenda Items for Conference with President Diem, August 63 (General Harkins)," Historians Background Materials Files, Box 1 206–02, RG 472, NARA. Defense Intelligence Agency report from *FRUS*, 1961–1963, IV: 707. On not affecting peasant support, see Asprey, *War in the Shadows*, 1031. Toczek discusses ARVN aggressiveness in *The Battle of Ap Bac*, 120–121, 127.

69. Harkins commentary in VNIT, CMH, 17. On poor cultural training, see Martin J. Dockery, *Lost in Translation, Vietnam: A Combat Advisor's Story* (New York: Ballantine Books, 2003),

13. On missing political and economic aspects of revolutionary war, see FitzGerald, *Fire in the Lake*, 143.

70. Jonathan F. Ladd, interviews, July 24 and September 25, 1984, LBJL, 2. On advisors not being accepted "with open arms by all provincial officials" see Heavner to Nolting, April 27, 1962, *FRUS*, 1961–1963, II: 353.

71. Dockery, *Lost in Translation*, 39. James Lawton Collins, Jr., *The Development and Training of the South Vietnamese Army, 1950–1972* (Washington, D.C.: U.S. Government Printing Office, 1975, 2002), 35.

72. On the origins of SAME reports see MACV Fact Sheet, "Requirement for Reporting on Effectiveness of RVNAF Units and Leaders," May 29, 1964, Historians Background Materials Files, Box 3, Book of Misc. Facts, RG 472, NARA. SAME reports in Entry MACV J3-05, Senior Advisor's Monthly Evaluation (SAME) of Proficiency, Combat Readiness, Morale, Leadership and Other Factors of ARVN, Boxes 1–3, RG 472, NARA.

73. Bert Fraleigh, Deputy Office of Rural Affairs in Vietnam, in Neese and O'Donnell, *Prelude to Tragedy*, 111, 115.

74. Neil Sheehan, "Crisis in Vietnam: Antecedents of the Struggle," *The New York Times*, August 27, 1964.

75. In *The Pentagon Papers*, II, 128. On origins of Operation Sunrise in Binh Duong province, see Blaufarb, *The Counterinsurgency Era*, 114. On influence of the Briggs Plan in Malaya, see Milton E. Osborne, *Strategic Hamlets in South Viet-Nam: A Survey and a Comparison* (Ithaca, N.Y.: Cornell University Department of Asian Studies, 1965), 14. On strategic hamlets as the primary means of achieving GVN's basic concept of operations, see *FRUS*, 1961–1963, II: 788.

76. Quotation in William A. Smith, Jr., "The Strategic Hamlet Program in Vietnam," *Military Review*, Vol. XVIV, No. 5 (May 1964): 19. American and British differences in Hunt and Shultz, *Lessons from an Unconventional War*, 5.

77. See Hilsman, *To Move a Nation*, 441, regarding oil blot principle. Quotation from Truehart, LBJL, 36.

78. Donlon in Christian G. Appy, *Patriots: The Vietnam War Remembered from All Sides* (New York: Viking, 2003), 13. On alienating the population and villagers moving reluctantly, see Osborne, *Strategic Hamlets in South Viet-Nam*, 6, 13. On officials rarely spending the night, see William R. Andrews, *The Village War: Vietnamese Communist Revolutionary Activities in Dinh Tuong Province, 1960–1964* (Columbia: University of Missouri Press, 1973), 58. On peasant dissatisfaction, see John C. Donnell and Gerald C. Hickey, *The Vietnamese "Strategic Hamlets": A Preliminary Report* (Santa Monica, Calif.: The RAND Corporation, August 1962), vii-viii.

79. *Wall Street Journal* observer quoted in Fall, *The Two Viet-Nams*, 378. On increased VC attacks against strategic hamlets, see "Viet Cong-Initiated Incident Capability and Recent Performance," October 1964, File # 101213, Box 18, Command Information Publications, RG 472, NARA.

80. Taylor, Impressions of South Vietnam, September 20, 1962, *FRUS*, 1961–1963, II: 660.

81. On Gia Dinh province, see Osborne, *Strategic Hamlets in South Viet-Nam*, 33. On willing support for the VC, see Kevin Ruane, *War and Revolution in Vietnam, 1930–75* (London: UCL Press, 1998), 56. Advisor comments from Ladd, LBJL, 16–17. On problems of defining the term "incident" see "Status Report, MACV Project (Definition of VC Incidents)," May 29, 1964, Historians Background Materials Files, Box 3, Book of Misc. Facts, RG 472, NARA. Hilsman, *To Move a Nation*, 522.

82. .Memorandum, September 10, 1963, *FRUS*, 1961–1963, IV: 161–162. Meeting overview in Halberstam, *The Best and the Brightest*, 275–279.

83. McNamara, *In Retrospect*, 79. For his trip report, see *The Pentagon Papers*, II, 751–757.

84. On Johnson's March trip, see Sorley, *Honorable Warrior*, 152. For his December trip, see "Memo for JCS, Trip Report, Vietnam, 8–12 December. 64," December 21, 1964, Historians Background Materials Files, Box 8, Memos & Misc. Studies, RG 472, NARA.

85. Rostow in *FRUS*, 1961–1963, I: 256. Forrestal in *FRUS*, 1964–1968, I: 386.

86. Paper prepared by Ambassador Taylor, n.d., *FRUS*, 1964–1968, I: 950.

87. Palmer, *Summons of the Trumpet*, 57. On U.S. troop increases, see Hunt, *Lyndon Johnson's War*, 83. On American casualties, see Young, *The Vietnam Wars*, 132.

88. On metrics not reflecting performance, see Christopher K. Ives, *US Special Forces and Counterinsurgency in Vietnam: Military Innovation and Institutional Failure, 1961–1963* (London and New York: Routledge, 2007), 129.

89. Quoted in Hilsman, *To Move a Nation*, 523.

Chapter 3

1. Command History, 1965, Headquarters, USMACV, Secretary of Joint Staff (MACJ03), Entry MACJ03, Military History Branch, Box 2, RG 472, NARA, 1–2. MACV put VC manpower between 93,000 and 113,000 at the opening of 1965. "The Joint Chiefs of Staff and the War in Vietnam, 1960–1968, Part II" (hereafter cited as JCS History), JCSHO, concluded that at "no time had the VC seemed so close to a decisive military victory over the RVN as in early 1965," p. 17–1.

2. Msg, COMUSMACV MAC 6191 to CJCS, November 29, 1964, in JCS History, Part I, JCSHO, 14–13.

3. Taylor, *FRUS*, 1964–1968, I: 948–949. Cooper quoted in Jeffrey P. Kimball, *To Reason Why: The Debate about the Causes of U.S. Involvement in the Vietnam War* (New York: McGraw-Hill, 1990), 228. DePuy quoted in George C. Herring, "'People's Quite Apart': Americans, South Vietnamese, and the War in Vietnam," *Diplomatic History*, Vol. 14, No. 1 (Winter 1990): 4.

4. On Johnson's advisors confidently arguing that "Vietnam represented for the United States the supreme test of its military might, its resolve against the Soviet Union and Asian communism, and its willingness to honor its solemn commitments" see Robert Mann, *A Grand Delusion: America's Descent into Vietnam* (New York: Basic Books, 2001), 458.

5. George C. Herring, "The 1st Cavalry and the Ia Drang Valley, 18 October–November 24, 1965," in *America's First Battles, 1776–1965*, eds. Charles E. Heller and William A. Stofft (Lawrence: University Press of Kansas, 1986), 300.

6. Lyndon Baines Johnson, *The Vantage Point: Perspectives on the Presidency, 1963–1969* (New York, Chicago, and San Francisco: Holt, Rinehart and Winston, 1971), 132. Embassy telegram, January 11, 1965, *FRUS*, 1964–1968, II: 47.

7. On exact numbers of RVNAF casualties, desertions, and weapons losses, see JCS History, Part II, JCSHO, 17–4. On Hanoi's decision to launch an increased political campaign in 1965 and target American forces in South Vietnam, see *Victory in Vietnam: The Official History of the People's Army of Vietnam, 1954–1975*, trans. Merle L. Pribbenow (Lawrence: University Press of Kansas, 2002), 155–156.

8. Taylor as quoted in Kaiser, *American Tragedy*, 386–387.

9. Alsop quoted in MACV Command History, 1965, NARA, 24.

10. Monthly Evaluation Report, January 1965, MACV Command Historian's Collection, Series II: Staff Sections, MACV J-3 Monthly Evaluation Reports, MHI, 1–2. In September 1967, the monthly eval reports changed to quarterly reports. On Lansdale's entreaty for a political solution, see Congressional Record—Senate, April 28, 1965, Box 249, Lansdale folder, OSDHO, 8491.

11. Results of bombing inside South Vietnam also were contentious. MACJ3, memorandum, April 23, 1965, "Evaluation Effectiveness of U.S. Fighter-Bombers in SVN," Historian's Background Materials Files, Box 8, Memos & Misc. Studies, RG 472, NARA. On Westmoreland's request for troops after Pleiku, see Larry Berman, *Planning a Tragedy: The Americanization of the War in Vietnam* (New York and London: W. W. Norton, 1982), 52.

12. McGeorge Bundy to Johnson, January 27, 1965, as quoted in Robert Buzzanco, *Masters of War: Military Dissent and Politics in the Vietnam Era* (Cambridge and New York: Cambridge University Press, 1996), 190. MACV Monthly Evaluation Reports, February, March, and April 1965, MHI. On Pleiku as a turning point, see JCS History, Part II, JCSHO, 17–25.

13. JCS History, Part I, JCSHO, 14–4.

14. For LBJ's Johns Hopkins speech, see *Major Problems in the History of the Vietnam War*, 2nd ed., ed. Robert J. McMahon (Lexington, Mass., and Toronto: D. C. Heath, 1995), 210–213. On Johnson not questioning the assumptions of containment, see Stephen E. Ambrose and Douglas G. Brinkley, *Rise to Globalism: American Foreign Policy Since 1938*, 8th ed. (New York: Penguin Books, 1997), 216.

15. Taylor report on Johnson's visit, March 7, 1965, in *FRUS*, 1964–1968, II: 408–411. On communists attacks, see "U.S. Officers Report Recent Gain in Vietnam War," *New York Times*, March 11, 1965. On quantitative analysis seeking patterns of activity, see Thayer, "How to Analyze a War Without Fronts," 807.

16. On communists moving to the "third stage," see Berman, *Planning a Tragedy*, 80, 135. On Westmoreland and Taylor's initial resistance to employing combat troops, see Buzzanco, *Masters of War*, 190. See Kinnard, *The War Managers*, 35, on Honolulu conference.

17. Fact Sheet on Statistical Indicators of Progress, SECDEF Saigon Trip, July 14, 1965, Items for Discussion, Section II, Tab 13, Historian's Background Materials, Box 9, RG 472, NARA. McNamara questioned numbers relating to VC losses. Meeting with Secretary of Defense & Party, July 16–17, 1965, MACV Emergency Actions Center Conference Room, Historian's Background Materials, Box 4, RG 472, NARA. For post-trip memorandum to Johnson see *FRUS*, 1964–1968, III: 171–179. On Westmoreland's 44 battalion request, see *The Pentagon Papers*, III: 390–391.

18. MACV Monthly Evaluation Report, July 1965, MHI, 1. Memo from Wheeler to McNamara, *FRUS*, 1964–1968, II: 670–671. On assumption that increased U.S. pressure would lead to a "breaking point" of North Vietnamese will, see John E. Mueller, "The Search for the 'Breaking Point' in Vietnam: The Statistics of a Deadly Quarrel," *International Studies Quarterly*, Vol. 24, No. 4 (December 1980): 499–500. On required troop numbers, see William Conrad Gibbons, *The U.S. Government and the Vietnam War: Executive and Legislative Roles and Relationships, Part III: January–July 1965* (Princeton, N.J.: Princeton University Press, 1989), 469, 476–477.

19. Undersecretary of State George Ball provided the most incisive rebuttals to the growing U.S. commitment to Vietnam. (Clark Clifford, a personal advisor to LBJ, also expressed his doubts.) David L. Di Leo, *George Ball, Vietnam, and the Rethinking of Containment* (Chapel

Hill and London: The University of North Carolina Press, 1991). Ball memo to president in Porter, *Vietnam*, 312–313. On troop ratios considered necessary for defeating the insurgency, see "A Tough Ground War Multiplies the Costs," *Business Week*, July 24, 1965, 22–23, and Cooper to Bundy, March 10, 1965, *FRUS*, 1964–1968, II: 433.

20. Memorandum, Ball to President Johnson, June 18, 1965, *FRUS*, 1964–1968, III: 16–19.

21. On the Americanization of the war being counterproductive, see Anthony James Joes, *The War for South Viet Nam, 1954–1975*, rev. ed. (Westport, Conn., and London: Praeger, 2001), 114–115, and JCS History, Part II, JCSHO, 21–22. On MACV trends and McNamara's visit, see "McNamara Questions, Taylor Answers," McNamara July 1965 Vietnam Trip Folder, Box 246, OSDHO.

22. Ball's dissent and Rusk's fears in McMahon, *Major Problems in the History of the Vietnam War*, 217–219.

23. Regarding security assistance coming to an end, see Andrew F. Krepinevich, "Vietnam: Evaluating the Ground War, 1965–1968," in Showalter and Albert, *An American Dilemma*, 89. Westmoreland's assessment of same in Larry H. Addington, *America's War in Vietnam: A Short Narrative History* (Bloomington and Indianapolis: Indiana University Press, 2000), 86.

24. Ernest B. Furgurson provides a sympathetic treatment in *Westmoreland: The Inevitable General* (Boston and Toronto: Little, Brown, 1968). More balanced is Samuel Zaffiri's *Westmoreland: A Biography of General William C. Westmoreland* (New York: William Morrow, 1994). Louis G. Michael, who taught at West Point from 1963 to 1965 and then served as a province advisor in Vietnam, recalled meeting Superintendent Westmoreland at his house to discuss counterinsurgency. Interview with author, April 15, 2008. On Westmoreland understanding the magnitude of his MACV assignment, see *Time*, February 19, 1965, 20, and David Halberstam, *The Best and Brightest* (New York: Random House, 1969), 547–562.

25. Lodge in *FRUS*, 1964–1968, III: 170. For the JCS's and MACV's early endorsement of an oil spot strategy, see *FRUS*, 1964–1968, I: 87 and Fact Sheet, "Steps to be Taken and Timetable for Future Implementation of 'Oil Spot' Concept Through End 1964," Secretary of Defense Conference, May 12–13, 1964, Historians Background Materials Files, Box 3, RG 472, NARA. On William Bundy's assessment of the ad hoc way in which decisions were made, see *The U.S. Government and the Vietnam War, Part III*, 118.

26. Westmoreland in Thompson and Frizzell, *The Lessons of Vietnam*, 60.

27. George C. Herring, *LBJ and Vietnam: A Different Kind of War* (Austin: University of Texas Press, 1994), 41. *The U.S. Government and the Vietnam War, Part IV*, 47–48. Bruce Palmer, Jr., *The 25-Year War: America's Military Role in Vietnam* (New York: Simon & Schuster, 1984), 42.

28. MACV Command History, 1965, NARA, 141–144. JCS History, Part II, JCSHO, 23–24 to 23–26.

29. Captain James F. Ray, "The District Advisor," *Military Review*, Vol. XLV, No. 5 (May 1965): 8.

30. Diversity of strategy in Laurence E. Grinter, "How They Lost: Doctrines, Strategies and Outcomes of the Vietnam War," *Asian Survey*, Vol. 15, No. 12 (December 1975): 1118, and Maxwell D. Taylor, *Swords and Plowshares* (New York: W. W. Norton, 1972), 370.

31. Mission statement in MACV Command History, 1965, NARA, 161. On Westmoreland's concern with pacification in late 1964, see JCS History, Part I, JCSHO, 14–13.

32. Westmoreland views in Graham A. Cosmas, *MACV: The Joint Command in the Years of Escalation, 1962–1967* (Washington, D.C.: Center of Military History, 2006), 238. VC "lie-low tactics" in *FRUS*, 1964–1968, III: 395, 414 and Department of the Army, Field Manual 31-16,

Counterguerrilla Operations, February 1963, 20. On escalation and renewed attention on pacification, see Herring, *LBJ and Vietnam*, 66–67. Lansdale quoted in "Lansdale Choice Stirs Washington," *The New York Times*, August 21, 1965. On Westmoreland's comprehensive view of security, see *A Soldier Reports*, 176.

33. On the enclave debate, see: U. S. Grant Sharp, *Strategy for Defeat: Vietnam in Retrospect* (San Rafael, Calif.: Presidio Press, 1978), 91–92; Davidson, *Vietnam at War*, 311–316; *The Pentagon Papers, III*, 394–395; and Herbert Y. Schandler, "America and Vietnam: the Failure of Strategy," in *Regular Armies and Insurgency*, ed. Ronald Haycock (London: Croom Helm, 1979), 89.

34. Vann quoted in *The U.S. Government and the Vietnam War*, IV, 62. Taylor's March assessment in *The U.S. Government and the Vietnam War*, III, 158.

35. On territorial versus population control, see Thompson and Frizzell, *The Lessons of Vietnam*, 73. On Westmoreland and GVN operations and governmental control, see Kaiser, *American Tragedy*, 324. "Employment of Forces" directive in John M. Carland, "Winning the Vietnam War: Westmoreland's Approach in Two Documents," *The Journal of Military History*, Vol. 68, No. 2 (April 2004): 558.

36. Gustav J. Gillert, Jr., "Counterinsurgency," *Military Review*, Vol. XLV, No. 4 (April 1965): 29. For General William E. DePuy's remarks on battle frequency and the attrition strategy, see *The U.S. Government and the Vietnam War*, IV, 50.

37. The historiographical debate is as fascinating as the actual development of strategy. Summers argued that "conventional tactics were militarily successful in destroying guerrilla forces" and that the U.S. Army failed to recognize that the insurgency was not the decisive element of the war. *On Strategy*, 90. Gabriel Kolko maintained the U.S. and GVN "had to rely increasingly on military means precisely to compensate for their already profound and growing political weakness." *Anatomy of a War: Vietnam, the United States, and the Modern Historical Experience* (New York: Pantheon Books, 1985), 142. Baritz contends that Westmoreland "knew that the guerrillas' effectiveness was at least as much political as military, and that fact helped to exonerate him from responsibility for their progress." *Backfire*, 161. On how winning popular support had little chance of success, see Charles Wolf, Jr., *Insurgency and Counterinsurgency: New Myths and Old Realities* (Santa Monica, Calif.: The Rand Corporation, 1965), 9. On lack of coordination between agencies, see Herring, *LBJ and Vietnam*, 69. On problems with escalation, see Chomsky, *Rethinking Camelot*, 58.

38. Westmoreland acknowledged the problem of measuring progress in U. S. Grant Sharp and William C. Westmoreland, *Report on the War in Vietnam* (Washington, D.C.: U.S. Government Printing Office, 1969), 105–106. Sector advisors' paperwork requirements in G. C. Hickey, *The American Military Advisor and his Foreign Counterpart: The Case of Vietnam* (Santa Monica, Calif.: The RAND Corporation, 1965), 42. Yardsticks in memorandum, "Interim Report of Progress Indicator Study; ARPA Project Agile: RAC Field Office, Vietnam," MACJ03, Historians Background Files, Box 22, RG 472, NARA, 4.

39. ARPA Project Agile, NARA, 10. Still left undecided was how best to measure yardsticks such as population or area control. On the heavy reliance on statistical indicators aimed at the military aspect of the war, see "Trends in Viet Cong Attacks on Hamlets," Command Information Publications, Folder 101251, Box 21, RG 472, NARA.

40. "Area war" and attrition in Westmoreland, *A Soldier Reports*, 185–186. Data limitations in ARPA Project Agile, NARA, C-3.

41. On forces deploying before an agreement on strategy, see JCS History, Part II, JCSHO, 23-1; 173rd deployment in Stanton, *The Rise and Fall of an American Army*, 46–47, and John M.

Carland, *Stemming the Tide: May 1965 to October 1966* (Washington, D.C.: Center of Military History, 2000), 21–29. Williamson quoted in Birtle, *U.S. Army Counterinsurgency and Contingency Operations Doctrine*, 374.

42. Theodore T. Mataxis, interview by Captain John Cash, CMH Library, 3. On intelligence being received too late to be effective, see USARV Battlefield Reports: A Summary of Lessons Learned, August 30, 1965, Vol. 1, Box. 1, RG 472, NARA, I-5-I-6.

43. On the 173rd's use of helicopters, see John J. Tolson, *Airmobility, 1961–1971* (Washington, D.C.: U.S. Government Printing Office, 1973), 64. James M. Gavin, "Cavalry, and I Don't Mean Horses," *Harper's*, Vol. 208, No. 1247 (April 1954): 54–60. Hamilton H. Howze, "Army Aviation 1955–1962: The Foundation of Air Mobility," *Army Aviation* (31 December 1992): 25–34. John M. Carland, "How We Got There: Air Assault and the Emergence of the 1st Cavalry Division (Airmobile), 1950–1965," *The Land Warfare Papers* No. 42 (May 2003).

44. McNamara to Secretary of the Army Stahr, April 19, 1962, in Shelby L. Stanton, *Anatomy of a Division: The 1st Cav in Vietnam* (Novato, Calif.: Presidio, 1987), 15–17. American pilots carrying ARVN paratroopers in Stephen Peter Rosen, *Winning the Next War: Innovation and the Modern Military* (Ithaca, N.Y., and London: Cornell University Press, 1991), 92.

45. Howze Board conclusions in Tolson, *Airmobility*, 24. Howze published three articles tracing the history of the board in the February ("The Howze Board"), March ("Airmobility Becomes More than a Theory"), and April ("Winding Up a 'Great Show'") editions of *Army*, Vol. 24, Nos. 2–4 (February–April 1974).

46. Ian Horwood, *Interservice Rivalry and Airpower in the Vietnam War* (Fort Leavenworth, Kans.: Combat Studies Institute Press, 2006), 30–31. Wheeler quoted in "What It Takes in Vietnam," *The Economist*, July 24, 1965, 333. Harry W. O. Kinnard, "Airmobility Revisited, Part I," *U.S. Army Aviation Digest*, Vol. 26, No. 6 (June 1980): 3.

47. Biographical sketch of Kinnard in Stanton, *Anatomy of a Division*, 25 and J.D. Coleman, *Pleiku: The Dawn of Helicopter Warfare in Vietnam* (New York: St. Martin's Press, 1988), 10. On field testing, see Carland, "How We Got There," 12. Wheeler quoted in Christopher C. S. Cheng, *Air Mobility: The Development of a Doctrine* (Westport, Conn., and London: Praeger, 1994), 186, citing "Army Moves Toward Mobility," *AID*, February 1964, 34–35. Redesignation to 1st Cavalry in Stanton, *Anatomy of a Division*, 36.

48. Harry W. O. Kinnard, "Airmobility Revisited, Part 2," *U.S. Army Aviation Digest*, Vol. 26, No. 7 (July 1980): 8. Emphasis in original. As an example of the growing media exposure, see "Vietnam War Proving Helicopter's Value as Weapon, Army Contends," *Aviation Week & Science Technology*, April 20, 1964, 104–106. On the "Reorganization Objectives Army Division" (ROAD), see Russell F. Weigley, *History of the United States Army* (New York: Macmillan, 1967), 540, 545. Helicopters as part of the counterinsurgency intelligence collection effort in 1st Aviation Brigade Operations Manual, February 1, 1967, Digital Archive Collection, USAAWCL, p. 10–15.

49. On early interest in the helicopter's counterinsurgency role in MAAG, see Rostow to Kennedy, April 3, 1961, *FRUS*, 1961–1963, I: 61.

50. U.S. Army Tactical Mobility Requirements Board, Fort Bragg, N.C., Annex O, Field Tests, July 31, 1962, Digital Archive Collection, USAAWCL, ii.

51. Operational Evaluation of Armed Helicopters, Concept Team, May 10, 1963, Tab I, 3–10, and Armed Helicopter Reconnaissance and Area Surveillance, January 15, 1965, Digital Archive Collection USAAWCL, vi.

52. Kinnard quoted in Lawrence H. Johnson III, *Winged Sabers: The Air Cavalry in Vietnam, 1965–1973* (Harrisburg, Pa.: Stackpole Books, 1990), 5. On American reliance on technology, see Kolko, *Anatomy of a War*, 188 and Baritz, *Backfire*, 51. On the capabilities of helicopters, see Department of the Army, Field Manual 57-35, *Airmobile Operations*, September 1963, 4.

53. French experience in Fall, *Street Without Joy*, 361. On ideology and technology, see Young, *The Vietnam Wars*, 112.

54. 1st Cavalry deployment in Carland, *Stemming the Tide*, 54–62. On central highlands encampment, see: Wilbur H. Morrison, *The Elephant and the Tiger: The Full Story of the Vietnam War* (New York: Hippocrene Books, 1990), 188; Asprey, *War in the Shadows*, 1112; and Mark Moyar, *Triumph Forsaken: The Vietnam War, 1954–1965* (Cambridge and New York: Cambridge University Press, 2006), 392. Shakedown exercises in Stanton, *Anatomy of a Division*, 46–47. North Vietnamese infiltration in JCS History, Part II, JCSHO, 22–1.

55. MACV Monthly Evaluation Report, October 1965, MHI, 2. Robert Mason, *Chickenhawk* (New York: The Viking Press, 1983), 101–102. Plei Me battle in Carland, *Stemming the Tide*, 99–104. Herring, *America's First Battles*, 309–313. The NVA regiments taking part in the campaign were the 32nd, 33rd, and the 66th, which was held in reserve.

56. Losses in the Plei Me battle from Herring, *America's First Battles*, 313. Brown quoted in Stanton, *Anatomy of a Division*, 55. On the lead up to Ia Drang, see Carland, *Stemming the Tide*, 104–111, and Stanton, *The Rise and Fall of an American Army*, 56–57.

57. Moore biographical sketch in Coleman, *Pleiku*, 187. Deal in Appy, *Patriots*, 131. Sheehan, *A Bright Shining Lie*, 573. The best account of the battle is Harold G. Moore and Joseph L. Galloway, *We Were Soldiers Once . . . and Young* (New York: HarperCollins, 1993). On artillery fires initially being ineffective, see John A. Cash, John Albright, and Allan W. Sandstrum, *Seven Firefights in Vietnam* (Mineola, N.Y.: Dover, 2007), 17.

58. Moore, *We Were Soldiers Once*, 133. On fighting three separate actions, see Coleman, *Pleiku*, 205. Use of B-52 bombers from Herring, *America's First Battles*, 319.

59. Quotation from Jack P. Smith, "Death in the Ia Drang Valley," *Saturday Evening Post* Vol. 240, No. 2 (January 28, 1967): 82. Harry W.O. Kinnard, "A Victory in the Ia Drang: The Triumph of a Concept," *Army* Vol. 17, No. 9 (September 1967): 89. Albany ambush in Carland, *Stemming the Tide*, 136–145 (casualties on p. 145).

60. Casualty numbers taken from After Action Report, Ia Drang Valley Operation, 1st Battalion, 7th Cavalry, November 14–16, 1965, 13. Copy of original report downloaded from www.lzxray.com. On low ratios confirming MACV's attrition strategy, see Leslie H. Gelb with Richard K. Betts, *The Irony of Vietnam: The System Worked* (Washington, D.C.: The Brookings Institution, 1979), 135.

61. Westmoreland, *A Soldier Reports*, 191 and *Report on the War in Vietnam*, 99.

62. Moore, *We Were Soldiers Once*, 399. For Hanoi's assessment of the fighting, see *Victory in Vietnam*, 159–160.

63. Hoang Anh Tuan quoted in Cecil B. Currey, *Victory at Any Cost: The Genius of Viet Nam's Gen. Vo Nguyen Giap* (Washington and London: Brassey's, 1997), 257. On early enemy reactions to U.S. helicopters in 1962, see Tolson, *Airmobility*, 26–27. On the enemy's capability at countering U.S. advantages in firepower, see Carland, *Stemming the Tide*, 149, and Rosen, *Winning the Next War*, 94.

64. Palmer noted "Victory in Vietnam was hard to measure." *Summons of the Trumpet*, 102. On success of 1st Cavalry's spoiling attack, see Kinnard, "A Victory in the Ia Drang," 72. On MACV

overlooking important facts, see Krepinevich in Showalter and Albert, *An American Dilemma*, 96. On Army Chief of Staff Harold K. Johnson's views of destruction versus control, see Sorley, *Honorable Warrior*, 201.

65. MACV Monthly Evaluation Report, November 1965, Annex E, 31–35, MHI. Although Moore acknowledged this issue in *We Were Soldiers Once . . . and Young*, 398–401.

66. Advisor quoted in Malcolm W. Browne, *The New Face of War*, rev. ed. (Indianapolis and New York: Bobbs-Merrill, 1968), 79. Hanson Baldwin, "U.S. First Cavalry is Sternly Tested," *The New York Times*, November 20, 1965. On asking how much increase in mobility helicopters actually provided, see James H. Pickerell, *Vietnam in the Mud* (Indianapolis and New York: Bobbs-Merrill, 1966), 45.

67. Johnson in *The U.S. Government and the Vietnam War, Part IV*, 101–102. On self-delusion in the army, see Herring, *LBJ and Vietnam*, 37.

68. Field Manual 31–16, 21.

69. On narrow lessons from the campaign, see Benjamin S. Silver and Francis Aylette Silver, *Ride at a Gallop* (Waco, TX.: Davis Brothers, 1990), 316. On conventional organizations potentially not being suited to counterinsurgency, see Boyd T. Bashore, "Organization for Frontless Wars," *Military Review*, Vol. XLIV, No. 5 (May 1964): 16. On discounting dangerous weaknesses, see Palmer, *Summons of the Trumpet*, 97.

70. Operations Report, Lessons Learned, 3–66, The Pleiku Campaign, May 10, 1966, CMH Library, 213. On MACV requiring no more feedback other than body counts, see Krepinevich, *The Army and Vietnam*, 169.

71. MACV Monthly Evaluation Report, November 1965, 2.

72. Air of defeatism in Asprey, *War in the Shadows*, 1113. MACV's command history called the year a "dramatic turn of events." MACV Command History, 1965, NARA, 1.

73. Westmoreland quoted in "Westmoreland Surveys Action," *The New York Times*, November 20, 1965.

74. Presidential Unit Citation from Stanton, *Vietnam Order of Battle*, 71. Examples of metrics from MACV Directive Number 88, MACV Adjutant General Administrative Division, MACV Directives, Box 5, RG 472, NARA. DoD message to MACV, November 1, 1965, "Reporting of VC Casualties in South Vietnam," Body Count Folder, Box 369, OSDHO.

75. "Smell of Victory: Success in Viet Nam Hangs on Two Vital Items," *The Evening Star*, November 4, 1965.

76. COMUSMACV memorandum, "Increased Emphasis on Rural Construction," December 8, 1965, Correspondence, 1965–1966, Box 35, Jonathan O. Seaman Papers, MHI. For response, see Seaman memorandum to 1st Infantry Division, December 27, 1965, ibid..

77. MACV Command History, 1965, NARA, 4. Advisors' perceptions of ARVN shortfalls in Jeffrey J. Clarke, *Advice and Support: The Final Years, 1965–1973* (Washington, D.C.: Center of Military History, 1988), 113.

78. On MACV's appraisals, see "MACV Briefing on Phase II Add-Ons," November 28, 1965, COMUSMACV Briefing to Secretary McNamara, Historians Background Files, Box 7, Materials Files, RG 472, NARA. On progress not being made with VC control, see JCS History, Part II, JCSHO, 27–13. On body counts gaining prominence, see "Memoirs," 2d rev., Part II, Box 9, Donald A. Seibert Papers, MHI, 854.

79. Westmoreland's evaluation in Carland, "Winning the Vietnam War," 570. On the media's take on these early battles, see "G.I.'s Found Rising to Vietnam Test," *New York Times*, December 26, 1965.

80. Memorandum to President Lyndon B. Johnson from Robert S. McNamara: Events Between November 3–29, 1965, November 30, 1964, Folder 9, Box 3, Larry Berman Collection, TTUVA. On McNamara being "shaken" by the meeting, see Sheehan, *A Bright Shining Lie*, 579–580.

Chapter 4

1. Kinnard in Maurer, *Strange Ground*, 143. 1st Cavalry's mission from "Combat After Action Report" (RCS MACV J3/32), April 28, 1966, Folder 18, Box 1, Operation Masher/Operation White Wing Collection, TTUVA.

2. On Masher/White Wing, see John Prados, *The Hidden History of the Vietnam War* (Chicago: Ivan R. Dee, 1995), 111–112; Sheehan, *A Bright Shining Lie*, 580–583; and Carland, *Stemming the Tide*, 202–215.

3. "Combat After Action Report," Headquarters, 3rd Brigade, 1st Cavalry Division, Operation Masher/White Wing folder, RG 472, NARA, 10–11. Division KIA numbers from Combat AAR, Folder 18, Box 1, Operation Masher/Operation White Wing Collection, TTUVA, 23. Kinnard estimated another 1,746 enemy killed and 1,348 wounded during Masher/White Wing. On the airmobile division's staying power, see Stanton, *Anatomy of a Division*, 77, and J. D. Coleman, ed., *Memoirs of the First Team: Vietnam, August 1965–December 1969* (Tokyo: Dia Nippon, 1970), 32.

4. On Larsen's views on pacification, see Sheehan, *A Bright Shining Lie*, 584. On hamlets destroyed, civilian casualties, and the enemy returning, see Young, *The Vietnam Wars*, 163–164. Moore quoted in Kuno Knoebl, *Victor Charlie: The Face of War in Viet-Nam*, trans. Abe Farbstein (New York and Washington: Frederick A. Praeger, 1967), 219. On the refugee problem created by Masher/White Wing, see Lewy, *America in Vietnam*, 58–59. On adverse affects of this operation on the pacification program, see Congressional Research Service, Library of Congress, *The U.S. Government and the Vietnam War: Executive and Legislative Roles and Relationships, Part IV, July 1965–January 1968* (Washington, D.C.: U.S. Government Printing Office, 1994), 189.

5. General Westmoreland's History Notes, December 31, 1965, History File December 20, 1965–January 29, 1966, Folder 3, Reel 6, WCWP. Westmoreland's guidance in "COMUSMACV Conference with FFORCEV Commanders and II Corps Advisors," December 30, 1965, ibid. On search-and-destroy operations dominating friendly actions, see MACV Monthly Evaluation Report, February 1966, MHI, 2.

6. JCS History, Part II, JCSHO, 33-1.

7. "Turn for Better Seen in War's Fortunes," *U.S. News & World Report*, March 7, 1966, 33. On eighteen operations in 1966 with over 500 enemy dead, see Palmer, *Summons of the Trumpet*, 120. Troop strength from News Release, Office of Assistant Secretary of Defense (Public Affairs), January 4, 1966, Mil Opns October–December 1965 folder, Box 248, OSDHO.

8. Carland, *Stemming the Tide*, 155–157. Telegram from Department of State to Embassy in Vietnam, *FRUS*, 1964–1968, IV: 14. Memorandum from NCS Staff to Bundy, ibid., 26–29. On Johnson's focus during the conference, see "The New Realism," *Time*, February 18, 1966, 19.

9. On discussion of the "other war" during Honolulu, see "Presidential Decisions: The Honolulu Conference, February 6–8, 1966," Folder 2, Box 4, Larry Berman Collection, TTUVA,

5, 19–20. "The Declaration of Honolulu" in *Public Papers of the Presidents, Lyndon B. Johnson, Book I—January 1 to June 30, 1966* (Washington, D.C.: U.S. Government Printing Office, 1967), 153–155. For how MACV portrayed "The Stakes in Vietnam," see "Ready Reference Facts on South Vietnam," Box 3, Joseph A. McChristian Papers, MHI.

10. Press Conference, February 6, 1966, Folder 4, Reel 6, WCWP. On protection of government and people, see Sharp and Westmoreland, *Report on the War in Vietnam*, 113.

11. On JCS and PACOM views, see Sharp to JCS, January 12, 1966, *FRUS*, 1964–1968, IV: 47 and "Command History, 1966," HQ, USMACV, Entry MACJ03, Box 3, RG 472, NARA, 339. On internal security, see Department of the Army, Field Manual 31–16, *Counterguerrilla Operations*, March 1967, 29.

12. "1966 Program to Increase the Effectiveness of Military Operations and Anticipated Results Thereof," February 8, 1966, Incl. 6, Folder 4, Reel 6, WCWP.

13. On Westmoreland's views on a long war and pacification in South Vietnam, see Alex Campbell, "'Our' War, 'Their' Peace: Who Wants What in South Vietnam?" *The New Republic*, Vol. 154, No. 12 (March 19, 1966): 19–21.

14. On bully boys and termites, see Westmoreland, *A Soldier Reports*, 175. On views in the U.S. military regarding ARVN effectiveness and the logic of search-and-destroy operations, see JCS History, Part II, JCSHO, 33-4-33-5. On the "shield of military protection" see Bell to Johnson, January 19, 1966, *FRUS*, 1964–1968, IV: 84–85.

15. Cyrus Vance quoted in *FRUS*, 1964–1968, IV: 345. Komer to Johnson, ibid., 375. McNamara to Johnson, ibid., 659. Frank L. Jones, "Blowtorch: Robert Komer and the Making of Vietnam Pacification Policy," *Parameters*, Vol. XXXV, No. 3 (Autumn 2005): 103–118.

16. JCS reporting to MACV on the pacification program in *FRUS*, 1964–1968, IV: 757. Johnson's failure to provide guidance in Herring, *LBJ and Vietnam*, 25.

17. On critics of Westmoreland's strategy, see Robert L. Gallucci, *Neither Peace Nor Honor: The Politics of American Military Policy in Viet-Nam* (Baltimore and London: The Johns Hopkins University Press, 1975), 116–117. PROVN summary statement from Lewis Sorley, "To Change a War: General Harold K. Johnson and the PROVN Study," *Parameters*, Vol. XXVIII, No. 1 (Spring 1998): 99. On depending on a "viable government" see *The U.S. Government and the Vietnam War, Part IV*, 206. See also Andrew J. Birtle, "PROVN, Westmoreland, and the Historians: A Reappraisal," *The Journal of Military History*, Vol. 72, No. 4 (October 2008): 1213–1247.

18. On Westmoreland's reaction to PROVN, see Davidson, *Vietnam at War*, 367–368. JCS views in *FRUS*, 1964–1968, IV: 591–592. On PROVN being downgraded to a "conceptual document," see Krepinevich, *The Army and Vietnam*, 182.

19. ARCOV Study in Folder 1, Box 5, Glenn Helm Collection, TTUVA. On "firepower doctrine" see Annex C, Folder 5, Box 5.

20. Brigade staff inadequacies in "Approval of Evaluation of U.S. Army Combat Operations in Vietnam (ARCOV)," Folder 1, Box 5, Glenn Helm Collection, TTUVA, 2-II-60. On flow of intelligence, see Annex A, Folder 3, Box 5, A-1-18.

21. L. W. Walt, interview by Paige E. Mulhollan, January 24, 1969, LBJL, 4. Lewis W. Walt, *Strange War, Strange Strategy: A General's Report on Vietnam* (New York: Funk & Wagnalls, 1970), 33. General discussions on Marine dissent can be found in *The U.S. Government and the Vietnam War, Part IV*, 197–201, and Buzzanco, *Masters of War*, 248–252.

22. Krulak quoted in Sheehan, *A Bright Shining Lie*, 636. On Marines' view of progress, see "The Marines Try a New Kind of War," *The Washington Star*, April 28, 1967, 2-F. On combined

action platoons, see Michael E. Peterson, *The Combined Action Platoons: The U.S. Marines' Other War in Vietnam* (Westport, Conn., and London: Praeger, 1989). MACV's response in "Command History, 1966," 347, and Westmoreland, *A Soldier Reports*, 200–202.

23. On Gavin's views, see "Vietnam Policy—Testimony at the Committee Hearings," *Congressional Digest*, Vol. 45, No. 4 (April 1966): 107–108 and "A Communication on Vietnam," *Harper's*, Vol. 232, No. 1389 (February 1966): 16–21. Robert Thompson, "Feet on the Ground," *Survival*, Vol. VIII, No. 4 (April 1966): 117. On the oil spot strategy, see John J. McCuen, *The Art of Counter-Revolutionary War* (Harrisburg, Pa.: Stackpole Books, 1966), 196–197.

24. JCS to McNamara, *FRUS*, 1964–1968, IV: 198–201. Wheeler testimony in *The U.S. Government and the Vietnam War, Part IV*, 241. MACV staff quoted in Westmoreland, *A Soldier Reports*, 156.

25. On the administration's failure to synchronize, see Karnow, *Vietnam*, 493, and Kolko, *Anatomy of a War*, 180–181. On problems with measurements, see Thayer, *War Without Fronts*, 55.

26. MACV Monthly Evaluation Report, March 1966, MHI. "Vietnam Status Report: Honolulu—Freeman, Gardner Recommendations and Suggestions," Planning Division, Office of Vietnam Affairs, May 26, 1966, Folder 18, Box 4, Larry Berman Collection (Presidential Archives Research), TTUVA.

27. CTZ information from Carland, *Stemming the Tide*, 5–7, and Stanton, *The Rise and Fall of an American Army*, 65–66.

28. "Hide-and-seek" in Anthony Harrigan, "Ground Warfare in Vietnam," *Military Review*, Vol. XLVII, No. 4 (April 1967): 62. Ground assault data from Thayer, *War Without Fronts*, 46. On few major battles see: Moss, *Vietnam*, 215; Gerard J. DeGroot, *A Noble Cause? America and the Vietnam War* (Harlow, Essex: Longman, 2000), 156–157; and Christian G. Appy, *Working-Class War: American Combat Soldiers and Vietnam* (Chapel Hill and London: The University of North Carolina Press, 1993), 153.

29. DePuy quoted in *Time*, May 27, 1966, 27. On the importance of gaining and maintaining contact, see "A Summary of Lessons Learned," June 30, 1966, Vol. 2, USARV Battlefield Reports, Box 1, RG 472, NARA, 38.

30. On enemy discipline, see Raoul H. Alcala, interview by Brian C. Bade, Box 1, Vietnam Company Command Oral History, MHI, LVI-15. Report on enemy initiating contact in Stanton, *The Rise and Fall of an American Army*, 86. Unpredictable nature of combat from Peter Braestrup, interview by Ted Gittinger, March 1, 1982, LBJL, I-4. On GIs living with constant fear and tension in this environment, see The Committee of Concerned Asian Scholars, *The Indochina Story*, 108.

31. Micheal Clodfelter, *Mad Minutes and Vietnam Months: A Soldier's Memoir* (Jefferson, N.C., and London: McFarland, 1988), 47, 77.

32. Putnam quoted in James R. Ebert, *A Life in a Year: The American Infantryman in Vietnam, 1965–1972* (Novato, Ca.: Presidio, 1993), 179. "Synopsis of the Battle of Lo Khe March 5, 1966" VNIT Folder 138, CMH.

33. James L. Estep, *Company Commander Vietnam* (Novato, Calif.: Presidio, 1996), 99.

34. Soldier quoted in Mark Baker, *Nam: The Vietnam War in the Words of the Men and Women Who Fought There* (New York: William Morrow, 1981), 101. On 1st Infantry Division generals, see Melvin Zais, interview by William L. Golden and Richard C. Rice, Senior Officers Oral History Program, Melvin Zais Papers, MHI, 475.

35. Victor K. Heyman memorandum to Mr. Nitze, December 4, 1967, Box 327, Vietnam War Statistical Data, OSDHO.

36. Systems Analysis office assessment from Enthoven and Smith, *How Much Is Enough?*, 295. On firepower reliance, see Robert H. Scales, Jr., *Firepower in Limited Warfare*, rev. ed. (Novato, Calif.: Presidio, 1995), 80.

37. James William Gibson, *The Perfect War: Technowar in Vietnam* (Boston and New York: The Atlantic Monthly Press, 1986), 113–115.

38. 1st Cavalry rifleman quoted in Al Santoli, *Everything We Had: An Oral History of the Vietnam War by Thirty-three American Soldiers Who Fought It* (New York: Random House, 1981), 42. "Walking arsenals" from "The Bloody Checkerboard," *Newsweek*, May 23, 1966, 64. 1966 casualty figures in "Vast U.S. Firepower Arrayed in Vietnam Against Guerrillas," *The New York Times*, June 28, 1966. On aggressiveness of American fighting in Vietnam, see Wesley R. Fischel, ed., *Vietnam: Anatomy of a Conflict* (Itasca, Ill.: F. E. Peacock, 1968), 497.

39. Veteran quoted in Jonathan Shay, *Achilles in Vietnam: Combat Trauma and the Undoing of Character* (New York: Antheneum, 1994), 96.

40. On balancing firepower in Vietnam, see "U.S. Forces Frustrated in Political Aspects of Vietnamese War," *The New York Times*, June 29, 1966. On killing as an end in itself, see Bergerud, *The Dynamics of Defeat*, 132. Making life more calculable in Elting E. Morison, *Men, Machines, and Modern Times* (Cambridge, Mass., and London: The M.I.T. Press, 1966), 93.

41. Robert S. McNamara, *In Retrospect: The Tragedy and Lessons of Vietnam* (New York: Times Books, 1995), 237–238.

42. Lansdale in Thompson and Frizzell, *The Lessons of Vietnam*, 77. McNamara's October visit in Bergerud, *Dynamics of Defeat*,162.

43. Charles Mohr, "Many in Vietnam Say Opinion in U.S. Is Key to Victory," *New York Times*, June 27, 1966.

44. On competition between units, see Lewy, *America in Vietnam*, 328. MACV Monthly Evaluation Report, October 1966, MHI. On commanders judged by number of kills, see Brigadier General Robert C. Taber, VNIT, CMH, 43.

45. Pearson, VNI Folder 17, CMH. On body counts and careerism, see Maureen Mylander, *The Generals* (New York: The Dial Press, 1974), 80–82, and Baritz, *Backfire*, 311.

46. Donald A. Siebert Papers, Box 9, MHI, 935–936. On firepower alienating the population, see Krepinevich, *The Army and Vietnam*,198. On ignoring the political infrastructure, see Schulzinger, *A Time for War*, 182.

47. Bong Son campaign in "Lessons Learned No 55: The Battle of Annihilation," DA AG Operations Report Lessons Learned, HQ, USARV, Command Historian, RG 472, NARA, 2–66. Difficulties in distinguishing forces in Palmer, *The 25-Year War*, 164. Collins's "Concept for Operations," Arthur S. Collins, Jr. Papers, Box 5, MHI.

48. "Operations Report—Lessons Learned, 1–66—Operation CRIMP," March 22, 1966, CMH Library.

49. John C. Bahnsen, *American Warrior: A Combat Memoir of Vietnam* (New York: Citadel Press, 2007), 109.

50. Melvin Zais, MHI interview, 477–478. On lessons from the French experience in Indochina, see Charles P. Biggio, "Let's Learn from the French," *Military Review*, Vol. XLVI, No. 10 (October 1966): 27–34.

51. 4th Infantry Division Commander's Notes Number 2, Arthur S. Collins, Jr., Papers, Box 6, MHI.

52. "Many in Vietnam Say Opinion in U.S. Is Key to Victory," *New York Times*, June 27, 1966.

53. MACV Monthly Evaluation Report, June 1966, MHI. On body counts not making "any difference as long as you have an enemy that's prepared to feed people into this meat grinder," see Stanley Karnow, interview by Ted Gittinger, April 30, 1984, LBJL, 51.

54. On problems in identifying combatants see: Jeffrey Record, *The Wrong War: Why We Lost in Vietnam* (Annapolis, Md: Naval Institute Press, 1998), 84; Lewy, *America in Vietnam*, 79; and Bergerud, *Dynamics of Defeat*, 168. On exaggerated reports, see Mueller, "The Search for the 'Breaking Point' in Vietnam," 503. Surveyed officers in Kinnard, *The War Managers*, 75. Westmoreland, *A Soldier Reports*, 332.

55. "A Systems Analysis View of the Vietnam War: 1965–1972," Vol. 8—Casualties and Losses, Geog. V. Vietnam-319.1, CMH, 4, 22.

56. S. L. A. Marshall, *Battles in the Monsoon: Campaigning in the Central Highlands Vietnam, Summer 1966* (New York: William Morrow, 1967), 149. On firepower making it difficult to produce accurate body counts, see Herring, *America's Longest War*, 153.

57. Alcala, MHI interview, LVI-31. On use of canteens, see Stanton, *The Rise and Fall of an American Army*, 272. See also Driskill, MHI interview, 38.

58. Correspondent views in *Newsweek*, May 23, 1966, and *New York Times*, June 29, 1966. Harvard University Professor George B. Kistiakowsky to McNamara, June 23, 1966, *FRUS, 1964–1968*, IV: 455–456.

59. McNamara concerns in *FRUS, 1964–1968*, IV: 852 and *The U.S. Government and the Vietnam War, Part IV*, 458–461. General Westmoreland's Historical Briefings, March 27, 1966, Folder 5, Reel 6 and November 25, 1966, Folder 11, Reel 8, WCWP. Komer raised his reservations about "undue optimism" to the President on April 13, 1966. See *FRUS, 1964–1968*, IV: 344–346.

60. ARPA Memorandum, "Indicators for Vietnam Progress; Past, Present, and Future," May 16, 1966, Folder 86, War Indicators SVN, Thomas C. Thayer Papers, CMH. Planning Research Corporation, "A Study of Factors Indicative of Progress of a Counterinsurgency Operation," ibid.

61. D. H. Armsby, "Proposed Study Project on Indicators of Political Success in South Vietnam," September 2, 1966, Folder 86, War Indicators SVN, Thomas C. Thayer Papers, CMH. Memorandum from Raymond Tanter, Northwestern University to Thomas Thayer, September 22, 1966, ibid.

62. MACV Monthly Evaluation Reports, November and December 1966, MHI. "Measurement of Progress" briefing, November 20, 1966, History File, Folder 11, Reel 8, WCWP. On heavy quantification and trivial analysis, see Thayer, *War Without Fronts*, 5.

63. On the need for collective judgment, see William G. Stewart, "Measuring Combat Effectiveness," Personal Correspondence, Box 2, 1969–1972, Donn A. Starry Papers, MHI, 6. On little consensus on enemy order of battle, see Davidson, *Vietnam at War*, 360 and Record, *The Wrong War*, 82. On defining enemy combatants, see Bruce Palmer, *The 25-Year War*, 79.

64. August 1966 figures from "Foe Put at 282,000 in South Vietnam," *New York Times*, August 10, 1966. See also National Intelligence Estimate, July 7, 1966, *FRUS, 1964–1968*, IV: 488–489. On MACV falsifying reports, see Sam Adams, *War of Numbers: An Intelligence Memoir* (South Royalton, Vt.: Steerforth Press, 1994), 212. MACV J2 assessment from Buzzanco, *Masters of War*, 259.

65. Sharp's assessment in MACV Command History, 1966, NARA, 347–348. Systems Analysis study in Enthoven and Smith, *How Much Is Enough?*, 297. On political and military influence, see "Ideas for Discussion with General Weyand," Box 7, Arthur S. Collins Papers, MHI.

66. Komer Memorandum to President Johnson, *FRUS, 1964–1968*, IV: 474–475. On problems with body count criteria, see "A Systems Analysis View of the Vietnam War: 1965–1972,"

Vol. 6—Rep. of Vietnam Armed Forces, Geog. V. Vietnam-319.1, CMH, 16–17. Moss discusses the problems of Westmoreland's strategy in *Vietnam*, 222–223. On MACV not questioning its approach, see Pickerell, *Vietnam in the Mud*, 33–34.

67. "A Symposium on Province Operations in South Vietnam, June 13–17, 1966," Command Information Publications, Folder 101217, Box 18, RG 472, NARA. The RAND Corporation published the final report in December.

68. Westmoreland cable to CINCPAC, "Concept of Military Operations in South Vietnam," August 26, 1966, Folder 3, Box 5, Larry Berman Collection, TTUVA. DePuy recollection as division commander in *Changing an Army*, 162.

69. On ramifications of firepower for the political side of the war, see Birtle, *U.S. Army Counterinsurgency and Contingency Operations Doctrine*, 381. On results, see George C. Herring, "American Strategy in Vietnam. The Postwar Debate," *Military Affairs* Vol. 46, No. 2 (April 1982): 59. On immune to military defeat, see Weigley, *History of the United States Army*, 547.

70. Remarks by General W. C. Westmoreland to Correspondents, September 13, 1966, Folder 524–2, Box 42, Westmoreland Personal Papers, RG 319, NARA. See also "Notes used for Address to Honolulu Press Club," August 12, 1966, Folder 8, Reel 7, WCWP.

71. On requirements of political insurgents, see Kinnard, *The War Managers*, 72.

72. Lodge to Johnson, *FRUS*, 1964–1968, IV: 412–413. On costs to the Great Society, see Buzzanco, *Masters of War*, 253. On gradual loss of public support, see Karnow, *Vietnam*, 505.

73. McNamara to Johnson, *FRUS*, 1964–1968, IV: 727–728.

Chapter 5

1. Westmoreland's year end assessment in *FRUS, 1964–1968*, V: 4–5, and *The U.S. Government and the Vietnam War, Part IV*, 529–531. On the Combined Campaign Plan for 1967, see JCS History, Part II, JCSHO, 42–1 to 42–2, and Davidson, *Vietnam at War*, 382–383.

2. On Cedar Falls mission statement and establishment of a strike zone, see Bernard W. Rogers, *Cedar Falls-Junction City: A Turning Point* (Washington, D.C.: U.S. Government Printing Office, 1974, 2004), 19 and MacGarrigle, *Taking the Offensive*, 96–99.

3. Sharp and Westmoreland, *Report on the War in Vietnam*, 133. On multidivisional assault and use of B-52s, see JCS History, Part III, JCSHO, 42–45.

4. Jonathan Schell, *The Village of Ben Suc* (New York: Alfred A. Knopf, 1967), 24. Ross quoted in Santoli, *Everything We Had*, 50. On Ben Suc, see Rogers, *Cedar Falls-Junction City*, 34–41.

5. DePuy quoted in Rogers, *Cedar Falls-Junction City*, 78. Emphasis in original. Cedar Falls results in MACV Monthly Evaluation Report, January 1967, MHI, A-28.

6. On Junction City goals, see Larry Cable, *Unholy Grail: The US and the Wars in Vietnam, 1965–8* (London and New York: Routledge, 1991), 188, and Rogers, *Cedar Falls-Junction City*, 83–90. On MACV's assessment of COSVN, see ST 67–023, "Central Office of South Vietnam," April 29, 1967, Box 3, Joseph A. McChristian Papers, MHI. On early positive assessments, see 173rd Airborne Brigade Combat After Action Report, Operation Junction City, August 8, 1967, Digital Archive Collection, USAAWCL, 38–39. MACV reported a total of 2,728 enemy casualties. MacGarrigle, *Taking the Offensive*, 141. VC moving into Cambodia in Stanton, *The Rise and Fall of an American Army*, 135. On the Vietcong eluding the Americans, see *Time*, March 3, 1967, 30.

7. Komer to Johnson, January 23, 1967, *FRUS, 1964–1968*, V: 56. Some officers shared Komer's views on "the guerrilla problem." *Outlook in Vietnam*, Folder 7, Box 8, Douglas Pike Collection, Unit 02: Military Operations, TTUVA. Iron Triangle quotation in Rogers, *Cedar Falls-Junction City*, 158. Shortfalls in MACV's expectations and assessments in Davidson, *Vietnam at War*, 384. On gaps between theory and practice, see Lewy, *America in Vietnam*, 88.

8. A number of Vietnam War histories state, incorrectly, that Westmoreland ignored pacification in 1967. On his acceptance of the pacification mission, see "Strategic Guidelines for 1967 in Vietnam," December 14, 1966, CSA Statements Folder, White House-State-DoD, October–December 1966, Reel 18, WCWP. Of the nine program areas for the year, "Press a Major Pacification Effort" ranked first. Westmoreland retained his belief that the bulk of ARVN should be employed in this effort. Balancing pacification with offensive operations in Zaffiri, *Westmoreland*, 187.

9. Westmoreland's assessments in *Report on the War in Vietnam*, 131, and *FRUS, 1964–1968*, V: 254. Johnson, *The Vantage Point*, 257–258.

10. Colonel A. L. Hamblin, Jr., Deputy Senior Advisor, CG I Corps, March 1, 1966–July 1, 1967, Senior Officer Debriefing Reports, Box #6, July 1, 1967, RG 472, NARA.

11. On McNamara's October 1966 visit, see SECDEF Visit, October 10–13, 1966, Historian's Background Material Files, Box 65, RG 472, NARA and memorandum on "Secretary McNamara's Meeting with General Thieu, Chairman, National Leadership Council," October 11, 1966, Folder 9, Reel 7, WCWP. McNamara quoted in Blaufarb, *The Counterinsurgency Era*, 236.

12. Richard H. Moorsteen, Memorandum to Ambassador Leonhart, May 18, 1967, State of the War: Sep 67 Assessment, Folder 96, Thayer Papers, CMH, 5–6. On the enemy recovering its losses, see *Southeast Asia Analysis Report*, July 1967, MHI, 8. CINCPAC strategy included three elements: destroying communist forces and nation building in the south and taking the war to the enemy in the north. See "CINCPAC Measurement of Progress in Southeast Asia," February 23, 1968, Folder 9, Box 10, Larry Berman Collection, (Presidential Archives Research), TTUVA, 2.

13. Rostow to Johnson, January 26, 1967, *FRUS, 1964–1968*, V: 62. 1967 Combined Campaign Plan in "USMACV Command History, 1967," Office of Secy, Joint Staff, Mil. Hist. Branch, Entry MACJ03, Box 5, RG 472, NARA, 317, 323–324. *Time*, February 3, 1967.

14. Strategic dialogue in Eliot A. Cohen, *Supreme Command: Soldiers, Statesmen, and Leadership in Wartime* (New York and London: The Free Press, 2002), 184. For arguments that American strategy had not changed in 1967, see Palmer, *Summons of the Trumpet*, 159, and Buzzanco, *Masters of War*, 275–277.

15. Komer biographical sketches in Sheehan, *A Bright Shining Lie*, 654–655, and Cosmas, *MACV: The Joint Command in the Years of Escalation*, 361–362. On influence with Johnson, see Colby, *Lost Victory*, 205.

16. "Excerpts from Remarks by the President before a Joint Session of the Congress on the State of the Union," January 10, 1967, #14 History File, Reel 9, WCWP. Komer's August 1966 staff paper, titled "Giving a New Thrust to Pacification: Analysis, Concept, and Management," in Dale Andrade and James H. Willbanks, "CORDS/Phoenix: Counterinsurgency Lessons from Vietnam for the Future," *Military Review*, Vol. LXXXVI, No. 2 (March–April 2006): 13. A "question of balance" from Robert W. Komer, interview (III) by Paige E. Mulhollan, November 15, 1971, LBJL, 59.

17. Westmoreland, *A Soldier Reports*, 260. Johnson's purposes for the Guam Conference in *The Vantage Point*, 259. On the conduct of the conference, see Larry Berman, *Lyndon Johnson's War:*

The Road to Stalemate in Vietnam (New York and London: W. W. Norton, 1989), 33–34, and Langguth, *Our Vietnam*, 441–442.

18. Robert W. Komer, interview (II) by Joe B. Frantz, August 18, 1970, LBJL, 46. On lack of coordination, see R. W. Komer, "Impact of Pacification on Insurgency in Vietnam," August 1970, Folder 5, Box 15, Douglas Pike Collection: Unit 01-Assessment and Strategy, TTUVA, 3; and "Civil Operations and Revolutionary Development Support (CORDS) Briefings, June–July 1967," Folder 065, US Marine Corps History Division, Vietnam War Documents Collection, TTUVA, 1–2.

19. MACV area control assessment in "Monthly Report of Revolutionary Development Progress: Population and Area Control from Period July 1 to July 31, 1966," August 16, 1966, MHI. Lawrence E. Grinter, "The Pacification of South Vietnam: Dilemmas of Counterinsurgency and Development" (Ph.D. diss., University of North Carolina at Chapel Hill, 1972), 593–599. Komer, *Bureaucracy at War*, 116–118. USAID and security of pacification efforts in "The War at the Grass Roots: 'Pacification' in Vietnam," *U.S. News and World Report*, September 26, 1966, 50, 52. On pacification implementation in 1966, see John H. Cushman, "Pacification: Concepts Developed in the Field by the RVN 21st Infantry Division," *Army*, Vol. 16, No. 3 (March 1966): 21–29.

20. Robert W. Komer, "Clear, Hold and Rebuild," *Army*, Vol. 20, No. 5 (May 1970): 19. On CORDS establishment, see National Security Action Memorandum No. 362, *FRUS*, 1964–1968, V: 398–399.

21. Ward Just, "New Army Role Dismays U.S. Civilians in Vietnam," *Washington Post*, May 12, 1967.

22. Remarks by Ambassador Komer, MACV Commanders' Conference, May 13, 1967, WCWP, Reel 9, #17 History File. On Westmoreland's views, see *A Soldier Reports*, 263. On action programs associated with CORDS, see "Goals of Project Takeoff," MACV Commanders' Conference, August 27, 1967, #21 History File, II, Reel 10, WCWP.

23. James W. Johnson and Charles Anello, "Measurement of Pacification Progress in Vietnam," Research Analysis Corporation Technical Paper, September 1968, CMH Library, 8.

24. On needing troops for pacification and attrition and the importance of American victories in 1965 and 1966, see Andrade and Willbanks, "CORDS/Phoenix," 10–11. On separation of tasks, see "Handbook for Military Support of Pacification," February 1968, Folder 14, Box 5, United States Armed Forces Manual Collection, TTUVA, 42. On Westmoreland's concerns over ARVN dealing with the civilian populace, see Grinter, "The Pacification of South Vietnam," 605.

25. Westmoreland, interview by Martin L. Ganderson, 1982, Box 1, Senior Officer Oral History Program, William C. Westmoreland Papers, MHI, 148. Pillars of strategy in "Strategy and Concept of Operations for 1967," January 1967, Folder 12, History File, Reel 8, WCWP. On Westmoreland accepting the administration's change in emphasis, see "Command Emphasis on Revolutionary Development/Civic Action Programs," October 22, 1966, Folder 10, Reel 7, WCWP.

26. For competing tasks within CORDS, see Chester L. Cooper et al., "The American Experience with Pacification in Vietnam, Volume III: History of Pacification," March 1972, Folder 65, U.S. Marine Corps History Division, Vietnam War Documents Collection, TTUVA, 271. LTC William C. Louisell, VNIT Folder 61, CMH, 27. On 90 percent turnover, see LTC Gerald R. McSpadden, VNIT Folder 85, CMH, 5.

27. General Westmoreland's Historical Briefing, January 1, 1967, Folder 12 History File, Reel 8, WCWP. Successive phases of joint military and civil RD actions in Annex B (Revolutionary Development) to Combined Campaign Plan, 1967, AB 142, Vietnam Materials, Box 1, WPSC,

B-6 to B-17. Expectations and capabilities in Louisell, VNIT, 21–22. On ARVN and pacification, see Hunt and Shultz, *Lessons from an Unconventional War*, xiv; Kinnard, *The War Managers*, 103; and Clarke, *Advice and Support*, 229.

28. Bunker, June 28, 1967, *FRUS*, 1964–1968, V: 557. Expectations for RF/PF in MACV Monthly Evaluation Report, February 1967, MHI, 12. On variations in RF/PF and ARVN leadership capabilities, see CPT Jay D. Menger, After Action Report, February 2, 1968, VNIT Folder 32, CMH, 4; COL Arndt L. Mueller, Senior Officer Debriefing Reports, July 15, 1967, Box 12, RG 472, NARA, 6; and Richard A. Hunt, *Pacification: The American Struggle for Vietnam's Hearts and Minds* (Boulder, San Francisco, and Oxford: Westview Press, 1995), 99.

29. Johnson and Anello, "Measurement of Pacification Progress in Vietnam," CMH, 1. On officers within MACV's Revolutionary Development Support Directorate appreciating these problems, see W. A. Knowlton to Thomas E. Griess, February 12, 1967, Vietnam Materials, Box 1, WPSC.

30. Control defined in Johnson and Anello, ibid., 2. On the importance of obtaining objective information, see Grinter, "The Pacification of South Vietnam," 650.

31. Bruce Palmer, Jr., VNIT Folder 185, CMH, 16. On problems of "criteria so general in wording as to force the evaluators to use subjective judgments" see Dorothy K. Clark and Charles R. Wyman, "An Exploratory Analysis of the Reporting, Measuring, and Evaluating of Revolutionary Development in South Vietnam," Research Analysis Corporation Technical Paper, November 1967, Command Information Publications, Folder #101243, Box 20, RG 472, NARA, 8. On correspondents questioning the validity of MACV reporting, see William Tuohy, "Military is Heavy-Handed with Statistics," *Los Angeles Times*, February 19, 1967.

32. On development of the HES, see Erwin R. Brigham, "Pacification Measurement in Vietnam: The Hamlet Evaluation System," Folder 18, Box 3, Glenn Helm Collection, TTUVA, 1–2 and MACRDS Fact Sheet, SECDEF Hamlet Evaluation System, December 15, 1966, Box 1, Vietnam Materials, WPSC. CIA perspective in George W. Allen, *None So Blind: A Personal Account of the Intelligence Failure in Vietnam* (Chicago: Ivan R. Dee, 2001), 219–224. On the Marine Corps point system for evaluating pacification status, see *Southeast Asia Analysis Report*, February 1967, MHI, 28. As an example of changes in categories under the old system, see MACV's "Monthly Report on Revolutionary Development Progress: Population and Area Control for Period December 1 to December 31, 1966," January 18, 1967, MHI, 2.

33. Brigham, "Pacification Measurement in Vietnam," TTUVA, 2. On the changing situation within the provinces, see Robert Komer in Thompson and Frizzell, *The Lessons of Vietnam*, 219.

34. "Text of Ambassador Komer's News Conference on the Hamlet Evaluation System, 1 December," HES Newsletter #2, HES Briefing for the Press, December 1, 1967, Amb. Komer to News Media Representatives in Saigon, Center of Military History refiles, RG 319, NARA.

35. HES worksheet description in Brigham, "Pacification Measurement in Vietnam," TTUVA, 4–6. On hamlet categories, see MACV's "Monthly Report on Revolutionary Development Progress: Hamlet, Population and Area Control for Period January 1 to January 31, 1967," March 15, 1967, MHI, 1–2. On how MACV determined an area secure, see *Southeast Asia Analysis Report*, February 1967, MHI, 29.

36. William A. Knowlton, interview with author, April 16, 2008.

37. Erwin R. Brigham, "Pacification Measurement," *Military Review*, Vol. L, No. 5 (May 1970): 55. On MACV using HES as a "public measurement of progress" see Hunt, *Pacification*, 96. On questions of HES's reliability, see MACRDS Fact Sheet, SECDEF Hamlet Evaluation System, December 15, 1966, WPSC.

38. Inventory of hamlets in "A Systems Analysis View of the Vietnam War: 1965–1972, Vol. 9-Population Security," Geog. V. Vietnam-319.1, CMH, 28. A July report noted that HES "still suffered from data turbulence," 35. On subjective judgments and advisors with different standards, see Brigham, "Pacification Measurement in Vietnam," TTUVA, 14, and Chester L. Cooper et al., "The American Experience with Pacification in Vietnam, Volume I: An Overview of Pacification," TTUVA, 26. Average number of hamlets under each advisor in Kolko, *Anatomy of a War*, 241.

39. William Lederer quoted in Asprey, *War in the Shadows*, 1200. On spectrum of matters, see Johnson and Anello, "Measurement of Pacification Progress in Vietnam," CMH, 12. Interpreters in John V. Tunney, *Measuring Hamlet Security in Vietnam: Report of a Special Study Mission* (Washington, D.C.: U.S. Government Printing Office, 1969), 7.

40. Grade creep from James Sewell, interview with author, April 21, 2008. Tense meeting from 1LT Mickey Hutchins, quoted in Michael Takiff, *Brave Men, Gentle Heroes. American Fathers and Sons in World War II and Vietnam* (New York: Morrow, 2003), 299–300.

41. Advisor quoted in Tunney, *Measuring Hamlet Security in Vietnam*, 8. General Westmoreland's History Notes, May 10, 1967, #17 History File, Reel 9, WCWP. On problems with MACV optimism being reported to the president, see McPherson to Johnson, June 13, 1967, *FRUS, 1964–1968*, V: 499. Continuing pressures to exaggerate body counts in *Southeast Asia Analysis Report*, November 1967, MHI, 2.

42. On problems assessing the failure of GVN to "develop and meaningful political structure in the villages" and how that related to Vietnamese culture, see Samuel L. Popkin, "Politics and the Village," *Asian Survey*, Vol. 10, No. 8 (August 1970): 668–669. On validity of HES data, see Thayer, *War Without Fronts*, 145–151.

43. General officer survey on HES in Kinnard, *The War Managers*, 108. Causal relations in Johnson and Anello, "Measurement of Pacification Progress in Vietnam," CMH, 6. On relativism in defining security, see Eric Wentworth, "'Secure Often Isn't in Vietnam Hamlets," *Washington Post*, January 8, 1967. On attitudes, aspirations, and loyalties, see Maurice D. Roush, "The Hamlet Evaluation System," *Military Review*, Vol. IL, No. 09 (September 1969): 17, and Tunney, *Measuring Hamlet Security in Vietnam*, 2.

44. Komer, "Impact of Pacification on Insurgency in Vietnam," TTUVA, 9. Alain Enthoven, memorandum on "Pacification indicators in Viet Nam," October 24, 1966, Folder 86, War Indicators, SVN, Thayer Papers, CMH. Number of HES reports in Brigham, "Pacification Measurement in Vietnam," TTUVA, 8. Daily pounds of reports in Kolko, *Anatomy of a War*, 194.

45. Absolute values of control and violence in Stathis N. Kalyvas and Matthew Kocher, "Violence and Control in Civil War: An Analysis of the Hamlet Evaluation System (HES)," paper presented at the American Political Association, Philadelphia, Pa., August 27, 2003, http://www.allacademic.com/meta/p.64584_index.html, p. 6. On the Chieu Hoi program, see J. M. Carrier and C. A. H. Thomson, *Viet Cong Motivation and Morale: The Special Case of Chieu Hoi* (Santa Monica, Calif.: RAND Corporation, 1966), and Lucian W. Pye, *Observations on the Chieu Hoi Program* (Santa Monica, Calif.: RAND Corporation, 1969).

46. Ears lighting up from LTC James S. Conklin, VNIT Folder 104-2, CMH, 36. Litmus quotation in Browne, *The New Face of War*, 46. On statistics as a "surrogate for genuine understanding and mastery" see Appy, *Working-Class War*, 159. Ideology and culture in Baritz, *Backfire*, 244. On revolution as a social process, see Jeffrey Race, "How They Won," *Asian Survey*, Vol. 10, No. 8 (August 1970): 629. Officers viewing security as a yardstick in Conklin, CMH, VNIT, 35, and

COL Leonard Daems, VNIT, Folder 109A, CMH, 20. On MACV's administrative approach, see Blaufarb, *The Counterinsurgency Era*, 245.

47. CBS News, *The People of South Vietnam: How They Feel about the War* (Princeton, N.J.: Opinion Research Corporation, 1967), 31. On lack of an effective attack on the VC political infrastructure, see BG Richard M. Lee, II CTZ, Senior Officer Debriefing Reports, July 28, 1967, Box 9, RG 472, NARA, 2. Karnow discusses the impenetrability of Vietnamese society in *Vietnam*, 468. Debrow Freed discussed MACV's attempts to designate values to intangibles, interview with author, April 12, 2008.

48. Gains in pacification from MACV Monthly Reports of Revolutionary Development Progress: Hamlet, Population and Area Control, March–October, 1967, MHI. Examples of Measurement of Progress Briefings in WCWP: Folder #12 History File, January 22, 1967, Reel 8; #15 History File, April 2, 1967, Reel 9; and #18 History File, June 11, 1967, Reel 10. Briefing officer observations from A.M. Robert Dean, interview with author, April 9, 2008. Komer to Johnson, October 4, 1967, *FRUS, 1964–1968*, V: 861.

49. On the establishment of MACEVAL, see "USMACV Command History, 1967," NARA, 1251–1252, and Cosmas, *MACV*, 291–295. On automation, see George C. Wilson, "Pacification Gets Help of Computer," *Washington Post*, February 16, 1968.

50. On summer operations in I CTZ, see JCS History, Part III, JCSHO, 45-1, 45-5. Enemy infiltration in Willard Pearson, *The War in the Northern Provinces, 1966–1968* (Washington, D.C.: U.S. Government Printing Office, 1975), 21. On Westmoreland's concerns, see General Westmoreland's Historical Briefing, January 1, 1967, Folder 12 History File, Reel 8, WCWP.

51. McNamara, *In Retrospect*, 283. On Con Thien, see R. W. Apple, Jr., "Westmoreland Asks M'Namara for More Troops," *New York Times*, July 8, 1967. Westmoreland's concerns for enough troops to conduct attrition and pacification in C. Dale Walton, *The Myth of Inevitable US Defeat in Vietnam* (London, Portland, Ore.: Frank Cass, 2002), 56. In mid-1967, Johnson authorized 47,000 more troops, imposing a ceiling of 525,000.

52. MG William DePuy quoted in Krepinevich, *The Army and Vietnam*, 190. For evaluation of enemy activities during this period, see MACV Monthly Evaluation Report, MHI, April 1967, p. 8 and August 1967, 4.

53. Westmoreland quoted in Lee Lescaze, "McNamara is Told War Is Being Won," *Washington Post*, July 8, 1967. Defense appraisal in *Southeast Asia Analysis Report*, MHI, May 1967, 13. Engagement percentages taken from Krepinevich, *The Army and Vietnam*, 192.

54. Transcript of S.O. Debriefing, Box 12, William R. Peers Papers, MHI, 40. On commanders understanding their mission in terms of security, see LTC Robert H. Nevins, Jr., VNIT Folder 62, CMH, 2. On lack of coordination between military and civil operations, see Thompson, *No Exit from Vietnam*, 146.

55. Following documents from J-3 Body Count File, Histories Div., Safe 78/1, CMH: MACJ2 Fact Sheet, "VC/NVA Personnel Losses," October 5, 1967; MACV J3 Report Survey of Body Count Procedures, November 9, 1967; MCJ343 Fact Sheet, "Enemy Body Count Survey," November 10, 1967.

56. Westmoreland quoted in Lescaze, *Washington Post*, July 8, 1967. On LBJ, McNamara, and the crossover point, see Johnson, *The Vantage Point*, 259; Frank E. Vandiver, *Shadows of Vietnam: Lyndon Johnson's Wars* (College Station: Texas A&M University Press, 1997), 235; Buzzanco, *Masters of War*, 282–283.

57. George W. Ashworth, "U.S. troop increase set for Vietnam," *The Christian Science Monitor*, August 5, 1967. Monthly cost of war in ibid. On spring analogy, see Moorsteen Trip Report, CMH, 2.

58. Holbrooke in *The U.S. Government and the Vietnam War, Part IV*, 712–713.

59. "Killing the enemy" in "CIIB Meeting," October 7, 1967, Body Counts File, Histories Div., Safe 78/1, CMH.

60. On security being essential to pacification, see: "A Systems Analysis View of the Vietnam War: 1965–1972, Vol. 9-Population Security," CMH, 21; Annex B to 1967 Combined Campaign Plan, WPSC, B-3; "Civil Operations and Revolutionary Development Support (CORDS) Briefings, June–July 1967," TTUVA, 4; and DePuy to Goodpaster, April 18, 1967, *FRUS, 1964–1968*, V: 321.

61. Samuel W. Smithers, Jr., "Combat Units in Revolutionary Development," *Military Review*, Vol. XLVII, No. 10 (October 1967): 40. On a lack of "preemptive social policies" and an obsession with security, see Jeffrey Race, *War Comes to Long An: Revolutionary Conflict in a Vietnamese Province* (Berkeley, Los Angeles, and London: University of California Press, 1972), 262–263.

62. Battalion commander quoted in Thomas G. Paterson, "Historical Memory and Illusive Victories: Vietnam and Central America," *Diplomatic History*, Vol. 12, No. 1 (Winter 1988): 5. On civil and military programs working against each other, see Grinter, "The Pacification of South Vietnam," 80, and Baritz, *Backfire*, 168–169. On commanders placing more attention on military planning, see Hoyt R. Livingston and Francis M. Watson, Jr., "Civic Action: Purpose and Pitfalls," *Military Review*, Vol. XLVII, No. 12 (December 1967): 22–23. For examples of American soldiers carrying out civic action on their own time, see Bernard Edelman, ed., *Dear America: Letters Home from Vietnam* (New York: Pocket Books, 1986), 208, and Bahnsen, *American Warrior*, 49.

63. Department of the Army, Field Manual 31–16, *Counterguerrilla Operations*, March 1967, 15. Westmoreland directed that ARVN coordinate operations against main forces with pacification activities; however, this proved a frustrating endeavor. See "Role of ARVN Division in CORDS," August 3, 1967, #19 History File, Reel 10, WCWP and William C. Westmoreland, interview by Charles B. McDonald, July 25, 1985, LBJL, 7. On ARVN reluctantly assuming pacification missions, see Cooper et al., "The American Experience with Pacification in Vietnam, Volume III," TTUVA, 274. Peter M. Dawkins discusses area security in "The United States Army and the 'Other' War in Vietnam: A Study of the Complexity of Implementing Organizational Change" (Ph.D. diss., Princeton University, 1979), 116.

64. Homeless figures from Pamela A. Conn, "Losing Hearts and Minds: U.S. Pacification Efforts in Vietnam during the Johnson Years" (Ph.D. diss., University of Houston, 2001), 22. Louis A. Wiesner, *Victims and Survivors: Displaced Persons and Other War Victims in Viet-Nam, 1954–1975* (New York and Westport, Conn.: Greenwood Press, 1988).

65. David W. P. Elliott and W. A. Stewart, *Pacification and the Viet Cong System in Dinh Tuong: 1966–1967* (Santa Monica, Calif.: Rand Corporation, 1969), 76.

66. Rostow to Johnson, August 1, 1967, *FRUS, 1964–1968*, V: 653. On political developments in South Vietnam not moving "at a rate commensurate with our own domestic political pressures," see Joshua Menkes and Raymond G. Jones, Trip Report, January 10, 1967, Folder 19-Advanced Research Project Agency, Thayer Papers, CMH, 6. Problems of building political consensus and a political community in John C. Donnell, "Pacification Reassessed," *Asian Survey*, Vol. 7, No. 8 (August 1967): 574, and Laurence E. Grinter, "How They Lost: Doctrine, Strategies and Outcomes of the Vietnam War," *Asian Survey*, Vol. 15, No. 12 (December 1975): 1115.

67. William Tuohy, "There Are No Certainties in Vietnam," *Los Angeles Times*, January 8, 1967. On growing uneasiness, see "Youth Questions the War," *Time*, January 6, 1967, 22; "Vietnam

Debate Escalates," *Washington News*, April 26, 1967; and "The No Strategy War," *New York Times*, April 30, 1967.

68. On Westmoreland's April visit, see "Westmoreland Tells Congress U.S. Will Prevail," *New York Times*, April 29, 1967, and "Westmoreland Says Protests Encourage Enemy in Vietnam," *Washington Post*, April 25, 1967. Address by General W. C. Westmoreland before Joint Session of Congress, April 28, 1967, Folder-Analysis of Public Statements II, Reel 18, WCWP. Speech to The Associated Press, Congressional Record, April 25, 1967, #16 History File, Reel 19, WCWP.

69. Jonathan Schell, *The Military Half: An Account of Destruction in Quang Ngai and Quang Tin* (New York: Alfred A. Knopf, 1968), 180. Joseph Kraft, "The True Failure in Saigon—South Vietnam's Fighting Force," *Los Angeles Times*, May 3, 1967. Stalemate due to the "disparity in the progress of the two wars" in *Time*, August 25, 1967, 21.

70. Ward Just, "This War May Be Unwinnable," *Washington Post, Outlook*, June 4, 1967. R. W. Apple, "Vietnam: The Signs of Stalemate," *New York Times*, August 7, 1967. On MACV and the press, see "Press Accused on War Reports," *Washington Post*, September 14, 1967, and MACJ343 Disposition Form, "Press Witnessing Body Counts," J-3 Body Count File, Histories Div., Safe 78/1, CMH. On MACV suppressing bad news, see Buzzanco, *Masters of War*, 283. September public opinion poll in Davidson, *Vietnam at War*, 404.

71. Clark Clifford with Richard Holbrooke, *Counsel to the President* (New York: Random House, 1991), 452. Westmoreland, memorandum for Clifford and Taylor, "Achievement of Objectives," WCWP, Reel 10, #19 History File.

72. Clifford, *Counsel to the President*, 453. On public relations and reporting, see Cooper et al., "The American Experience with Pacification in Vietnam, Volume I," TTUVA, 53, and Rowland Evans and Robert Novak, "U.S. Mania for Statistical 'Progress' In South Vietnam Reversed by Komer," *Washington Post*, October 5, 1967.

73. Johnson quoted in Herring, *America's Longest War*, 183. Assessments from MACV Monthly Evaluation Report, September 1967, MHI. Komer's reply can be found in his memorandum to Ambassador Bunker on "Pacification Status and Prospects," October 1, 1967, #23 History File, Reel 11, WCWP. Bunker's positive assessment to the Secretary of State reported "steady progress in security, pacification, and population control." Message, "Measurements of Progress," November 7, 1967, Folder 86, War Indicators SVN, Thayer Papers, CMH.

74. Bundy quoted in Berman, *Lyndon Johnson's War*, 99.

75. Westmoreland special communication to Abrams, November 23, 1967, #25 History File, Reel 12, WCWP. On looking for evidence, see Hanson W. Baldwin, "Vietnam War Evaluation Being Made for Johnson," *New York Times*, November 15, 1967. As to whether LBJ knew statistical indicators were unreliable, see Ruane, *War and Revolution in Vietnam*, 82.

76. McNamara, *In Retrospect*, 307–308. See also Clifford, *Counsel to the President*, 456–458, and Berman, *Lyndon Johnson's War*, 93–95. Walt Rostow responded unfavorably to McNamara's evaluation. Rostow to Johnson, November 2, 1967, *FRUS*, 1964–1968, V: 971–973.

77. Interview with General William C. Westmoreland, USA, and Steve Rowan, CBS, November 17, 1967, Folder 524–2, Box 42, Westmoreland Personal Papers, RG 319, NARA. On Westmoreland's visit setting the stage for "a new chorus of official optimism," see "A Clouded Crystal Ball," *New York Times*, November 19, 1967.

78. William C. Westmoreland, "Progress Report on the War in Viet-Nam," Mil Opns in RVN, October–December 1967 Folder, Box 261, OSDHO. Meet the Press, transcript, November 19, 1967, COMUSMACV (WCW) Public Statements, July–December 1967 Folder, Reel 18,

WCWP. On media receiving optimistic reports with caution, see Hedrick Smith, "Optimists vs. Skeptics," *New York Times*, November 24, 1967, and Ward Just, "President's Hard-Sell on Vietnam," *Washington Post*, November 26, 1967.

79. Col. Francis J. Kelly, Senior Officer Debriefing Reports, May 30, 1967, Box 8, RG 472, NARA, 27–28. On use of statistics see BG Linton S. Boatwright, Senior Officer Debriefing Reports, September 19, 1967, Box 1, ibid., B-1-B-3. "CINCPAC Measurement of Progress in Southeast Asia," TTUVA, 6–7.

80. McNamara, May 19, 1967, memorandum to the president, *In Retrospect*, 267. Michael Herr, *Dispatches* (New York: Alfred A. Knopf, 1968, 1978), 47.

81. "Westy's 1967 End of Year Report," Folder 95, Thayer Papers, CMH, 2.

82. MACV Quarterly Evaluation Report, December 1967, MHI, 4–6. In December, the Monthly Evaluation Report became a quarterly evaluation. JCS in Herbert Y Schandler, *The Unmaking of a President: Lyndon Johnson and Vietnam* (Princeton, N.J.: Princeton University Press, 1977), 58, and Herring, *LBJ and Vietnam*, 58. CIA "Capabilities of the Vietnamese Communists for Fighting in South Vietnam," November 13, 1967, in Porter, *Vietnam: A History in Documents*, 351–352.

83. Komer's disappointment in Hunt, *Pacification*, 135. Mueller, Senior Officer Debriefing, NARA, 5. David Halberstam, "Return to Vietnam," *Harper's*, Vol. 235, No. 1411 (December 1967): 49.

84. Elliott and Stewart, *Pacification and the Viet Cong System in Dinh Tuong*, 64. On HES not being able to evaluate morale or loyalty, see David W. P. Elliott, *The Vietnamese War: Revolution and Social Change in the Mekong Delta, 1930–1975*, concise ed. (Armonk, N.Y., and London: M. E. Sharpe, 2003, 2007), 253, 293.

85. James Megellas, interview with author, July 29, 2008. Megellas served as the Deputy for Revolutionary Development Support in II Corps.

86. VC responses in Elliott and Stewart, *Pacification and the Viet Cong System in Dinh Tuong*, 64; MACV Monthly Evaluation Report, June 1967, MHI, 12; *Southeast Asia Analysis Report*, September 1967, MHI, 19.

87. "USMACV Command History, 1967," NARA, 109, noted that the "VC infrastructure persists as a significant influence over portions of the population." Wayne L. Cooper, VNIT Folder 381–383, CMH, 17.

88. Cooper, *The Lost Crusade*, 423. On changing yardsticks, see Jack Foisie, "Where We Stand in a Changing War," in *Outlook in Vietnam*, TTUVA.

89. General Westmorland History Notes, December 8, 1967, #26 History File, Reel 12, WCWP.

90. Don Oberdorfer, "War Becomes a Numbers Game," *Chicago Daily News*, November 23, 1967. On failing to break the enemy's morale, see Cable, *Unholy Grail*, 159.

91. Katzenbach to Johnson, November 16, 1967, FRUS, 1964–1968, V: 1032.

Chapter 6

1. Troop strength from Stanton, *Vietnam Order of Battle*, 333. Westmoreland to Sharp, "Military Operations in Vietnam," December 10, 1967, #25 History File, Reel 12, WCWP. On the 1968 Combined Campaign Plan, see JCS History, Part III, JCSHO, 51–51. For MACV's strategic study in late 1967, see *The U.S. Government and the Vietnam War, Part IV*, 928–932.

2. "USMACV Command History, 1968," Office of Secy, Joint Staff, MACV, Mil. Hist. Branch, Entry MACJ03, Box 6, RG 472, NARA, 20–21. Senior Officer quoted in "General Is Optimistic on Delta," *Washington Post*, January 10, 1968. Rostow to Johnson, January 4, 1968, *FRUS, 1964–1968*, VI: 6–9.

3. For a day-by-day account of Dak To, see "The Battle for Dak To," Box 7, William R. Peers Papers, MHI. Casualty figures from Edward F. Murphy, *Dak To: The 173d Airborne Brigade in South Vietnam's Central Highlands, June–November 1967* (Novato, Calif.: Presidio, 1993), 305. On American firepower in the hinterlands, see Karnow, *Vietnam*, 538–539. Westmoreland's assessment in *A Soldier Reports*, 287–291.

4. On enemy intentions puzzling Americans, see Don Oberdorfer, *Tet!* (Garden City, N.Y.: Doubleday, 1971), 107, and Phillip B. Davidson, interview by Ted Gittinger, March 30, 1982, LBJL, 49. For the enemy's perspective on these battles, see *Victory in Vietnam*, 212. "The State of the Union—In the President's Own Words," *U.S. News & World Report*, January 29, 1968, 84.

5. "How Goes the War?" *Newsweek*, January 1, 1968, 17. Public opinion poll results in Mann, *A Grand Delusion*, 568. On lack of decisive victory leading to public dissatisfaction, see Carter Malkasian, *A History of Modern Wars of Attrition* (Westport, Conn.: Praeger, 2002), 193. On correspondents noting the disparity between headquarters briefings and the battlefield, see Peter Arnett, *Live from the Battlefield: From Vietnam to Baghdad, 35 Years in the World's War Zones* (New York and London: Simon & Schuster, 1994), 226.

6. On differences between strategic and operational measures of effectiveness, see Rosen, *Winning the Next War*, 35.

7. Ronald H. Spector argues convincingly that "Abrams and his staff were well aware that their ability to control and influence the war was limited." *After Tet: The Bloodiest Year in Vietnam* (New York: The Free Press, 1993), 216. Enemy's pain threshold in Richard H. Immerman, "'A Time in the Tide of Men's Affairs': Lyndon Johnson and Vietnam," in *Lyndon Johnson Confronts the World: American Foreign Policy, 1963–1968*, eds. Warren I. Cohen and Nancy Bernkopf Tucker (New York: Cambridge University Press, 1994), 63.

8. On Hanoi's views and their policy for a decisive victory, see *Victory in Vietnam*, 206–207. On the war in 1967 being perceived as a stalemate, see Thompson, *No Exit from Vietnam*, 67, and Joes, *The War for South Viet Nam*, 96. On overriding political goals, see James J. Wirtz, *The Tet Offensive: Intelligence Failure in War* (Ithaca and London: Cornell University Press, 1991), 10, 20–21; Ronnie E. Ford, *Tet 1968: Understanding the Surprise* (London: Frank Cass, 1995), 70–71; and Kolko, *Anatomy of a War*, 303.

9. Giap quoted in Karnow, *Vietnam*, 535. On the importance of surprise and coordination, see Wirtz, *The Tet Offensive*, 61. Strategic objectives of TCK-TKN in *Victory in Vietnam*, 214–215. James H. Willbanks, *The Tet Offensive: A Concise History* (New York: Columbia University Press, 2007), 11. Merle L. Pribbenow II, "General Võ Nguyên Giáp and the Mysterious Evolution of the Plan for the 1968 Tết Offensive," *Journal of Vietnamese Studies*, Vol. 3 (Summer 2008): 1–33.

10. Fighting while negotiating and TCK-TKN phases in Ford, *Tet 1968*, 93.

11. The Office of the Secretary of Defense Southeast Asia Programs Division, *Southeast Asia Analysis Report*, December 1967, MHI, 21. On purpose for the border battles, see Ford, ibid., 92.

12. Wheeler to the President, January 29, 1968, *FRUS, 1964–1968*, VI: 69. CIA, ibid., 44. Emphasis in original. Pearson, *The War in the Northern Provinces*, 30.

13. On Operation Niagara, see Pearson, ibid., 31, 97. On multiple sources of intelligence, see Colonel Sidney B. Berry, Jr., "Observations of a Brigade Commander, Part I," *Military Review*,

Vol. XLVIII, No. 1 (January 1968): 7–8, and Joes, *The War for South Viet Nam*, 97. Differences between MACV and CIA collection priorities in James J. Wirtz, "Intelligence to Please? The Order of Battle Controversy during the Vietnam War," *Political Science Quarterly*, Vol. 106, No. 2 (Summer 1991): 246.

14. Davidson, *Secrets of the Vietnam War*, 105. On uncertainty in the enemy's strategy complicating the intelligence struggle, see John Prados, "Impatience, Illusion, and Asymmetry: Intelligence in Vietnam," in *Why the North Won the Vietnam War*, ed. Marc Jason Gilbert (New York: Palgrave, 2002), 138. Debates over enemy strength figures in Sam Adams, "Vietnam Cover-Up: Playing War with Numbers," *Harper's*, Vol. 250, No. 1500 (May 1975): 64.

15. Charles A. Morris, Chief of Intelligence Production, MACV-J2, interview by Ted Gittinger, November 19, 1982, LBJL, 39. Westmoreland, *A Soldier Reports*, 381.

16. Intelligence officer quoted in Palmer, *Summons of the Trumpet*, 180.

17. CIA report in *FRUS*, 1964–1968, VI: 73. On captured documents during the Dak To battle, see Ford, *Tet 1968*, 99–100.

18. Ethnocentrism in Davidson, *Secrets of the Vietnam War*, 109. On differences between gathering indicators and predicting enemy intentions, see Prados, *The Hidden History of the Vietnam War*, 134.

19. Charles A. Krohn, *The Lost Battalion: Breakout of the 2/12th Cavalry at Hue* (Annapolis, Md.: Naval Institute Press, 2008), 20. Numbers of intelligence officers in Vietnam in Oberdorfer, *Tet!*, 117.

20. Frederick C. Weyand, "Troops to Any Equal," *Vietnam* (August 1998): 38.

21. On progress reports, see Oberdorfer, *Tet!*, 120. Westmoreland blaming the president in *A Soldier Reports*, 391, and Davidson, *Vietnam at War*, 435. White House not receiving a sense of "immediacy and intensity which was present in Saigon" in Wirtz, *The Tet Offensive*, 234.

22. "Mild surprise" in Davidson, *Secrets of the Vietnam War*, 104. In *Vietnam at War*, Davidson contended that "Giap's offensive did gain *tactical* surprise," p. 430. Issue of control in Daniel C. Hallin, *The "Uncensored War" The Media and Vietnam* (New York, Oxford: Oxford University Press, 1986), 173, and. Hunt, *Lyndon Johnson's War*, 114.

23. On opening days of Tet, see *FRUS*, 1964–1968, VI: 74; David F. Schmitz, *The Tet Offensive: Politics, War, and Public Opinion* (Lanham, Boulder, and New York: Rowman & Littlefield, 2005), 83; and Moss, *Vietnam*, 272–273. Moss describes the shock over the shattered sense of security on p. 273.

24. Embassy attack in Peter Braestrup, *Big Story: How the American Press and Television Reported and Interpreted the Crisis of Tet 1968 in Vietnam and Washington*, Vol. 1 (Boulder, Colo.: Westview Press, 1977), 86. Can Tho and Vinh Long in Oberdorfer, *Tet!*, 152. U.S. official quoted in *Newsweek*, February 19, 1968, 33.

25. Westmoreland to Sharp, February 3, 1968, *FRUS*, 1964–1968, VI: 117.

26. Enemy coordination problems in Ford, *Tet 1968*, 140. Enemy casualties in JCS History, Part III, JCSHO, 48-12 to 48-13. Allied casualties in Walter LaFeber, *The Deadly Bet: LBJ, Vietnam, and the 1968 Election* (Lanham, Boulder, and New York: Rowman & Littlefield, 2005), 24.

27. Ronald Laramy, "GIs Say 3-Day Pass Given for Killing Foe," *Washington Post*, March 21, 1968. 1LT James Simmen quoted in Edelman, *Dear America*, 96. Journalist questioning in Hugh Lunn, *Vietnam: A Reporter's War* (New York: Stein and Day, 1986), 233. Westmoreland defending body counts in William M. Hammond, *Reporting Vietnam: Media and Military at War* (Lawrence: University Press of Kansas, 1998), 113, and Memorandum, "Recommended Press Statement

by General Westmoreland on Casualty Reporting," March 15, 1968, J-3 Body Count File, Safe 78/1, CMH.

28. Vann quoted in Buzzanco, *Masters of War*, 331. Ben Tre in Arnett, *Live from the Battlefield*, 255–256; Moss, *Vietnam*, 279–280; and Willbanks, *The Tet Offensive*, 41. Enemy casualties through March in Backgrounder, March 6, 1968, History File, I, Reel 13, #30, WCWP.

29. HES figures from "USMACV Command History, 1968," NARA, 524. Lack of security and Westmoreland in James Landers, *The Weekly War: Newsmagazines and Vietnam* (Columbia and London: University of Missouri Press, 2004), 191. On correspondents' views see Ward Just, "Guerrillas Wreck Pacification Plan," *Washington Post*, February 4, 1968; Stanley Karnow, "Future of Pacification is Questioned," *Washington Post*, February 16, 1968; and "Pacification 'Will Take Years,'" *U.S. News & World Report*, February 19, 1968, 42–43.

30. Gene Roberts, "Komer Optimistic over Pacification Despite Foe's Drive," *New York Times*, April 19, 1968. Province official quoted in Schmitz, *The Tet Offensive*, 107. District advisors in Province Report: "SA DEC Province—CORDS Report 2/68," February 29, 1968, Folder 08, Box 10, Douglas Pike Collection: Unit 01-Assessment and Strategy, TTUVA.

31. Don Oberdorfer, interview (II) by Ted Gittinger, September 17, 1981, LBJL, 10. On confusion over enemy intentions, see "More than a Diversion," *New York Times*, February 2, 1968, and Cable, *Unholy Grail*, 221.

32. "Report of Chairman of the Joint Chiefs of Staff Gen. Earle G. Wheeler on the Situation in Vietnam, February 27, 1968," in Porter, *Vietnam: A History in Documents*, 357–361. On paying such a heavy price, see Robert Shaplen, *The Road from War: Vietnam 1965–1970* (New York and Evanstown: Harper & Row, 1970), 193. Lee Lescaze, "Question in Assessing Casualties is Effect on Enemy Capability," *Washington Post*, February 29, 1968.

33. "Desperate effort" in "Special Report from Vietnam," *Army*, Vol. 18, No. 5 (May 1968): 20. Comparisons to Pearl Harbor in Address by LTG Frederick L. Weyand to the National Guard Association of the United States, October 10, 1968, Officials, Weyand, Frederick L., Folder #73, Westmoreland Personal Papers, Box 3, RG 319, NARA. Westmoreland's assessment in Sharp and Westmoreland, *Report on the War in Vietnam*, 170–173, 235.

34. Bright spots of Tet in USMACV Quarterly Evaluation Report, January–March 1968, MHI, 4–5. Press Briefing, 1968 Tet Offensive in II CTZ, April 17, 1968, Folder 01, Bud Harton Collection, TTUVA, 7. Weyand, "Troops to Any Equal," 39. Dinh Tuong uprising in Elliott, *The Vietnamese War*, 303. Refugees in "Assessment of Refugee Problem," CORDS/Refugee Division, Folder 06, Box 31, Douglas Pike Collection: Unit 03-Refugees and Civilian Casualties, TTUVA. Inconsistencies in reporting in Schmitz, *The Tet Offensive*, 108.

35. Westmoreland to Sharp, February 9, 1968, *FRUS, 1964–1968*, VI: 153–157. Westmoreland to Sharp and Wheeler, ibid., 183–185. Westmoreland, interview by Wes Gallagher, February 25, 1968, in Braestrup, *Big Story*, Vol. II, 155. On Westmoreland not challenging administration policies of the "doctrine of civilian supremacy," see Blair Clark, "Westmoreland Appraised," *Harper's* (November 1970): 101.

36. McNamara, *FRUS, 1964–1968*, VI: 179. Clifford, ibid., 167.

37. Hedrick Smith and Neil Sheehan, "Westmoreland Requests 206,000 More Men, Stirring Debate in Administration," *New York Times*, March 10, 1968. Bruce Palmer, interview (II) by Ted Gittinger, November 9, 1982, LBJL, 1. Press briefings in Ward Just, *To What End: Report from Vietnam* (Boston: Houghton Mifflin, 1968; New York: Public Affairs, 2000), 77. Uncertainty of American aims in Vietnam in Sir Robert Thompson, "Squaring the Error," *Foreign Affairs*, Vol.

46, No. 3 (April 1968): 448. Westmoreland recalled that Johnson told Wheeler "very bluntly that he does not have the horses to change our strategy." *A Soldier Reports*, 435.

38. Byrd dissent in D. Michael Shafer, ed., *The Legacy: The Vietnam War in the American Imagination* (Boston: Beacon Press, 1990), 23. Tom Wickers, "Kennedy Asserts U.S. Cannot Win," *New York Times*, February 9, 1968, and "Kennedy on Vietnam: An Unwinnable War," *U.S. News & World Report*, February 19, 1969.

39. "Big Setback for U.S. in the Countryside," *Newsweek*, March 4, 1968. Gallup poll results in Berman, *Lyndon Johnson's War*, 185. Background on LBJ's March 31 speech in Mann, *A Grand Delusion*, 600–602; Langguth, *Our Vietnam*, 492–493; and Kolko, *Anatomy of a War*, 320–321. Decision on troop levels in Mann, 576.

40. Col. Marvin D. Fuller, VNIT 277, CMH, 18.

41. Mohr in *The American Experience in Vietnam: A Reader*, ed. Grace Sevy (Norman and London: University of Oklahoma Press, 1989), 150. On journalists accepting that the VC were defeated during Tet, see Hallin, *The "Uncensored War,"* 171. On Americans failing to realize the importance of public information and politics, see "Why U.S. Isn't Winning a 'Little' War," *U.S. News & World Report*, April 1, 1968, 43. For the army's definitions on military strategy and the purpose of battle, see Department of the Army, Field Manual 100–105, *Operations of Army Forces in the Field*, September 1968, 1–2, 6–1.

42. On government tensions with the media, see Mohr in Sevy, ibid., 147 and Schmitz, *The Tet Offensive*, 159. Officer views in "Special Report from Vietnam," *Army*, 18.

43. Full transcript of Cronkite's February 27, 1968, "Report from Vietnam" in Braestrup, *Big Story*, Vol. II, 180–189. Cronkite quoted in Oberdorfer, *Tet!*, 249.

44. Zorthian quoted in Appy, *Patriots*, 293. On Tet legitimizing the war as a political issue, see Schandler, *The Unmaking of a President*, 220.

45. Polls in Schmitz, *The Tet Offensive*, 112, and "Johnson's Rating on Vietnam Drops," *New York Times*, February 14, 1968. *U.S. News & World Report* found the impact of television limited in changing attitudes toward the war. See "'Living Room War'—Impact of TV," March 4, 1968, 28–29.

46. Herr, *Dispatches*, 218. Media pressures in Lunn, *Vietnam*, 63, and Clarence R. Wyatt, *Paper Soldiers: The American Press and the Vietnam War* (New York, London: W. W. Norton, 1993), 183. Cultural barriers in Davidson, *Vietnam at War*, 438, and Kathleen J. Turner, *Lyndon Johnson's Dual War: Vietnam and the Press* (Chicago and London: The University of Chicago Press, 1985), 218. On difficulties defining the war, see Shafer, *The Legacy*, 126, and Braestrup, *Big Story*, Vol. I, 23.

47. Media's focus on battles in Braestrup, Vol. I, 287, and Turner, ibid., 217–218. In February, a record 636 reporters were accredited to MACV. Hammond, *Reporting Vietnam*, 120.

48. Steady progress versus lost cause in "The 'War without a Goal': Mood of Americans in Vietnam," *U.S. News & World Report*, June 24, 1968, 31. Arnett recalled Harkins in *Live from the Battlefield*, 245. See also Oberdorfer, *Tet!*, 34, 183. On the credibility gap being "inevitable" see James S. Olson, *The Vietnam War: Handbook of the Literature and Research* (Westport, Conn., and London: Greenwood Press, 1993), 55.

49. Message, Wheeler to Westmoreland, Sharp, March 8, 1968, #30 History File, I, Reel 13, WCWP. Statement by General Westmoreland upon Departure from Washington, April 7, 1958, Folder 524-2, Box 42, Westmoreland Personal Papers, RG 319, NARA. Statement by General Westmoreland at LBJ Ranch, May 30, 1968, Analysis of Public Statements, Folder III, Reel 18, WCWP. Five O'clock Follies in Lunn, *Vietnam*, 13.

50. Media doubts in Jack Gould, "U.S. Is Losing War in Vietnam, N.B.C. Declares," *New York Times*, March 11, 1968, and "Million Americans Soon in Vietnam?" *U.S. News & World Report*, March 18, 1968. On confidence among GVN and ARVN, see Weyand, Address to National Guard Association, October 10, 1968, NARA.

51. Gene Roberts, "New Optimism in War in Vietnam," *New York Times*, June 4, 1968. Westmoreland's "Post-Tet Pacification Assessment" in Chester L. Cooper et al., "The American Experience with Pacification in Vietnam, Volume III: History of Pacification," TTUVA, 292.

52. Johnson, *The Vantage Point*, 384. Press secretary in Landers, *The Weekly War*, 189.

53. Earl G. Wheeler, interview (II) by Dorothy Pierce McSweeny, May 7, 1970, LBJL, 2. General Westmoreland's History Notes, February 1, 1968, #29 History File, I, Reel 12, WCWP. MG Charles P. Stone, Commanding General, 4th Infantry Division, Senior Officer Debriefing Reports, Box 16, RG 472, NARA. Bahnsen, *American Warrior*, 145. Davidson, *Vietnam at War*, 436.

54. Clifford, *Counsel to the President*, 493. Media reflecting official viewpoints in William M. Hammond, "The Press in Vietnam as Agent of Defeat: A Critical Examination," *Reviews in American History*, Vol. 17, No. 2 (June 1989): 318 and Melvin Small, *Covering Dissent: The Media and the Anti-Vietnam War Movement* (New Brunswick, N.J.: Rutgers University Press, 1994), 165.

55. Johnson quoted in Cohen and Tucker, *Lyndon Johnson Confronts the World*, 79. Townsend Hoopes wrote to Clifford on the infeasibility of military victory on March 14. *The Limits of Intervention: An Inside Account of the Johnson Policy of Escalation in Vietnam Was Reversed* (New York: David McKay, 1969), 187–196. Clifford's account in "A Viet Nam Reappraisal," *Foreign Affairs*, Vol. 47, No. 4 (July 1969): 601–622.

56. The decision to improve and modernize ARVN forces was a political decision made prior to Abrams's assumption of command. See JCS History, Part III, JCSHO, 51–56; W. W. Rostow, *The Diffusion of Power: An Essay in Recent History* (New York: Macmillan, 1972), 520; Clarke, *Advice and Support*, 298; and Herring, "'People's Quite Apart,'" 15. On establishing timetables for American withdrawal, see "War Take-Over by South Vietnam—When?" *U.S. News & World Report*, May 13, 1968, 58–59.

57. Notes of meeting, March 26, 1968, *FRUS*, 1964–1968, VI: 463.

58. Biography of Abrams in Lewis Sorley, *Thunderbolt: General Creighton Abrams and the Army of His Times* (New York and London: Simon & Schuster, 1992) and Davidson, *Vietnam at War*, 517–526. Assignments in Biography, General Creighton W. Abrams, Folder 06, Box 01, Van Michael Davidson Collection, TTUVA. Mini-Tet in *FRUS*, 1964–1968, VI: 673; Westmoreland, *A Soldier Reports*, 437; and Willbanks, *The Tet Offensive*, 66–67.

59. Zeb B. Bradford, "With Creighton Abrams During Tet," *Vietnam* (February 1998): 45. Media reports in Landers, *The Weekly War*, 145–146. As an example, see A. J. Langguth, "General Abrams Listens To a Different Drum," *New York Times*, May 5, 1968, and "A 'Different' War Now, With Abrams in Command," *U.S. News & World Report*, August 26, 1968, 12. On Abrams's "one-war" concept, see Sorley, *A Better War*, 18. On interlocking system, see Sorley, *Thunderbolt*, 238. The Westmoreland-Abrams strategy debate is among the more contentious within Vietnam War historiography. In his admiration of Abrams, Sorley is most vocal in supporting a change in strategic concept. See, as an example, *Vietnam Chronicles: The Abrams Tapes, 1968–1972* (Lubbock, Tex.: Texas Tech University Press, 2004), xix. Others are less certain. Phillip Davidson served under both commanders, as did Robert Komer—neither subscribed to a change in strategy under Abrams. Davidson, *Vietnam at War*, 512, and Komer in Thompson and Frizzell, *The Lessons of Vietnam*, 79. Hunt takes a more balanced approach in *Pacification*, 222. Andrew Birtle's argument

on the change being "more in emphasis than in substance" seems most compelling. "As MACV admitted in 1970, 'the basic concept and objectives of pacification, to defeat the VC/NVA and to provide the people with economic and social benefits, have changed little since the first comprehensive GVN plan was published in 1964.'" In *U.S. Army Counterinsurgency and Contingency Operations Doctrine*, 367.

60. On similar problems with enemy, see Andrew J. Goodpaster, Senior Officers Debriefing Program, May 1976, MHI, 40. On peace replacing military victory, see Hallin, *The "Uncensored War,"* 178. Johnson's commitment in LaFeber, *The Deadly Bet*, 63.

61. *FRUS*, 1964–1968, VI: July 18, 1968, 876. Lewy, *America in Vietnam*, 134. Problems of finding and fixing the enemy in John H. Hay, Jr., VNIT Folder 205, CMH, 28. On enemy infiltration, see IDA Study S-316, "The Productivity of Major Military Forces in Vietnam: A Statistical Analysis of Three Years of War," Box 2, 1969–1972, Donn A. Starry Papers, MHI.

62. Decreasing quality of enemy reported in Roy K. Flint, VNIT Folder 92B, CMH, 34, and Gene Roberts, "Saigon General Says Foe Has Replaced His Losses," *New York Times*, March 10, 1968. Changes to Abrams's tactical approach reported in *US News & World Report*, August 26, 1968, 12, and *Time*, September 20, 1968, 45. MACV Quarterly Evaluation Report, April 1–June 30, 1968, MHI. On Abrams assessing ARVN using kill ratios, see Sorley, *Vietnam Chronicles*, 6.

63. Officer quoted in William Tuohy, "Pacification Is Tied to Security," *Washington Post*, June 27, 1968.

64. Infiltration numbers in William Tuohy, "U.S., Saigon Tallies Often Are at Odds," *Washington Post*, August 22, 1968. In mid-August, MACV estimated 128,000 infiltrators had entered South Vietnam since February 1, 1968. See Sorley, *Vietnam Chronicles*, 27. On problems with ARVN, see JCS History, Part III, JCSHO, 51–23, and III CTZ Senior Officer Debriefing Program memorandum, June 6, 1968, Box 14, RG 472, NARA. Bunker, *FRUS*, 1964–1968, VI: 769.

65. On increasing ARVN strength, see JCS History, Part III, JCSHO, 51–58. The June 3, 1968, edition of *U.S. News & World Report* noted that one in every eleven persons in South Vietnam was officially a refugee. See "Vietnam's 1.5 Million Refugees," p. 59. On negotiations, see Gene Roberts, "Each Side in War Claiming Big Gains as Parley Opens," *New York Times*, May 13, 1968; "In Paris, Talk of Peace; In Vietnam, a Hotter War," *U.S. News & World Report*, June 10, 1968, 52; and Hammond, *Reporting Vietnam*, 127–128. Advisor quoted in Gibson, *The Perfect War*, 313.

66. Komer quoted in Sorley, *Vietnam Chronicles*, 21. The 45 percent figure was much higher than that portrayed to the press. On conflict between Komer and Abrams, see Hunt, *Pacification*, 214, and Sorley, *A Better War*, 62.

67. On HES studies, see Anders Sweetland, "Item Analysis of the HES (Hamlet Evaluation System)" (Santa Monica, Calif.: RAND, August 20, 1968) and "Village Defense Study—Vietnam," November 1968, Digital Archive Collection, USAAWCL. Quotation from "Hamlet Evaluation System Study," May 1, 1968, Command Information Publications, Folder #101222, Box 19, RG472, NARA, 22. MACV did attempt to ascertain local attitudes after Tet, yet contained their efforts to Saigon. See "Saigon Attitude Survey," July 7, 1968, Folder 0615, Box 04, Vietnam Archive Collection, TTUVA.

68. Pacification Priority Area Summary, September 3, 1968, prepared by CORDS, Folder 65, US Marine Corps History Division, Vietnam War Documents Collection, TTUVA. On increase of 1.7 million people, see Hunt, *Pacification*, 197. Countryside depopulation in Charles Mohr, "Saigon Tries to Recover from the Blows," *New York Times*, May 10, 1968, and Elliot, *The Vietnamese War*, 331, 336.

69. Division commander in Bergerud, *The Dynamics of Defeat*, 225. Official quoted in ibid., 234. Thieu and contested hamlets in Hunt, *Pacification*, 195.

70. Vietnam Lessons Learned No. 73, "Defeat of VC Infrastructure," November 20, 1968, MACV Lessons Learned, Box 1, RG 472, NARA. MACV defined the VCI "as the political organization through which the Viet Cong control or seek to control the South Vietnamese people." MACV Commander's Conference, August 27, 1967, #21 History File, II, Reel 10, WCWP.

71. Phoenix operations in Annex A, Phung Hoang Advisors Handbook, November 20, 1970, Folder 06, Box 04, United States Armed Forces Manuals Collection, TTUVA. Phung Hoang was the South Vietnamese name for the program. Dale Andrade and James H. Willbanks, "CORDS/Phoenix: Counterinsurgency Lessons from Vietnam for the Future," *Military Review*, Vol. LXXXVI, No. 2 (March–April 2006):17–21. "The Phoenix Program" January 1975, Folder 05, Box 25, Douglas Pike Collection: Unit 02-Military Operations, TTUVA.

72. Number of reports in Lt. Col. Erik G. Johnson, VNIT Folder 100, CMH, 12. Robert S. Meehan spoke on the problems of HES not dealing with the structure of the insurgency in interview with author, April 13, 2008. On problems estimating popular attitudes and passive resistance, see Special National Intelligence Estimate, June 6, 1968, *FRUS*, 1964–1968, VI: 763 and Just, *To What End*, 68. Bing West and Charles Benoit found that HES was not measuring pacification, only control. "A Brief Report from Rural Vietnam," October 31, 1968, Strategy File #1, Folder 24, Thayer Papers CMH, 3.

73. CIA field assessment in *FRUS*, 1964–1968, VII: 762–763. Advisor quoted in Mark Moyar, *Phoenix and the Birds of Prey: Counterinsurgency and Counterterrorism in Vietnam* (Lincoln and London: University of Nebraska Press, 1997, 2007), 187. On quotas, see Dale Andradé, *Ashes to Ashes: The Phoenix Program and the Vietnam War* (Lexington, Mass.: Lexington Books, 1990),123–124, and Wayne L. Cooper, "Operation Phoenix: A Vietnam Fiasco Seen from Within," June 18, 1972, Folder 05, Box 24, Douglas Pike Collection: Unit 01-Assessment and Strategy, TTUVA.

74. Bunker weekly message, October 19, 1968, *FRUS*, 1964–1968, VII: 247–259. The 25 November National Security Council Meeting relied on similar figures to illustrate positive trends in South Vietnam. Ibid., 697. On Bunker's views on Thieu, see JCS History, Part III, JCSHO, 52–45. For the political intrigue associated with the bombing campaign halt during the November election, see Jeffrey Kimball, *Nixon's Vietnam War* (Lawrence: University Press of Kansas, 1998), 56–62.

75. "How Goes Thieu's Government?" *Time*, August 16, 1968, 30. Challenges confronting GVN in "USMACV Command History, 1968," NARA, 33, and MACV Quarterly Evaluation Report, July 1–September 30, 1968, MHI, 12.

76. Following documents in MACV Joint Message Forms, MACV Operational Guidance, MHI: fixing forces in Operational Guidance, July 27, 1968; counteroffensive in Operational Guidance, August 27, 1968; all types of operations in Operational Guidance, October 13, 1968; spirit of the offensive in Operational Guidance-4th Quarter CY 68, September 28, 1968.

77. Just, *To What End*, 80. On conventional mindedness in MACV's staff, see David T. Zabecki, *Chief of Staff: The Principal Officers behind History's Great Commanders*, Vol. 2 (Annapolis, Md.: Naval Institute Press, 2008), 214. On reluctance for pacification, see LTC Louis C. Menetrey, VNIT Folder 348, CMH, 8. Reliance on firepower in BG George H. Young, VNIT Folder 71, CMH, 18. 3X5 cards in memorandum, March 3, 1970, Olinto M. Barsanti Papers, MHI.

78. Little improvement in intelligence in BG William S. Coleman, VNIT Folder 308, CMH, 2. Fred C. Weyand, Senior Officer Debriefing Reports, Box 17, RG 472, NARA, 4. On no change to tactics, see Col. Eugene P. Forrester, VNIT Folder 206, CMH, 13–14.

79. Obderdorfer, *Tet!*, 111. On foreign policy concerns, see Johnson, *The Vantage Point*, 385; Schmitz, *The Tet Offensive*, 94; and Davidson, *Vietnam at War*, 446. On dollar and gold crisis in relation to Vietnam, see Kolko, *Anatomy of a War*, 313–314. Convention riots in Small, *Covering Dissent*, 88.

80. On enemy attacking from "pacified" villages, see Col. Hubert S. Campbell, VNIT Folder 96, CMH, 8–9. On public opinion after Tet and Americans not understanding the war, see Robert B. Rigg, "How Not to Report a War," *Military Review*, Vol. IL, No. 6 (June 1969): 14, and Gartner, *Strategic Assessment in War*, 136. Suppression of violence in Frank E. Armbruster, Raymond D. Gastil, Herman Kahn, William Pfaff, and Edmund Stillman, *Can We Win in Vietnam?* (New York: Frederick A. Praeger, 1968), 23.

81. Ward Just, "Saigon Yardstick: Eye of Beholder," *Washington Post*, October 25, 1968. Andrew Goodpaster, MACV's Deputy Commander, quoted in Sorley, *Vietnam Chronicles*, 85. LTC Charles P. Graham, Commander, 2nd Squadron, 1st Cavalry Regiment, VNIT Folder 3, CMH, 30.

82. Analysis of NVA infiltration in Thayer, "How to Analyze a War Without Fronts," 835. On problems associated with Abrams's new approach, see Moss, *Vietnam*, 310–311.

83. Memorandum for General Abrams, July 07, 1968, Folder 0615, Box 04, Vietnam Archive Collection, TTUVA. Figures in MACJ3-051 memorandum, "Measurement of Progress," November 25, 1968, MHI. On MACV staff problems, see Walter T. Kerwin, "Inside MACV Headquarters," *Vietnam* (February 2001): 28 and Zabecki, *Chief of Staff*, 211–212. On Abrams relying on statistics, see Sorley, *A Better War*, 35.

84. Bunker to Johnson, January 16, 1969, *FRUS, 1964–1968*, VII: 826. On other additional positive assessments, see Sorley, ibid., 94–95. HES end of year figures in "USMACV Command History, 1968," NARA, 523. U.S. casualty figures for 1968 in Stanton, *Vietnam Order of Battle*, 349.

85. On 1968 ending in stalemate, see Graham A. Cosmas, *MACV: The Joint Command in the Years of Withdrawal, 1968–1973* (Washington, D.C.: Center of Military History, 2007), 139, and Spector, *After Tet*, 311–312.

Chapter 7

1. Charles Mohr, "Optimism Emerges in Saigon as Allies Make Major Gains," *New York Times*, January 3, 1969. On the "surprising success" of the Accelerated Pacification Campaign, see Dave Warsh, "'Great Leap Forward': Success or Failure?" *Pacific Stars & Stripes*, February 3, 1969. Abrams, Operational Guidance #1-1st Qtr CY69, January 17, 1969, MACV Joint Message Forms, MACV Operational Guidance, MHI.

2. On Dewey Canyon, see Stanton, *The Rise and Fall of an American Army*, 295–297, and Samuel Zaffiri, *Hamburger Hill: May 11–20, 1969* (Novato, Calif.: Presidio, 1988), 48–51. MACV assessment of these "preemptive operations" in USMACV Quarterly Evaluation Report, January 1–March 31, 1969, MHI, 3 and Headquarters, USMACV, "One War," MACV Command Overview, 1968–1972, Historians Files, CMH, 4–46, 4–48.

3. "One War" concept in USMACV Quarterly Evaluation, ibid., 7. Operational Report-Lessons Learned, Headquarters, 1st Infantry Division, Period Ending January 31, 1969, May 21, 1969, Digital Archive Collection, USAAWCL.

4. On changes to enemy organization and tactics, see MG Elvy B. Roberts, Senior Officer Debriefing Report, April 18, 1970, Box 1, Elvy B. Roberts Papers, MHI and USMACV, "One War," CMH, 1–18. Officer quoted in "Vietcong Terrorism Up 30% in January; Allied Forces Prepare for 'All Possibilities' at Tet Holiday," *New York Times*, February 5, 1969.

5. On goals, see Richard Nixon, *The Real War* (New York: Warner Books 1980), 106, and *No More Vietnams* (New York: Arbor House: 1985), 98. Henry Kissinger, *The White House Years* (London: Weidenfeld and Nicolson and Michael Joseph, 1979), 298. See also Larry Berman, *No Peace, No Honor: Nixon, Kissinger, and Betrayal in Vietnam* (New York and London: The Free Press, 2001), 50.

6. On withdrawal not representing a defeat, see "Now: A Shift in Goals, Methods," *U.S. News & World Report*, January 6, 1969, 16. On global perspective, see Kimball, *Nixon's Vietnam War*, 62.

7. Bunker, January 11, 1969, quoted in Sorley, *Vietnam Chronicles*, 100. CIA Special National Intelligence Estimate, January 16, 1969, *FRUS*, 1969–1976, VI: 1. For an example of the numerous areas measured as part of Vietnamization, see USMACV, "Vietnamization," Lessons Learned No. 76, November 28, 1969, Digital Archive Collection, USAAWCL. Lack of consensus in "Americans See War Going Well, But Tet Is a Time for Testing," *Washington Post*, February 15, 1969. On GVN's "lack of will to reform" see Andrew Wiest, *Vietnam's Forgotten Army: Heroism and Betrayal in the ARVN* (New York and London: New York University Press, 2008), 156.

8. USMACV, "One War," CMH, 7–43. On changing definition of success, see Anderson, *The Vietnam War*, 84.

9. On problems of different types of threats, see Viet-Nam Info Series 20: "The Armed Forces of the Republic of Viet Nam," from Vietnam Bulletin, 1969, Folder 09, Box 13, Douglas Pike Collection: Unit 02-Military Operations, TTUVA, 8, 25.

10. Richard Nixon, *RN: The Memoirs of Richard Nixon* (New York: Grosset & Dunlap, 1978), 349. On realizing limits to U.S. power, see Lawrence W. Serewicz, *America at the Brink of Empire: Rusk, Kissinger, and the Vietnam War* (Baton Rouge: Louisiana State University Press, 2007), 10. On containing communism, see U.S. Embassy Statement, "Objectives and Courses of Action of the United States in South Viet-Nam," *FRUS*, 1964–1968, VII: 719 and "USMACV Command History, 1969," Digital Archive Collection, USAAWCL, II-1.

11. On credibility, see Ward S. Just, "Notes on a Losing War," *The Atlantic*, Vol. 223, No. 1 (January 1969): 40, and Jeffrey Kimball, *The Vietnam War Files: Uncovering the Secret History of Nixon-Era Strategy* (Lawrence: University Press of Kansas, 2004), 45. On "insurmountable problems" facing Nixon, see Robert Dalleck, *Nixon and Kissinger: Partners in Power* (New York: HarperCollins Publishers, 2007), 126–127. On Nixon's strategy, see Addington, *America's War in Vietnam*, 127.

12. Henry A. Kissinger, "The Viet Nam Negotiations," *Foreign Affairs*, Vol. 47, No. 2 (January 1969): 211. National Security Study Memorandum 1, January 21, 1969, OSDHO. On intent to seek divergent views, see James H. Willbanks, *Abandoning Vietnam: How America Left and South Vietnam Lost Its War* (Lawrence: University Press of Kansas, 2004), 10, and Showalter and Albert, *An American Dilemma*, 161.

13. Kissinger quoted in Kimball, *Nixon's Vietnam War*, 95. On disagreements, see Willard J. Webb, *The Joint Chiefs of Staff and The War in Vietnam: 1969–1970* (Washington, D.C.: Office

of Joint History, 2002), 8–9. (Hereafter cited as *JCS History, 1969–1970*) On MACV leaving out adverse comments, see Clarke, *Advice and Support*, 344. Kimball argues that "Abrams suppressed the most negative analyses." Ibid.

14. Nixon, *No More Vietnams*, 104–107 (definition of pacification on p. 132). On strategy being developed before NSSM 1, see Kimball, ibid., 98.

15. Westmoreland quoted in Larry A. Niksch, "Vietnamization: The Program and Its Problems," Congressional Record Service, January 5, 1972, Folder 01, Box 19, Douglas Pike Collection: Unit 02-Military Operations, TTUVA, CRS-5. On the phases of Vietnamization, see Willbanks, *Abandoning Vietnam*, 21–22. On plans in 1968, see Nguyen Duy Hinh, "Vietnamization and The Cease Fire," Folder 15, Box 4, Douglas Pike Collection: Unit 11-Monographs, TTUVA, 31.

16. Quoted in Cosmas, *MACV: The Joint Command in the Years of Withdrawal*, 157. "Pullout from Vietnam: Timetable for U.S.," *U.S. News & World Report*, January 27, 1969.

17. Nixon, *RN*, 380. On enemy offensive see: "A Time of Testing in Viet Nam," *Time*, March 7, 1969, 29; *JCS History, 1969–1970*, 25; and Davidson, *Vietnam at War*, 532. On the secret bombing campaign, see Kimball, *The Vietnam War Files*, 79, and *Nixon's Vietnam War*, 131–137.

18. Laird quoted in *JCS History, 1969–1970*, 10. "What Secretary Laird Learned in Vietnam," *U.S. News & World Report*, March 24, 1969, 26, and Showalter and Albert, *An American Dilemma*, 161–162.

19. Laird to Nixon, March 13, 1969, *FRUS*, 1969–1976, VI: 113. On Wheeler's recommendations, see ibid., 105–107. On troop redeployment numbers, see *JCS History, 1969–1970*, 11.

20. On the Guam Doctrine, see Langguth, *Our Vietnam*, 549, and Kimball, *Nixon's Vietnam War*, 154.

21. Kissinger, *The White House Years*, 276. Cosmas, *MACV*, 251. Development of MACV strategy under Abrams in USMACV, "One War," CMH, 2–14 to 2–19. Abrams and offensive operations in *JCS History, 1969–1970*, 57.

22. Henry Kissinger, *Ending the Vietnam War: A History of America's Involvement in and Extrication from the Vietnam War* (New York: Simon & Schuster, 2003), 85.

23. Analyst quoted in "Next Turn in Vietnam," *U.S. News & World Report*, March 3, 1969, 29. On problems in the enemy camp, see Elliott, *The Vietnamese War*, 343, 349.

24. Enemy threat tied to troop withdrawals in Collins, *The Development and Training of the South Vietnamese Army*, 88. On enemy views of pacification and Vietnamization, see *Victory in Vietnam*, 237–244. Strategy of waiting in Berman, *No Peace, No Honor*, 51.

25. Westmoreland address, Alfred M. Landon Lecture, Kansas State University, April 9, 1969, OSDHO, p. 7. MACV Joint Message Forms, MACV Operational Guidance No. 5, April 5, 1969, MHI.

26. USMACV, MACJ3-051, "Measurement of Progress" memorandum, August 26, 1969, MHI.

27. Laird quoted in "Maximum Military Pressure," *New York Times*, May 28, 1969. On officers supporting offensive operations, see *JCS History, 1969–1970*, 52. Kissinger to Nixon, April 3, 1969, *FRUS*, 1969–1976, VI: 181.

28. Abrams in Sorley, *Vietnam Chronicles*, 300. Combined Campaign Plan objectives in "USMACV Command History, 1969," USAAWCL, II-9.

29. Combat After Action Report of Operation Speedy Express, June 14, 1969, Historians Files, CMH. Lewy, *America in Vietnam*, 142–143. On dispersed combat see Ewell and Hunt, *Sharpening the Combat Edge*, 77.

30. After Action Report quoted in Dale Andradé, "Presidential Unit Citation for 9th Infantry Division," July 27, 1993, Historians Files, CMH, 4. Contributing factors in message, "Speedy Express," MG Sidle to ODCSOPS, January 17, 1972, Historians Files, CMH.

31. On reporter queries and CORDS allegations, see "Pacification's Deadly Price," *Newsweek*, June 19, 1972, 42–44.

32. Activity versus results in Ewell and Hunt, *Sharpening the Combat Edge*, 150. Contacts in Julian J. Ewell, "Impressions of a Division Commander in Vietnam," September 17, 1969, Box 1, Elvy B. Roberts Papers, MHI, 5. On productivity, see Senior Officers Debriefing Program, Transcripts of Debriefing, Box 1, Julian J. Ewell Papers, MHI, 92. Success defined in Julian J. Ewell, interview by Ted Gittinger, November 7, 1985, LBJL, 14.

33. On Ewell's briefing, see Douglas Kinnard in Appy, *Patriots*, 323.

34. David H. Hackworth and Eilhys England, *Steel My Soldiers' Hearts: The Hopeless to Hardcore Transformation of 4th Battalion, 39th Infantry, United States Army, Vietnam* (New York, London: Simon & Schuster, 2002), 15. On intelligence and language problems, see Colonel John A. Hemphill, commander, 3rd Brigade, 9th Infantry Division, VNIT Folder 455, CMH, 14–17, 32–35.

35. 3x5 cards in Hackworth, ibid., 99. Booby trap threat in Ewell, interview, October 15, 1991, Historians Files, CMH, p. 33. SP4 Dennis R. Moss, VNIT 379, CMH, 8, 12.

36. "Summary of Action and Results," memorandum of May 24, 1969, Melvin Zais Papers, MHI. See also "The Battle for Hamburger Hill," *Time*, May 30, 1969, 27–28. For Zais's decision to fight and enemy reactions, see Zaffiri, *Hamburger Hill*, 168, 197. Casualty figures for this battle range widely. I have relied on Lewy, *America in Vietnam*, 144.

37. Trooper quoted in "Woe to the Victors," *Newsweek*, June 2, 1969, 42. On media storm, see "A Question of Casualties," *Newsweek*, June 9, 1969, 45.

38. Kennedy's reactions in "Teddy on the Stump," *Newsweek*, June 2, 1969, 33. Mahon and "aggressive posture" both in "Action at Apbia," *New York Times*, May 22, 1969. State Department official quoted in "Woe to the Victors."

39. News release, May 24, 1969, Melvin Zais Papers, MHI. Body counts in Senior Officers Oral History Program, Volume III, Melvin Zais Papers, MHI, 581. Westmoreland in Zaffiri, *Hamburger Hill*, 276.

40. Kevin Buckley, "General Abrams Deserves a Better War," *New York Times*, October 5, 1969. Aggressiveness in Box 9, Donald A. Seibert Papers, MHI, p. 1015. On terminology, see Wheeler, *FRUS, 1969–1976*, VI: 313. On the continuing influence of body counts, see Richard A. McMahon, "Bury the Body Count, an Army Officer Says," *Baltimore Sun*, June 29, 1969.

41. Ewell, "Impressions," MHI, 12. Ira A. Hunt, Jr., discussed the 9th Infantry linking combat operations to HES in interview with author, April 23, 2008. On the 9th Infantry Division's impact on the population, see Elliott, *The Vietnamese War*, 345–346.

42. MACEVAL Studies, December 14, 1968, Research Task M.E. #1, Technical Reports, Box 1, RG 472, NARA. Part of this study included a technical report entitled, "An Optimum Transfer Study Survey."

43. On combined combat operations, see USMACV Quarterly Evaluation, April 1–June 30, 1969, MHI, 5–6 and *JCS History, 1969–1970*, 75–76. Laird's report to Nixon in *FRUS, 1969–1976*, VI: 361.

44. On size increases, see Niksch, "Vietnamization: The Program and Its Problems," TTUVA, CRS-21, and "Vietnam: December 1969," A Staff Report Prepared for the Use of the Committee

on Foreign Relations, United States Senate, February 2, 1970, Folder 06, Box 07, Douglas Pike Collection: Unit 11-Monographs, TTUVA, 10. Political problems within ARVN in Joes, *The War for South Viet Nam, 1954–1975*, 93.

45. "The Laird Plan," *Newsweek*, June 2, 1969, 44. On ARVN lacking experience, see Willbanks, *Abandoning Vietnam*, 51 and Zaffiri, *Westmoreland*, 211. In December 1969, MACV listed 20 percent of ARVN's infantry battalions as "non-aggressive." See USMACV, "One War," CMH, 7–24.

46. Program Review and Analysis for RVNAF Progress, briefing to USMACV Commanders' Conference, September 24, 1967, #22 History File II, Reel 11, WCWP. MACV Directive 18–3, January 13, 1968, "Army Information and Data Systems Program Review and Analysis for RVNAF Progress," MHI. USMACV, Program Review and Analysis for RVNAF Progress report, August 31, 1968, MHI. On ARVN military training and education, see Vinh Loc, "Search for Professional Excellence," *Military Review*, Vol. XLVIII, No. 12 (December 1968): 51–55.

47. Laird to Nixon, June 2, 1969, *FRUS, 1969–1976*, VI: 263. On ARVN's ability to handle the threat, see "Can U.S. Get Out of the War Now?" *U.S. News & World Report*, May 5, 1969. On problems of using desertion to assess ARVN effectiveness, see Marilyn B. Young, and Robert Buzzanco, eds., *Companion to the Vietnam War* (Malden, Mass.: Blackwell Publishing, 2002), 148.

48. Major Lawrence D. Silvan, memorandum, "Handout Material Collected at the MACV/CORDS Advisor Orientation Course," December 2, 1969, VNIT Folder 558, CMH. Linguistic and cultural problems in Robert D. Ramsey, *Advising Indigenous Forces: American Advisors in Korea, Vietnam, and El Salvador* (Fort Leavenworth, Kans.: Combat Studies Institute Press, 2006), 46.

49. Problems with the 25th Infantry in David Hoffman, "Pacification: Merely a 'Numbers Game'?" *Washington Post*, January 28, 1969. Advisors as "glue" in Palmer, *The 25-Year War*, 94. On withdrawing faster than ARVN could improve, see Kolko, *Anatomy of a War*, 179.

50. Epithets in "Can Vietnamization Work?" *Time*, September 26, 1969, 25. "Their Lions—Our Rabbits," *Newsweek*, October 9, 1967, 20. Lack of motivation in DePuy, *Changing an Army*, 123. Paul Kelly in Edelman, *Dear America*, 109.

51. "GI's in Battle: The 'Dink' Complex," *Newsweek*, December 1, 1969, 37. On differences in attitudes between combat units and advisors, see Senior Officers Oral History Program, Volume II, Melvin Zais Papers, MHI, 478. Years of criticism in Showalter and Albert, *An American Dilemma*, 163.

52. Westmoreland quoted in *JCS History, 1969–1970*, 122. On SAME reports, see BG John W. Barnes, Deputy Senior Advisor, II Corps Tactical Zone, Senior Officer Debriefing Reports, December 15, 1968, Box 1, RG 472, NARA. Clarke, *Advice and Support*, 241–243.

53. Advisor quoted in Clarke, ibid., 325. Distribution of effort chart in MACV SEER Report, 4th Quarter, CY 69, USAAWCL, Digital Archive, 19. On problems with report, see Clarke, ibid., 387–389.

54. Territorial Forces Evaluation System (TFES) Handbook, November 1969, Folder 10, Box 43, Douglas Pike Collection: Unit 03-Statistical Data, TTUVA.

55. Pacification Data Bank-November 1969, Folder 10, Box 43, Douglas Pike Collection: Unit 03-Statistical Data, TTUVA. MACCORDS Field Reporting System, July 1, 1969, Folder 02, Box 01, Douglas Pike Collection: Unit 03-Civil Operations, Revolutionary Development Support, TTUVA.

56. KIAs and "improved leadership" in USMACV, "Command History, 1969," USAAWCL, VI-136. On using body counts as a metric for ARVN, see also Jack Walsh, "ARVN—Bigger, Better,

Bolder Than Year Ago," *Pacific Stars & Stripes*, March 22, 1969. Advisor views on ARVN leadership from Senior Officer Debriefing Program, BG Donald D. Dunlop, April 30, 1969, Folder 01, Bud Harton Collection, TTUVA, 3.

57. ARVN missions in "A Systems Analysis View of the Vietnam War: 1965–1972, Vol. 7-Rep. of Vietnam Armed Forces," Geog. V. Vietnam-319.1, CMH,2. On different dimensions of measurement, see W. G. Prince, "Analysis of Vietnamization: Summary and Evaluation," Final Report, Vol. I, November 1973, Digital Archive Collection, USAAWCL, II-23. Diverse threats in Sorley, *Vietnam Chronicles*, 256. Building ARVN in American image in James Walker Trullinger, Jr., *Village at War: An Account of Revolution in Vietnam* (New York and London: Longman, 1980), 176 and Scales, *Firepower in Limited Warfare*, 148.

58. Clifford noted the problem of dramatizing ARVN participation to LBJ on July 18, 1968. See *FRUS, 1964–1968*, VI: 881. Officer quoted in Tom Buckley, "The ARVN Is Bigger And Better, But—," *New York Times*, October 12, 1969. Wheeler to Abrams in Clarke, *Advice and Support*, 389. "Mediocre" assessment in Maynard Parker, "The Illusion of Vietnamization," *Newsweek*, September 29, 1969, 33.

59. Tran Von Don, *Our Endless War: Inside Vietnam* (San Rafael, Calif., and London: Presidio Press, 1978), 163. William Beecher, "The Problem Is How to Disengage Without Causing a Collapse," *New York Times*, June 22, 1969. On pace of withdrawal, see *FRUS, 1969–1976*, VI: 15 and Schulzinger, *A Time for War*, 279.

60. Quotation in Buckley, "The ARVN Is Bigger And Better, But—." John Prados, "Vietnamization: Success or Failure?" *The VVA Veteran* (November/December 2007): 39.

61. Desertion figures in Hunt and Shultz, *Lessons from an Unconventional War*, 101. Training percentages in "A Systems Analysis View of the Vietnam War: 1965–1972, Vol. 7-Rep. of Vietnam Armed Forces," CMH, 1–2. On general ARVN weaknesses, see *JCS History, 1969–1970*, 124 and Moss, *Vietnam*, 340.

62. Shaplen's report appeared in *The New Yorker* on September 21, 1969. *The Road from War*, 312. On the GVN being out of touch, see Brigham, *ARVN*, 27, 72. On political competition, see Allan E. Goodman, "South Vietnam: Neither War Nor Peace," *Asian Survey*, Vol. 10, No. 2 (February 1970): 114.

63. Abrams quoted in Sorley, *Vietnam Chronicles*, 152. On "working the system" see also "Hold Your Breath," *Newsweek*, July 14, 1969, 41, and USMACV, "One War," CMH, 19.

64. On coordination difficulties, see: "Lessons from the Vietnam War," Report of a Seminar Held at the Royal United Service Institution, February 12, 1969, Folder 77, Public Documents, William C. Westmoreland Papers, RG 319, NARA, 5; "Vietnam Dilemma: A First-Hand Explanation," *U.S. News & World Report*, June 16, 1969, 26–29.

65. Abrams, MACV Commanders' Conference, January 11, 1969, in USMACV, "One War," CMH, 3–25. Positive pacification indicators in "Vietnam: December 1969," A Staff Report, TTUVA, 3–4. On relationship between Vietnamization and pacification, see Colby, *Lost Victory*, 307.

66. Donn Starry, letter to A. L. West, Jr., April 15, 1969, Box 2, Personal Correspondence, Donn A. Starry Papers, MHI. "Widespread skepticism" in "Easy Come . . .," *Newsweek*, March 3, 1969, 32. RF/PF analysis in "A Systems Analysis View of the Vietnam War: 1965–1972, Vol. 7-Rep. of Vietnam Armed Forces," CMH, 169. 90 percent figure in Report by Subcommittee of the House Committee on Armed Services Following a Visit to the Republic of Vietnam, January 15–17, 1970, on the Progress of the Pacification Program (Washington, D.C.: U.S. Government Printing Office, 1970), 5417–5418.

67. General quoted in "Vietnam: As Shooting Dies Down . . .," *U.S. News & World Report*, October 27, 1969, 35. On "lull" see Hedrick Smith, "Debate Continues on Combat Tactics," *New York Times*, July 7, 1969, and "Behind the Vietnam 'Lull'—The Shifts in Strategy," *U.S. News & World Report*, August 11, 1969, 29–30. On resiliency of the NLF, see Brian M. Jenkins, "A People's Army for South Vietnam: A Vietnamese Solution," November 1971, Folder 05, Box 04, Douglas Pike Collection: Unit 11-Monographs, TTUVA, v.

68. "Three clingings" in Marc Jason Gilbert and William Head, eds., *The Tet Offensive* (Westport, Conn.: Praeger, 1996), 119. Hanoi fears in USMACV, "Command History, 1969," USAAWCL, III-14 and USMACV, "One War," CMH, 4–36.

69. Kissinger, *The White House Years*, 971. See also: Nixon, *RN*, 408; Karnow, *Vietnam*, 593; and Dale Van Atta, *With Honor: Melvin Laird in War, Peace, and Politics* (Madison: The University of Wisconsin Press, 2008), 183.

70. On Nixon's dilemma, see Max Frankel, "Nixon Is Forced to 'Negotiate' on Three Fronts," *New York Times*, March 23, 1969. Doubting simultaneous efforts in Guy J. Pauker, *An Essay on Vietnamization* (Santa Monica, Calif.: Rand, March 1971), v. Officer concerns in Mark M. Boatner, "Withdrawal, Redeployment or Cop Out," *Army*, Vol. 21, No. 4 (April 1971): 16, and USMACV, "Command History, 1969," USAAWCL, I-1.

71. Nixon, *No More Vietnams*, 115. B. Drummond Ayres, Jr., "South Vietnamese Troops Showing Uneven Progress," *New York Times*, June 2, 1969. *Time* report in Landers, *The Weekly War*, 251. "Baby-Sitting with ARVN," *Newsweek*, November 10, 1969, 61.

72. Zais to Abrams, message dated October 1, 1969, Melvin Zais Papers, MHI. Poor media relations in Cosmas, *MACV*, 219. Lack of criticism directed toward Hanoi in Kissinger, *The White House Years*, 293.

73. Jonathan Schell, December 6, 1969, in *Observing the Nixon Years* (New York: Pantheon Books, 1989), 12. On the Moratorium, see "Strike Against the War," *Time*, October 17, 1969, 17–19, and Mann, *A Grand Delusion*, 641.

74. After action report quoted in Appy, *Working-Class War*, 275. Body count commendation in Colin L. Powell with Joseph E. Persico, *My American Journey* (New York: Random House, 1995), 146. On news release of My Lai, see Mann, *A Grand Delusion*, 648–649.

75. Mansfield and McGovern quoted in Mann, ibid., 645, 649. Budget considerations in *JCS History, 1969–1970*, 38. Nixon's views on progress of Vietnamization as a criterion for withdrawal in Niksch, "Vietnamization: The Program and Its Problems," TTUVA, CRS-13.

76. "Now a New Kind of War," *U.S. News & World Report*, May 26, 1969, 29. Combat Lessons Bulletin, July 15, 1969, Computerization of Data for Operational Planning, USARV Combat Lessons Bulletin, Box 1, RG 472, NARA.

77. Force withdrawals in Sorley, *Vietnam Chronicles*, 230 and *JCS History, 1969–1970*, 98. 1st ARVN Division in "As Saigon Gets Set to Fight Its Own War—," *U.S. News & World Report*, October 6, 1969, 61. See also "Officials See Hope of Winning War," *Washington Post*, October 14, 1969, and "Vietnamization: Will It Work?" *Newsweek*, February 9, 1970, 31–33. On the vulnerability of ARVN, see Scott Sigmund Gartner, "Differing Evaluations of Vietnamization," *Journal of Interdisciplinary History*, Vol. 29, No. 2 (Autumn 1998): 260–261.

78. Kissinger, *The White House Years*, 273.

79. Senior Officers Oral History Program, Volume II, Melvin Zais Papers, MHI, 478. On ARVN's various missions, see Don, *Our Endless War*, 219. "The War: Testing Vietnamization," *Time*, January 5, 1970, 30.

80. "Behind Optimism about Vietnam," *U.S. News & World Report*, December 1, 1969, 40–42. "Vietnam: The New Underground Optimism," *Time*, December 12, 1969, 14–15. 1LT William R. Mayfield, letter to LTC James C. Torrence, August 16, 1969, Adventure Board, Box 2, Vietnam Letters, Torrence Collection, WPSC.

81. Kissinger to Nixon, January 19, 1970, *FRUS*, 1969–1976, VI: 536. On problems with reporting, see Cosmas, *MACV*, 203. Defending statistics in George W. Nelson, Jr., "The Numbers Game," *Army*, Vol. 19, No. 2 (February 1969): 54. Supporting any case with any evidence from "Vietnam: December 1969," A Staff Report, TTUVA, 2.

82. Address by General W. C. Westmoreland to the Opening Session of the Annual Convention, American Association of School Administrators, February 15, 1969, Speech File Service, Office of the Chief of Information, OSDHO, 9. On consistency of "one war" approach, see Ellis W. Williamson, Senior Officer Debriefing Reports, Box 18, RG 472, NARA. On sustainability of ARVN, see Jenkins, "A People's Army for South Vietnam," v, 3.

83. On worries about redeployment, see Boatner, "Withdrawal, Redeployment or Cop Out," 15.

Chapter 8

1. Arthur S. Collins, Jr., Senior Officers Oral History Program, interview by Chandler P. Robbins III, 1982, MHI, 347. LTC Lee Roberts, battalion commander, quoted in Donald Kirk, "Who Wants to Be the Last American Killed in Vietnam?" *New York Times*, September 19, 1971.

2. Captain Brian Utermahlen, company commander, quoted in John Sarr, "You Can't Just Hand Out Orders," *Life*, October 23, 1970, 32. 1st Platoon, D Company, 506th Infantry, 101st Airborne Division AAR, February 11, 1970, VNI Folder 302, CMH. On the gap between performance expected and actual performance see Kurt Lang, "American Military Performance in Vietnam: Background and Analysis," *Journal of Political & Military Sociology*, Vol. 8, No. 2 (Fall 1980): 273.

3. Robert D. Heinl, Jr., "The Collapse of the Armed Forces," *Armed Forces Journal*, Vol. 108, No. 19 (June 7, 1971): 31, 36. Nixon at West Point in Dalleck, *Nixon and Kissinger*, 253. For a discussion blaming the American army's failures on "ineptitude at the top," see Cincinnatus, *Self-Destruction: The Disintegration and Decay of the United States Army During the Vietnam Era* (New York and London: W. W. Norton, 1981), 10.

4. Charles C. Moskos, Jr., "Military Made Scapegoat for Vietnam," in *A Short History of the Vietnam War*, ed. Allan R. Millett (Bloomington and London: Indiana University Press, 1978), 70. Article originally published August 30, 1970. Lawrence M. Baskir and William A. Strauss, *Chance and Circumstance: The Draft, the War, and the Vietnam Generation* (New York: Alfred A. Knopf, 1978), 6. Paul L. Savage and Richard A. Gabriel, "Cohesion and Disintegration in the American Army: An Alternative Perspective," in Sevy, *The American Experience in Vietnam*, 95. *Armed Forces and Society* originally published the Savage and Gabriel essay in May 1976.

5. Richard A. Gabriel and Paul L. Savage, *Crisis in Command: Mismanagement in the Army* (New York: Hill and Wang, 1978), 39.

6. Charles C. Moskos, Jr., "Vietnam: Why Men Fight," in *The American Military*, ed. Martin Oppenheimer (Chicago: Aldine, 1971), 17.

7. McCaffrey quoted in Lewy, *America in Vietnam*, 154. On worries over effectiveness decreasing with lower quality soldiers, see James R. Holbrook, "Volunteer Army: Military Caste?" *Military Review*, Vol. LI, No. 8 (August 1971): 95. Disintegration in Edward L. King, *The Death of The Army: A Pre-Mortem* (New York: Saturday Review Press, 1972), vi.

8. Congressman L. Mendel Rivers quoted in Michael S. Foley, *Confronting the War Machine: Draft Resistance during the Vietnam War* (Chapel Hill and London: The University of North Carolina Press, 2003), 37. On low monthly draft calls after Korea, see David L. Anderson, *The Columbia Guide to the Vietnam War* (New York: Columbia University Press, 2002), 113.

9. Peak troop strength in "Vietnam Warriors: A Statistical Profile," *VFW* (March 1993): 20. On draft numbers, see George Q. Flynn, *The Draft, 1940–1973* (Lawrence: University Press of Kansas, 1993), 168–169. On 1966 levels, see Foley, *Confronting the War Machine*, 54.

10. Moynihan quoted in Appy, *Working-Class War*, 31.

11. Paul R. Camacho and David Coffey, "Project 100,000," in *Encyclopedia of the Vietnam War: A Political, Social, and Military History*, Vol. 2, ed. Spencer C. Tucker (Santa Barbara, Calif.: ABC-CLIO, 1998), 587.

12. McNamara quoted in Lisa Hsiao, "Project 100,000: The Great Society's Answer to Military Manpower Needs in Vietnam," *Vietnam Generation*, Vol. 1, No. 2 (1989): 14.

13. New Standards Men statistics from Charles R. Coble, Jr., "Social Action Programs in the Department of Defense" (Ph.D. diss., University of North Carolina at Chapel Hill, 1969), 47–48. African American statistics from Camacho and Coffey, "Project 100,000," 587.

14. In Edward Bernard Glick, *Soldiers, Scholars, and Society: The Social Impact of the American Military* (Pacific Palisades, Calif.: Goodyear Publishing Company, 1971), 44–45.

15. McNamara quoted in Hsiao, "Project 100,000," 17.

16. Charles Cooper quoted in Appy, *Patriots*, 445.

17. The National Advisory Commission on Selective Service, *In Pursuit of Equity: Who Serves When Not All Serve?* (Washington, D.C.: U.S. Government Printing Office, 1967), 4–7, 41.

18. Hershey in John Helmer, *Bringing the War Home: The American Soldier in Vietnam and After* (New York: The Free Press, 1974), 6. For a detailed description of channeling and attendant deferments, see "Channeling," reprinted from *Ramparts* (December 1967).

19. On correlation between AFQT, race, and combat arms assignments, see Cynthia Gimbel and Alan Booth, "Who Fought in Vietnam?" *Social Forces*, Vol. 74, No. 4 (June 1996): 1143, 1147–1149. On educational levels and percentages of those serving in Vietnam, see Gary L. Long, "A Sociology for Special Circumstances: Using the Vietnam War in the Classroom," *Teaching Sociology*, Vol. 21, No. 3 (July 1993): 262. On draftees compared to volunteers, see John Moddell and Timothy Haggerty, "The Social Impact of War," *Annual Review of Sociology*, Vol. 17 (1991): 210.

20. Fitt, LBJL, 26. Occupational group percentages from Coble, "Social Action Programs in the Department of Defense," 91. On good management sense in placing higher IQ soldiers in assignments outside of the infantry, see Baskir and Strauss, *Chance and Circumstance*, 52.

21. As an example, see James Fallows, "What Did You Do in the Class War, Daddy?" in *Against the Vietnam War: Writings Published by Activists*, ed. Mary Susannah Robbins (Syracuse, N.Y.: Syracuse University Press, 1999), 205, originally published in *The Washington Monthly*, October 1975.

22. 1963 high school data from Charles C. Moskos, Jr., *The American Enlisted Man: The Rank and File in Today's Military* (New York: Russell Sage Foundation, 1970), 196. AFQT percentages

in 1966 from Roger W. Little, ed., *Selective Service and American Society* (New York: Russell Sage Foundation, 1969), 19. College educational data and percentage of high school dropouts from Appy, *Working-Class War*, 26.

23. "USMACV Command History, 1970," Digital Archive Collection, USAAWCL, 1970, p. XII-1.

24. Herbert Y. Schandler, interview with author, April 7, 2008. First sergeant quoted in "The Troubled U.S. Army in Vietnam," *Newsweek*, January 11, 1971, 30, 34. On avoiding risks in a withdrawing army, see Saar, "You Can't Just Hand Out Orders," 31.

25. Westmoreland, "From the Army of the '70s: 'A Flawless Performance,'" *Army*, Vol. 20, No. 10 (October 1970): 27. On permissiveness, see Donald A. Seibert Papers, MHI, Box 9, 1049 and Robert Rivikin, "Is Discipline Bad for the Army?" *New York Times*, December 21, 1970. On spillover debate, see William L. Hauser, *America's Army in Crisis: A Study in Civil-Military Relations* (Baltimore and London: The Johns Hopkins University Press, 1973), 124–125.

26. Pacific Command report in "Armed Forces: Disorder in the Ranks," *Time*, August 9, 1971, 21. Brigadier General Theodore C. Mataxis, "This Far, No Farther," *Military Review*, Vol. L, No. 3 (March 1970): 75.

27. Colonel Robert B. Rigg, "Future Military Discipline," *Military Review* Vol. L, No. 9 (September 1970): 16. Douglas E. Kneeland, "War Stirs Debate among G.I.'s," *New York Times*, June 21, 1970. David Cortright, *Soldiers in Revolt: GI Resistance during the Vietnam War* (Chicago: Haymarket Books, 1975, 2005), 50–51.

28. "3 Ex-Officers Attack Viet Body Count," *Washington Post*, April 16, 1971. William A. Gouveia, Jr., "An Analysis of Moral Dissent: An Army Officer's Public Protest of the Vietnam War," *Journal of Military Ethics*, Vol. 3, No. 1 (March 2004): 55–57. David H. Hackworth, "Army Leadership Is Ineffective," *Washington Post*, June 29, 1971.

29. Richard Halloran, "Army Orders the Seizure of Antiwar Mail Sent to G.I.'s in Vietnam," *New York Times*, March 31, 1971. For underground press, see Dick Cluster, ed., *They Should Have Served That Cup of Coffee* (Boston: South End Press, 1979), 150, and Hauser, *America's Army in Crisis*, 83.

30. 1st Infantry Division soldier quoted in "A New GI: For Pot and Peace," *Newsweek*, February 2, 1970, 24. GI organizations in Richard R. Moser, *The New Winter Soldier: GI and Veteran Dissent during the Vietnam War* (New Brunswick, N.J.: Rutgers University Press, 1996), 58–59.

31. "The Alpha Incident," *Newsweek*, September 8, 1969, 17.

32. "Soldiers Who Refuse to Die," *Newsweek*, October 25, 1971, 67–68. Guenter Lewy, "The American Experience in Vietnam," in *Combat Effectiveness: Cohesion, Stress, and the Volunteer Military*, ed. Sam C. Sarkesian (Beverly Hills and London: Sage Publications, 1980), 97–98. Terry H. Anderson, "The GI Movement and the Response from the Brass," in *Give Peace a Chance: Exploring the Vietnam Antiwar Movement*, eds. Melvin Small and William D. Hoover (Syracuse, N.Y.: Syracuse University Press, 1992), 105–106. Captain Pete Zastrow quoted in Moser, *The New Winter Soldier*, 54.

33. Mathias quoted in Cortright, *Soldiers in Revolt*, 43. Eugene Linden, "Fragging and Other Withdrawal Symptoms," *Saturday Review*, January 8, 1972, 12–17, 55. Iver Peterson, "Major Arguing with G.I.'s Shot to Death in Vietnam," *The New York Times*, January 11, 1971.

34. Moser, *The New Winter Soldier*, 48, 50. William Thomas Allison, *Military Justice in Vietnam: The Rule of Law in an American War* (Lawrence: University Press of Kansas, 2007), 78–79.

35. CINCPAC study quoted in Cosmas, *MACV: The Joint Command in the Years of Withdrawal*, 233.

36. "The Troubled U.S. Army in Vietnam," *Newsweek*, 30. Benjamin E. Smith, interview by Joel D. Meyerson, CMH, VNIT 9819, 5.

37. On whites receiving better jobs, see Wallace Terry, *Bloods: An Oral History of the Vietnam War by Black Veterans* (New York: Random House, 1984), 219. On racial unrest being more prevalent in rear areas, see James S. White, "Race Relations in the Army," *Military Review*, Vol. L, No. 7 (July 1970): 5, and Philip D. Beidler, *Late Thoughts on an Old War: The Legacy of Vietnam* (Athens and London: The University of Georgia Press, 2004), 73.

38. Barnes quoted in Herman Graham III, *The Brothers' Vietnam War: Black Power, Manhood, and the Military Experience* (Gainesville and Tallahassee: University Press of Florida, 2003), 113. On the army reflecting a racist society at home, see George C. Wilson and Haynes Johnson, "GI Crime, Violence Climb Overseas," *Washington Post*, September 13, 1971. Salutes in "Whites Against Blacks in Vietnam," *The New Republic*, Vol. 160, No. 3 (January 18, 1969): 15. Black Liberation Front in David Cortright, "Black GI Resistance during the Vietnam War," *Vietnam Generation*, Vol. 2, No. 1 (Spring 1990): 57. Friction in Rigg, "Future Military Discipline," 16.

39. On "blaming civilian attitudes for black radicalism in the army," see James E. Westheider, *The African American Experience in Vietnam: Brothers in Arms* (Lanham, Boulder, and New York: Rowman & Littlefield, 2008), 81. Medical officer quoted in "Marijuana—The Other Enemy in Vietnam," *U.S. News & World Report*, January 26, 1970, 69. For MACV's response, see Hauser, *America's Army in Crisis*, 114–119.

40. Defense statistics in Sarkesian, *Combat Effectiveness*, 95. Hospital statistics in Landers, *The Weekly War*, 113. BG DeWitt C. Armstrong, Senior Officer Debriefing Report, HQ, U.S. Army Pacific, Military Historian's Office, Command Reporting Files, 1963–1972, Box 193, RG 550, NARA, p. 4. Stanley F. Cherrie, 17th Cavalry, Americal Division, interview by Jerry Felder, 1985, Box 7, Vietnam Company Command Collection, MHI, 4. Abrams's response in "Drive Against G.I. Drug Abuse In Vietnam Ordered by Abrams," *New York Times*, January 7, 1971 and "What Army Is Doing About GI's on Drugs," *U.S. News & World Report*, January 18, 1971, 37.

41. "Hearings before the Committee on Foreign Relations, United States Senate, Ninety-First Congress, Second Session on Moral and Military Aspects of the War in Southeast Asia," (Washington, D.C.: U.S. Government Printing Office, 1970), 4.

42. Jack Crouchet, *Vietnam Stories: A Judge's Memoir* (Niwot: University Press of Colorado, 1997), 171–173.

43. Hackworth, "Army Leadership Is Ineffective." Armstrong, Debriefing Report, NARA, 4. Officer ethical problems in Stuart H. Loory, *Defeated: Inside America's Military Machine* (New York: Random House, 1973), 54, and King, *The Death of the Army*, 76–77. Iver Peterson, "Medals System under Study by U.S.; Many Awarded Though War Wanes," *New York Times*, November 20, 1970.

44. Training performance statistics from Coble, "Social Action Programs in the Department of Defense," 50, and Janice H. Laurence and Peter F. Ramsberger, *Low-Aptitude Men in the Military: Who Profits, Who Pays?* (New York, Westport, Conn., and London: Praeger, 1991), 43–49.

45. For a discussion on the increased costs of training "marginal personnel," see Samuel H. Hays, "Military Conscription in a Democratic Society," in *Draftees or Volunteers: A Documentary History of the Debate over Military Conscription in the United States, 1787–1973*, ed. John Whiteclay Chambers II (New York and London: Garland, 1975), 511.

46. By 1969, nine out of every ten draftees were serving in Vietnam. See Flynn, *The Draft*, 234. DoD statistics in Appy, *Working-Class War*, 164, and Helmer, *Bringing the War Home*, 26.

47. As quoted in Appy, *Working-Class War*, 163.

48. 101st soldier quoted in Kirk, "Who Wants to Be the Last American Killed in Vietnam?" Intelligence officer in Santoli, *Everything We Had*, 194. Frank Hart pointed out the differences between enemy-initiated contact against patrols and firebases in correspondence with author, October 21, 2008.

49. George C. Wilson, "Hard-Learned Lessons in a Military Laboratory" in Millett, *A Short History of the Vietnam War*, 63.

50. As quoted in Paul Starr, *The Discarded Army: Veterans after Vietnam* (New York: Charterhouse, 1973), 192.

51. Not changing to account for inferior officers in William R. Corson, *Consequences of Failure* (New York: W. W. Norton, 1974), 84. Personnel officer quoted in "The Troubled U.S. Army in Vietnam," *Newsweek*, 29. Casualty briefing in Kirk, "Who Wants to Be the Last American Killed in Vietnam?"

52. Kill ratios in John M. Shaw, *The Cambodian Campaign: The 1970 Offensive and America's Vietnam War* (Lawrence: University Press of Kansas, 2005), 48. On indicators of the "disintegration of U.S. military forces in South Vietnam," see Allison, *Military Justice in Vietnam*, 67–68. For continuity in field indicators between 1966 and 1970–1971, see Birtle, "PROVN, Westmoreland, and the Historians," especially charts on 1230–1232.

53. Benjamin E. Smith, VNIT 9819, CMH, 13. Commander's conference and statistical measures in Memorandum, "Military Discipline," June 15, 1971, Folder 01, Box 14, George J. Veith Collection, TTUVA.

54. "Study on Military Professionalism," U.S. Army War College, June 30, 1970, MHI Library, iii-v, 14, 17, 20. See also Kinnard, *The War Managers*, 109–111.

55. Company commander quoted in Ronald H. Spector, "The Vietnam War and the Army's Self-Image," in *The Second Indochina War*, ed. Schlight, 179. On the influence of careerism, see Hauser, *America's Army in Crisis*, 173, and Lewy, *America in Vietnam*, 161.

56. Gimbel and Booth, "Who Fought in Vietnam?" 1143. On racial and drug problems and their link to Vietnamization, see Herring, *America's Longest War*, 243. Motto in Cluster, *They Should Have Served That Cup of Coffee*, 151. On boredom, see "Eyewitness Report on Drugs, Race Problems and Boredom," *U.S. News & World Report*, January 25, 1971, 30. Fighting versus surviving in Small and Hoover, *Give Peace a Chance*, 105. Soldier quoted in "As Fighting Slows in Vietnam: Breakdown in GI Discipline," *U.S. News & World Report*, June 7, 1971, 16. Draftees conditioned by home front from Douglas Kinnard, interview with author, October 23, 2008.

57. Bruce Palmer, interview (II) by Ted Gittinger, November 9, 1982, LBJL, 36. Army survey team report from Sorley, *A Better War*, 297.

58. On criticism of short tours, see Holbrook, "Volunteer Army: Military Caste?" 95, and Charles C. Moskos, Jr., *Soldiers and Sociology* ([Alexandria, Va.]: United States Army Research Institute for Behavioral and Social Sciences, 1988), 7. On lack of adequate training, see Lewy, *America in Vietnam*, 331. Decreasing effectiveness of NCO corps and decline in officer professionalism from Frank Hart, correspondence with author, October 25, 2008, and Paul Miles, interview with author, October 24, 2008. On too much emphasis on combat power, see Cincinnatus, *Self-Destruction*, 101.

59. In Stanton, *The Rise and Fall of an American Army*, 293.

60. Disengaging while fighting in Westmoreland, "From the Army of the '70s," 26. Rifleman quoted in Kirk, "Who Wants to Be the Last American Killed in Vietnam?"

Chapter 9

1. Laird quoted in "How Goes the War? A Colloquy in Saigon," *Time*, February 23, 1970, 20. On results of his trip, see "Ahead—Faster Withdrawal from Vietnam," *U.S. News & World Report*, February 23, 1970, 29–30. Laird, Memorandum to President, February 17, 1970 in Porter, *Vietnam: A History in Documents*, 388–390. Abrams, "Assessment of the Situation in Vietnam," memorandum, January 28, 1970, Historians Files, CMH.

2. Case Study, Operation "Randolph Glen," December 7, 1969–March 31, 1970, Drawer 1, Box 1, Unit History Files, 101st Airborne Division, MACV Command Historian's Collection, MHI. Enemy-initiated actions in "Observations after One Month in Command of I FFORCEV," memorandum dated March 24, 1970, Box 5, A.S. Collins Papers, MHI, 2.

3. Frank Hart discussed the disaster of Ripcord in correspondence with author, October 22, 2008. Keith W. Nolan, *Ripcord: Screaming Eagles under Siege, Vietnam 1970* (Novato, Calif.: Presidio, 2000). On enemy protracted war strategy, see DeGroot, *A Noble Cause?* 213.

4. Bunker, message to Secretary of State, April 24, 1970, Folder 21, Box 01, Douglas Pike Collection: Ellsworth Bunker Papers, TTUVA, 8–9. CIA assessment in memorandum, "Study: Improving South Vietnam's Internal Security Scene," May 5, 1970, Folder 16, Box 15, Douglas Pike Collection: Unit 01-Assessment and Strategy, TTUVA. On VC resilience, see Samuel L. Popkin, "Pacification: Politics and the Village," *Asian Survey* Vol. 10, No. 8 (August 1970): 664; Hammond, *Reporting Vietnam*, 201; and Stuart A. Herrington, *Silence Was a Weapon: The Vietnam War in the Villages, A Personal Perspective* (Novato, Calif.: Presidio, 1982), 65.

5. Abrams in Sorley, *Vietnam Chronicles*, 397. Soldier observations on secured areas in Maurer, *Strange Ground*, 246. John W. Finney, "War-Policy Basis is Called Dubious," *New York Times*, February 2, 1970. Robert W. Komer, Trip Report, "Vietnam Revisited," Folder 20, Box 01, Ogden Williams Collection, TTUVA.

6. On Kissinger's staff linking population control to U.S. troop withdrawals, see HAK Talking Points, VSSG [Vietnam Special Studies Group] Meeting, April 22, 1970, Richard Hunt VSSG Folder, OSDHO, p. 5. Officer warnings in "If Cambodia Falls to the Reds—Why Nixon Acted," *U.S. News & World Report*, May 11, 1970, 16. Communists exploiting rebellion in Wilfred P. Deac, *Road to the Killing Fields: The Cambodian War of 1970–1975* (College Station: Texas A&M University Press, 1997), 55. For Henry Kissinger's view, see *The White House Years* (London: Weidenfeld and Nicolson and Michael Joseph, 1979), 484–485.

7. Nixon, *The Real War*, 109. Max Frankel, "Purpose in Laos: A Shorter War," *New York Times*, February 9, 1971.

8. Abrams in Sorley, *Vietnam Chronicles*, 363.

9. "Results Uncertain in First Cambodian Forays," *New York Times*, May 10, 1970. "Balance Sheet on Laos—Victory or Defeat?" *U.S. News & World Report*, April 5, 1971, 15–17. "South Vietnam's Chances of Making It Alone," *U.S. News & World Report*, September 13, 1971, 30–31. Optimists and pessimists in William Beecher, "Vietnamization: A Few Loose Ends," *Army*, Vol. 20, No. 11 (November 1970): 14.

10. Taber, *The War of the Flea*, 13, 18–19.

11. Trinquier, *Modern Warfare*, 34, 54.

12. Galula, *Counterinsurgency Warfare*, 79.

13. Dilemma and intelligence in McCuen, *The Art of Counter-Revolutionary War*, 79, 113. On Mao and coordination of all aspects of counterinsurgency, see J. Bowyer Bell, *The Myth of the Guerrilla: Revolutionary Theory and Malpractice* (New York: Alfred A. Knopf, 1971), 23. Initiative and integration of political-military affairs in Pustay, *Counterinsurgency Warfare*, 110, 136, and Andrew W. Scott, *Insurgency* (Chapel Hill: University of North Carolina Press, 1970), 127.

14. Department of the Army, Field Manual 31–16, *Counterguerrilla Operations*, March 1967, 39. On doctrinal continuity, see Birtle, *U.S. Army Counterinsurgency and Contingency Operations Doctrine*, 431–432, and Richard H. Shultz, Jr. "The Vietnamization-Pacification Strategy of 1969–1972: A Quantitative and Qualitative Analysis," in Hunt and Shultz, *Lessons from an Unconventional War*, 26.

15. Scott, *Insurgency*, 10–11. Baljit Singh and Ko-Wang Mei, *Theory and Practice of Modern Guerrilla Warfare* (New York: Asia Publishing House, 1971), 68.

16. Nathan Leites and Charles Wolf, Jr., *Rebellion and Authority: An Analytic Essay on Insurgent Conflicts* (Chicago: Markham, 1970), 86–89. On insurgency as a system, see ps. 28–35.

17. Potential of operational analysis in MG Harris W. Hollis, Senior Officer Debriefing Report, April 1, 1970, Box 7, RG 472, NARA. MACV Chief of Staff memorandum, "Indicators to Supplant 'Body Count' As a Measure of Progress," January 26, 1970, Body Counts File, Safe 78/1, Histories Division, CMH. MACCORDS memorandum, "Requirements for Data for Measurement of Progress of the 1971 Plan," June 29, 1971, CORDS Historical Working Group Files, 1967–1973, Box 39, Plans and Reports, RG 472, NARA.

18. HES/70 in "USMACV Command History, 1970," Digital Archive Collection, USAAWCL, VIII–15 to VIII–23, and Thayer, "How to Analyze a War Without Fronts," 873. Advisor doubts in LTC Cecil K. Simmons, Senior Officer Debriefing Report, July 8, 1972, Box 15, RG 472, NARA.

19. "The U.S. Maps Its Progress," *Newsweek*, October 26, 1970, 33. MACV Directive 335–2, "Reports and Statistics—Ground Operations Reporting Guide," July 31, 1971. MACV Directive 335–22, "Reports and Statistics—Measurement of Progress," May 29, 1970. Updated on July 21, 1971. All three reports from MACV Directives, MACV Command Historian's Collection, Series I, MACV General HQ, MHI. Directive 335–22 contained more than 100 indices requiring input from all of MACV's staff agencies.

20. Col. Arthur D. Moreland, Senior Officer Debrief Report, August 1, 1972, Box 11, RG 472, NARA, 12. On useless feedback, see Col. Robert W. Springman, Senior Officer Debrief Report, August 19, 1972, Box 16, ibid., 7.

21. "What the Vietnamese Peasant Thinks," Pacification Attitudes Analysis System, Folder 151, Thayer Papers, CMH. Memorandum, "Analysis of Pacification Attitude Analysis System Results," January 10, 1970, Safe 71, Historians Files, CMH. The PAAS reports are housed at MHI.

22. "G.I. Publications Asked Not to Stress Fighting," *New York Times*, February 13, 1970. R.W. Komer, memorandum for Dr. Henry Kissinger, July 29, 1970, R. Hunt VSSG Folder, OSDHO.

23. T. H. Moorer, memorandum for the Secretary of the Army, "Credibility," October 5, 1971, Body Count Folder, Box 369, OSDHO. LTG Charles A. Corcoran, Senior Officer Debriefing Report, April 22, 1970, Box 3, RG 472, NARA, 7. MACV SEER Report, Part I, 4th Qrtr CY 70, File HRC, Geog V Vietnam 319.1, CMH, 2.

24. Westmoreland's views from Paul Miles, correspondence with author, August 22, 2008. Strategic guidance and goals in USMACV Command History 1970, T.S. Supplement, HQ

USMACV, Secy. of Joint Staff (MACJ03), Mil. Hist. Branch, Box 8, RG 472, NARA. Kissinger, *Ending the Vietnam War*, 177.

25. Henry Kissinger, *Diplomacy* (New York: Simon & Schuster, 1994), 693. MACV's 1970 Command History noted that "the success of Vietnamization allowed the US to adhere to the Nixon Doctrine." USAAWCL, I–1. On Congressional debate on this, see "Widening the War to Wind It Down?" *Newsweek*, February 8, 1971, 19. "Quarantine" in William Shawcross, *Sideshow: Kissinger, Nixon, and the Destruction of Cambodia*, rev. ed. (New York: Cooper Square Press, 1979, 2002), 91.

26. Potential consequences if Cambodia fell in Keith William Nolan, *Into Cambodia: Spring Campaign, Summer Offensive, 1970* (Novato, Calif.: Presidio, 1990), 77. American credibility in Tran Dinh Tho, *The Cambodian Incursion* (Washington, D.C.: U.S. Army Center of Military History, 1979), 33. Limited JCS involvement in Palmer, *The 25-Year War*, 100.

27. Strategic unity in William S. Turley, *The Second Indochina War: A Short Political and Military History, 1954–1975* (Boulder, Colo.: Westview Press, 1986), 135. See also Norman B. Hannah, *The Key to Failure: Laos and the Vietnam War* (Lanham and New York: Madison Books, 1987), 277. On the need for U.S. involvement outside of South Vietnam, see "If You Wonder What U.S. Is Doing in Laos—," *U.S. News & World Report*, January 5, 1970, 28–29.

28. Karnow, *Vietnam*, 626, 635. Col. Edwin W. Chamberlain, Jr., Senior Officer Debriefing Report, March 10, 1973, Digital Archive Collection, USAAWCL, 8.

29. Zais to Abrams, June 12, 1970, Melvin Zais Papers, MHI, 3. Terence Smith, "U.S. Vietnam Policy: An Assessment," *New York Times*, June 3, 1970.

30. Percentages in DeGroot, *A Noble Cause?*, 210, and Alexander Haig, Jr., with Charles McCarry, *Inner Circles: How America Changed the World, A Memoir* (New York: Warner Books, 1992), 235. MACV SEER Report, 4th Qtr CY70, CMH, 77.

31. A. S. Collins, Jr., to Abrams, "Observations on Dak Seang-Dak Pek Operations," May 7, 1970, Box 5, A.S. Collins Papers, MHI. Memorandum, "Ideas on Vietnam," Fall 1970, Box 7, ibid. LTG A.S. Collins, Jr., Senior Officer Debriefing Report, January 18, 1971, Box 2, RG472, NARA, 6.

32. Haig, *Inner Circles*, 236. South Vietnam's internal problems in "Vietnamization: Policy under Fire," *Time*, February 9, 1970, 25–26. PRG defined in Stanley I. Kutler, ed., *Encyclopedia of the Vietnam War* (New York: Simon & Schuster Macmillan, 1997), 461. On difficulties in determining the phase of revolutionary warfare, see McCuen, *The Art of Counter-Revolutionary War*, 79.

33. Quotations from Kissinger, *The White House Years*, 485. Ho Chi Minh Trail in Tho, *The Cambodian Incursion*, 18, 21. Bombing tonnage and convoy numbers from John Prados, *The Blood Road: The Ho Chi Minh Trail and the Vietnam War* (New York: John Wiley & Sons, 1999), 303, 314.

34. On events leading to American troops in Cambodia, see Malcolm Caldwell and Lek Tan, *Cambodia in the Southeast Asia War* (New York and London: Monthly Review Press, 1973), 308–310; Nolan, *Into Cambodia*, 72–75; and Tho, *The Cambodian Incursion*, 32–33.

35. Full text of presidential address in "The President Explains His Decision On Indo-China," *U.S. News & World Report*, May 11, 1970, 22–24. "Defensive raid" quoted in Keith William Nolan, *Into Laos: The Story of Dewey Canyon II/Lam Son 719; Vietnam 1971* (Novato, Calif.: Presidio, 1986), 11. On major objectives, see Joseph R. Cerami, "Presidential Decisionmaking and Vietnam: Lessons for Strategists," *Parameters*, Vol. XXVI, No. 4 (Winter 1996–97): 70. On internal debate among Nixon's advisors, see H. R. Haldeman, *The Haldeman Diaries: Inside the Nixon White House* (New York: G.P. Putnam's Sons, 1994), 155.

36. On hasty planning, see J. D. Coleman, *Incursion: From America's Chokehold on the NVA Lifelines to the Sacking of the Cambodian Sanctuaries* (New York: St. Martin's Press, 1991), 222–224, and Nolan, *Into Cambodia*, 78–81. See also *JCS History, 1969–1970*, 158–159.

37. On NVA avoiding contact, see Deac, *Road to the Killing Fields*, 79. Laird in George C. Wilson, "GI Casualty Rate Held 'Top Concern,'" *Washington Post*, May 9, 1970. Limits in Shaw, *The Cambodian Campaign*, 76.

38. Vietnamization working in Nixon, *RN*, 467. Most successful operation in Nixon, *No More Vietnams*, 122. Haig, *Inner Circles*, 239.

39. II FFORCEV Commander's Evaluation Report-Cambodian Operations, July 31, 1970, Folder 10, Box 01, Vietnam Helicopters Association Collection: Unit Histories, TTUVA, 8. Statistics from Coleman, *Incursion*, 265; Willbanks, *Abandoning Vietnam*, 85; and DeGroot, *A Noble Cause?*, 223. Driving enemy main force units away in Tho, *The Cambodian Incursion*, 175. "USMACV Command History, 1970," USAAWCL, I–2 supports this point.

40. II FFORCEV Commander's Evaluation Report, TTUVA, 2. Col. Carter Clarke quoted in "Cambodia: 'We're Cache Counters,'" *Newsweek*, May 25, 1970, 43. Percentage of areas searched in "Just How Important Are Those Caches?" *Time*, June 1, 1970, 27.

41. Operational Report-Lessons Learned, 1st Cavalry Division, August 14, 1970, notes that one of its brigade's missions was to locate and neutralize COSVN Headquarters. Folder 02, Box 01, Vietnam Helicopter Pilot Association Collection: Unit Histories-1st Cavalry Division, TTUVA, 12. On Abrams's use of B-52s, see Shaw, *The Cambodian Campaign*, 142.

42. Headquarters, USMACV, "One War," MACV Command Overview, 1968–1972, Historians Files, CMH, 3–50. Nixon's views on Kent State and campus protests in *RN*, 458–459. On loss of domestic and congressional support, see Willbanks, *Abandoning Vietnam*, 85–86.

43. Joseph Kraft, "Cambodia Operation Is Not 'Greatest Victory Yet Achieved,'" *Washington Post*, June 30, 1970. On refugees, see Marquis Childs, "Nixon Military Balance Sheet Ignores Misery in Cambodia," *Washington Post*, July 4, 1970, and Shawcross, *Sideshow*, 151. Presidential progress report in *JCS History, 1969–1970*, 181–182.

44. Schell, *Observing the Nixon Years*, 53. Questions over incursion in "As U.S. Leaves Cambodia—Success or Failure?" *U.S. News & World Report*, July 6, 1970, 99–11. On differing assessments, see: "Cambodia: A Cocky New ARVN," *Time*, June 8, 1970, 30 and "Fighting Slows Down, But Saigon's Woes Increase," *U.S. News & World Report*, August 17, 1970, 24–25.

45. Troop strengths in Stanton, *Vietnam Order of Battle*, 334. Kissinger's concerns in *The White House Years*, 971.

46. Nguyen Duy Hinh, *Lam Son 719* (Washington, D.C.: U.S. Army Center of Military History, 1979), 8. ARVN assuming responsibilities in Larry A. Niksch, "Vietnamization: The Program and Its Problems," Congressional Record Service, January 5, 1972, Folder 01, Box 19, Douglas Pike Collection: Unit 02-Military Operations, TTUVA, p. CRS-25.

47. For interpretations on the Cooper-Church Amendment, see Mann, *A Grand Delusion*, 659–666, and Hannah, *The Key to Failure*, 282–283. Planning for Lam Son 719 in "USMACV Command History, 1971," Digital Archive Collection, USAAWCL, E-15 to E-17, and Willard J. Webb and Walter S. Poole, *The Joint Chiefs of Staff and The War in Vietnam, 1971–1973* (Washington, D.C.: Office of Joint History, 2007), 3–5. (Hereafter cited as *JCS History, 1971–1973*) For U.S. role, see "Final Report: Airmobile Operations in Support of Operation Lam Son 719," Vol. II, May 1, 1971, Box 00, Folder 01, Bud Harton Collection, TTUVA, I–1 to I–2 and Nolan, *Into Laos*,

16–17. Grace period in "Why U.S. Stepped Up War in Indo-China," *U.S. News & World Report*, February 15, 1971, 22.

48. Kissinger, *The White House Years*, 1002. Sorties in Nolan, *Into Laos*, 125.

49. Nixon, *RN*, 498. Soldier quoted in John Saar, "An Ignominious and Disorderly Retreat," *Life*, April 2, 1971, 28. Lam Son 719 problems in: USMACV, "One War," CMH, 4–98; Hinh, *Lam Son 719*, 101–102; and *JCS History, 1971–1973*, 6, 10–13. NVA preparations in *Victory in Vietnam*, 271–275.

50. MACV results reported in USMACV, "One War," CMH, 4–99. Abrams quoted in Sorley, *Vietnam Chronicles*, 570. Thieu quoted in Willbanks, *Abandoning Vietnam*, 111. Bunker assessment in Memorandum for the President, March 30, 1971, Folder 21, Box 01, Douglas Pike Collection: Ellsworth Bunker Papers, TTUVA, p. 6. Nixon quoted in "Assessing the Laos Invasion," *Newsweek*, April 5, 1971, 25.

51. Kissinger, *The White House Years*, 1010. Abrams's concerns in Sorley, *Vietnam Chronicles*, 565. Coordination and planning issues in Nolan, *Into Laos*, 360–361. See also *JCS History, 1971–1973*, 100–103. Hanoi's confidence in "Answers to a Mystery: Why North Vietnam Fights On," *U.S. News & World Report*, August 9, 1971, 40.

52. Nixon, *RN*, 499. For similar arguments against the press, see Bunker, ibid., 26–27, and Haig, *Inner Circles*, 277. On the campaign results being linked to elections, see Stephen P. Randolph, *Powerful and Brutal Weapons: Nixon, Kissinger, and the Easter Offensive* (Cambridge, Mass.: Harvard University Press, 2007), 17 and "A Hollow Triumph?" *Newsweek*, October 11, 1971, 49.

53. Official quoted in "Vietnamization: The Reality and the Myth," *Newsweek*, August 2, 1971, 38–39. On Nixon refusing to acknowledge failure in Laos, see Dalleck, *Nixon and Kissinger*, 260–261. Iver Peterson, "Resor, in Vietnam, Expects Difficulties as Troops Pull Out," *New York Times*, May 4, 1971.

54. LTG James W. Sutherland, Jr., Debrief Report, June 1, 1971, Folder 06, Box 17, Douglas Pike Collection: Unit 02-Military Operations, TTUVA, 17. Alexander Haig acknowledged that "ARVN was beset by fundamental problems" in the wake of Lam Son 719. *Inner Circles*, 279.

55. "USMACV Command History, 1971," USAAWCL, VII–5. Bunker, Memorandum for the President, March 30, 1971, TTUVA, 7, 19. Officers briefed Abrams on the non-military aspects of MACV strategy for 1972 yet never altered their metrics of progress to support potential strategic changes during U.S. redeployment. See Sorley, *Vietnam Chronicles*, 619.

56. MACV assessments in "USMACV Command History, 1972–1973," Digital Archive Collection, USAAWCL, 9–10. On negotiations, see Allan E. Goodman, *The Lost Peace: America's Search for a Negotiated Settlement of the Vietnam War* (Stanford, Calif.: Hoover Institution Press, 1978), 111; Ruane, *War and revolution in Vietnam*, 96; and Kimball, *The Vietnam War Files*, 203–205. Deadlock in "The Last Peace Plan," *The Economist*, January 29, 1972, 13. Infiltration and terrorist attacks in Peter A. Jay, "Vietnam: The Optimism Has Faded," *The Washington Post*, January 16, 1972.

57. Politburo quoted in *Victory in Vietnam*, 283. Abrams to CINCPAC, Military Situation in the RVN, March 8, 1972, Box 3, Folder 12, Glenn Helm Collection, TTUVA. On Hanoi's strategic motives, see Kimball, *Nixon's Vietnam War*, 324; Randolph, *Powerful and Brutal Weapons*, 28–29; and Ngo Quang Truong, *The Easter Offensive of 1972* (Washington, D.C.: U.S. Army Center of Military History, 1980), 157–158.

58. Politburo quoted in *Victory in Vietnam*, ibid. On uncertainty over Hanoi's intentions, see Berman, *No Peace, No Honor*, 124; Goodman, *The Lost Peace*, 117–118; and Anthony T.

Bouscaren, ed., *All Quiet on the Eastern Front: The Death of South Vietnam* (Old Greenwich, Conn.: The Devin-Adair Company, 1977), 44. Nixon viewed the invasion "as a sign of desperation." In *RN*, 587.

59. Advisor quoted in G.H. Turley, *The Easter Offensive: Vietnam, 1972* (Novato, Calif.: Presidio, 1985), 87. MACV's account can be found in "USMACV Command History, 1972–1973," USAAWCL, 33–37.

60. ARVN untrained in defensive operations in F.P. Serong, "The 1972 Easter Offensive," *Southeast Asian Perspectives*, No. 10 (Summer 1974): 25. On debates between the White House and MACV over the best use of B-52s, see Randolph, *Powerful and Brutal Weapons*, 119–120; Kimball, *Nixon's Vietnam War*, 314–315; and Haldeman, *The Haldeman Diaries*, 435.

61. James H. Willbanks, *The Battle of An Loc* (Bloomington and Indianapolis: Indiana University Press, 2005), 45. Thieu's order in Ian Ward, "Why Giap Did It: Report from Saigon," *Conflict Studies*, No. 27 (October 1972): 5. On symbolic importance, see "The Fierce War on the Ground," *Time*, May 1, 1972, 17.

62. Walter F. Ulmer, Jr., interview with author, October 26, 2008. Casualty figures from Willbanks, *The Battle of An Loc*, 147. On campaign ending with "no culminating battles and mass retreats, just the gradual erosion of NVA strength and the release of pressure against defending ARVN troops," see Randolph, *Powerful and Brutal Weapons*, 270.

63. Vann quoted in Dale Andradé, *America's Last Vietnam Battle: Halting Hanoi's 1972 Easter Offensive* (Lawrence: University Press of Kansas, 1995, 2001), 266.

64. Advisor quoted in "Why the Burst of Optimism on Ground War in Vietnam," *U.S. News & World Report*, June 12, 1972, 34. NVA errors in Truong, *The Easter Offensive of 1972*, 160, and DeGroot, *A Noble Cause?*, 228.

65. "USMACV Command History, 1972–1973," USAAWCL, 33. NVA casualties in Lewis Sorley, "Courage and Blood: South Vietnam's Repulse of the 1972 Easter Offensive," *Parameters*, Vol. XXIX, No. 2 (Summer 1999): 53.

66. Pacification quotation in "Who's Ahead Now?" *Newsweek*, October 16, 1972, 57. U.S. Embassy views in "Assessment of Easter Offensive: June 24, 1972," Folder 04, Box 24, Douglas Pike Collection: Unit 01-Assessment and Strategy, TTUVA. On villager reticence, see Andradé, *America's Last Vietnam Battle*, 485–486. NVA troop numbers in Berman, *No Peace, No Honor*, 142.

67. BG DeWitt C. Armstrong, Senior Officer Debriefing Report, HQ, U.S. Army Pacific, Military Historian's Office, Command Reporting Files, 1963–1972, Box 193, RG 550, NARA, 2. On continuing problems in South Vietnam, see Haig, *Inner Circles*, 292 and Arnold R. Isaacs, *Without Honor: Defeat in Vietnam and Cambodia* (Baltimore and London: The Johns Hopkins University Press, 1983), 118.

68. Differing pacification evaluations in Sydney H. Schanberg, "Control of Mekong Delta a Matter of Perspective," *New York Times*, August 25, 1972. Maxwell D. Taylor, "No Victory in Sight for Either Side in Vietnam," *Washington Post*, September 16, 1972.

69. Craig R. Whitney, "Abrams Leaves Vietnam after Transforming War," *New York Times*, July 2, 1972. Troop levels in Sorley, *Vietnam Chronicles*, 739.

70. Thieu quoted in "Can South Vietnam Survive a Cease-Fire?" *U.S. News & World Report*, November 13, 1972, 26. October negotiations in Kimball, *The Vietnam War Files*, 254–255, and Dalleck, *Nixon and Kissinger*, 422–423.

71. Thieu's defiance and Hanoi's intransigence in Dalleck, ibid., 443. Linebacker II goals in Kimball, *Nixon's Vietnam War*, 364–365. Press quoted in ibid., 366.

72. Paris agreement in Kimball, ibid., 366–368. Nixon to Thieu in Kimball, *The Vietnam War Files*, 276–277.

73. Nixon, *The Real War*, 114. Weyand quoted in Isaacs, *Without Honor*, 124.

74. Julian Paget explained the importance of tying together political and military aims in *Counter-Insurgency Operations: Techniques of Guerrilla Warfare* (New York: Walker, 1967), 156. Insurgent access in Kolko, *Anatomy of a War*, 397. Hanoi's tenacity in Ward, "Why Giap Did It," 9.

75. Hanoi's actions in Van Tien Dung, *Our Great Spring Victory*, trans. John Spragens, Jr. (New York and London: Monthly Review Press, 1977), 18–19; Goodman, *The Lost Peace*, 169–170; and Isaacs, *Without Honor*, 83. Paris agreement violations in Bouscaren, *All Quiet on the Eastern Front*, 48.

76. COL Edwin W. Chamberlain, Jr., Senior Officer Debrief Report, May 10, 1973, Digital Archive Collection, USAAWCL, 2. On Operation Enhance, see "USMACV Command History, 1972–1973," USAAWCL, 37, 69 and *JCS History, 1971–1973*, 213–215.

77. ARVN facing a multitude of threats in Sorley, *A Better War*, 374. On the period between the Paris agreement and the 1975 offensive, see William E. Le Gro, *Vietnam from Cease-Fire to Capitulation* (Washington, D.C.: U.S. Army Center of Military History, 1981).

78. Government official quoted in Isaacs, *Without Honor*, 392. ARVN general quoted in Stephen T. Hosmer, Konrad Kellen, and Brian M. Jenkins, *The Fall of South Vietnam: Statements by Vietnamese Military and Civilian Leaders* (New York: Crane, Russak, 1980), 159. ARVN problems in ibid., 11–13. Hanoi's planning for the final offensive in Merle L. Pribbenow, "North Vietnam's Final Offensive: Strategic Endgame Nonpareil," *Parameters*, Vol. XXIX, No. 4 (Winter 1999–2000): 58–71.

79. Final NVA assaults in Turley, *The Second Indochina War*, 182. On not addressing ARVN's fundamental weaknesses, see Andradé, *America's Last Vietnam Battle*, 489, and Willbanks, *Abandoning Vietnam*, 89, 155.

80. "Vietnamization is working" in "Vietnamization: Is It Working or Isn't It?" *New York Times*, June 10, 1972. Thompson, *No Exit from Vietnam*, 176.

81. June 3, 1972, briefing in Sorley, *Vietnam Chronicles*, 860–862. On continuity in metrics, see MACV Directive 335–22, Reports and Statistics, Measurement of Progress, June 25, 1972, MACV Directives, MHI. On reservations over the meaningfulness of yardsticks, see LTG William McCaffrey, CMH, VNIT Folder 1048, 57.

Conclusion

1. On army failures, see "Why We Didn't Win in Vietnam," *U.S. News & World Report*, February 9, 1970, 44–45, and Robert E. Osgood, *Limited War Revisited* (Boulder, Co.: Westview Press, 1979), 37–48.

2. Ward Just, "Progress in Viet War: Roads Become Safe for Driving," *Washington Post*, March 5, 1967.

3. Sharp and Westmoreland, *Report on the War in Vietnam*, 189.

4. James Farmer, *Counterinsurgency: Principles and Practices in Viet-Nam* (Santa Monica, Calif.: The RAND Corporation, 1964), 4. Measurements being wrongly applied from William Fred Long, interview with author, October 26, 2008. Long served on the MACV operational planning staff from July 1963 to July 1964.

5. MACV staff officer Colonel Donn Starry to A. L. West, Jr., April 15, 1969, Personal Correspondence, Box 2, Donn A. Starry Papers, MHI. Julian J. Ewell, interview by Ted Gittinger, November 7, 1985, LBJL, 5.

6. Quoted in DoD paper "Alternate Strategies." In *The Pentagon Papers*, IV: 557. On warnings, see LTC Richard W. Hobbs, "All the Answers Are Not in the Statistics," *Army*, Vol. 18, No. 3 (March 1968): 77–78.

7. On "numerical rationality," see Alex Abella, *Soldiers of Reason: The RAND Corporation and the Rise of the American Empire* (New York: Harcourt, 2008), 181. Statistics dominating a hierarchical organization from Walter F. Ulmer, Jr., interview with author, October 26, 2008.

8. BG H.S. Cunningham, Senior Officer Debriefing Report, November 10, 1970, Digital Archive Collection, USAAWCL, 2. Mandate of Heaven in FitzGerald, *Fire in the Lake*, 238. The U.S. Army's newest field manual includes an appendix on social network analysis. Department of the Army, Field Manual 3–24, *Counterinsurgency*, December 2006, Appendix B.

9. Operations Report, Lessons Learned, 3–66, The Pleiku Campaign, May 10, 1966, CMH Library, 213.

10. Edward G. Lansdale, "Viet Nam: Do We Understand Revolution?" *Foreign Affairs*, Vol. 43, No. 1 (October 1964): 77. On language problems, see William J. Lederer, *Our Own Worst Enemy* (New York: W. W. Norton, 1968), 27.

11. James R. McDonough, *Platoon Leader* (Novato, Calif.: Presidio, 1985), 1.

12. As an example, see Harkins to President Diem, May 15, 1963, *FRUS*, 1961–1963, III: 299. On the necessity to strike a "balance between the need for standardization of metrics and the need for nuance and detail" see Austin Long, *The "Other War": Lessons from Five Decades of RAND Counterinsurgency Research* (Santa Monica, Calif.: The RAND Corporation, 2006), 64.

13. Phillip B. Davidson, interview by Ted Gittinger, March 30, 1982, LBJL, 7. Abrams quoted in Sorley, *Vietnam Chronicles*, 407. On lack of data analysis, see Komer, *Bureaucracy at War*, 74, and Thayer in Thompson and Frizzell, *The Lessons of Vietnam*, 196.

14. VSSG [Vietnam Special Studies Group] Meeting Notes, memorandum for Mr. Kissinger, November 18, 1969, Richard Hunt VSSG Folder, OSDHO, 4. Contradictory assessments in Jeffrey S. Milstein, *Dynamics of the Vietnam War: A Quantitative Analysis and Predictive Computer Simulation* (Columbus: Ohio State University Press, 1974), 174.

15. Rice example taken from Dennis J. Vetock, *Lessons Learned: A History of US Army Lesson Learning* (Carlisle Barracks, Pa.: US Army Military History Institute, 1988), 107. On not questioning validity, see Farmer, *Counterinsurgency*, 4. On importance of feedback mechanisms, see Cable, *Unholy Grail*, viii. Kissinger's VSSG Working Group found "several of the most widely used data series are quite unreliable." VSSG Meeting Notes, OSDHO, 2.

16. Recording tape in Brian M. Jenkins, *The Unchangeable War*, RM-6278-ARPA, November 1970, CMH Library, 8. On problems of institutional memory, see COL W.F. Ulmer, Jr., Senior Officer Debriefing Report, January 10, 1973, Box 16, RG 472, NARA. Day-to-day problems in Komer, *Bureaucracy at War*, 77.

17. Memorandum from Counselor for Public Affairs to Ambassador Lodge, August 24, 1963 *FRUS*, 1961–1963, III: 623. On masking realities, see Milstein, *Dynamics of the Vietnam War*, 173.

18. LTG Julian Ewell, interview, October 15, 1991, Historians Files, CMH, 31. On setting political and military aims, see Julian Paget, *Counter-Insurgency Operations: Techniques of Guerrilla Warfare* (New York: Walker, 1967), 156.

19. Jenkins, *The Unchangeable War*, 5.

20. Palmer, *The 25-Year War*, 176.

21. "The Strategy and Tactics of Peace in Viet Nam," *Time*, March 28, 1969, 19. Administration doubts in "Cambodian Balance Sheet," *New York Times*, May 17, 1970.

22. Robert G. Kaiser, "Guide to Assessing State of the War," *Washington Post*, March 5, 1970.

23. On the army interested in more than body counts, see Bergerud, *The Dynamics of Defeat*, 332. Intellectual resources and unpreparedness in: Bouscaren, *All Quiet on the Eastern Front*, 13, and Builder, *The Masks of War*, 130.

24. Peter M. Dawkins, "The United States Army and the 'Other' War in Vietnam: A Study of the Complexity of Implementing Organizational Change" (Ph.D. diss., Princeton University, 1979), 102.

25. Paul F. Gorman, interview with author, March 27, 2008. On immediate results, see CPT Edward J. Haydash, letter to MAJ Torrence, April 9, 1969, Adventure Board, Box 2, Torrence Collection, WPSC.

26. Need for success in diverse areas from Paul Miles, interview with author, September 20, 2008. There was nothing new about Abrams's systems approach. See 1963 National Campaign Plan discussion in chapter 2.

27. Pickerell, *Vietnam in the Mud*, 114.

28. Walt, *Strange War, Strange Strategy*, 80. Control versus security in VSSG Meeting Notes, OSDHO, 3 and Fall, "Insurgency Indicators," 3.

29. On difficulty in defining success, see Farmer, *Counterinsurgency*, 2. Clear and hold issues in Taber, *The War of the Flea*, 85. "Definitional morass" in Robert Mandel, *The Meaning of Military Victory* (Boulder, London: Lynne Rienner, 2006), 4.

30. Long, interview with author. Dispersion of critical information in Barry D. Watts, *Clausewitzean Friction and Future War* (Washington, D.C.: Institute for National Strategic Studies, 1996), 69–78.

31. Conrad C. Crane, *Avoiding Vietnam: The U.S. Army's Response to Defeat in Southeast Asia* (Carlisle, Pa.: Strategic Studies Institute, 2002). George Herring, "Preparing *Not* to Refight the Last War: The Impact of the Vietnam War on the U.S. Military," in *After Vietnam: Legacies of a Lost War*, ed. Charles E. Neu (Baltimore and London: The Johns Hopkins University Press, 2000). For performance metrics used in the early 1980s, see "Extracts from the Green Book" (Greensboro, N.C.: Center for Creative Leadership, 1989). Copy provided to author by Walter F. Ulmer, Jr.

32. Field Manual 3-24, 5-26 to 5-28.

33. French experience in James Clancy and Chuck Crossett, "Measuring Effectiveness in Irregular Warfare," *Parameters*, Vol. XXXVII, No. 2 (Summer 2007): 88–100. Jim Baker, "Systems Thinking and Counterinsurgencies," *Parameters*, Vol. XXXVI, No. 4 (Winter 2006-07): 26–43. On statistics, see Frederick W. Kagan, "Measuring Success," *Armed Forces Journal* (January 2006): 20–24.

34. Ian Westerman, "Pacifying Afghanistan: Enduring Lessons from CORDS in Vietnam," *RUSI*, Vol. 153, No. 5 (October 2008): 14–21. Eric P. Wendt, "Strategic Counterinsurgency Modeling," *Special Warfare*, Vol. 18, No. 2 (September 2005): 2–13.

35. Karen DeYoung, "What Defines a Killing as Sectarian?" *Washington Post*, September 25, 2007, and "U.S. Sets Metrics to Assess War Success," *Washington Post*, August 20, 2009. On commander problems in Iraq, see Peter R. Mansoor, *Baghdad at Sunrise: A Brigade Commander's War in Iraq* (New Haven and London: Yale University Press, 2008), 47, 123, 164. Colonel Gian

Gentile discussed the problems of interpreting data in Iraq in interview with author, November 4, 2008.

36. Seema Patel and Steven Ross, *Breaking Point: Measuring Progress in Afghanistan* (Washington, D.C.: Center for Strategic and International Studies, 2006), 5. On the various indicators used by General David Petraeus to describe progress in Iraq, see transcript of special presentation, October 7, 2008, AUSA Annual Meeting, Washington, D.C. Available at http://www.ausa.org/news/.../Documents/2008AnnualMeetingPetraeusTranscript.pdf. On examples of problems with progress, see Nina Kamp, Michael O'Hanlon, and Amy Unikewicz, "The State of Iraq: An Update," *New York Times*, June 16, 2006, and Jim Rutenberg, "A New Phrase Enters Washington's War of Words over Iraq," *New York Times*, December 21, 2006.

37. David E. Sanger, Eric Schmitt, Thom Shanker, "White House Struggles to Gauge Afghan Success," *New York Times*, August 6, 2009.

38. *Poems and Ballads of Goethe*, trans. W. Edmondstoune Aytoun and Theodore Martin, 3rd ed. (London: William Blackwood and Sons, 1907), 104–108.

39. Voluntary information in Galula, *Counterinsurgency Warfare*, 131, and Thompson, *No Exit from Vietnam*, 142. Freedom of movement in Palmer, *Summons of the Trumpet*, 224. Surrendering in LTC J.R. Meese, interview, July 30, 1968, VNIT Folder 239, CMH. Village leaders sleeping in villages from Robert S. Meehan, interview with author, April 9, 2008.

40. Kissinger, memorandum for President Ford, "Lessons of Vietnam," in Berman, *No Peace, No Honor*, 279. On how officers tend to use history for illustrating "lessons," see Robert M. Cassidy, "Back to the Street without Joy: Counterinsurgency Lessons from Vietnam and Other Small Wars," *Parameters*, Vol. XXXIV No. 2 (Summer 2004): 73–83.

Bibliography

PRIMARY SOURCES

Manuscripts and Archival Sources

Combined Arms Research Library, U.S. Army Command and General Staff College, Fort Leavenworth, Ks.
Joint Chiefs of Staff History Office, The Pentagon, Washington, D.C.
Lester, Robert E., ed. *The War in Vietnam: The Papers of William C. Westmoreland*. Bethesda, Md.: University Publications of America, 1993, microfiche.
Lyndon B. Johnson Library Oral History Collection. Austin, Tx.
National Archives and Records Administration. College Park, Md.
Office of the Secretary of Defense Historical Office. Washington, D.C.
U.S. Army Armor School Library, Special Collections, Fort Knox, Ky.
U.S. Army Aviation Warfighting Center, Aviation Technical Library. Fort Rucker, Ala.
U.S. Army Center of Military History. Fort MacNair, Washington, D.C.
U.S. Army Military History Institute, Carlisle Barracks, Pa.
United States Military Academy Library, Special Collections, West Point, N.Y.
The Vietnam Archive, Texas Tech University. Lubbock, Tex.

Interviews by Author

Larry D. Budge, March 28, 2008
Al Costanzo, April 14, 2008
A.M. Robert Dean, April 8, 9, 2008
William T. Dillinger, April 18, 2008
DeBow Freed, April 12, 2008

Gian P. Gentile, November 4, 2008
Paul F. Gorman, March 27, 2008
Franklin Hart, March 31, 2008
Ira A. Hunt, Jr., April 23, 2008
Douglas Kinnard, March 24, October 23, 2008
William A. Knowlton, April 16, 2008
William Fred Long, Jr., October 26, 2008
Robert S. Meehan, April 13, 2008
James Megellas, July 29, 2008
Louis G. Michael, April 15, 2008
Paul Miles, March 8, April 26, September 20, October 24, 2008
Herbert Y. Schandler, April 7, 2008
James Sewell, April 21, 2008
Donn A. Starry, October 27, 2008
Walter F. Ulmer, Jr., October 26, 2008
Volney Warner, March 25, 2008

U.S. Government Publications

"Cambodia: May 1970, A Staff Report Prepared for the Use of the Committee on Foreign Relations, United States Senate." Washington, D.C.: U.S. Government Printing Office, 1970.

Congressional Research Service, Library of Congress. *The U.S. Government and the Vietnam War: Executive and Legislative Roles and Relationships, Part IV, July 1965–January 1968*. Washington, D.C.: U.S. Government Printing Office, 1994.

"Hearings before the Committee on Foreign Relations, United States Senate, Ninety-First Congress, Second Session on Moral and Military Aspects of the War in Southeast Asia." Washington, D.C.: U.S. Government Printing Office, 1970.

Jennings, Allen B., ed. "Readings in Counterinsurgency." West Point, N.Y.: USMA Department of Social Sciences, 1962.

The Pentagon Papers: The Defense Department History of United States Decisionmaking in Vietnam [Senator Gravel ed.] 5 vols. Boston: Beacon Press, 1971–1972.

Public Papers of the Presidents, Lyndon B. Johnson, Book I—January 1 to June 30, 1966. Washington, D.C.: U.S. Government Printing Office, 1967.

National Advisory Commission on Selective Service, *In Pursuit of Equity: Who Serves When Not All Serve?* Washington, D.C.: U.S. Government Printing Office, 1967.

Sharp, U. S. Grant, and William C. Westmoreland. *Report on the War in Vietnam*. Washington, D.C.: U.S. Government Printing Office, 1969.

Tunney, John V. *Measuring Hamlet Security in Vietnam: Report of a Special Study Mission*. Washington, D.C.: U.S. Government Printing Office, 1969.

U.S. Army Infantry School. *Selected Readings on Guerrilla Warfare*. Fort Benning, Ga.: U.S. Army Infantry School, 1962.

U.S. Army Special Warfare School. Special Text Number 31–176, "Counterinsurgency Planning Guide." Fort Bragg, N.C.: Department of Counterinsurgency, 1963.

U.S. Department of the Army. Field Manual 3–24, *Counterinsurgency Operations*. Washington, D.C., December 2006.

U.S. Department of the Army. Field Manual 31–15, *Operations Against Airborne Attack, Guerrilla Action, and Infiltration*. Washington, D.C., January 1953; May 1961.

U.S. Department of the Army. Field Manual 31–16, *Counterguerrilla Operations*. Washington, D.C., February 1963; March 1967.

U.S. Department of the Army. Field Manual 31–20, *Operations Against Guerrilla Forces*. Washington, D.C., February 1951.

U.S. Department of the Army. Field Manual 31–21, *Guerrilla Warfare*. Washington, D.C., May 1955.

U.S. Department of the Army. Field Manual 57–35, *Airmobile Operations*. Washington, D.C., September 1963.

U.S. Department of the Army. Field Manual 90–98, *Counterguerrilla Operations*, Washington, D.C., August 1986.

U.S. Department of the Army. Field Manual 100–105, *Field Service Regulations, Operations*. Washington, D.C., February 1962.

U.S. Department of the Army. Field Manual 100–105, *Operations of Army Forces in the Field*, Washington, D.C., September 1968.

U.S. Department of the Army. Field Manual 100–120, *Low Intensity Conflict*, Washington, D.C., January 1981.

U.S. Department of State. *Foreign Relations of the United States*. Washington, D.C., 1988–2006.

Webb, Willard J. *The Joint Chiefs of Staff and the War in Vietnam: 1969–1970*. Washington, D.C.: Office of Joint History, 2002.

Webb, Willard J., and Walter S. Poole. *The Joint Chiefs of Staff and the War in Vietnam, 1971–1973*. Washington, D.C.: Office of Joint History, 2007.

Books

Adams, Sam. *War of Numbers: An Intelligence Memoir*. South Royalton, Vt.: Steerforth Press, 1994.

Allen, George W. *None So Blind: A Personal Account of the Intelligence Failure in Vietnam*. Chicago: Ivan R. Dee, 2001.

American University Special Operations Research Office. *Undergrounds in Insurgent, Revolutionary, and Resistance Warfare*. Washington, D.C.: The American University, 1963.

Armbruster, Frank E., and Raymond D. Gastil, Herman Kahn, William Pfaff, and Edmund Stillman. *Can We Win in Vietnam?* New York: Frederick A. Praeger, 1968.

Arnett, Peter. *Live from the Battlefield: From Vietnam to Baghdad 35 Years in the World's War Zones*. New York, London: Simon & Schuster, 1994.

Baclagon, Uldarico S. *Lessons from the Huk Campaign in the Philippines*. Manila: M. Colcol, 1960.

Bahnsen, John C. *American Warrior: A Combat Memoir of Vietnam*. New York: Citadel Press, 2007.

Beidler, Philip D. *Late Thoughts on an Old War: The Legacy of Vietnam*. Athens and London: The University of Georgia Press, 2004.

Bradley, Omar. *A Soldier's Story*. New York: Henry Holt, 1951, 271.

Browne, Malcolm W. *The New Face of War*, rev. ed. Indianapolis, New York: Bobbs-Merrill, 1968.

Callwell, C. E. *Small Wars: Their Principles and Practice*. London: H.M.S.O, 1906; Lincoln: University of Nebraska Press, 1996.

CBS News. *The People of South Vietnam: How They Feel About the War*. Princeton, N.J.: Opinion Research, 1967.

Clausewitz, Carl von. *On War*. Edited and translated by Michael Howard and Peter Paret. New York and Toronto: Alfred A. Knopf Everyman's Library, 1976, 1993.

Clifford, Clark, with Richard Holbrooke. *Counsel to the President*. New York: Random House, 1991.

Clodfelter, Micheal. *Mad Minutes and Vietnam Months: A Soldier's Memoir*. Jefferson, N.C., and London: McFarland, 1988.

Colby, William, with James McCargar. *Lost Victory: A Firsthand Account of America's Sixteen-Year Involvement in Vietnam*. Chicago and New York: Contemporary Books, 1989.

Coleman, J. D., ed. *Memoirs of the First Team: Vietnam, August 1965–December 1969*. Tokyo: Dia Nippon, 1970.

Collins, J. Lawton. *Lightning Joe: An Autobiography*. Baton Rouge: Louisiana State University, 1979.

Committee of Concerned Asian Scholars. *The Indochina Story: A Fully Documented Account*. New York: Pantheon Books, 1970.

Cooper, Chester L. *The Lost Crusade: America in Vietnam*. New York: Dodd, Mead & Company 1970.

Corson, William R. *Consequences of Failure*. New York: W. W. Norton, Inc., 1974.

Crouchet, Jack. *Vietnam Stories: A Judge's Memoir*. Niwot: University Press of Colorado, 1997.

de Lattre, Marshal Jean. *Ne Pas Subir, Écrits, 1914–1952*. Edited by Élisabeth du Réau, et al. Paris: Plon, 1984.

DePuy, William E. *Changing an Army: An Oral History of General William E. DePuy, USA Retired*. Washington, D.C.: U.S. Army Center of Military History, 1988.

Dockery, Martin J. *Lost in Translation, Vietnam: A Combat Advisor's Story*. New York: Ballantine Books, 2003.

Don, Tran Von. *Our Endless War: Inside Vietnam*. San Rafael, Calif., and London: Presidio Press, 1978.

Dung, Van Tien. *Our Great Spring Victory*. Translated by John Spragens, Jr. New York and London: Monthly Review Press, 1977.

Elliott, David W.P., and W.A. Stewart. *Pacification and the Viet Cong System in Dinh Tuong: 1966–1967*. Santa Monica, Calif.: RAND Corporation, 1969.

Guevara, Che. *Guerrilla Warfare*. New York: Monthly Review Press, 1961; Lincoln: University of Nebraska Press, 1998.

Eisenhower, Dwight D. *Crusade in Europe*. Garden City, N.Y.: Doubleday, Inc., 1948.

Enthoven, Alain, and K. Wayne Smith. *How Much Is Enough? Shaping the Defense Program, 1961–1969*. New York and London: Harper & Row, 1971.

Estep, James L. *Company Commander Vietnam*. Novato, Calif.: Presidio, 1996.

Ewell, Julian J., and Ira A. Hunt. *Sharpening the Combat Edge: The Use of Analysis to Reinforce Military Judgment*. Washington, D.C.: Department of the Army, 1974.

Fall, Bernard B. *Street Without Joy*. Mechanicsburg, Pa.: Stackpole Books, 1994.

Fall, Bernard B. *The Two Viet-Nams: A Political and Military Analysis*. New York and London: Frederick A. Praeger, 1963.

Fall, Bernard B. *Viet-Nam Witness: 1953–66*. New York and Washington: Frederick A. Praeger, 1966.

Farmer, James. *Counterinsurgency: Principles and Practices in Viet-Nam*. Santa Monica, Calif.: The RAND Corporation, 1964.

Farmer, James. *Counter-Insurgency: Viet-Nam 1963–1963*. Santa Monica, Calif.: The RAND Corporation, 1963.
FitzGerald, Frances. *Fire in the Lake: The Vietnamese and the Americans in Vietnam*. Boston, Toronto: Little, Brown, 1972.
Galula, David. *Counterinsurgency Warfare: Theory and Practice*. New York, Washington, and London: Frederick A. Praeger, 1964, 2005.
Galula, David. *Pacification in Algeria: 1956–1958*. Santa Monica, Calif.: RAND Corporation, 1963, 2006.
Greene, T. N., ed. *The Guerrilla—and How to Fight Him*. New York: Frederick A. Praeger Publisher, 1962.
Griffith, Samuel B. *Mao Tse-Tung on Guerrilla Warfare*. New York and Washington: Praeger Publishers, 1961.
Grivas, George. *General Grivas on Guerrilla Warfare*. Translated by A. A. Pallis. NewYork, Washington: Frederick A. Praeger, 1965.
Hackworth, David H., and Eilhys England. *Steel My Soldiers' Hearts: The Hopeless to Hardcore Transformation of 4th Battalion, 39th Infantry, United States Army, Vietnam*. New York and London: Simon & Schuster, 2002.
Haig, Alexander, Jr., with Charles McCarry. *Inner Circles: How America Changed the World, A Memoir*. New York: Warner Books, 1992.
Haldeman, H. R. *The Haldeman Diaries: Inside the Nixon White House*. New York: G. P. Putnam's Sons, 1994.
Heilbrum, Otto. *Partisan Warfare*. New York: Frederick A. Praeger, 1962.
Herr, Michael. *Dispatches*. New York: Alfred A. Knopf, 1968, 1978.
Herrington, Stuart A. *Silence Was a Weapon: The Vietnam War in the Villages, A Personal Perspective*. Novato, Calif.: Presidio, 1982.
Hickey, G. C. *The American Military Advisor and his Foreign Counterpart: The Case of Vietnam*. Santa Monica, Ca.: The RAND Corporation, 1965.
Hilsman, Roger. *To Move a Nation: The Politics of Foreign Policy in the Administration of John F. Kennedy*. Garden City, N.Y.: Doubleday, 1964, 1967.
Hitch, Charles J. *Decision-Making for Defense*. Berkeley and Los Angeles: University of California Press, 1965.
Hoopes, Townsend. *The Limits of Intervention: An Inside Account of How the Johnson Policy of Escalation in Vietnam Was Reversed*. New York: David McKay, 1969.
Hosmer, Stephen T., and Sibylle O. Crane. *Counterinsurgency: A Symposium, April 16–20, 1962*. Santa Monica, Calif.: RAND Corporation, 1963; reprint 2006.
"Isolating the Guerrilla," Vol. 1. Washington, D.C.: Historical Evaluation and Research Organization, February 1966.
Johnson, Lyndon Baines. *The Vantage Point: Perspectives on the Presidency, 1963–1969*. New York, Chicago, and San Francisco: Holt, Rinehart and Winston, 1971.
Just, Ward. *To What End: Report From Vietnam*. Boston: Houghton Mifflin, 1968; New York: Public Affairs, 2000.
Kissinger, Henry. *Ending the Vietnam War: A History of America's Involvement in and Extrication from the Vietnam War*. New York: Simon & Schuster, 2003.
Kissinger, Henry. *The White House Years*. London: Weidenfeld and Nicolson and Michael Joseph, 1979.

Komer, Robert W. *Bureaucracy at War: U.S. Performance in the Vietnam Conflict.* Boulder and London: Westview Press, 1986.

Krohn, Charles A. *The Lost Battalion: Breakout of the 2/12th Cavalry at Hue.* Annapolis, Md.: Naval Institute Press, 2008.

Lansdale, Edward Geary. *In the Midst of Wars: An American's Mission to Southeast Asia.* New York: Harper & Row, 1972.

Lunn, Hugh. *Vietnam: A Reporter's War.* New York: Stein and Day Publishers, 1986.

Marshall, S. L. A. *Ambush: The Battle of Dau Tieng.* Nashville, Tenn.: The Battery Press, 1969.

Marshall, S. L. A. *Battles in the Monsoon: Campaigning in the Central Highlands Vietnam, Summer 1966.* New York: William Morrow, 1967.

Mason, Robert. *Chickenhawk.* New York: The Viking Press, 1983.

McCuen, John J. *The Art of Counter-Revolutionary War.* Harrisburg, Pa.: Stackpole Books, 1966.

McDonough, James R. *Platoon Leader.* Novato, Calif.: Presidio, 1985.

McKean, Roland N. *Efficiency in Government Through Systems Analysis: With Emphasis on Water Resources Development.* New York: John Wiley & Sons, 1958.

McNamara, Robert S. *The Essence of Security: Reflections in Office.* New York and London: Harper & Row, 1968.

McNamara, Robert S. *In Retrospect: The Tragedy and Lessons of Vietnam.* New York: Times Books, 1995.

Melnik, Constantin. "Insurgency and Counterinsurgency in Algeria." Santa Monica, Calif: RAND Corporation, April 23, 1964.

Moore, Harold G., and Joseph L. Galloway. *We Were Soldiers Once . . . and Young.* New York: HarperCollins, 1993.

Morison, Elting E. *Men, Machines, and Modern Times.* Cambridge, Mass., and London: The M.I.T. Press, 1966.

Moskos, Charles C., Jr. *The American Enlisted Man: The Rank and File in Today's Military.* New York: Russell Sage Foundation, 1970.

Moskos, Charles C., Jr.. *Soldiers and Sociology.* United States Army Research Institute for Behavioral and Social Sciences, 1988.

Navarre, Henri. *Agonie de L'Indochine (1953–1954).* Paris: Librarie Plon, 1956.

Nixon, Richard. *No More Vietnams.* New York: Arbor House: 1985.

Nixon, Richard. *The Real War.* New York: Warner Books 1980.

Nixon, Richard. *RN: The Memoirs of Richard Nixon.* New York: Grosset & Dunlap, 1978.

Nolting, Frederick. *From Trust to Tragedy: The Political Memoirs of Frederick Nolting, Kennedy's Ambassador to Diem's Vietnam.* New York, Westport, Conn., and London: Praeger, 1988.

Osborne, Milton E. *Strategic Hamlets in South Viet-Nam: A Survey and a Comparison.* Ithaca, N.Y.: Cornell University Department of Asian Studies, 1965.

Osgood, Robert E. *Limited War: The Challenge to American Security.* Chicago: The University of Chicago Press, 1957.

Osgood, Robert E. *Limited War Revisited.* Boulder, Co.: Westview Press, 1979.

Paget, Julian. *Counter-Insurgency Operations: Techniques of Guerrilla Warfare.* New York: Walker and Company, 1967.

Palmer, Bruce, Jr. *The 25-Year War: America's Military Role in Vietnam.* New York: Simon & Schuster, 1984.

Pauker, Guy J. *An Essay on Vietnamization.* Santa Monica, Calif.: Rand, March 1971.

Pauker, Guy J. "Notes on Non-Military Measures in Control of Insurgency." Santa Monica, Calif.: RAND Corporation, October 1962.
Pickerell, James H. *Vietnam in the Mud*. Indianapolis and New York: Bobbs-Merrill, 1966.
Powell, Colin L., with Joseph E. Persico. *My American Journey*. New York: Random House, 1995.
Pustay, John S. *Counterinsurgency Warfare*. New York: The Free Press, 1965.
Pye, Lucian W. *Observations on the Chieu Hoi Program*. Santa Monica, Calif.: RAND Corporation, 1969.
Quade, E. S., ed. *Analysis for Military Decisions*. Chicago: Rand McNally, 1966.
Quade E. S., and W. I. Boucher, eds. *Systems Analysis and Policy Planning: Application in Defense*. New York: American Elsevier, 1968.
Rostow, W. W. *The Diffusion of Power: An Essay in Recent History*. New York: Macmillan, 1972.
Schell, Jonathan. *The Military Half: An Account of Destruction in Quang Ngai and Quang Tin*. New York: Alfred A. Knopf, 1968.
Schell, Jonathan. *The Village of Ben Suc*. New York: Alfred A. Knopf, 1967.
Servan-Schreiber, Jean-Jacques. *Lieutenant in Algeria*. New York: Alfred A. Knopf, 1957.
Shaplen, Robert. *The Road from War: Vietnam 1965–1970*. New York and Evanston: Harper & Row, 1970.
Sharp, U. S. Grant. *Strategy for Defeat: Vietnam in Retrospect*. San Rafael, Calif.: Presidio Press, 1978.
Taber, Robert. *The War of the Flea: The Classic Study of Guerrilla Warfare*. New York: Lyle Stuart, 1965; Washington, D.C.: Potomac Books, 2002.
Tanham, George K. *Communist Revolutionary Warfare: The Vietminh in Indochina*. New York: Frederick A. Praeger, 1961.
Taylor, Maxwell D. *Swords and Plowshares*. New York: W. W. Norton, 1972.
Taylor, Maxwell D. *The Uncertain Trumpet*. New York: Harper & Brothers, 1960.
Thompson, Robert. *Defeating Communist Insurgency: The Lessons of Malaya and Vietnam*. New York, Washington: Frederick A. Praeger, Publishers, 1966.
Thompson, Robert. *No Exit from Vietnam*. New York: David McKay, 1969.
Trinquier, Roger. *Modern Warfare: A French View of Counterinsurgency*. Westport, Conn., and London: Praeger Security International, 1964, 2006.
Valeriano, Napoleon D., and Charles T. R. Bohannan. *Counter-Guerrilla Operations: The Philippine Experience*. Westport, Conn., and London: Praeger Security International, 1962, 2006.
Walt, Lewis W. *Strange War, Strange Strategy: A General's Report on Vietnam*. New York: Funk & Wagnalls, 1970.
Westmoreland, William C. *A Soldier Reports*. Garden City, N.Y.: Doubleday, 1976.

Articles

Adams, Sam. "Vietnam Cover-Up: Playing War with Numbers." *Harper's*, Vol. 250, No. 1500 (May 1975): 41–73.
Bashore, Boyd T. "Organization for Frontless Wars." *Military Review*, Vol. XLIV, No. 5 (May 1964): 3–16.
Beebe, John E. "Beating the Guerrilla." *Military Review*, Vol. XXXV, No. 9 (December 1955): 3–18.
Beecher, William. "Vietnamization: A Few Loose Ends." *Army*, Vol. 20, No. 11 (November 1970): 12–17.

Berry, Sidney B., Jr. "Observations of a Brigade Commander, Part I." *Military Review*, Vol. XLVIII, No. 1 (January 1968): 3–21.

Biggio, Charles P. "Let's Learn from the French." *Military Review*, Vol. XLVI, No. 10 (October 1966): 27–34.

Boatner, Mark M., III "The Unheeded History of Counterinsurgency." *Army*, Vol. 16, No. 9 (September 1966): 31–36.

Boatner, Mark M., III. "Withdrawal, Redeployment or Cop Out." *Army*, Vol. 21, No. 4 (April 1971): 14–19.

Braestrup, Peter. "Partisan Tactics—Algerian Style." *Army*, Vol. 11, No. 1 (August 1960): 33–44.

Brigham, Erwin R. "Pacification Measurement." *Military Review*, Vol. L, No. 5 (May 1970): 47–55.

Clark, Blair. "Westmoreland Appraised." *Harper's* (November 1970): 96–101.

Clifford, Clark. "A Viet Nam Reappraisal." *Foreign Affairs*, Vol. 47, No. 4 (July 1969): 601–622.

Clutterback, Richard L. "Communist Defeat in Malaya: A Case Study." *Military Review*, Vol. XLIII, No. 9 (September 1963): 63–78.

Cunningham, Robert K. "The Nature of War." *Military Review*, Vol. XXXIX, No. 8 (November 1959): 48–57.

Cushman, John H. "Pacification: Concepts Developed in the Field by the RVN 21st Infantry Division." *Army*, Vol. 16, No. 3 (March 1966): 21–29.

D'Arezzo, Joseph P. "Systems Analysis in the Army." *Military Review*, Vol. XLVII, No. 7 (July 1967): 89–95.

Donnell, John C. "Pacification Reassessed." *Asian Survey*, Vol. 7, No. 8 (August 1967): 567–576.

Dunn, Jerry F. "A New Look at Pacification." *Military Review*, Vol. L, No. 1 (January 1970): 84–87.

East, C. H. A. "Guerrilla Warfare." *Military Review*, Vol. XXXVII, No. 6 (September 1957): 95–101.

Enthoven, Alain. "Systems Analysis and Decision Making." *Military Review*, Vol. XLIII, No. 1 (January 1963): 7–17.

Fall, Bernard B. "Insurgency Indicators." *Military Review*, Vol. XLVI, No. 4 (April 1966): 3–11.

Fall, Bernard B. "South Viet-Nam's Internal Problems." *Pacific Affairs*, Vol. 31, No. 3 (September 1958): 241–260.

Fowler, Delbert M. "Strategy and Systems Analysis." *Military Review*, Vol. XLV, No. 6 (June 1965): 3–7.

Gavin, James M. "Cavalry, and I Don't Mean Horses." *Harper's* Vol. 208, No. 1247 (April 1954): 54–60.

Gavin, James M. "A Communication on Vietnam." *Harper's*, Vol. 232, No. 1389 (February 1966): 16–21.

Gillert, Gustav J., Jr. "Counterinsurgency." *Military Review*, Vol. XLV, No. 4 (April 1965): 25–33.

Goodman, Allan E. "South Vietnam: Neither War Nor Peace." *Asian Survey*, Vol. 10, No. 2 (February 1970): 107–132.

Guezlo, Carl M. "The Communist Long War." *Military Review*, Vol. XL, No. 9 (December 1960): 14–22.

Halberstam, David. "Return to Vietnam." *Harper's*, Vol. 235, No. 1411 (December 1967): 47–58.

Hammer, Ellen J. "Progress Report on Southern Viet Nam." *Pacific Affairs*, Vol. 30, No. 3 (September 1957): 221–235.

Hammond, Paul Y. "A Functional Analysis of Defense Department Decision-Making in the McNamara Administration." *The American Political Science Review*, Vol. 62, No. 1 (March 1968): 57–69.

Hare, Robert R., Jr. "Models and Systems Effectiveness." *Military Review*, Vol. XLV, No. 11 (November 1965): 26–30.

Harrigan, Anthony. "Ground Warfare in Vietnam." *Military Review*, Vol. XLVII, No. 4 (April 1967): 60–67.

Hartness, William M. "Social and Behavioral Sciences in Counterinsurgency." *Military Review*, Vol. XLVI, No. 1 (January 1966): 3–10.

Hayes, James H. "Basic Concepts of Systems Analysis." *Military Review*, Vol. XLV, No. 4 (April 1965): 4–13.

Heinl, Robert D., Jr. "The Collapse of the Armed Forces." *Armed Forces Journal*, Vol. 108, No. 19 (June 7, 1971): 30–37.

Hobbs, Richard W. "All the Answers Are Not In The Statistics." *Army*, Vol. 18, No. 3 (March 1968): 77–78.

Holbrook, James R. "Volunteer Army: Military Caste?" *Military Review*, Vol. LI, No. 8 (August 1971): 91–95.

Just, Ward S. "Notes on a Losing War." *The Atlantic*, Vol. 223, No. 1 (January 1969): 39–44.

Kelly, George A. "Footnotes on Revolutionary War." *Military Review*, Vol. XLII, No. 9 (September 1962): 31–39.

Kinnard, Harry W. O. "Airmobility Revisited, Part I," *U.S. Army Aviation Digest*, Vol. 26, No. 6 (June 1980): 1–5, 26–27.

Kinnard, Harry W. O. "Airmobility Revisited, Part 2." *U.S. Army Aviation Digest*, Vol. 26, No. 7 (July 1980): 8–14.

Kinnard, Harry W. O. "A Victory in the Ia Drang: The Triumph of a Concept." *Army*, Vol. 17, No. 9 (September 1967): 71–91.

Kissinger, Henry A. "The Viet Nam Negotiations." *Foreign Affairs*, Vol. 47, No. 2 (January 1969): 211–234.

Komer, Robert W. "Clear, Hold and Rebuild," *Army*, Vol. 20, No. 5 (May 1970): 16–24.

Ladd, Jonathan F. "Some Reflections on Counterinsurgency." *Military Review*, Vol. XLIV, No. 10 (October 1964): 72–78.

Lansdale, Edward G. "Viet Nam: Do We Understand Revolution?" *Foreign Affairs*, Vol. 43, No. 1 (October 1964): 75–86.

Lawrence, T. E. "The Evolution of a Revolt." *Army Quarterly and Defence Journal*, 1 (October 1920): 1–22.

Lincoln, G. A., and Amos A. Jordan, Jr. "Limited War and the Scholars." *Military Review*, Vol. XXXVII, No. 10 (January 1958): 50–60.

Lindsay, Franklin A. "Unconventional Warfare." *Foreign Affairs*, Vol. 40, No. 2 (January 1962): 264–274.

Livingston, Hoyt R., and Francis M. Watson, Jr. "Civic Action: Purpose and Pitfalls." *Military Review*, Vol. XLVII, No. 12 (December 1967): 21–25.

Loc, Vinh. "Search for Professional Excellence." *Military Review*, Vol. XLVIII, No. 12 (December 1968): 51–55.

Long, William F. "Counterinsurgency: Some Antecedents for Success." *Military Review*, Vol. XLIII, No. 10 (October 1963): 90–97.

Mataxis, Theodore C. "This Far, No Farther." *Military Review*, Vol. L, No. 3 (March 1970): 74–82.

Nelson, George W., Jr. "The Numbers Game." *Army*, Vol. 19, No. 2 (February 1969): 52–55.

Odom, William E. "Output Measurement." *Military Review*, Vol. XLVI, No. 1 (January 1966): 43–51.

Popkin, Samuel L. "Pacification: Politics and the Village." *Asian Survey*, Vol. 10, No. 8 (August 1970): 662–671.

Race, Jeffrey. "How They Won." *Asian Survey*, Vol. 10, No. 8 (August 1970): 628–650.

Ray, James F. "The District Advisor." *Military Review*, Vol. XLV, No. 5 (May 1965): 3–8.

Rice, Irvin R., and McGlachlin Hatch. "Firepower: Tool for Systems Analysis?" *Army*, Vol. 16, No. 2 (February 1966): 28–36.

Rigg, Robert B. "Future Military Discipline." *Military Review*, Vol. L, No. 9 (September 1970): 15–23.

Rigg, Robert B. "How Not to Report a War." *Military Review*, Vol. IL, No. 6 (June 1969): 14–24.

Seigle, John W. "The Myth of Decision by Computer." *Army*, Vol. 14, No. 10. (May 1964): 67–73.

Shuffer, George M., Jr. "Finish Them with Firepower." *Military Review*, Vol. XLVII, No. 12 (December 1967): 11–15.

Smith, Robert Ross. "The Hukbalahap Insurgency." *Military Review*, Vol. XLV, No. 6 (June 1965): 35–42.

Smith, William A., Jr., "The Strategic Hamlet Program in Vietnam." *Military Review*, Vol. XVIV, No. 5 (May 1964): 17–23.

Smithers, Samuel W., Jr. "Combat Units in Revolutionary Development." *Military Review*, Vol. XLVII, No. 10 (October 1967): 37–41.

Thayer, Thomas C. "How to Analyze a War Without Fronts: Vietnam, 1965–72." *Journal of Defense Research, Series B: Tactical Warfare*, Vol. 7B, No. 3 (Fall 1975).

Thompson, Robert. "Feet on the Ground." *Survival*, Vol. VIII, No. 4 (April 1966): 117–118.

Thompson, Robert. "Squaring the Error." *Foreign Affairs*, Vol. 46, No. 3 (April 1968): 442–453.

Wainhouse, Edward R. "Guerrilla War in Greece, 1946–49: A Case Study." *Military Review*, Vol. XXXVII, No. 3 (June 1957): 25.

Westmoreland, William C. "From the Army of the '70s: 'A Flawless Performance.'" *Army*, Vol. 20, No. 10 (October 1970): 23–27.

Weyand, Frederick C. "Troops to Any Equal." *Vietnam* (August 1998): 34–40.

Weyand, Frederick C.. "Winning the People in Hau Nghia Province." *Army*, Vol. 17, No. 1 (January 1967): 52–55.

White, James S. "Race Relations in the Army." *Military Review*, Vol. L, No. 7 (July 1970): 3–12.

Yale, Wesley W. "The Evaluation of Combat Effectiveness." *Army*, Vol. 12, No. 10 (May 1962): 68–73.

Newspapers and Periodicals

Aviation Week and Science Technology
Baltimore Sun
Business Week
Chicago Daily News
The Christian Science Monitor
The Economist
The Evening Star
Life
Los Angeles Times
Minnesota Tribune

The Nation
Newsweek
The New Republic
New York Times
Pacific Stars & Stripes
Saturday Evening Post
Saturday Review
The Spectator
Time
Washington Post
Washington Star
U.S. News & World Report

SECONDARY SOURCES

Books

Abella, Alex. *Soldiers of Reason: The RAND Corporation and the Rise of the American Empire*. New York: Harcourt, , 2008.

Addington, Larry H. *America's War in Vietnam: A Short Narrative History*. Bloomington and Indianapolis: Indiana University Press, 2000.

Allison, William Thomas. *Military Justice in Vietnam: The Rule of Law in an American War*. Lawrence: University Press of Kansas, 2007.

Ambrose, Stephen E., and Douglas G. Brinkley. *Rise to Globalism: American Foreign Policy since 1938*, 8th ed. New York: Penguin Books, 1997.

Anderson, David L. *The Columbia Guide to the Vietnam War*. New York: Columbia University Press, 2002.

Anderson, David L. *The Vietnam War*. New York: Palgrave Macmillan, 2005.

Andradé, Dale. *America's Last Vietnam Battle: Halting Hanoi's 1972 Easter Offensive*. Lawrence: University Press of Kansas, 1995, 2001.

Andradé, Dale. *Ashes to Ashes: The Phoenix Program and the Vietnam War*. Lexington, Mass.: Lexington Books, 1990.

Andrews, William R. *The Village War: Vietnamese Communist Revolutionary Activities in Dinh Tuong Province, 1960–1964*. Columbia: University of Missouri Press, 1973.

Appy, Christian G. *Patriots: The Vietnam War Remembered from All Sides*. New York: Viking, 2003.

Appy, Christian G. *Working-Class War: American Combat Soldiers and Vietnam*. Chapel Hill and London: The University of North Carolina Press, 1993.

Asprey, Robert B. *War in the Shadows: The Guerrilla in History*. Garden City, N.Y.: Doubleday, 1975.

Bacevich, A. J. *The Pentomic Era: The U.S. Army Between Korea and Vietnam*. Washington, D.C.: National Defense University Press, 1986.

Baker, Mark. *Nam: The Vietnam War in the Words of the Men and Women Who Fought There*. New York: William Morrow, 1981.

Balkoski, Joseph. *Beyond the Beachhead: The 29th Infantry Division in Normandy*. Harrisburg, Pa.: Stackpole Books, 1989.

Baritz, Loren. *Backfire: A History of How American Culture Led Us into Vietnam and Made Us Fight the Way We Did*. Baltimore and London: The Johns Hopkins University Press, 1985.

Baskir, Lawrence M., and William A. Strauss. *Chance and Circumstance: The Draft, the War, and the Vietnam Generation*. New York: Alfred A. Knopf, 1978.

Beckett, Ian F. W., and John Pimlott, ed. *Armed Forces and Modern Counter-Insurgency*. New York: St. Martin's Press, 1985.

Bell, J. Bowyer. *The Myth of the Guerrilla: Revolutionary Theory and Malpractice*. New York: Alfred A. Knopf, 1971.

Bergerud, Eric M. *The Dynamics of Defeat: The Vietnam War in Hau Nghia Province*. Boulder, Colo.: Westview Press, 1991.

Berman, Larry. *Lyndon Johnson's War: The Road to Stalemate in Vietnam*. New York, London: W.W. Norton, 1989.

Berman, Larry. *No Peace, No Honor: Nixon, Kissinger, and Betrayal in Vietnam*. New York, London: The Free Press, 2001.

Berman, Larry. *Planning a Tragedy: The Americanization of the War in Vietnam*. New York, London: W.W. Norton 1982.

Birtle, Andrew J. *U.S. Army Counterinsurgency and Contingency Operations Doctrine, 1942–1976*. Washington, D.C.: Center of Military History, 2006.

Blair, Clay. *The Forgotten War: America in Korea, 1950–1953*. New York: Times Books, 1987.

Blaufarb, Douglas S. *The Counterinsurgency Era: U.S. Doctrine and Performance, 1950 to the Present*. New York: The Free Press, 1977.

Borklund, Carl W. *Men of the Pentagon: From Forrestal to McNamara*. New York, Washington, and London: Frederick A. Praeger, 1966.

Boulding, Kenneth E. *Conflict and Defense: A General Theory*. New York and London: Harper Torchbooks, 1963.

Bouscaren, Anthony T., ed. *All Quiet on the Eastern Front: The Death of South Vietnam*. Old Greenwich, Conn.: Devin-Adair, 1977

Braestrup, Peter. *Big Story: How the American Press and Television Reported and Interpreted the Crisis of Tet 1968 in Vietnam and Washington*, 2 vols. Boulder, Colo.: Westview Press, 1977.

Brigham, Robert K. *ARVN: Life and Death in the South Vietnamese Army*. Lawrence: University Press of Kansas, 2006.

Builder, Carl H. *The Masks of War: American Military Styles in Strategy and Analysis*. Baltimore and London: The Johns Hopkins University Press, 1989.

Buzzanco, Robert. *Masters of War: Military Dissent and Politics in the Vietnam Era*. Cambridge and New York: Cambridge University Press, 1996.

Cable, Larry E. *Conflict of Myths: The Development of American Counterinsurgency Doctrine and the Vietnam War*. New York and London: New York University Press, 1986.

Cable, Larry E. *Unholy Grail: The US and the wars in Vietnam, 1965–8*. London and New York: Routledge, 1991.

Caldwell, Malcolm, and Lek Tan. *Cambodia in the Southeast Asia War*. New York and London: Monthly Review Press, 1973.

Carland, John M. "How We Got There: Air Assault and the Emergence of the 1st Cavalry Division (Airmobile), 1950–1965." *The Land Warfare Papers* No. 42 (May 2003).

Carland, John M. *Stemming the Tide: May 1965 to October 1966*. Washington, D.C.: Center of Military History, 2000.

Carrier, J. M., and C. A. H. Thomson. *Viet Cong Motivation and Morale: The Special Case of Chieu Hoi*. Santa Monica, Calif.: RAND Corporation, 1966.

Cash, John A., John Albright, and Allan W. Sandstrum. *Seven Firefights in Vietnam*. Mineola, N.Y.: Dover, 2007.

Chambers, John Whiteclay, II, ed. *Draftees or Volunteers: A Documentary History of the Debate Over Military Conscription in the United States, 1787–1973*. New York and London: Garland, 1975.

Cheng, Christopher C.S. *Air Mobility: The Development of a Doctrine*. Westport, Conn., London: Praeger, 1994.

Chomsky, Noam. *Rethinking Camelot: JFK, the Vietnam War, and U.S. Political Culture*. Boston, Mass.: South End Press, 1993.

Cincinnatus. *Self-Destruction: The Disintegration and Decay of the United States Army During the Vietnam Era*. New York and London: W. W. Norton 1981.

Clarke, Jeffrey J. *Advice and Support: The Final Years, 1965–1973*. Washington, D.C.: Center of Military History, 1988.

Clodfelter, Mark. *The Limits of Airpower: The American Bombing of North Vietnam*. New York and London: The Free Press, 1989.

Cluster, Dick, ed. *They Should Have Served That Cup of Coffee*. Boston: South End Press, 1979.

Cohen, Eliot A. *Supreme Command: Soldiers, Statesmen, and Leadership in Wartime*. New York and London: The Free Press, 2002.

Cohen, Warren I., and Nancy Bernkopf Tucker, ed. *Lyndon Johnson Confronts the World: American Foreign Policy, 1963–1968*. New York: Cambridge University Press, 1994.

Coleman, J. D. *Incursion: From America's Chokehold on the NVA Lifelines to the Sacking of the Cambodian Sanctuaries*. New York: St. Martin's Press, 1991.

Coleman, J. D. *Pleiku: The Dawn of Helicopter Warfare in Vietnam*. New York: St. Martin's Press, 1988.

Collins, James Lawton, Jr., *The Development and Training of the South Vietnamese Army, 1950–1972*. Washington, D.C.: U.S. Government Printing Office, 1975, 2002.

Cortright, David. *Soldiers in Revolt: GI Resistance During the Vietnam War*. Chicago: Haymarket Books, 1975, 2005.

Cosmas, Graham A. *MACV: The Joint Command in the Years of Escalation, 1962–1967*. Washington, D.C.: Center of Military History, 2006.

Cosmas, Graham A. *MACV: The Joint Command in the Years of Withdrawal, 1968–1973*. Washington, D.C.: Center of Military History, 2007.

Crane, Conrad C. *Avoiding Vietnam: The U.S. Army's Response to Defeat in Southeast Asia*. Carlisle, Pa.: Strategic Studies Institute, 2002.

Currey, Cecil B. *Victory at Any Cost: The Genius of Viet Nam's Gen. Vo Nguyen Giap*. Washington and London: Brassey's, Inc., 1997.

Dalleck, Robert. *Nixon and Kissinger: Partners in Power*. New York: HarperCollins Publishers, 2007.

Dastrup, Boyd L. *The US Army Command and General Staff College: A Centennial History*. Manhattan, Kans.: Sunflower University Press, 1982.

Davidson, Phillip B. *Secrets of the Vietnam War*. Novato, Ca.: Presidio Press, 1990.

Davidson, Phillip B. *Vietnam at War, The History: 1946–1975*. Novato, Calif.: Presidio Press, 1988.

Deac, Wilfred P. *Road to the Killing Fields: The Cambodian War of 1970–1975*. College Station: Texas A&M University Press, 1997.

DeGroot, Gerard J. *A Noble Cause? America and the Vietnam War*. Harlow, Essex: Longman, 2000.

Di Leo, David L. *George Ball, Vietnam, and the Rethinking of Containment*. Chapel Hill and London: The University of North Carolina Press, 1991.

Donnell, John C., and Gerald C. Hickey. *The Vietnamese "Strategic Hamlets": A Preliminary Report*. Santa Monica, Calif.: The RAND Corporation, August 1962.

Doughty, Robert A. *The Evolution of US Army Tactical Doctrine, 1946–1976*. Fort Leavenworth, Kans.: Combat Studies Institute, 1979.

Downie, Robert Duncan. *Learning from Conflict: The U.S. Military in Vietnam, El Salvador, and the Drug War*. Westport, Conn., and London: Praeger, 1998.

Drez, Ronald J., ed. *Voices of D-Day: The Story of the Allied Invasion Told by Those Who Were There*. Baton Rouge: Louisiana State University Press, 1994.

Dupuy, T. N. *Numbers, Predictions and War: Using History to Evaluate and Predict the Outcome of Armed Conflict*, rev. ed. Fairfax, Va.: Hero Books, 1985.

Dupuy, T. N.. *Understanding War: History and Theory of Combat*. New York: Paragon Publishers, 1987.

Ebert, James R. *A Life in a Year: The American Infantryman in Vietnam, 1965–1972*. Novato, Calif.: Presidio, 1993.

Edelman, Bernard, ed. *Dear America: Letters Home from Vietnam*. New York: Pocket Books, 1986.

Elliott, David W.P. *The Vietnamese War: Revolution and Social Change in the Mekong Delta, 1930–1975*, concise ed. Armonk, N.Y., and London: M. E. Sharpe, 2003, 2007.

Fehrenbach, T. R. *This Kind of War: The Classic Korean War History*. Washington and London: Brassey's, 1963, 1994.

Fischel, Wesley R., ed. *Vietnam: Anatomy of a Conflict*. Itasca, Ill.: F. E. Peacock, 1968.

Flynn, George Q. *The Draft, 1940–1973*. Lawrence: University Press of Kansas, 1993.

Foley, Michael S. *Confronting the War Machine: Draft Resistance during the Vietnam War*. Chapel Hill and London: The University of North Carolina Press, 2003.

Ford, Ronnie E. *Tet 1968: Understanding the Surprise*. London: Frank Cass, 1995.

Furgurson, Ernest B. *Westmoreland: The Inevitable General*. Boston, Toronto: Little, Brown, 1968.

Gabriel, Richard A., and Paul L. Savage. *Crisis in Command: Mismanagement in the Army*. New York: Hill and Wang, 1978.

Gaddis, John Lewis. *Strategies of Containment: A Critical Appraisal of Postwar American National Security Policy*. New York and Oxford: Oxford University Press, 1982.

Gallucci, Robert L. *Neither Peace Nor Honor: The Politics of American Military Policy in Viet-Nam*. Baltimore and London: The Johns Hopkins University Press, 1975.

Gartner, Scott Sigmund. *Strategic Assessment in War*. New Haven and London: Yale University Press, 1997.

Gelb, Leslie H., with Richard K. Betts. *The Irony of Vietnam: The System Worked*. Washington, D.C.: The Brookings Institution, 1979.

Gibbons, William Conrad. *The U.S. Government and the Vietnam War: Executive and Legislative Roles and Relationships, Part III: January–July 1965*. Princeton, N.J.: Princeton University Press, 1989.

Gibson, James William. *The Perfect War: Technowar in Vietnam*. Boston and New York: The Atlantic Monthly Press, 1986.
Gilbert, Marc Jason, ed. *Why the North Won the Vietnam War*. New York: Palgrave, 2002.
Gilbert, Marc Jason, and William Head, ed. *The Tet Offensive*. Westport, Conn.: Praeger, 1996.
Glick, Edward Bernard. *Soldiers, Scholars, and Society: The Social Impact of the American Military*. Pacific Palisades, Calif.: Goodyear, 1971.
Goodman, Allan E. *The Lost Peace: America's Search for a Negotiated Settlement of the Vietnam War*. Stanford, Calif.: Hoover Institution Press, 1978.
Gordon, David F., ed. *Estimative Products on Vietnam, 1948–1975*. Pittsburgh, Pa.: National Intelligence Council, 2005.
Graham, Herman, III. *The Brothers' Vietnam War: Black Power, Manhood, and the Military Experience*. Gainesville, Tallahassee: University Press of Florida, 2003.
Guide to the Evaluation of Educational Experiences in the Armed Services, 1954–1989, Vol. 1. Washington, D.C: American Council on Education, n.d.
Halberstam, David. *The Best and the Brightest*. New York: Random House, 1969.
Halberstam, David. *The Making of a Quagmire: America and Vietnam During the Kennedy Era*. New York: Alfred A. Knopf, 1964, 1988.
Hallin, Daniel C. *The "Uncensored War" The Media and Vietnam*. New York and Oxford: Oxford University Press, 1986.
Hamilton, Donald W. *The Art of Insurgency: American Military Policy and the Failure of Strategy in Southeast Asia*. Westport, Conn., andLondon: Praeger, 1998.
Hammer, Ellen J. *The Struggle for Indochina, 1940–1955*. Stanford, Calif.: Stanford University Press, 1954, 1966.
Hammond, William M. *Reporting Vietnam: Media and Military at War*. Lawrence: University Press of Kansas, 1998.
Hannah, Norman B. *The Key to Failure: Laos and the Vietnam War*. Lanham, New York: Madison Books, 1987.
Hastings, Max. *Overlord: D-Day and the Battle for Normandy*. New York: Simon and Schuster, 1984.
Hauser, William L. *America's Army in Crisis: A Study in Civil-Military Relations*. Baltimore and London: The Johns Hopkins University Press, 1973.
Haycock, Ronald, ed. *Regular Armies and Insurgency*. London: Croom Helm, 1979.
Heggoy, Alf Andrew. *Insurgency and Counterinsurgency in Algeria*. Bloomington and London: Indiana University Press, 1972.
Heller, Charles E., and William A. Stofft, ed. *America's First Battles, 1776–1965*. Lawrence: University Press of Kansas, 1986.
Helmer, John. *Bringing the War Home: The American Soldier in Vietnam and After*. New York: The Free Press, 1974.
Herring, George C. *America's Longest War: The United States and Vietnam, 1950–1975*, 2nd ed. New York: Alfred A. Knopf, 1979, 1986.
Herring, George C. *LBJ and Vietnam: A Different Kind of War*. Austin: University of Texas Press, 1994.
Hinh, Nguyen Duy. *Lam Son 719*. Washington, D.C.: U.S. Army Center of Military History, 1979.
Horwood, Ian. *Interservice Rivalry and Airpower in the Vietnam War*. Fort Leavenworth, Kans.: Combat Studies Institute Press, 2006.

Hosmer, Stephen T., and Konrad Kellen, and Brian M. Jenkins. *The Fall of South Vietnam: Statements by Vietnamese Military and Civilian Leaders.* New York: Crane, Russak, 1980.

Hunt, Michael H. *Lyndon Johnson's War: America's Cold War Crusade in Vietnam, 1945–1968.* New York: Hill and Wang, 1996.

Hunt, Richard A. *Pacification: The American Struggle for Vietnam's Hearts and Minds.* Boulder, San Francisco, and Oxford: Westview Press, 1995.

Hunt, Richard A., and Richard H. Shultz, Jr., ed. *Lessons from an Unconventional War: Reassessing U.S. Strategies for Future Conflicts.* New York and Oxford: Pergamon Press, 1982.

Hutchinson, Martha Crenshaw. *Revolutionary Terrorism: The FLN in Algeria, 1954–1962.* Stanford, Calif.: Hoover Institution Press, 1978.

Isaacs, Arnold R. *Without Honor: Defeat in Vietnam and Cambodia.* Baltimore and London: The Johns Hopkins University Press, 1983.

Ives, Christopher K. *US Special Forces and Counterinsurgency in Vietnam: Military innovation and institutional failure, 1961–1963.* London and New York: Routledge, 2007.

Joes, Anthony James. *The War for South Viet Nam, 1954–1975*, rev. ed. Westport, Conn., and London: Praeger, 2001.

Johnson, Lawrence H., III. *Winged Sabers: The Air Cavalry in Vietnam, 1965–1973.* Harrisburg, Pa.: Stackpole Books, 1990.

Kahin, George McTurnan, and John Wilson Lewis. *The United States in Vietnam*, rev. ed. New York: The Dial Press, 1967, 1969.

Kaiser, David. *American Tragedy: Kennedy, Johnson, and the Origins of the Vietnam War.* London and Cambridge, Mass.: The Belknap Press of Harvard University Press, 2000.

Kaplan, Fred. *The Wizards of Armageddon.* New York: Simon and Schuster, 1983.

Karnow, Stanley. *Vietnam: A History.* New York: The Viking Press, 1983.

Kaufman, William W. *The McNamara Strategy.* New York, Evanston, London: Harper & Row, 1964.

Kimball, Jeffrey. *Nixon's Vietnam War.* Lawrence: University Press of Kansas, 1998.

Kimball, Jeffrey. *To Reason Why: The Debate about the Causes of U.S. Involvement in the Vietnam War.* New York: McGraw-Hill, 1990.

Kimball, Jeffrey. *The Vietnam War Files: Uncovering the Secret History of Nixon-Era Strategy.* Lawrence: University Press of Kansas, 2004.

King, Edward L. *The Death of The Army: A Pre-Mortem.* New York: Saturday Review Press, 1972.

Kinnard, Douglas. *The War Managers: American Generals Reflect on Vietnam.* Hanover, N.H.: University Press of New England, 1977; DaCapo Press, 1991.

Kissinger, Henry. *Diplomacy.* New York: Simon & Schuster, 1994.

Klare, Michael T. *War Without End: American Planning for the Next Vietnams.* New York: Alfred A. Knopf, 1972.

Knoebl, Kuno. *Victor Charlie: The Face of War in Viet-Nam.* Translated by Abe Farbstein. New York and Washington: Frederick A. Praeger, 1967.

Kolko, Gabriel. *Anatomy of a War: Vietnam, the United States, and the Modern Historical Experience.* New York: Pantheon Books, 1985.

Krepinevich, Andrew F., Jr. *The Army and Vietnam.* Baltimore and London: The Johns Hopkins University Press, 1986.

Kutler, Stanley I., ed. *Encyclopedia of the Vietnam War.* New York: Simon & Schuster Macmillan, 1997.

LaFeber, Walter. *America, Russia, and the Cold War, 1945–1984*, 5th ed. New York: Alfred A. Knopf, 1985.

LaFeber, Walter. *The Deadly Bet: LBJ, Vietnam, and the 1968 Election*. Lanham, Boulder, and New York: Rowman & Littlefield, 2005.

Landers, James. *The Weekly War: Newsmagazines and Vietnam*. Columbia and London: University of Missouri Press, 2004.

Langguth, A. J. *Our Vietnam: The War, 1954–1975*. New York and London: Simon & Schuster, 2000.

Laurence, Janice H., and Peter F. Ramsberger. *Low-Aptitude Men in the Military: Who Profits, Who Pays?* New York, Westport, Conn., and London: Praeger, 1991.

Lawrence, Mark Atwood. *Assuming the Burden: Europe and the American Commitment to War in Vietnam*. Berkeley, Los Angeles, and London: University of California Press, 2005.

Lederer, William J. *Our Own Worst Enemy*. New York: W. W. Norton, 1968.

Le Gro, William E. *Vietnam from Cease-Fire to Capitulation*. Washington, D.C.: U.S. Army Center of Military History, 1981.

Leites, Nathan, and Charles Wolf, Jr. *Rebellion and Authority: An Analytic Essay on Insurgent Conflicts*. Chicago: Markham, 1970.

Lewy, Guenter. *America in Vietnam*. New York: Oxford University Press, 1978.

Lind, Michael. *Vietnam: The Necessary War*. New York: The Free Press, 1999.

Linn, Brian McAllister. *The U.S. Army and Counterinsurgency in the Philippine War, 1899–1902*. Chapel Hill and London: The University of North Carolina Press, 1989.

Little, Roger W., ed. *Selective Service and American Society*. New York: Russell Sage Foundation, 1969.

Logevall, Fredrik. *The Origins of the Vietnam War*. Harlow, England: Longman, 2001.

Lomperis, Timothy J. *The War Everyone Lost—and Won: America's Intervention in Viet Nam's Twin Struggles*. Washington, D.C.: CQ Press, 1993.

Long, Austin. *The "Other War": Lessons from Five Decades of RAND Counterinsurgency Research*. Santa Monica, Calif.: The RAND Corporation, 2006.

Loory, Stuart H. *Defeated: Inside America's Military Machine*. New York: Random House, 1973.

Luttwak, Edward, and Stuart Koehl. *The Dictionary of Modern War*. New York: HarperCollins, 1991.

MacGarrigle, George L. *Taking the Offensive: October 1966 to October 1967*. Washington, D.C.: Center of Military History, 1998.

Malkasian, Carter. *A History of Modern Wars of Attrition*. Westport, Conn.: Praeger, 2002.

Mandel, Robert. *The Meaning of Military Victory*. Boulder and London: Lynne Rienner, 2006.

Mann, Robert. *A Grand Delusion: America's Descent into Vietnam*. New York: Basic Books, 2001.

Mansoor, Peter R. *Baghdad at Sunrise: A Brigade Commander's War in Iraq*. New Haven and London: Yale University Press, 2008.

Maurer, Harry, ed. *Strange Ground: Americans in Vietnam, 1945–1975, An Oral History*. New York: Henry Holt, 1989.

McMahon, Robert J., ed. *Major Problems in the History of the Vietnam War*, 2d ed. Lexington, Mass., Toronto: D. C. Heath, 1995.

McMaster, H.R. *Dereliction of Duty: Lyndon Johnson, Robert McNamara, the Joint Chiefs of Staff, and the Lies That Led to Vietnam*. New York: Harper Perennial, 1997.

Millett Allan R., ed. *A Short History of the Vietnam War*. Bloomington and London: Indiana University Press, 1978.

Millett, Allan R., and Williamson Murray, eds. *Military Effectiveness*, Volume I: *The First World War*. Boston: Unwin Hyman, 1988.

Millett, Allan R., and Williamson Murray, eds.. *Military Effectiveness*, Volume III: *The Second World War*. Boston: Allen & Unwin, 1988.

Milstein, Jeffrey S. *Dynamics of the Vietnam War: A Quantitative Analysis and Prediction Computer Simulation*. Columbus: Ohio State University Press, 1974.

Momyer, William W. *Airpower in Three Wars*. Maxwell Air Force Base, Ala.: Air University Press, 1978, 2003.

Moran, Daniel. *Wars of National Liberation*. London: Cassell, 2001.

Morrison, Wilbur H. *The Elephant and the Tiger: The Full Story of the Vietnam War*. New York: Hippocrene Books, 1990.

Moser, Richard R. *The New Winter Soldier: GI and Veteran Dissent during the Vietnam War*. New Brunswick, N.J.: Rutgers University Press, 1996.

Moss, George Donelson. *Vietnam: An American Ordeal*, 5th ed. Upper Saddle River, N.J.: Pearson Prentice Hill, 1990, 2006.

Moyar, Mark. *Phoenix and the Birds of Prey: Counterinsurgency and Counterterrorism in Vietnam*. Lincoln and London: University of Nebraska Press, 1997, 2007.

Moyar, Mark. *Triumph Forsaken: The Vietnam War, 1954–1965*. Cambridge, New York: Cambridge University Press, 2006.

Murphy, Edward F. *Dak To: The 173d Airborne Brigade in South Vietnam's Central Highlands, June-November 1967*. Novato, Calif.: Presidio, 1993.

Mylander, Maureen. *The Generals*. New York: The Dial Press, 1974.

Nagl, John. *Learning to Eat Soup with a Knife: Counterinsurgency Lessons from Malaya and Vietnam*. Chicago and London: The University of Chicago Press, 2002.

Neese, Harvey, and John O'Donnell, ed. *Prelude to Tragedy: Vietnam, 1960–1965*. Annapolis, Md.: Naval Institute Press, 2001.

Neu, Charles E., ed. *After Vietnam: Legacies of a Lost War*. Baltimore and London: The Johns Hopkins University Press, 2000.

Nolan, Keith William. *Into Cambodia: Spring Campaign, Summer Offensive, 1970*. Novato, Calif.: Presidio, 1990.

Nolan, Keith William. *Into Laos: The Story of Dewey Canyon II/Lam Son 719; Vietnam 1971*. Novato, Calif.: Presidio, 1986.

Nolan, Keith William. *Ripcord: Screaming Eagles Under Siege, Vietnam 1970*. Novato, Calif.: Presidio, 2000.

O'Ballance, Edgar. *The Indo-China War, 1945–1954: A Study in Guerrilla Warfare*. London: Faber and Faber, 1964.

Oberdorfer, Don. *Tet!* Garden City, N.Y.: Doubleday, 1971.

Olson, James S. *The Vietnam War: Handbook of the Literature and Research*. Westport, Conn., and London: Greenwood Press, 1993.

O'Neill, Bard E. *Insurgency and Terrorism: From Revolution to Apocalypse*, 2nd ed. Washington, D.C.: Potomac Books, Inc., 2005.

Oppenheimer, Martin, ed. *The American Military*. Chicago: Aldine, 1971.

Palmer, Dave Richard. *Summons of the Trumpet: U.S.-Vietnam in Perspective*. San Rafael, Calif.: Presidio Press, 1978.

Palmer, Gregory. *The McNamara Strategy and the Vietnam War: Program budgeting in the Pentagon, 1960–1968*. Westport, Conn., and London: Greenwood Press, 1978.

Paret, Peter. *French Revolutionary Warfare from Indochina to Algeria: The Analysis of a Political and Military Doctrine*. New York, Washington, and London: Frederick A. Praeger, 1964.

Patel, Seema, and Steven Ross. *Breaking Point: Measuring Progress in Afghanistan*. Washington, D.C.: Center for Strategic and International Studies, 2006.

Pearson, Willard. *The War in the Northern Provinces, 1966–1968*. Washington, D.C.: U.S. Government Printing Office, 1975.

Peterson, Michael E. *The Combined Action Platoons: The U.S. Marines' Other War in Vietnam*. Westport, Conn., and London: Praeger, 1989.

Porter, Gareth, ed. *Vietnam: A History in Documents*. New York and Scarborough, Ontario: New American Library, 1981.

Prados, John. *The Blood Road: The Ho Chi Minh Trail and the Vietnam War*. New York: John Wiley & Sons,, 1999.

Prados, John. *The Hidden History of the Vietnam War*. Chicago: Ivan R. Dee, 1995.

Race, Jeffrey. *War Comes to Long An: Revolutionary Conflict in a Vietnamese Province*. Berkeley, Los Angeles, and London: University of California Press, 1972.

Record, Jeffrey. *The Wrong War: Why We Lost in Vietnam*. Annapolis, Md: Naval Institute Press, 1998.

Robbins, Mary Susannah, ed. *Against the Vietnam War: Writings Published by Activists*. Syracuse, N.Y.: Syracuse University Press, 1999.

Randolph, Stephen P. *Powerful and Brutal Weapons: Nixon, Kissinger, and the Easter Offensive*. Cambridge, Mass.: Harvard University Press, 2007.

Rogers, Bernard W. *Cedar Falls-Junction City: A Turning Point*. Washington, D.C.: U.S. Government Printing Office, 1974, 2004.

Rosen, Stephen Peter. *Winning The Next War: Innovation and the Modern Military*. Ithaca and London: Cornell University Press, 1991.

Ruane, Kevin. *War and Revolution in Vietnam, 1930–75*. London: UCL Press, 1998.

Sanders, Ralph. *The Politics of Defense Analysis*. New York, London: Dunellen, 1973.

Santoli, Al. *Everything We Had: An Oral History of the Vietnam War by Thirty-three American Soldiers Who Fought It*. New York: Random House, 1981.

Sarkesian, Sam C., ed. *Combat Effectiveness: Cohesion, Stress, and the Volunteer Military*. Beverly Hills and London: Sage Publications, 1980.

Scales, Robert H., Jr. *Firepower in Limited Warfare*, rev. ed. Novato, Calif.: Presidio, 1995.

Schalk, David L. *War and the Ivory Tower: Algeria and Vietnam*. New York and Oxford: Oxford University Press, 1991.

Schandler, Herbert Y. *The Unmaking of a President: Lyndon Johnson and Vietnam*. Princeton, N.J.: Princeton University Press, 1977.

Schell, Jonathan. *Observing the Nixon Years*. New York: Pantheon Books, 1989.

Schlight, John, ed. *The Second Indochina War: Proceedings of a Symposium Held at Airlie, Virginia, November 7–9, 1984*. Washington, D.C.: Center of Military History, 1986.

Schmitz, David F. *The Tet Offensive: Politics, War, and Public Opinion*. Lanham, Boulder, and New York: Rowman & Littlefield, 2005.

Schulzinger, Robert D. *A Time for War: The United States and Vietnam, 1941–1975*. New York and Oxford: Oxford University Press, 1997.

Scott, Andrew W. *Insurgency*. Chapel Hill: The University of North Carolina Press, 1970.

Serewicz, Lawrence W. *America at the Brink of Empire: Rusk, Kissinger, and the Vietnam War*. Baton Rouge: Louisiana State University Press, 2007.

Sevy, Grace, ed. *The American Experience in Vietnam: A Reader*. Norman and London: University of Oklahoma Press, 1989.

Shaw, John M. *The Cambodian Campaign: The 1970 Offensive and America's Vietnam War*. Lawrence: University Press of Kansas, 2005.

Shawcross, William. *Sideshow: Kissinger, Nixon, and the Destruction of Cambodia*, rev. ed. New York: Cooper Square Press, 1979, 2002.

Shay, Jonathan. *Achilles in Vietnam: Combat Trauma and the Undoing of Character*. New York: Antheneum, 1994.

Sheehan, Neil. *A Bright Shining Lie: John Paul Vann and America in Vietnam*. New York: Random House, 1988.

Showalter, Dennis E., and John G. Albert, ed. *An American Dilemma: Vietnam, 1964–1973*. Chicago: Imprint Publications, 1993.

Shultz, Richard H., Jr., and Robert L. Pfaltzgraff, Jr., Uri Ra'anan, William J. Olson, and Igor Lukes, eds. *Guerrilla Warfare and Counterinsurgency*. Lexington, Mass., and Toronto: Lexington Books, 1989.

Silver, Benjamin S. and Francis Aylette. *Ride at a Gallop*. Waco, Tex.: Davis Brothers, 1990.

Singh, Baljit, and Ko-Wang Mei. *Theory and Practice of Modern Guerrilla Warfare*. New York: Asia Publishing House, 1971.

Small, Melvin. *Covering Dissent: The Media and the Anti-Vietnam War Movement*. New Brunswick, N.J.: Rutgers University Press, 1994.

Small, Melvin, and William D. Hoover, ed. *Give Peace a Chance: Exploring the Vietnam Antiwar Movement*. Syracuse, N.Y.: Syracuse University Press, 1992.

Sorley, Lewis. *A Better War: The Unexamined Victories and Final Tragedy of America's Last Years in Vietnam*. New York, San Diego, and London: Harcourt Brace, 1999.

Sorley, Lewis. *Honorable Warrior: General Harold K. Johnson and the Ethics of Command*. Lawrence: University Press of Kansas, 1998.

Sorley, Lewis. *Thunderbolt: General Creighton Abrams and the Army of his Times*. New York and London: Simon & Schuster, 1992.

Sorley, Lewis. *Vietnam Chronicles: The Abrams Tapes, 1968–1972*. Lubbock, Tex.: Texas Tech University Press, 2004.

Spector, Ronald H. *After Tet: The Bloodiest Year in Vietnam*. New York: The Free Press, 1993.

Stanton, Shelby L. *Anatomy of a Division: The 1st Cav in Vietnam*. Novato, Calif.: Presidio, 1987.

Stanton, Shelby L. *The Rise and Fall of an American Army: U.S. Ground Forces in Vietnam, 1965–1973*. Novato, Calif.: Presidio Press, 1985.

Stanton, Shelby L. *Vietnam Order of Battle: A Complete Illustrated Reference to U.S. Army Combat and Support Forces in Vietnam, 1961–1973*. Mechanicsburg, Pa.: Stackpole Books, 2003.

Starr, Paul. *The Discarded Army: Veterans after Vietnam*. New York: Charterhouse, 1973.

Starry, Donn A. *Armored Combat in Vietnam*. New York: Arno Press, 1980.

Sweetland, Anders. "Item Analysis of the HES (Hamlet Evaluation System)." Santa Monica, Calif.: RAND, August 20, 1968.

Summers, Harry G., Jr. *On Strategy: A Critical Appraisal of the Vietnam War*. Novato, Calif.: Presidio, 1982.

Takiff, Michael. *Brave Men, Gentle Heroes: American Fathers and Sons in World War II and Vietnam.* New York: Morrow, 2003.

Terry, Wallace. *Bloods: An Oral History of the Vietnam War by Black Veterans.* New York: Random House, 1984.

Thayer, Thomas C. *War Without Fronts: The American Experience in Vietnam.* Boulder and London: Westview Press, 1985.

Tho, Tran Dinh. *The Cambodian Incursion.* Washington, D.C.: U.S. Army Center of Military History, 1979.

Thompson, W. Scott, and Donaldson D. Frizzell, ed. *The Lessons of Vietnam.* New York: Crane, Russak, 1977.

Toczek, David M. *The Battle of Ap Bac, Vietnam: They Did Everything but Learn from It.* Westport, Conn., and London: Greenwood Press, 2001.

Tolson, John J. *Airmobility, 1961–1971.* Washington, D.C.: U.S. Government Printing Office, 1973.

Trullinger, James Walker, Jr. *Village at War: An Account of Revolution in Vietnam.* New York and London: Longman, 1980.

Truong, Ngo Quang. *The Easter Offensive of 1972.* Washington, D.C.: U.S. Army Center of Military History, 1980.

Tucker, Spencer C., ed. *Encyclopedia of the Vietnam War: A Political, Social, and Military History,* 2 vols. Santa Barbara, Ca: ABC-CLIO, 1998.

Turley, G. H. *The Easter Offensive: Vietnam, 1972.* Novato, Calif.: Presidio, 1985.

Turley, William S. *The Second Indochina War: A Short Political and Military History, 1954–1975.* Boulder, Colo.: Westview Press, 1986.

Turner, Kathleen J. *Lyndon Johnson's Dual War: Vietnam and the Press.* Chicago and London: The University of Chicago Press, 1985.

Van Atta, Dale. *With Honor: Melvin Laird in War, Peace, and Politics.* Madison: The University of Wisconsin Press, 2008.

Vandiver, Frank E. *Shadows of Vietnam: Lyndon Johnson's Wars.* College Station: Texas A&M University Press, 1997.

Vetock, Dennis J. *Lessons Learned: A History of US Army Lesson Learning.* Carlisle Barracks, Pa.: US Army Military History Institute, 1988.

Victory in Vietnam: The Official History of the People's Army of Vietnam, 1954–1975. Translated by Merle L. Pribbenow. Lawrence: University Press of Kansas, 2002.

Walton, C. Dale. *The Myth of Inevitable US Defeat in Vietnam.* London and Portland, Ore.: Frank Cass, 2002.

Watts, Barry D. *Clausewitzean Friction and Future War.* Washington, D.C.: Institute for National Strategic Studies, 1996.

Weigley, Russell F. *Eisenhower's Lieutenants: The Campaign of France and Germany, 1944–1945.* Bloomington: Indiana University Press, 1990.

Weigley, Russell F. *History of the United States Army.* New York: Macmillan, 1967.

Westheider, James E. *The African American Experience in Vietnam: Brothers in Arms.* Lanham, Boulder, and New York: Rowman & Littlefield, 2008.

Wiesner, Louis A. *Victims and Survivors: Displaced Persons and Other War Victims in Viet-Nam, 1954–1975.* New York and Westport, Conn.: Greenwood Press, 1988.

Wiest, Andrew. *Vietnam's Forgotten Army: Heroism and Betrayal in the ARVN.* New York and London: New York University Press, 2008.

Willbanks, James H. *Abandoning Vietnam: How America Left and South Vietnam Lost Its War*. Lawrence: University Press of Kansas, 2004.

Willbanks, James H. *The Battle of An Loc*. Bloomington and Indianapolis: Indiana University Press, 2005.

Willbanks, James H. *The Tet Offensive: A Concise History*. New York: Columbia University Press, 2007.

Wirtz, James J. *The Tet Offensive: Intelligence Failure in War*. Ithaca and London: Cornell University Press, 1991.

Wolf, Charles, Jr. *Insurgency and Counterinsurgency: New Myths and Old Realities*. Santa Monica, Calif.: The RAND Corporation, 1965.

Wyatt, Clarence R. *Paper Soldiers: The American Press and the Vietnam War*. New York and London: W. W. Norton, 1993.

Young, Marilyn B. *The Vietnam Wars, 1945–1990*. New York: HarperCollins, 1991.

Young, Marilyn B., and Robert Buzzanco, ed. *Companion to the Vietnam War*. Malden, Mass.: Blackwell Publishing, 2002.

Zabecki, David T. *Chief of Staff: The Principal Officers Behind History's Great Commanders*, Vol. 2. Annapolis, Md.: Naval Institute Press, 2008.

Zaffiri, Samuel. *Hamburger Hill: May 11–20, 1969*. Novato, Calif.: Presidio, 1988.

Zaffiri, Samuel. *Westmoreland: A Biography of General William C. Westmoreland*. New York: William Morrow, 1994.

Articles

Andradé, Dale, and James H. Willbanks. "CORDS/Phoenix: Counterinsurgency Lessons from Vietnam for the Future." *Military Review*, Vol. LXXXVI, No. 2 (March–April 2006): 9–23.

Baker, Jim. "Systems Thinking and Counterinsurgencies." *Parameters*, Vol. XXXVI, No. 4 (Winter 2006–07): 26–43.

Birtle, Andrew J. "PROVN, Westmoreland, and the Historians: A Reappraisal." *The Journal of Military History*, Vol. 72, No. 4 (October 2008): 1213–1247.

Carland, John M. "Winning the Vietnam War: Westmoreland's Approach in Two Documents." *The Journal of Military History*, Vol. 68, No. 2 (April 2004): 553–574.

Cassidy, Robert M. "Back to the Street Without Joy: Counterinsurgency Lessons from Vietnam and Other Small Wars." *Parameters*, Vol. XXXIV No. 2 (Summer 2004): 73–83.

Cerami, Joseph R. "Presidential Decisionmaking and Vietnam: Lessons for Strategists." *Parameters*, Vol. XXVI, No. 4 (Winter 1996–97): 66–80.

Clancy, James, and Chuck Crossett. "Measuring Effectiveness in Irregular Warfare." *Parameters*, Vol. XXXVII, No. 2 (Summer 2007): 88–100.

Cortright, David. "Black GI Resistance During the Vietnam War." *Vietnam Generation*, Vol. 2, No. 1 (Spring 1990): 51–64.

Gartner, Scott Sigmund. "Differing Evaluations of Vietnamization." *Journal of Interdisciplinary History*, Vol. 29, No. 2 (Autumn 1998): 243–262.

Gartner, Scott S., and Marissa E. Myers. "Body Counts and 'Success' in the Vietnam and Korean Wars." *Journal of Interdisciplinary History*, Vol. 25, No. 3 (Winter, 1995): 377–395.

Gimbel, Cynthia, and Alan Booth. "Who Fought in Vietnam?" *Social Forces*, Vol. 74, No. 4 (June 1996): 1137–1157.

Gouveia, William A., Jr. "An Analysis of Moral Dissent: An Army Officer's Public Protest of the Vietnam War." *Journal of Military Ethics*, Vol. 3, No. 1 (March 2004): 53–60.

Grinter, Laurence E. "How They Lost: Doctrines, Strategies and Outcomes of the Vietnam War." *Asian Survey*, Vol. 15, No. 12 (December 1975): 1114–1132.

Hammond, William M. "The Press in Vietnam as Agent of Defeat: A Critical Examination." *Reviews in American History*, Vol. 17, No. 2 (June 1989): 312–323.

Herring, George C. "American Strategy in Vietnam: The Postwar Debate." *Military Affairs*, Vol. 46, No. 2 (April 1982): 57–63.

Herring, George C. "'People's Quite Apart': Americans, South Vietnamese, and the War in Vietnam." *Diplomatic History*, Vol. 14, No. 1 (Winter 1990): 4.

Howze, Hamilton H. "Army Aviation 1955–1962: The Foundation of Air Mobility." *Army Aviation* (December 31, 1992): 25–34.

Hsiao, Lisa. "Project 100,000: The Great Society's Answer to Military Manpower Needs in Vietnam." *Vietnam Generation*, Vol. 1, No. 2 (1989): 14–37.

Jones, Frank L. "Blowtorch: Robert Komer and the Making of Vietnam Pacification Policy." *Parameters*, Vol. XXXV, No. 3 (Autumn 2005): 103–118.

Kagan, Frederick W. "Measuring Success." *Armed Forces Journal* (January 2006): 20–24.

Lang, Kurt. "American Military Performance in Vietnam: Background and Analysis." *Journal of Political & Military Sociology*, Vol. 8, No. 2 (Fall 1980): 269–286.

Long, Gary L. "A Sociology for Special Circumstances: Using the Vietnam War in the Classroom." *Teaching Sociology*, Vol. 21, No. 3 (July 1993): 269–270.

Moddell, John, and Timothy Haggerty. "The Social Impact of War." *Annual Review of Sociology*, Vol. 17 (1991): 205–224.

Mueller, John E. "The Search for the 'Breaking Point' in Vietnam: The Statistics of a Deadly Quarrel." *International Studies Quarterly*, Vol. 24, No. 4 (December 1980): 499–500.

Paterson, Thomas G. "Historical Memory and Illusive Victories: Vietnam and Central America." *Diplomatic History*, Vol. 12, No. 1 (Winter 1988): 1–18.

Prados, John. "Vietnamization: Success or Failure?" *The VVA Veteran* (November/December 2007): 37–40.

Pribbenow, Merle L., II. "General Võ Nguyên Giáp and the Mysterious Evolution of the Plan for the 1968 Tết Offensive." *Journal of Vietnamese Studies*, Vol. 3 (Summer 2008): 1–33.

Pribbenow, Merle L., II. "North Vietnam's Final Offensive: Strategic Endgame Nonpareil." *Parameters*, Vol. XXIX, No. 4 (Winter 1999–2000): 58–71.

Serong, F. P. "The 1972 Easter Offensive." *Southeast Asian Perspectives*, No. 10 (Summer 1974): 1–62.

Shy, John, and Thomas W. Collier. "Revolutionary War." In *Makers of Modern Strategy: From Machiavelli to the Nuclear Age*, ed. Peter Paret, 815–862. Princeton, N.J.: Princeton University Press, 1986.

Sorley, Lewis. "Courage and Blood: South Vietnam's Repulse of the 1972 Easter Offensive." *Parameters*, Vol. XXIX, No. 2 (Summer 1999): 38–56.

Sorley, Lewis. "To Change a War: General Harold K. Johnson and the PROVN Study." *Parameters*, Vol. XXVIII, No. 1 (Spring 1998): 93–109.

Ward, Ian. "Why Giap did it: report from Saigon." *Conflict Studies*, No. 27 (October 1972): 1–10.

Wendt, Eric P. "Strategic Counterinsurgency Modeling." *Special Warfare*, Vol. 18, No. 2 (September 2005): 2–13.

Westerman, Ian. "Pacifying Afghanistan: Enduring Lessons from CORDS in Vietnam," *RUSI*, Vol. 153, No. 5 (October 2008): 14–21.

Wirtz, James J. "Intelligence to Please? The Order of Battle Controversy during the Vietnam War." *Political Science Quarterly*, Vol. 106, No. 2 (Summer 1991): 239–263.

Dissertations and Theses

Coble, Charles R., Jr. "Social Action Programs in the Department of Defense." Ph.D. diss., University of North Carolina at Chapel Hill, 1969.

Conn, Pamela A. "Losing Hearts and Minds: U.S. Pacification Efforts in Vietnam during the Johnson Years." Ph.D. diss., University of Houston, 2001.

Dawkins, Peter M. "The United States Army and the 'Other' War in Vietnam: A Study of the Complexity of Implementing Organizational Change." Ph.D. diss., Princeton University, 1979.

Duffy, David A. "A Reflection of the Army: West Point and Counterinsurgency, 1962–1968." LD720 Research Paper, United States Military Academy Tactical Officer Education Program, 1995.

Grinter, Lawrence E. "The Pacification of South Vietnam: Dilemmas of Counterinsurgency and Development." Ph.D. diss., University of North Carolina at Chapel Hill, 1972.

Walmsley, John K. "US Military Advisers in Greece: The Development of United States Military Assistance and Counterinsurgency Operations During the Greek Civil War." Master's thesis, The Ohio State University, 2003.

Illustration Credits

All maps taken from Richard W. Stewart, ed., American Military History, Vol. II, The United States in a Global Era, 1917–2003 (Washington, D.C.: Center of Military History, 2005).

All photos are from the archives of the U.S. Army Military History Institute, Carlisle Barracks, Pa. Specific source data accompanies each photo.

Index

Abrams, Creighton, W.: Army Chief of Staff, 218; Cambodia and, 200, 203; casualties and, 166–167, 188, 196, 210; conflicting guidance and, 167, 196; counter-drug programs and, 192; evaluations of war and, 201, 203, 231; Laos and, 213–214; media and, 149; military discipline and, 189, 196; "one war" concept and, 135, 147–153, 157–158, 163–164, 166–168, 174, 202, 205, 215; pacification and, 148–150, 152, 163; statistics and, 154, 172, 224, 227; tactics and, 135, 148–149, 157, 162, 164, 167–168, 188, 196, 202, 215–216; Tet Offensive and, 144; U.S. withdrawal and, 162, 178; Vietnamization and, 161, 168–170, 176, 179, 214; Westmoreland, William and, 13, 128, 148, 152, 161
Accelerated Pacification Campaign (APC), 150–151, 175
Acheson, Dean, 128
Advanced Research Projects Agency (ARPA), 103
Agency for International Development (USAID), 106, 114
airmobility, 64, 74–78, 81–85, 94, 224
Algeria, 22, 24, 26, 29, 32, 39, 77, 233
Alsop, Joseph, 66
An Loc, 216–217
Ap Bac, Battle of, 55–56, 106, 145, 228

Armed Forces Qualification Test (AFQT), 183–187
Army Concept Team, 76
Army of the Republic of Vietnam (ARVN), 15, 17, 45, 55, 57, 61, 68, 73, 88, 92, 94–95, 109, 112–113, 116, 120, 123–128, 130–133, 135, 146, 148–149, 152, 163, 168–173, 176–179, 181, 198, 200–201, 206, 208, 220; 1st Division, 178; 2nd Division, 56; 7th Division, 55; Cambodia and, 203, 210–212, 228; desertions and, 49, 65, 68, 149, 168, 170, 173, 208; Easter Offensive and, 203, 219–220; Laos and, 213–215, 228; measuring effectiveness of, 145, 158–162, 170–173, 179, 202–203, 205–209, 213–214, 218–222, 224, 226–229; revolutionary development and, 113; Tet Offensive and, 139; *See also* Vietnamization
Army War College, 36, 197–199

Baldwin, Hanson, W., 81
Ball, George, 68
Beckwith, Charles, 99
Ben Tre, 140
body counts, 7, 9–10, 14, 15, 65, 80, 83–85, 88–89, 91–92, 95–105, 106–108, 123–124, 127, 131, 140, 149, 153–154, 157, 164–166, 172, 189, 190, 198, 203, 205–206, 226, 230
Bradley, Omar N., 3–4, 128
Brown, Thomas W., 78

Browne, Malcolm W., 82
Bundy, McGeorge, 67, 128
Bunker, Ellsworth, 114, 116, 128–129, 149, 152, 155, 159, 161, 202, 214, 215
Byrd, Robert, 142

Callwell, C.E., 21
Cambodia: bombing of, 161, 209–210; border with Vietnam, 6–7, 77–79, 111, 134, 209; discussions of invasion, 142, 162; incursions into, 189, 200, 203, 207–208, 210–214, 216–218, 228; internal rebellion in, 203, 207, 210; sanctuaries in, 208–211, 213
Central Intelligence Agency (CIA), 43, 46, 105, 114, 118, 130, 135–138, 159, 160, 202
Central Office of South Vietnam (COSVN), 110–111, 211
Chieu Hoi, 115, 121, 151
Civil Operations and Revolutionary Development Support (CORDS), 17, 115–119, 121–122, 125–126, 131, 140, 145, 150–151, 165, 170, 175
Clausewitz, Carl von, 21
Clifford, Clark, 127, 142, 146–147
Colby, William, 52, 150
Collins, Arthur S. Jr., 100, 181, 209
Collins, J. Lawton, 4
Combined Action Platoons (CAPs), 17, 93
Combined Campaign Plan (1967), 109
Combined Campaign Plan (1969), 164
Command and General Staff College (CGSC), 32–33
Cooper–Church Amendment, 213
Cooper, Chester L., 53, 64, 131
Cronkite, Walter, 144
"crossover point," 91, 92, 98, 102, 105, 124, 164
Cushman, John H., 51–52

Dak To, 134, 136, 137
Davidson, Phillip B., 139
Davydov, Denis, 21
de Saussure, Edward H., 6, 8
de Tassigny, Jean de Lattre, 23
Decker, George, C., 29
Democratic Republic of Vietnam (DRV), 60
DePuy, William E., 7, 64, 95
Diem, Ngo Dinh, 37, 41–43, 45–47, 54, 57, 59
Dien Bien Phu, 24, 41, 136, 137
Dockery, Martin, 56
dominant indicators, 9, 15, 61, 104, 163, 207, 231, 234

Donlon, Roger, 58
Dupuy, Trevor N., 11

Easter Offensive, 203, 219–220
Eisenhower, Dwight D., 4, 42
Enhance Operation, 219
Enthoven, Alain C., 35, 121–122
Ewell, Julian J., 164–166, 168, 225

Fall, Bernard B., 11, 26, 27, 33, 37, 42, 79
Field Manual 100–5, 40
Field Manual 31–15, 22, 31
Field Manual 31–16, 13–14, 32
Field Manual 31–20, 29, 31, 32
Field Manual 31–21, 31
Fitt, Alfred B., 186
flexible response, 11
Forrestal, Michael V., 60
Fort Benning Infantry School, 21, 33
"fragging," 190–191, 197
Free World Military Assistance Forces (FWMAF), 83

Galula, David, 25–26, 30, 39, 49, 101, 204
Gavin, James, 74–75, 94, 127
Geneva Conference, 24, 37, 41, 63
Giap, Vo Nguyen, 23, 136, 137, 139, 149, 157
Government of South Vietnam (GVN), 47, 49–51, 53–54, 58–60, 63–65, 67–68, 70–73, 83, 85, 87–89, 106–107, 109, 112, 114–116, 118–119, 121–122, 124–126, 128–131, 140, 142, 145, 150, 152, 159–161, 173, 178, 202–203, 207–209, 217, 219, 223–224, 231
Greek Civil War, 27–28
Griffith, Samuel B., 22
Grivas, George, 28
Guam Doctrine, 162
guerre révolutionnaire, 24
Guevara, Che, 11, 30
Gulf of Tonkin, 46

Hackworth, David, 166, 189, 193
Haig, Alexander, 209, 211
Halberstam, David, 43, 46, 53, 57, 130
Hamburger Hill, 167–168, 176
Hamlet Evaluation System (HES), 118–122, 126, 130–131, 140–141, 149–151, 155, 165, 168, 174, 231
Harkins, Paul D., 44, 49–50, 52, 55–57, 61, 63–64, 66, 69, 71, 74, 134, 145, 193, 224, 228

Hatfield, Mark, 177
Heinl, Robert D. Jr., 182, 187
Herbert, Anthony, 189
Herr, Michael, 145
Hershey, Lewis B., 186
Hilsman, Roger, 58
Hitch, Charles J., 35–36
Ho Chi Minh Trail, 42, 61, 161, 209, 213
Ho Chi Minh, 23, 41
Holbrooke, Richard, 124
Honolulu Conference, 5–6, 67, 89–92, 102, 104–105
Hoopes, Townsend, 147
Howze Board, 75, 76
Hue, 137, 139, 144, 145
Humphrey, Hubert, 151

Ia Drang, 5–6, 65, 79–85, 87–88, 101, 112, 231
Iron Triangle, 110–111

Johnson, Harold K., 52, 59–60, 67, 82
Johnson, Lyndon B., 6, 46, 64–68, 85, 87, 106, 112, 114, 124, 126–128, 132, 134, 142–144; Great Society Program and, 108; Honolulu Conference and, 89–90, 92; media and, 144, 146
Joint Chiefs of Staff, 43, 47, 59, 67, 71, 74, 89–90, 92–94, 101, 108, 113, 118, 124, 127, 130, 145–146, 160, 177, 194, 206–207, 229
Just, Ward, 127, 154

Karnow, Stanley, 43
Katzenbach, Nicholas, 132
Kennedy, Edward, 167, 176, 190
Kennedy, John F., 11, 42–43, 46, 59
Kennedy, Robert, 143, 153
Kent State, 211
Khe Sanh, 136–137, 139, 145
Khrushchev, Nikita, 11
King, Martin Luther Jr., 153
Kinnard, Harry W., 75–83, 87–89, 231
Kissinger, Henry, 158–160, 162, 164, 173, 175, 178–179, 202, 206–209, 213–215, 218, 227, 234
Knowlton, William A., 119
Komer, Robert, W., 46, 95, 106, 117, 128, 130, 132, 156, 216; Abrams, Creighton and, 150; Hamlet Evaluation System and, 119, 121, 150; Johnson, Lyndon and, 113–114; pacification and, 105–106, 113–116, 119, 125, 130; Tet Offensive and, 140–141

Korean War, 6, 19, 30, 42–43, 75, 79, 164, 175, 183
Krulak, Victor, 59, 70, 93
Ky, Nguyen Cao, 70, 90

Ladd, Jonathan, 56
Laird, Melvin, 158–159, 162, 164, 168, 170–172, 175, 177, 201, 207–208, 210
Lam Son 719, 213–215, 220
Lansdale, Edward G., 12, 48–49, 66, 72, 99, 100, 101, 226
Laos, 76, 166, 189, 200, 203, 208, 213–215, 218, 220, 228
Larsen, Stanley, 88
Lawrence, T. E., 21
Le Duan, 136
LeMay, Curtis E., 36
Lemnitzer, Lyman, 43
Linebacker II, Operation, 218
Lodge, Henry Cabot, 46, 70, 92, 108, 128

Magsaysay, Ramón, 28
Malaya, 12, 26–27, 57, 69
Man, Chu Huy, 78–79
Mansfield, Mike, 45, 176–177
Marshall, S. L. A., 117
Mathias, Charles, 190
McCaffrey, William J., 183
McDade, Robert A., 80–81
McGarr, Lionel, C., 33, 42, 43, 48
McGovern, George, 177
McNamara, Robert S.: airmobility and, 75–76; body counts and, 95; doubts on Vietnam War and, 85, 112, 128–129; enemy morale and, 103; Hamlet Evaluation System and, 121; Honolulu Conference and, 6, 90; pacification and, 92, 108, 111; Project 100,000 and, 185; strategy and, 91, 94, 106; systems analysis and quantitative reporting, 10, 34–36, 50, 52, 91, 93, 85, 98, 102, 118, 225–226; troop increases and, 67–68, 85, 123, 142; visits to Vietnam, 49, 59, 67–68, 85, 99, 108, 112, 123; "Wise Men" and, 128; World War II and, 52
Measurement of Progress Reports, 8, 104, 122
Mekong Delta, 10, 44, 53, 55–56, 95, 133, 139–140, 164, 169, 177, 196, 218, 228
Mendenhall, Joseph A., 59
Military Assistance Advisory Group (MAAG), 33, 41–43, 46, 48

Military Assistance Command, Vietnam (MACV): air power and, 83; Army of the Republic of Vietnam (ARVN) and, 15, 45–46, 52, 169–170, 172, 174, 178–179, 181, 198–201, 206–209, 219; attrition strategy and, 91–92, 105; body counts and, 88–89, 91–92, 96, 99–104, 124, 140; Cambodia and, 207–211, 215; casualties and, 80, 108, 195–196; command changes and, 13, 44, 69, 147–148, 152, 218; criticism of, 94, 126–127, 130, 132, 144–146, 152, 167, 175–177, 189, 202, 230; counterinsurgency and, 9, 12, 44, 55, 69–70, 82–83, 85, 153; Hamlet Evaluation System and, 119–122, 172, 175; Honolulu Conference, 89–90, 92; intelligence and, 15, 118, 137–139; Laos and, 166, 208, 214–215; media and, 126–127, 130, 132, 134, 144–146, 167, 175–176; mission statement, 44–45, 49, 162–163, 177; pacification and, 51–53, 91–92, 104, 108, 110, 114–117, 119, 122, 124–125, 130–131, 140, 150–151, 163, 168, 174, 202, 206, 211–212; revolutionary development and, 111, 123; search and destroy and, 87–88, 96, 98, 152, 168; statistics and metrics and, 7–10, 14–18, 40–41, 47–56, 58–61, 64–66, 68, 71, 73–74, 78, 80–82, 84–85, 88–89, 91, 93–94, 96, 98–106, 112, 115, 118, 121–122, 124, 126, 129–130, 133–135, 138, 141, 145, 147, 149–150, 153–155, 157–160, 163–164, 169–173, 177, 179, 181–182, 193, 195, 202–209, 214–215, 220–221, 223–232, 234–235; strategy and, 7, 9–10, 44–45, 47–48, 50, 54, 66, 71–74, 90–92, 112–113, 115, 122–123, 133, 136, 141–142, 149–150, 157, 174, 202, 207, 228–229; systems analysis office (MACEVAL), 122; Territorial Forces Evaluation System (TFES), 171–172; Tet Offensive and, 134–135, 138, 140–141, 143, 147, 153–154; troop quality and morale, 182–183, 187–192, 195, 197, 199; troop withdrawals and, 162, 202; Vietnamization and, 56, 161–162, 168, 173, 177–178, 181–182, 188, 192, 198–201, 203, 215, 220; war assessments, 10, 14, 16–17, 44, 48, 50, 52, 54, 57, 63, 66, 81, 83, 85, 104, 108–109, 111, 127–128, 130–132, 141, 143, 160, 163, 171, 173, 213–215, 219, 223, 225, 228, 235
Mohr, Charles, 99, 101–102
Moore, Harold G., 79–81, 83–84, 88, 231
Moskos, Charles, 182–183
Moynihan, Daniel P., 184–185
My Lai massacre, 176–177

National Front for the Liberation of South Vietnam (NLF), 42, 52, 70, 141, 151, 175, 178, 231
Navarre, Henri, 23
Nhu, Ngo-Dinh, 57–59
Nixon, Richard, 151, 163, 182; Cambodia and, 189, 200, 208–212; Congress and, 176–177; Laos and, 200, 208; media and, 175–176, 214; Nixon Doctrine, 162, 207; peace negotiations and, 175, 218–219; public opinion and, 176; victory and, 207–209, 218–219; Vietnam strategy and, 158–161, 170, 175, 179, 202–203, 208, 212–214, 216, 218
North Vietnamese Army (NVA), 61, 67, 72, 77–82, 91, 95, 98–100, 102, 105–107, 112–113, 124–125, 129, 132, 136–137, 139, 149, 154, 166, 174–175, 178, 194, 202, 207–211, 213, 215–218, 220
NSC-68, 29
NSSM1, 160

oil spot theory, 23, 58, 70
Omaha Beach, 3–4
Omanski, Frank A., 54
Osborn, Robert B., 106–107
Osgood, Robert, 19–20, 37

Pacification Attitude Analysis System (PAAS), 206
pacification: 6, 10, 15, 17, 23–26, 40, 43, 47, 51–53, 57, 63–64, 66, 71–73, 81, 83–84, 88–94, 98–99, 101–106, 108–126, 130–131, 133, 140, 144–146, 148–152, 158–160, 162–165, 167–168, 172–175, 177, 202, 205–206, 209, 211–212, 217–218, 224, 228, 231 *See also* Abrams, Creighton; Accelerated Pacification Campaign (APC); Komer, Robert; McNamara, Robert; Military Assistance Command, Vietnam (MACV); Pacification Attitude Analysis System (PAAS); and Westmoreland, William
Palmer, Bruce, 199, 229
Palmer, Dave R., 16
Paris peace negotiations, 149–151, 154, 160, 175, 177, 211, 213, 215, 218–219
Pearson, Willard, 99

Peers, William R., 123
People's Liberation Armed Forces (PLAF), 6, 7, 14, 81, 111
Philippines, 27–28
Phoenix program, 151, 202, 209
Pike, Douglas, 45
Pleiku, 66, 77–78, 81–82, 84–85, 99
Project 100,000, 185–187, 189, 193–195, 199
Provisional Revolutionary Government (PRG), 209, 218–219
PROVN, 92–93
public opinion (United States), 127, 132, 134, 141, 143–144, 146–147, 175–177, 190

quadrillage, 23

RAND, 24–25, 34, 35, 39–40, 50, 53, 106, 113, 124, 125, 130, 204, 229
Regional Forces/Popular Forces (RF/PF), 56, 116, 137, 174
Republic of Vietnam Armed Forces (RVNAF), 63, 66, 71–72, 170–171, 213, 229
Research Analysis Corporation, 73, 117
Resor, Stanley R. 214
revolutionary development, 101, 104, 106, 111, 113–114, 116, 118, 121, 122–127, 131, 140
Ridgway, Matthew B., 30
Rivers, L. Mendel, 184
Rolling Thunder, Operation, 66
Rostow, Walt, 43, 59–60, 113, 126, 133
Rusk, Dean, 6, 69, 90–91, 128

Schandler, Herbert Y., 188
Schell, Jonathan, 126, 176, 212
search and destroy, 10, 71–72, 88, 94–96, 101–102, 110, 125, 131, 149, 157–158, 168, 176, 190
SEER Reports, 171–172
Selective Service, 183–184, 186
Senior Advisor Monthly Evaluation (SAME), 50, 56, 171
Shaplen, Robert, 173
Sharp, U. S. Grant, 70, 105
Sheehan, Neil, 57, 79
Siebert, Donald A., 100
Starry, Donn, 174
Stillwell, Richard G., 33
strategic hamlet program, 54, 57, 58 *See also* Hamlet Evaluation System (HES)
"Study on Military Professionalism," 197–198
Sunrise, Operation, 57

Taber, Robert, 34, 203–204
Taylor, Maxwell, 42–43, 47–49, 58–60, 64–67, 69, 72, 127, 218
Tet Offensive (1968), 112, 132–147, 149–150, 152–154, 157, 161, 163, 167–169, 175–176, 194, 195
TFES Reports, 171, 172
Thayer, Thomas, 47, 51, 53
Thieu, Nguyen, 93, 119, 149, 158, 178, 225, 228–229
Thompson, Robert, 11, 12, 94, 221
Timmes, C. J., 46
Trinquier, Roger, 25–26, 30, 101, 204
Truman Doctrine, 29
Tse Tung, Mao, 20, 22, 23, 30, 204

Ulmer, Walter F. Jr., 216
United States Army,
  Brigades: 173rd Airborne, 74, 100, 110; 196th Infantry 8, 190
United States Army,
  Divisions: 1st Cavalry, 5–6, 65, 76–78, 80–85, 87–88, 130, 138, 181, 190, 210; 7th Cavalry, 79–80; 11th Armored Cavalry, 110; 12th Cavalry, 190; 1st Infantry, 3, 7, 95–96, 110, 158, 189; 4th Infantry, 7; 9th Infantry, 140, 164–166, 177–178, 196; 25th Infantry, 7, 97, 148, 170; 29th Infantry, 3; 83rd Infantry, 4; 101st Airborne, 95–96, 99
United States Army,
  Operations: Attleboro, 5–9, 14, 110; Cedar Falls, 109–111, 131, 193, 228; Cobra, 4; Dewey Canyon, 157–158; Junction City, 111, 131, 193; Masher/White Wing, 87–89, 92, 95, 228; Niagara, 137; Randolph Glen, 202; Speedy Express, 164, 166
United States Army,
  drug use in, 16, 182, 188, 191–192, 197–198, 224
United States Army,;
  race relations in, 16, 186, 191, 197, 198, 224
United States Marine Corps, 5, 17, 59, 70, 93, 136, 139, 177, 182, 231

Van Fleet, James, 27
Vance, Cyrus, 92
Vann, John Paul, 55, 57, 72, 106–107, 140, 165, 217
Vietcong (VC): air power and, 78, 82; Army of the Republic of Vietnam (ARVN) and, 55, 57, 60, 70, 72, 116; attrition and, 107, 112–113, 129, 151; body counts and, 94–96, 102, 106, 164, 166; Cambodia and, 210–211; guerilla tactics and, 158, 191,

Vietcong (VC) (*continued*)
202, 218; infiltration of South Vietnam, 41–42, 44–45, 51–52, 54, 65–67, 78, 85, 114, 136, 149, 163, 168, 178; Iron Triangle and, 110–111; Military Assistance Command, Vietnam (MACV) and, 6, 52–53, 57, 60, 73–74, 85, 87, 91, 104–105, 124, 131, 149, 151, 160, 164, 194, 227; Mekong Delta and, 55–56, 164–165; pacification and, 115–116, 119; propaganda, 49, 58, 140; resilience of, 60, 132; rural areas and, 49–50, 57–58, 141, 226, 228; taxes and, 52, 131, 150, 218; Tet Offensive and, 134–135, 139, 144, 146, 149; U.S. military and, 88, 98, 231; Vietnamese population and, 42, 64, 125, 157, 202, 219, 226; Vietminh, 23–25, 32, 72

Vietnamization, 17, 56, 158–159, 161–162, 167–169, 171, 173–179, 181–183, 188–189, 192, 195, 198–199, 201, 203, 205–211, 213–215, 217–220, 221, 228–229, 231

Volckmann, Russell W., 31

Walt, Lewis W., 93, 231
Warren, Earl, 158
West Point, 33, 69, 79, 147, 182, 189
Westmoreland, William C.: 1st Cavalry and, 77–78, 78, 80, 87; Army Chief of Staff, 147–148, 163, 167, 171, 179, 188–189, 197, 218; Army of the Republic of Vietnam (ARVN) and, 72; attrition strategy and, 92, 98, 108, 123–124, 141–142; background, 69; body counts and, 7, 102–106, 124; counterinsurgency and, 6, 33, 69, 72, 91, 93–95, 103, 109, 113, 123, 125, 135, 231; criticisms of, 111–117; Hamlet Evaluation System and, 120; Honolulu Conference and, 5–6, 91–92; Ia Drang and, 82, 84; intelligence collection and, 118, 136–138; MACV command and, 13, 64, 69–70, 83–85, 88, 94; Malaya counterinsurgency and, 12, 27, 75; media and, 126–129, 146; military discipline and, 179, 188, 197; Operation Attleboro and, 6–7; pacification and, 15, 64, 84, 90–92, 94, 102, 110–111, 113–114, 116–117, 123, 133 140; revolutionary development and, 111, 115; search and destroy and, 88, 101, 152; statistics and metrics, 37, 94, 98, 104–105, 111, 122, 127, 129–130, 137, 140, 147, 154, 171, 224; strategy and, 6, 64, 70–73, 83, 85, 88–93, 98, 105–107, 112–113, 133, 135, 138; Tet Offensive and, 139–141, 146; troop requests and, 66, 68, 85, 106, 123, 133, 141–143; victory and, 207, 231; Vietnamization and, 161; war assessments, 67, 73–74, 81, 108–109, 123, 126–127, 145; West Point Superintendent, 33

Weyand, Frederick C., 14, 138, 141, 153, 218–219
Wheeler, Earle G., 33, 75, 76, 94, 136, 141–142, 146–147, 162, 172
Williamson, Ellis W., 74, 100
"Wise Men," 128, 147

Zais, Melvin, 166–167, 176, 178, 208
Zorthian, Barry, 144